Intellectual Talent

Psychometric
and
Social Issues

Intellectual
Talent

Edited by
Camilla Persson Benbow
and
David Lubinski

THE JOHNS HOPKINS
UNIVERSITY PRESS

Baltimore and London

© 1996 The Johns Hopkins University Press

All rights reserved. Published 1996
Printed in the United States of America on acid-free paper
05 04 03 02 01 00 99 98 97 96   5 4 3 2 1

The Johns Hopkins University Press
2715 North Charles Street
Baltimore, Maryland 21218–4319
The Johns Hopkins Press Ltd., London

Library of Congress Cataloging-in-Publication Data will be found at the
end of this book.
A catalog record for this book is available from the British Library.

ISBN 0-8018-5301-X
ISBN 0-8018-5302-8 (pbk.)

Contents

Contributors

BETSY JANE BECKER, Ph.D., Professor of Education, Department of Counseling, Educational Psychology, and Special Education, Michigan State University, East Lansing, Michigan

CAMILLA PERSSON BENBOW, Ed.D., Distinguished Professor of Psychology, Department of Psychology, Iowa State University, Ames, Iowa

CAROL C. BLACKBURN, Ph.D., Senior Research Associate, Study of Exceptional Talent, Institute for the Academic Advancement of Youth, Johns Hopkins University, Baltimore, Maryland

THOMAS J. BOUCHARD, JR., Ph.D., Professor of Psychology and Director, Minnesota Twin and Adoption Study, Department of Psychology, University of Minnesota, Minneapolis, Minnesota

LINDA E. BRODY, Ed.D., Director, Study of Exceptional Talent, Institute for the Academic Advancement of Youth, Johns Hopkins University, Baltimore, Maryland

JAMES S. COLEMAN, Ph.D., University Professor of Sociology Emeritus (deceased), Department of Sociology, University of Chicago, Chicago, Illinois

LEE J. CRONBACH, Ph.D., Vida Jacks Professor of Education Emeritus, School of Education, Stanford University, Stanford, California

MICHELE ENNIS, Ph.D., Associate Research Scientist, American Institutes for Research, Palo Alto, California

JOHN F. FELDHUSEN, Ph.D., Robert B. Kane Distinguished Professor of Education, Department of Educational Studies and Gifted Education Resource Institute, Purdue University, West Lafayette, Indiana

N. L. GAGE, Ph.D., Margaret Jacks Professor of Education Emeritus, School of Education, Stanford University, Stanford, California

JAMES J. GALLAGHER, Ph.D., Kenan Professor of Education, Frank Porter Graham Child Development Center, University of North Carolina, Chapel Hill, North Carolina

LYNN W. GLASS, Ph.D., University Professor of Education, Department of Curriculum and Instruction, Iowa State University, Ames, Iowa

LLOYD G. HUMPHREYS, Ph.D., Professor of Psychology Emeritus, Department of Psychology, University of Illinois, Champaign, Illinois

ARTHUR R. JENSEN, Ph.D., Professor of Educational Psychology, School of Education, University of California, Berkeley, California

TIMOTHY Z. KEITH, Ph.D., Professor of School Psychology, Alfred University, Alfred, New York

HERBERT J. KLAUSMEIER, Ph.D., V. A. C. Henmon Professor of Educational Psychology Emeritus, Department of Educational Psychology, University of Wisconsin, Madison, Wisconsin

DAVID LUBINSKI, Ph.D., Associate Professor of Psychology, Department of Psychology, Iowa State University, Ames, Iowa

DAVID T. LYKKEN, Ph.D., Professor of Psychology, Department of Psychology, University of Minnesota, Minneapolis, Minnesota

MATTHEW McGUE, Ph.D., Professor of Psychology, Department of Psychology, University of Minnesota, Minneapolis, Minnesota

LOLA L. MINOR, M.A., Graduate Student of Psychology (deceased), Department of Psychology, Johns Hopkins University, Baltimore, Maryland

ELLIS B. PAGE, Ed.D., Professor of Educational Psychology and Research, Program in Education, Duke University, Durham, North Carolina

A. HARRY PASSOW, Ed.D., Jacob H. Schiff Professor of Education Emeritus (deceased), Teachers College, Columbia University, New York, New York

NANCY M. ROBINSON, Ph.D., Director, Halbert Robinson Center for the Study of Capable Youth, University of Washington, Seattle, Washington

ARNOLD E. ROSS, Ph.D., Professor of Mathematics Emeritus, Department of Mathematics, Ohio State University, Columbus, Ohio

RICHARD E. SNOW, Ph.D., Howard H. and Jesse T. Watkins University Professor, School of Education, Stanford University, Stanford, California

JULIAN C. STANLEY, Ed.D., Professor of Psychology and Director, Study of Mathematically Precocious Youth, Department of Psychology, Johns Hopkins University, Baltimore, Maryland

BABETTE SUCHY, B.A., Graduate Student in Psychology, Department of Psychology, Iowa State University, Ames, Iowa

ABRAHAM J. TANNENBAUM, Ph.D., Professor of Education Emeritus, Teachers College, Columbia University, New York, New York

JOYCE VAN TASSEL-BASKA, Ed.D., Jody and Layton Smith Professor of Education, School of Education, College of William and Mary, Williamsburg, Virginia

AUKE TELLEGEN, Ph.D., Professor of Psychology, Department of Psychology, University of Minnesota, Minneapolis, Minnesota

LEROY WOLINS, Ph.D., Professor of Psychology Emeritus, Department of Psychology, Iowa State University, Ames, Iowa

Preface

On April 19, 1992, almost a hundred individuals made a pilgrimage to San Francisco to attend a symposium conducted in honor of Julian C. Stanley and his career achievements. The symposium was entitled "From Psychometrics to Giftedness," a fitting description of Julian's career path. It was attended by many of his former as well as current colleagues and students, including a research participant in his Study of Mathematically Precocious Youth.

This book grew out of that symposium. All but four of the presentations were expanded upon and developed into chapters for this volume. Eight chapters were added to round out the book's coverage of the subject matter. The book is meant to tell an important story, and we believe it does. It begins with a discussion of IQ and the educational acceleration of gifted children, and how work in this area is affected by the *Zeitgeist*. A major theme is how political climates and emotions influence scientific inquiry by limiting both the questions posed and what knowledge obtained from social science research is actually put into practice. What we have learned is that little of what is applied is consistent with what research informs us are good practices. Rather, we are attracted to fads with insufficient empirical support.

This leads to two questions: what do we actually know, and what would happen if our knowledge were applied? We decided to approach these issues by having several contributors examine one problem: how properly to educate children with exceptional academic talents. There is much that we know about this topic and have known for quite some time, as the chapters reveal. When this knowledge is applied, as it was by Julian Stanley through his Study of Mathematically Precocious Youth, the results are simply striking. This leads one to wonder more generally what could the state of education in the United States be if we actually applied what works and resisted the temptation to jump on the next bandwagon. The current state of affairs in education and the social sciences could be considered malpractice.

The book comes to a close with several chapters dealing with psychometric issues and the crucial differences between genius and giftedness. Often the concepts of genius and giftedness are conflated, but true genius is much more than giftedness; this idea is explored in some surprising and thought-provoking ways.

It has been exciting putting the symposium and book together. We have learned a great deal. It was a pleasure to work with all the contributors, who patiently responded to all our requests and editorial feedback. We also thank Wilma Bucklin, Hossain Eftekhari-Sanjani, and Mildred Peterson for their assistance in first organizing the symposium and then preparing the final manuscript. Finally, we owe special gratitude to Sanford J. Cohn, as he not only served as a discussant at the symposium but also handled the videotaping of the event.

Intellectual Talent

I   Political Correctness and the *Zeitgeist*

Genetic Antecedents to Human Behavior

Policy formation is basically directed by values, not by evidence. Values can and should at times override evidence that suggests a contrary course of action. One's values, however, may direct action in different directions. Hence data concerning consequences become highly relevant to a decision. Courses of action are also frequently buttressed by mythical or completely inadequate data. Such data should be criticized, and dependable data, when available, should be made known. In a democracy the electorate and their representatives should be well informed, and they have the right not to be sold a bill of goods on the basis of mythical evidence.

Humphreys, 1989

In the chapters of this section of the volume, the importance of distinguishing evidence from values is underscored, as is the need for scientific examination of socially sensitive topics. One might question why such an emphasis is required. Is this kind of examination not what academicians are trained to undertake? Unfortunately, when dealing with sensitive topics, scholars (and others) frequently violate many canons of scientific reasoning, as the contributions in this section document. This is especially the case when academicians are faced with genotypic *and* phenotypic inquiries into human variation, a situation in which values have come to conflict with the resultant empirical evidence. Passionate arguments often have ensued, especially when the findings indicate genetic antecedents to prized, value-laden traits.

We start off the volume with a description of one of the most intriguing psychological investigations of our time—the Minnesota Twin Study of monozygotic and dizygotic twins reared apart. The authors of the first chapter (Bouchard, Lykken, Tellegen, and McGue) are the individuals responsible for the study, a study that has produced a spate of interesting findings on a variety of topics. Here, they choose to focus on the magnitude of the heritabilities of a variety of well-known psychological traits and then begin developing a

1

possible theoretical basis for them by drawing on concepts and findings in sociobiology.

The relative influence of nature and nurture on the manifestation of human traits has for centuries produced speculation by philosophers and scholars of all kinds. Yet twin and adoption methodologies (coupled with highly developed statistical techniques) now have allowed us to separate into distinct sources of variance the intertwined influences of heredity and environment. Consequently, speculation about nature and nurture is being transformed into theorizing based on facts, and the facts are pretty firmly in place. To be sure, the influence of our biological heritage on physical and psychological attributes is undeniable, and this includes human abilities, personality, vocational interests, religiosity, and even divorce. Yet theorizing has taken a leap forward, not just because of these findings but also because of recent results demonstrating that a number of conventional "environmental measures" frequently employed in social science research actually assess (to a degree) genetic variation (Plomin & Bergman, 1991).

Findings of this sort, although robust and of major importance, are not always received warmly (just ask anyone who has tried to secure funding for such research through conventional granting agencies or who has tried to publish such results); many members of the scientific community find these data emotionally troubling. Proposals to examine genetic influences on human behavior empirically all too frequently meet with tempestuous resistance. The chapters in this section certainly document this phenomenon. In contrast, causal inferences based on environmental sources of influence tend to be cheerfully accepted by social scientists. The developmental psychologist Sandra Scarr captures the situation well: "Even if biologically inclined psychologists admit some shortcomings, the sins of omission by mainstream psychology of biological factors are far more egregious. Few, if any, journals require environmental explanations to be countered by alternative genetic or sociobiological hypotheses; nearly all psychological journals require the reverse" (1993, p. 461).

Indeed, Bouchard et al. provide in their chapter a splendid illustration of a causal-environmental interpretation of data (from the Terman studies) that confounded environmental and genetic components of variance but, nonetheless, appeared in a highly respected scientific outlet (the *Journal of Educational Psychology* in 1990) and received wide attention. The pointing out by Bouchard et al. of the erroneous inferences drawn therein is valuable and should induce caution in all psychologists wishing to make environmentally causal attributions based on nonexperimental correlational findings.

To provide an opportunity for the other viewpoint to be heard, we conclude this section with a contribution from Abraham Tannenbaum. Tannenbaum sees himself as an "IQ basher" and is especially concerned with behavior-genetic analyses of human abilities and the findings about group differences in our society that intelligence testing has revealed. Consequently, he calls for a moratorium on intelligence testing and refers to behavior-genetic analyses as a form of sophistry. Although most contemporary scholars of individual differences in human behavior would not endorse all of Tannenbaum's views and conclusions, ideas such as his are what make research interesting and thought provoking.

References

Humphreys, L. G. (1989). Intelligence: Three kinds of instability and their consequences for policy. In R. L. Linn (Ed.), *Intelligence: Measurement, theory, and public policy*, pp. 193–216. Urbana: University of Illinois Press.

Lubinski, D., & Dawis, R. V. (1992). Aptitudes, skills, and proficiencies. In M. D. Dunnette & L. M. Hough (Eds.), *The handbook of industrial/organizational psychology* (2nd ed., Vol. 3, pp. 1–59). Palo Alto: Consulting Psychologists Press.

Plomin, R., & Bergeman, C. S. (1991). The nature of nurture: Genetic influences on "environmental" measures. *Behavioral and Brain Sciences* 14:414–424.

Scarr, S. (1993). Ebbs and flows of evolution in psychology. *Contemporary Psychology* 38:458–462.

Figure 1.1. A pair of ninety-four-year-old monozygotic twins reared together.

1 Genes, Drives, Environment, and Experience

EPD Theory Revised

THOMAS J. BOUCHARD, JR.,

DAVID T. LYKKEN, AUKE TELLEGEN,

AND MATTHEW MCGUE

Human twins, particularly identical or monozygotic (MZ) twins, have fascinated both laypersons and scholars since time immemorial. The ancient literature is dotted with references to twins (Gedda, 1961). The principal reason for this fascination is the remarkable morphological and behavioral similarity of such twins. For an example of the morphological similarity one often sees in MZ twins, see figure 1.1.

This picture also tells an ontogenetic tale. These women began life as a single fertilized egg. At some point the developing blastula divided into two parts and gave rise to two genetically identical individuals. They have undergone obvious morphological changes over the course of their ninety-four years, yet they remain remarkably alike. This single observation illustrates a fundamental biological fact: within the normal range of environments, morphological development is to a considerable degree under the influence of a "genetic program." The degree of genetic influence at any time is significant and can be quantified. Change is, of course, greater in the early years than in the later years. The process of genetically influenced morphological change can be appreciated if one simply looks at photographs of the same twins taken over the course of their lives (see Bouchard, 1991). Genetic influences on psychological change can similarly be observed if one plots the growth spurts and lags in mental ability for dizygotic (DZ) and MZ twins (Wilson, 1983). Virtually any morpho-

5

logical feature of human beings shows a significant genetic influence (Bernhard, Hancke, Brauer, & Chopra, 1980; Dupae, Defries-Gussenhoven, & Susanne, 1982). This, however, is not to deny the existence of environments that are deficient generally (malnutrition) or specifically (vitamin C deficiency) in a way that affects the individual's pattern of growth. Growth can be stunted or deflected from its natural course.

Genetic influence on the course of development and most features of biological organisms is taken for granted in biology and generalized to behavioral traits by behavioral biologists (Trivers, 1985). These scientists presume that the human species evolved just as all the other species did, and that human behavior reflects, in part, our evolutionary history. Many psychologists, however, become upset, if not apoplectic, when evolutionary and genetic facts are proposed as part of the framework necessary to understand the etiology of human behavior and development (see Gottlieb, 1991; Oyama, 1985, 1988; for the contrary position, see Barkow, Cosmides, & Tooby, 1992; Charlesworth, 1992; Plomin, 1988; Wright, 1994). We believe, however, that a framework informed by quantitative genetics and evolutionary theory is both highly appropriate and extremely useful. It allows for a quantitative description of some significant facts, it is consistent with standard practice in a variety of scientific disciplines, it incorporates our understanding that human beings are biological organisms whose functional and developmental mechanisms operate under the same biological constraints as do other organisms, and it provides a solid frame of reference for reexamining the validity of the implicit and often deliberately unstated argument that human beings somehow are a unique species that has evolved beyond ordinary forms of scientific understanding. This view permeates many segments of psychology and is redolent with the kind of mysticism that the scientific mind has had to battle for centuries. The fact is, human beings are, in the words of Foley (1987), just "another unique species." Any attempt fully to understand this species apart from its biological and evolutionary heritage is, in our opinion, doomed to failure. The history of this view, which was once taken for granted in psychology and was subsequently abandoned, has been brilliantly reviewed by Richards in his book *Darwin and the Emergence of Evolutionary Theories of Mind and Behavior* (1987). (See also Degler, 1991.)

Below we review selected findings from research in behavioral genetics in the domains of IQ, personality, and psychological interests. The focus is on twin and adoption studies, with a special emphasis on our own work with twins reared apart. We then attempt to integrate the findings into the framework of evolutionary psychology.

Models of Genetic and Environmental Influence

We begin by briefly sketching the logic of the basic twin and adoption designs that provide the data we plan to review. Path analysis is a powerful and relatively straightforward tool for illustrating the logic underlying the methodology of behavioral genetics (Loehlin, 1989, 1992a, 1992b). For the path diagram for monozygotic twins reared together (MZTs), see figure 1.2.

The notation in figure 1.2 is as follows: Items in circles indicate underlying latent variables; items in boxes indicate measurable phenotypes (scores) for the kinships indicated (e.g., MZ_1 is the score, on the trait under consideration, for the first member of a twin pair); G = genotype, UE = unique (unshared) environment; and CE = common (shared) environment; h, c, e = genetic, shared environmental, and unshared environmental paths (standardized partial regressions between latent and observed variables).

The phenotype of each twin is influenced by both the genotype and the environment. That is, the single-headed arrows in the figure denote causal influences, with the lowercase letters representing the degree to which the phenotype is a function of the latent causal entities. The expected correlation between any two measured traits can be derived using the tracing rules of path analysis.[1] There are two paths influencing the correlation between MZTs: a path that reflects common environmental influences and a genetic path (r_{GG}). The coefficient of genetic relationship is set at 1.00 for MZ twins, .50 for DZ twins and siblings, .25 for half siblings, and .00 for unrelated individuals reared together. The MZT correlation ($r_{mzt} = h^2 + c^2$) confounds two sources of variance. It is possible to represent developmental change by means of a series of diagrams with theoretically relevant paths connecting the latent variables from different times.

We can generate the static model for all the other interesting kinships by simply modifying or removing components of this diagram. As indicated above, if we set r_{GG} at .50 it represents the correlation between fraternal twins reared together. The observed correlation still confounds two sources of variance, but it is reduced by precisely half the genetic variance; thus $r_{dzt} = .5h^2 + c^2$. The difference between the correlations for MZ and DZ twins estimates half the genetic variance. If we multiply this difference by two, we have calculated the Falconer heritability estimate. This particular model makes a number of assumptions; it assumes that *(a)* genetic effects are additive, *(b)* assortative mat-

---

1. The correlation is the product of the values of the constituent arrows (paths) connecting the phenotypes. There are, however, additional rules; no loops, no going forward and then backward, a maximum of one curved arrow per path (see Li, 1975; Loehlin, 1992b).

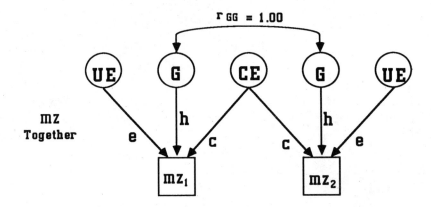

Figure 1.2. Path diagram for monozygotic twins reared together.

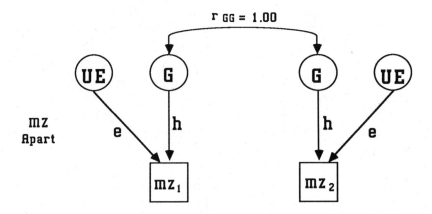

Figure 1.3. Path diagram for monozygotic twins reared apart.

ing is not relevant, and *(c)* the CEs are the same for both types of twins (the "equal environments assumption").

If we remove CE, the model represents the correlation between monozygotic twins reared apart (MZAs), which is $r_{mza} = h^2$; for the path diagram, see figure 1.3. The observed correlation reflects the influence only of genetic factors. This diagram illustrates why the correlation between MZA twins is not squared. The observed correlation directly estimates variance accounted for by genetic factors. The expected DZA correlation, under the stated assumptions, reflects half the influence of genetic factors.

Many psychologists argue that genes are irrelevant and do not influence the development of behavior; they assert that the similarity of MZA twins arises

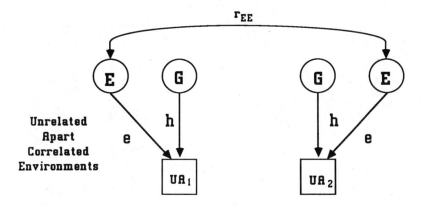

Figure 1.4. Path diagram for unrelated individuals reared apart and reared in correlated environments.

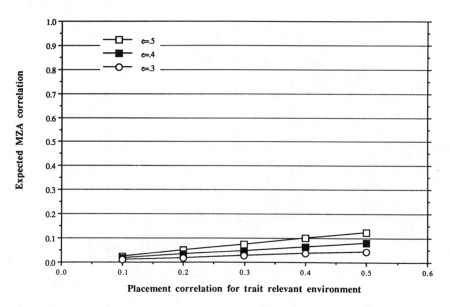

Figure 1.5. The effects of selective placement on MZA correlations under the assumption of zero heritability.

because their environments are correlated. This assertion is examined in the "unrelated apart" model; see figure 1.4. This model is eminently testable and generates the predictions presented in figure 1.5.

Figure 1.5 presents the values expected for MZAs under the hypothesis that there is no genetic influence on the MZA correlation (genes are irrelevant

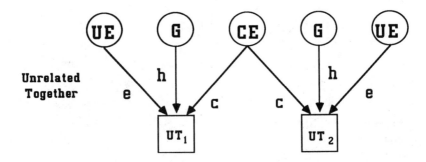

Figure 1.6. Path diagram for unrelated individuals reared together.

and any behavioral similarity is due simply to correlated environmental influences) and some rational values of r_{EE} and e. To account for the correlations between twins reared apart by considering environmental factors only, the features of the environment with regard to which the twins are correlated must be trait relevant, and e must be substantially greater than zero; see figures 1.4 and 1.5. The estimate of influence—the value of e for a particular environmental feature with respect to a particular trait—must be estimated in an adoption study. In our study of twins reared apart, the placement correlation (r_{EE}) for the father's socioeconomic status (SES) was .267 and the value of e (the correlation between SES and the adoptee's IQ) was .174. The predicted value of the MZA correlation was thus .008, a value well below the lowest line in the chart. Despite what appears to be a sizable placement coefficient (.267), only the minuscule figure of .008 needed to be subtracted from the MZA IQ correlation to take account of placement on SES.

For unrelated individuals reared together, $r_{EE} = 1.00$. This is often represented in the path diagram by having the arrows flow from a single latent variable; see figure 1.6. The correlation for a trait in this design is a direct estimate of c^2.

These models are somewhat simplified; for example, one could add a dominance parameter connecting the phenotypes and set it at the appropriate genetic values (MZ = 1, Sib = .25, P-O = .0) and one could also represent the effect of assortative mating; still, these models represent the basic principles.

Intelligence

The data on intelligence relevant to our discussion can be summarized succinctly in a single graph. Figure 1.7 presents the correlations for IQ, for adults, for five critical kinship relationships under two conditions of rearing, together and apart. These results are quite similar to summaries found in all the studies

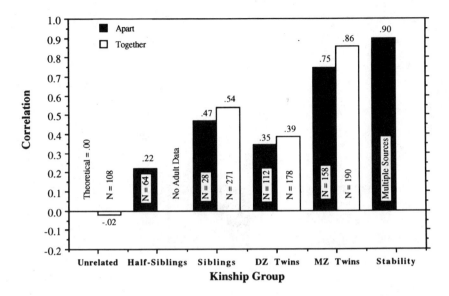

Figure 1.7. Correlations and sample sizes for adult samples from five kinship groups reared apart and reared together.

that include children (Bouchard & McGue, 1981) except for the group of unrelated individuals reared together. If the intellectual assessment is carried out in childhood, unrelated individuals reared together show modest degrees of similarity (see fig. 1.8).[2]

There are some inconsistencies in these data. These are brought out nicely in figure 1.9, where we show simple heritability estimates for adults, using the data from figure 1.7. The first four estimates, which are based on different groups, are entirely independent of each other and are direct estimates. Following the logic of the path diagram, for the reared-apart kin the half-sibling correlation is simply multiplied by four; the sibling and DZ twin correlations are multiplied by two, and the MZA correlation is taken as a direct estimate of h^2. The estimates of half siblings reared apart and siblings reared apart are based on small sample sizes and consequently have large standard errors. The high Falconer heritabilities suggest that perhaps nonadditive genetic variance may be important for IQ; this suggestion is confirmed in the study by Pedersen, Plomin, Nesselroade, and McClearn (1992) discussed below.

Plomin and Loehlin (1989) fit models to the large body of kin IQ data,

2. An additional study of unrelated individuals reared together has appeared since figure 1.8 was prepared. Scarr, Weinberg, & Waldman (1993) report a correlation of .19. The weighted average used in the figure changes very little with the addition of this new datum.

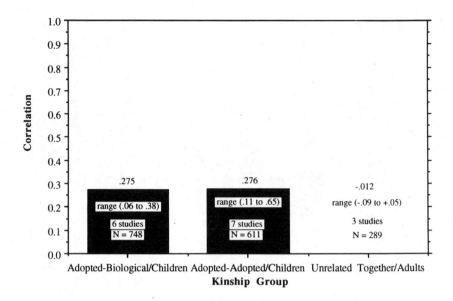

Figure 1.8. Correlations and sample sizes for unrelated individuals reared together by type of pairing (adopted-biological and adopted-adopted) in childhood and adulthood.

which includes children, and show that direct and indirect heritability estimates differ, with direct estimates being somewhat higher (.58 versus .47). Much as we favor model fitting as a primary method for the analysis of complex data sets, the process does not take into account the various threats to validity discussed by Campbell and Stanley (1966). Only a careful analysis in which studies were coded for artifacts could begin to address such problems, and there are simply not enough studies. Until there are enough studies, judgmental estimates, if they are labeled as such, are legitimate. These data suggest that a judgmental estimate of a heritability of about .70 for adult IQ is reasonable. Chipuer, Rovine, and Plomin (1990) fit models to the entire set of data and estimate the heritability to be .51.

The data presented in figure 1.7 clearly suggest, at best, a modest amount of shared environmental influence. The MZ twin data suggest something in the range of 11 percent. The sibling and DZ twin data suggest something closer to 7 percent and 4 percent, respectively. The data on unrelated individuals reared together suggest virtually no shared environmental influence. A partial explanation of these discrepant results would be a common environmental effect for twins and siblings. Loehlin (1989) reports such an effect in his analysis of the

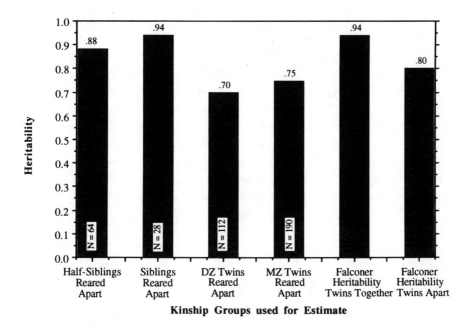

Figure 1.9. Heritabilities estimated from adult data using four comparable-in-age kinship groups.

world literature, which includes subjects of all ages. Chipuer, Rovine, and Plomin (1990), again fitting data from all ages, report similar results. Consistent with the age effect for unrelated individuals reared together presented in figure 1.8, McCartney, Harris, and Bernieri (1990) show that with twins the influence of common family environment declines as they move apart. McGue, Bouchard, Iacono, and Lykken (1993) have shown that adult twins yield higher heritability estimates than young twins. Nevertheless, the results are not entirely consistent. Included in figure 1.7 are the data from Pedersen, Plomin, Nesselroade, and McClearn (1992). They report an MZA intraclass correlation of .78 ($N = 45$), a DZA intraclass correlation of .32 ($N = 88$), an MZT intraclass correlation of .80 ($N = 63$), and a DZT intraclass correlation of .22 ($N = 79$) for the first principal component of thirteen tests of special mental ability. The MZA correlation of .78 exactly replicates the MZA correlation for a similar first principal component reported by Bouchard, Lykken, McGue, Segal, and Tellegen (1990). These authors note that a model with a sizable amount of nonadditive variance fits the IQ (first principal component) data best.

No matter how one looks at these results, it appears that for adult IQ, the influence of a common family environment is of modest importance. Scarr (1992) comes to a similar conclusion. Citing Plomin and Thompson (1987), she correctly argues that, contrary to the beliefs of most psychologists, the family is not the "unit of environmental transmission" (p. 14). When genetic influences are controlled, psychologists have been unable to locate important common family environmental correlates of adult IQ (Bouchard, Lykken, McGue, Segal, & Tellegen, 1990; Bouchard & Segal, 1985; Scarr, in press; Willerman, 1979). It is difficult to overestimate the importance of this finding. It confirms the old maxim that "correlation does not mean causation." Studies of correlations within families, which make up a large proportion of the correlational studies carried out in developmental psychology, if carried out alone rather than in conjunction with twin or adoption studies, are ambiguous with respect to causation.

We are sometimes asked, "What is the big issue, since no one makes that mistake anymore?" This is simply not true. An example was published by Tomlinson-Keasey and Little (1990) in the *Journal of Educational Psychology*. Their analysis was carried out on the Terman longitudinal data (Terman & Oden, 1959), a sample that should be of special interest to the readers of this book.

The study by Tomlinson-Keasey and Little clearly illustrates the poverty of a purely environmental approach. Using teacher and parent ratings gathered from eleven- and twelve-year-olds, they derived measures of three childhood personality characteristics, which they called Social Responsibility (probably constraint, or impulse control), Intellectual Determination (a rated IQ factor), and Sociability (a personality trait). Two family-of-origin predictors were derived: Parental Education and Family Harmony. The latter measure was based on eight retrospective items concerning the quality of the early family environment. Three outcome variables were created: Educational Attainment, Intellectual Skill (scores on the Concept Mastery Test, straightforward measures of verbal IQ), and Personal Adjustment (from various mental health measures). A structural equation model was developed and tested to evaluate the role of the three childhood and two family variables as they related to the intermediate variables—Educational Attainment, Intellectual Skill, and Personal Adjustment—and then finally the more distal outcome variable of Occupational Achievement.

These authors consider the variables they are studying to be proximal causes. "As educational psychologists, it behooves us to try to ascertain what factors promote the educational and occupational achievements that should accompany intellectual skill. Delineating the childhood variables critical to positive adult outcomes requires longitudinal information on individuals that spans a lifetime" (p. 442). Yet there is no discussion of (never mind testing of) the competing genetic model. What do they conclude about their measures regarding "influences" on intellectual skills?

> How well did these children, identified as gifted at age 11 or 12, maintain their intellectual superiority as adults, and what variables predicted their continuing interest in the intellectual sphere? For both sexes, three factors predicted Intellectual Skill in adulthood. Parental Education and Intellectual Determination were positively associated with maintaining intellectual skill; Sociability was negatively associated with maintaining intellectual skill. . . . Parental Education has appeared repeatedly in the literature as one of several indicators of the family's socioeconomic status and is often depicted as an indicator of the value parents place on education (see Henderson, 1981; White, 1982; Willerman, 1979). When parents place a premium on education, this attitude pervades the home environment and becomes part of the child's value structure. (P. 452)

It is worth emphasizing that the authors did not measure parental values or the children's value structure. Nor did they relate either to adult intellectual skills. Their claim is based on the use of Parental Education as a proxy for educational values, and it goes well beyond the data. This claim, in our opinion, deserves a true test. Their conclusion rests on an average correlation of .15 between Parental Education and the offspring's adult IQ. This is a within-family correlation in which genetic and environmental factors are confounded. If we take the model seriously, Tomlinson-Keasey and Little account for about 2.25 percent of the variance in adult IQ.

Not only is this a modest amount of explanatory power, it is probably not even real. To test this claim fully we would need a comparable sample of adult adoptees. Such a sample is not available, but we can approximate one. In the Scarr and Weinberg adoption study (1978), in which the average age is about eighteen years, the correlation between parental education and IQ is .26 for biological offspring and .08 for adopted children. (See Scarr, 1981, p. 395.) The biological correlation is higher than in the Terman sample (a sample that is far from optimal for this type of analysis because the Terman children were selected for their extreme IQ scores and because as Keating [1975] showed, the sampling was peculiar), but similar to those found in large-sample surveys.

The adopted children in the Scarr and Weinberg study still live with their parents, and the evidence suggests that the correlation between parental education and an adopted child's IQ will drop over time (McGue, Bouchard, Iacono, & Lykken, 1993). In our study of adult adoptees (Bouchard, Lykken, McGue,

TABLE 1.1. Correlations among Parental Characteristics, Childhood Environmental Factors, and Special Mental Abilities

Variable	Average Parental Education	Adoptive Parents' Occupation	Number of Residences	Material Possessions	Childhood Environmental Factors		
					Scientific/ Technical	Cultural	Mechanical
Verbal reasoning							
Vocabulary	.07	.04	−.05	−.12	.14	.14	−.08
Word beginning and ending	−.06	.01	−.07	−.07	.15	.09	−.27
Pedigrees	.00	.09	.05	−.11	.10	.15	−.14
Things	−.05	.03	−.01	−.16[a]	.12	.28	−.01
Subtraction and multiplication	−.13	−.12	−.05	−.04	−.08	.11	−.03
Mean	−.03	.01	−.03	−.10	.09	.15	−.11
Verbal factor	−.02	−.01	−.05	−.11	.15	.16	−.20
Spatial ability							
Card rotations	.03	.16	.04	−.05	.00	.03	.01
Cubes	.01	.02	.07	−.05	−.02	.15	.06
Mental rotations	−.01	.06	−.04	−.06	.01	.00	.04
Paper form board	−.16	−.08	.07	−.20	.04	.14	.01
Paper folding	−.19	−.16	−.08	−.13	.02	.02	.05
Hidden patterns	−.06	.04	.05	−.12	−.03	.13	−.07
Mean	−.06	.01	.02	−.10	.00	.08	.02
Spatial factor	−.02	.08	.04	−.10	.03	.05	.04
Perceptual speed and accuracy							
Lines and dots	−.05	.05	.11	−.01	.01	.06	.07
Identical pictures	−.05	−.09	−.02	−.08	−.07	.11	.00
Mean	−.05	−.02	.05	−.05	−.03	.09	.04
PSA factor	−.08	−.05	.07	−.06	−.02	.12	.09
Visual memory							
Delayed	−.08	−.03	.12	−.11	−.05	.02	−.08
Immediate	−.04	−.01	.07	−.10	−.04	−.07	−.04
Mean	−.06	−.02	.10	−.11	−.05	−.02	−.06
Visual memory factor	−.11	−.05	.11	−.12	−.07	−.01	−.09

Source: McGue & Bouchard (1989).
Note: Sample sizes range from 111 to 135. Correlations significant at $p < .05$ are indicated in boldface type.

Segal, & Tellegen, 1990), the average correlation between IQ and parental education is .05. Consistent with a genetic interpretation of the Tomlinson-Keasey and Little data, in large-scale studies of biological families, the mother's education is seldom correlated more highly with the child's IQ than the father's education is. The weighted mean values are .303 for fathers' education and .295 for mothers' education ($N = 34,714$, from four studies; Bouchard & Segal, 1985). This is also true in both the Terman data and the Scarr and Weinberg data. We would argue that an environmental explanation along the lines suggested by Tomlinson-Keasey and Little would require at least a slightly higher correlation between mother and offspring than between father and offspring. Genetic theory does not make this prediction. The same lack of difference holds for the correlation between parents' IQ and their children's IQ (Bouchard & McGue, 1981). Again, this outcome is expected on the basis of a genetic model, but not on the basis of an environmental one. The Tomlinson-Keasey and Little results are also incompatible with the very modest correlations between the IQ scores of unrelated children reared together, as reported above. The specifics of the argument are unimportant. This study employs a sample of individuals reared by their biological parents; consequently, all of the parent-offspring correlations are ambiguous. An adult sample of adoptees is mandatory if the authors wish to draw causal inferences. (See Scarr, in press, for a detailed discussion of this important methodological point.)

To add some breadth to this picture, we offer in table 1.1 the correlations among parental characteristics, childhood environmental factors, and special mental abilities in our adult adoptee sample (McGue & Bouchard, 1989). Except that reported cultural amenities do correlate positively with verbal skills and mechanical amenities correlate negatively with them (verbal fluency measures show the strongest effect in both cases, but different fluency measures are involved in each case), there is precious little in this table. Notice that parental education is unrelated to any of the mental-ability factors, a finding similar to that reported for IQ above. Recall also that these correlations must be squared to estimate variance accounted for.

With respect to the explanation of variance in adult intellectual skill, the Tomlinson-Keasey and Little model performs as follows: *(a)* childhood sociability explains 3.8 percent of the variance, and *(b)* intellectual determination (childhood ratings of IQ) explains 3.45 percent (for women) and 3.21 percent (for men) of the variance. The predictive value of childhood sociability is consistent with the known correlations between personality variables and IQ (Bayley, 1970). It is possible that much of the reliable variance in childhood sociability is determined by IQ, and the cross-correlation between the variables at either time or across time may also be genetic in origin. These are hypotheses to be tested, not facts to be assumed (Bouchard, 1995). We are currently engaged in an evaluation of this model with our MZA/DZA data set.

The Tomlinson-Keasey and Little paper illustrates the double standard that permeates the editorial process in psychology with respect to the publication of data that purportedly support an environmental theory as opposed to data that support a genetic theory. If comparable data had been collected on a twin or adoption sample and a paper submitted for publication to the *Journal of Educational Psychology*, the reviewers and editors would, rightly, have required the authors to discuss competing environmental explanations and possible confounds.

The systematic failure of psychologists to appreciate the confounded nature of within-family correlations (see Bouchard [1993a] for a critique of Hoffman [1991], who repeatedly commits this error) reflects a deep-seated bias, not just ignorance. The problem was pointed out in 1869 by Galton, who proposed the adoption design to avoid it; Burks, perhaps Terman's most brilliant student, dealt with it quantitatively in 1938 in the context of estimating genetic and environmental parameters for an adoption study. She was one of the first psychologists to use the method of path analysis, which had been invented by Sewall Wright (see Wright, 1921). It is a sad commentary on our discipline that Tomlinson-Keasey and Little did not even see fit to cite her work. A similar observation can be made regarding the otherwise brilliant analysis of the correlation between SES and achievement by White (1982). White fails to mention that these correlations confound genetic and environmental factors. The omission in both cases seems inexplicable. This problem has been repeatedly brought to our attention in recent years—for example, by Jensen (1973, ch. 11) under the heading "the sociologists' fallacy"—and it is discussed repeatedly in the developmental literature by Scarr (1981, in press) and in textbooks on behavioral genetics (Plomin, DeFries, & McClearn, 1990). Wright's classic 1931 paper, which contains a path analysis of Burks's adoption data, is cited in the standard works on structural equation modeling (Bollen, 1989; Jöreskog & Sörbom, 1989). We do not appear to participate in a cumulative scientific enterprise.

Personality

The literature in behavioral genetics on personality has been reviewed by a number of people over the years. An early comprehensive analysis is that of Nichols (1978). He organizes the data into nine traits on an intuitive basis and reports a mean MZ correlation of .48 and a mean DZ correlation of .29. A more recent and methodologically sophisticated analysis by Eaves, Eysenck, and Martin (1989, p. 39) organizes the data according to the Eysenckian paradigm—Neuroticism, Extraversion, and Psychoticism—and finds similar results. The MZ correlations are .44, .53, and .46. The DZ correlations are all .22, giving mean values of .49 and .22.

These findings, based largely on samples of young people, clearly suggest that about half the variance in most personality-trait measures is associated with genetic factors (more than half when error of measurement is taken into account). They also suggest that shared environments do not have any lasting effect on the resemblance between first-degree relatives. In terms of our model, if the MZ correlation is close to twice the difference between the MZ and the DZ correlations, then there is no excess similarity to be explained by the twins having grown up together. The assumptions of this model have been criticized (see Kamin, 1974). These criticisms are repeated regularly in introductory textbooks even though a large body of evidence has accumulated to refute them (Bouchard, 1984, 1993b). The twins-reared-apart design, however, directly surmounts this problem because it makes entirely different assumptions, many of which can be tested (see Bouchard, Lykken, McGue, Segal, & Tellegen, 1990).

An analysis of the California Psychological Inventory (CPI) using our adult sample of MZA and DZA twins and an adult male sample of MZT and DZT twins from a previous study by Horn, Plomin, and Rosenman (1976) yields results that are largely consistent with the overall findings of numerous recent large-scale twin studies. The results for the original eighteen CPI scales are provided in table 1.2.

The twins reared apart differ minimally in similarity from the twins reared together. The mean correlations hardly differ from those of Eaves, Eysenck, and Martin (1989). In addition, we correlated the MZA intraclass correlations for the eighteen primary scales, considered as estimates of broad heritability, with the heritability estimates for the same scales published by Loehlin (1985). Loehlin's estimates of heritability are based on seventeen subgroups (kinships), which include the adult twins reared together discussed above, but not the twins reared apart. Even with a highly restricted range of variation in the MZA correlations and the Loehlin heritabilities the correlation is .78.

Thus, consistent with conclusions based on studies of twins reared together, we can conclude that common family environment is of negligible importance for personality development. Environmental variance is important for the development of personality traits, but it consists of experiences that are not shared by sibling pairs. We have reported virtually identical results with the Multidimensional Personality Questionnaire (Tellegen et al., 1988; Bouchard,

TABLE 1.2. *Intraclass Correlations for the Eighteen Primary Scales of the California Psychological Inventory*

CPI Scale	Kinship			
	MZA	DZA	MZT	DZT
Dominance	.47	.21	.54	.26
Capacity for status	.55	.35	.53	.22
Sociability	.31	.32	.48	.16
Social presence	.47	.44	.50	.19
Self-acceptance	.51	.04	.48	.21
Well-being	.59	.21	.44	.08
Responsibility	.48	.37	.45	.32
Socialization	.59	.19	.43	.24
Self-control	.62	−.07	.47	.09
Tolerance	.57	.26	.47	.16
Good impression	.52	−.04	.41	.15
Communality	.02	−.04	.20	.07
Achievement via conformance	.43	.22	.41	.00
Achievement via independence	.55	.23	.49	.23
Intellectual efficiency	.49	.46	.48	.29
Psychological mindedness	.26	.35	.35	.19
Flexibility	.24	.01	.47	.11
Femininity	.26	.11	.26	.16
Means	.44	.20	.44	.17
S.D.	.16	.17	.09	.08

Sources: Bouchard & McGue (1990); Horn, Plomin, & Rosenman (1976).
Note: MZA = Monozygotic twin pairs reared apart (N = 60 pairs and 1 set of triplets). DZA = Dizygotic twin pairs reared apart (N = 42 pairs). All data from twins reared apart are corrected for age and sex. MZT = Monozygotic twin pairs reared together (N = 99 pairs). DZT = Dizygotic twin pairs reared together (N = 99 pairs).

1994). Eaves, Eysenck, and Martin (1989), working with large twin samples from London and Australia, come to a similar conclusion.

Loehlin and Nichols (1976), working with a younger sample of twins, examine unshared environmental influences directly. They note that differences in treatment of MZ twins as reported by their mothers do not explain a significant number of the differences between the twins, differences that must be entirely environmental in origin. They conclude that "in short, in the personality domain we seem to see environmental effects that operate almost randomly with respect to the sorts of variables that psychologists (and other people) have traditionally deemed important in personality development." After discussing a number of possible environmental factors that might influence twins reared together, but that are excluded by the data on twins reared apart, they continue: "It seems to us that one is thrown back on the view that the major, consistent, directional factors in personality development are the genes and the important environmental influences are highly variable situational inputs" (pp. 92–93). We will return to this line of argument shortly.

In the Tomlinson-Keasey and Little study (1990), a measure of personal adjustment is predicted from a retrospective measure of family harmony, and this variable alone explains 7.88 percent of the variance for females and 6.93 percent of the variance for males. This correlation within the biological family confounds genetic and environmental sources of variance. It can be studied, however, in the context of adoption. Using a methodology similar to that of Loehlin and Nichols, we (Bouchard & McGue, 1990) correlate differences in self-reported scores regarding child rearing on the Family Environment Scale (FES; Moos & Moos, 1986) with CPI score differences in the MZA sample. We find few substantial effects. Because we are also working with an adoption sample, the correlations between FES scores and personality traits can provide a direct measure of environmental influence. Again the effects are meager, and more importantly, there is virtually no replication of the few findings obtained with the difference-score analysis; this suggests that the few significant but modest correlations in each analysis are chance findings. Specifically, a correlation of .30 (9 percent of the variance) between our family harmony measure (Cohesion versus Conflict) on the FES and the CPI Well-Being scale initially confirms the Tomlinson-Keasey and Little results, but it drops to .08 when the difference-score analysis is applied. Failure to replicate the results within our study suggests that the initial results were due to chance. Consequently our findings suggest that the Tomlinson-Keasey and Little (1990) results are indeed confounded by genetic factors.

In table 1.2, the DZ twin correlations are on average a bit less than half as high as the MZ twin correlations. This finding characterizes most studies of adult twins, as well as results from models fit to multiple kinships (Eaves, Eysenck, & Martin, 1989, p. 148). The findings all suggest that nonadditive genetic factors contribute to the variability in personality traits. This may explain why twin and adoption studies suggest different heritabilities for personality. Scarr, Webber, Weinberg, and Wittig (1981) report adoptive-sibling correlations near zero, as expected, but their biological-sibling correlations for many measures are lower than would be expected based on twin data. Low sibling correlations may also, in part, be due to age differences in the expression of genetic influences during development (Eaves, Eysenck, & Martin, 1989, ch. 7).

Loehlin (1992a) compiles published kinship correlations for personality and reports them as they relate to the Big Five personality traits (Extraversion, Neuroticism, Openness, Agreeableness, and Conscientiousness). The results when models are fitted to these multiple kinships indicate that (a) genetic factors account for approximately 40 to 50 percent of the variance in each of the Big Five personality traits as measured by self-report, and (b) nonadditive

TABLE 1.3. *Intraclass Correlations, Mean Squares within, and Degrees of Freedom from MZA and DZA Twins and Heritabilities for the Ten Principal Components Underlying the Thirty-Four Work Roles and Work Style Scales of the Jackson Vocational Interest Survey and the Twenty-Three Basic Interest Scales of the Strong Campbell Interest Inventory*

| Scale | Intraclass Correlation | | MZA | | DZA | | Heritability (sc) | χ^2 for Test of | |
	MZA (N = 45)	DZA (N = 22)	MSB (df = 44)	MSW (df = 46)	MSB (df = 21)	MSW (df = 22)		No Genetic Effect (3 df)	General Model (2 df)
Enterprising	.41	.30	1.285	.534	1.775	.950	.50 ± .122	**10.04**	2.21
Academic orientation	.73	.19	1.487	.233	1.789	1.223	.82 ± .062	**17.04**	**6.58**
Artistic	.52	−.07	1.894	.572	.836	.970	.50 ± .109	**13.03**	2.12
Investigative	.68	.02	2.088	.389	.972	.934	.66 ± .086	**18.00**	1.92
Work style	.25	−.03	1.129	.675	.884	.934	.22 ± .140	*2.76*	*.48*
Realistic	.44	−.09	1.506	.584	.716	.858	.41 ± .118	**9.85**	1.90
Social	.54	.02	1.730	.508	.965	.936	.52 ± .109	**12.50**	1.27
Adventure	.54	.04	1.723	.515	1.383	1.280	.53 ± .126	**10.44**	2.43
Medical	.47	.14	1.316	.469	1.402	1.057	.49 ± .139	**9.10**	2.19
Conventional	.38	.17	1.215	.549	1.170	.839	.38 ± .129	**6.28**	*.29*

Source: Moloney, Bouchard, & Segal (1991).

Note: For the No Genetic Effect Model, $\chi^2 > 7.82$ is significant at 0.5 for 3 df. For the General Model, $\chi^2 > 5.99$ is significant at .05 for 2 degrees of freedom. Significant χ^2 values are indicated in boldface type. Nonsignificant χ^2 values that differ significantly are indicated in italic type.

variance contributes significantly to most of these traits (in the range from .02 to .17). Loehlin cannot, however, rule out the competing hypothesis of a more modest heritability based on only additive variance (28 to 46 percent) and special monozygotic and sibling environments. We believe that the available evidence from designs other than simple kinship correlations (e.g., the Loehlin and Nichols [1976] and Lytton [1977] studies of differential treatment of MZ and DZ twins) makes the hypothesis of special monozygotic and sibling environments less tenable than the hypothesis of sizable heritability and nonadditive variance.

Psychological Interests

Given the background already developed, it is easy to present our results in the domain of psychological interests. The variables in table 1.3 were derived from a factor analysis of the Strong Campbell Interest Inventory (SCII; Hansen & Campbell, 1985) and the Jackson Vocational Interest Survey (JVIS; Jackson, 1977), instruments chosen for their dramatically different item content and item structure. Only two factors do not yield significant heritabilities, and only one heritability (.22) could be considered low. Sample sizes slightly larger than the modest ones used in the study would probably result in of both of them reaching statistical significance. The six Holland "types" (Holland, 1973) are clearly in evidence (Enterprising, Artistic, Investigative, Realistic, Social, and Conventional). The Academic Orientation and Work Style factors are defined solely by JVIS scales. The striking findings presented in this table are the low DZA correlations. Because of modest sample sizes, they do not differ significantly from half the MZA correlations, but in absolute magnitude they do stand out in contrast to our data on special mental ability. The DZA correlations of special mental ability are systematically higher than half the MZA correlations. This is a welcome differentiation. It will, however, require interpretation because the DZT correlations from adult interests (different tests) are generally around .21 in our own work (Lykken, Bouchard, McGue, & Tellegen, 1993; but see also Betsworth et al., 1993).

Table 1.4 provides correlations between the interest factors and the FES measures. There are few meaningful and significant correlations. The largest single correlation ($-.23$) is between encouragement of individual growth and the Artistic Interest factor. On general psychological grounds one would expect the correlation to be positive rather than negative.

Table 1.5 presents the correlations between the interest factors and our four environmental factors derived from the Physical Facilities Questionnaire. Even if one agrees that the few significant correlations make sense, and one

TABLE 1.4. *Correlations among the Ten Interest Factors Derived from the Jackson Vocational Interest Survey and the Strong Campbell Interest Inventory and Environmental Factors from the Family Environment Scales for Adoptive MZA and DZA Individuals* $(N = 120)$

| | Environmental Factor | | |
Interest Factor	Cohesion versus Conflict	Positive Constraint	Encouragement of Individual Growth
Enterprising	.02	−.05	−.02
Academic orientation	.15	.04	−.10
Artistic	.09	.11	**−.23**
Investigative	−.06	.05	.05
Work style	−.03	**.16**	−.01
Realistic	−.04	.02	−.08
Social	.05	−.01	−.05
Adventure	.15	.00	−.07
Medical	.09	.03	**−.16**
Conventional	−.05	−.04	−.05

Sources: Moloney, Bouchard, & Segal (1991).
Note: Correlations significant at $p > .05$ are indicated in boldface type.

TABLE 1.5. *Correlations among the Ten Interest Factors Derived from the Jackson Vocational Interest Survey and the Strong Campbell Interest Inventory and Environmental Factors from the Physical Facilities Questionnaire for Adoptive MZA and DZA Individuals* $(N = 104)$

| | Environmental Factor | | | |
Interest Factor	Material Possessions	Cultural	Scientific/ Technical	Mechanical/ Outdoor
Enterprising	.13	.03	−.08	.05
Academic orientation	−.10	.07	−.03	−.06
Artistic	−.07	**.34**	.08	**−.17**
Investigative	−.08	−.09	−.02	**.19**
Work style	.03	−.01	−.10	−.11
Realistic	−.06	.09	**.20**	.04
Social	.06	−.05	.01	−.03
Adventure	−.02	−.12	−.15	−.10
Medical	**.20**	.05	.07	−.06
Conventional	.04	−.07	−.06	.02

Sources: Moloney, Bouchard, & Segal (1991).
Note: Correlations significant at $p < .05$ are indicated in boldface type.

correlation clearly does (Cultural Amenities reported in the home × Artistic Interests equals .34), the amount of variance accounted for is modest. Note, however, that any psychologist would predict different correlations for Investigative × Mechanical/Outdoors (.19) and Realistic × Scientific/Technical (.20). The obvious prediction would be a high Investigative × Scientific/Technical correlation (it is −.02) and a high Realistic × Mechanical/Outdoors correlation (it is .04).

Now that we have demonstrated that genes are involved in the shaping of behavior, and that differences in rearing environment are not nearly so influential as most psychologists have believed, let us turn to the problem of explaining these results. The assertion that genetic factors are important is just a beginning. Fundamental explanation requires a theory and the specification of mechanisms. What mechanisms might underlie the development of psychological traits?

The Theory of Experience-Producing Drives—Revised

Two hypotheses that are not necessarily incompatible have been proposed to characterize the nature of genetic involvement in psychological traits, although most often they have been proposed for cognitive skills rather than for traits such as personality and interests. The first is called the theory of innate neurological structure (INS) and the second is called the theory of experience-producing drives (EPD; McGue & Bouchard, 1989).

Wilson (1983) argues, for example, that genetic influences on IQ largely reflect inherited differences in the structure and function of the brain. Reed (1984) argues that there may be considerable variability in the genes specifying such factors as "transmission proteins" at neural synapses. In support of this view, the speed of information processing has been repeatedly related to intelligence (Bouchard, 1993a; Deary, Langan, Graham, & Hepburn, 1992), and the covariance between intelligence and the speed of cognitive processing appears to reflect a common underlying genetic mechanism (Baker, Vernon, & Ho, 1991). In addition, there is evidence that reaction time (McGarry-Roberts, Stelmack, & Campbell, 1992) and brain nerve conduction velocity correlates with IQ (Reed & Jensen, 1992; Vernon, 1987; Vernon & Mori, 1992). Nevertheless, there are failures to replicate (Barrett, Daum, & Eysenck, 1990; Reed & Jensen, 1991; Rijsdijk, Boomsma, & Vernon, 1995), and some investigators have expressed considerable pessimism about the information-processing approach (Lohman, 1994; Snow, 1995). This model does not, however, explain all individual differences in intelligence. In addition, it proposes a general mechanism, one perhaps influencing the entire nervous system. Such a mechanism addresses neither the problem of special mental abilities nor the common evolutionary argument that biological adaptations are necessarily numerous and highly specific (Tooby & Cosmides, 1990, 1992).

EPD Theory

EPD theory was developed by Hayes (1962), who, with his wife as a collaborator, raised a chimpanzee in their home (Hayes, 1951). It is of considerable interest that Hayes does not see his theory as an environmental theory. Rather, he argues, it is a motivational-experiential theory. Hayes's theory is heavily influenced by comparative psychology, behavioral genetics, and evolutionary theory. He explicitly takes the broad evolutionary view that living organisms are not passive recipients of environmental stimuli, but rather are active agents "designed" by the forces of nature (natural selection) to survive in the environments in which they have evolved. He cites the growing body of literature on behavioral genetics that demonstrates strain differences in various drives, measures of emotional responsiveness, and preferences. He makes it quite clear that he is trying to explicate fundamental biological mechanisms shaped by evolution. As he correctly points out, "the biological nature of modern man is still that of the primitive hunter, farmer, and handscraftsman" (1962, p. 332).

Although it was formulated to deal with the trait of intelligence, the general applicability of EPD theory is readily apparent. It can be reduced to two essential propositions: "(a) manifest intelligence is nothing more than an accumulation of learned facts and skills; and (b) innate intellectual potential consists of tendencies to engage in activities conducive to learning, rather than inherited intellectual capacities, as such. These tendencies are referred to here as experience-producing drives (EPDs)" (p. 337). According to Hayes, these inherent propensities to engage in different types of activities result in extended practice and the formation of stable psychological structures (abilities, in the case of intellectual structures).

EPD theory was built on the observation that a great deal of animal behavior can best be understood in terms of drives that have evolved to fit particular environmental niches. Such drives are designed to be adaptive in the environments in which they have evolved. They can be manipulated by environmental contingencies (operant schedules), but drift in the direction of species typicality when the reinforcement schedules are relaxed (Breland & Breland, 1961).

We have adopted a version of this theory, developed largely by Scarr (Scarr & McCartney, 1983; Scarr, 1992), and it has been our contention that individual differences in psychological traits arise because human beings create their own environments and thus control, to some extent, their own experiences. "It is a plausible conjecture that a key mechanism by which the genes affect the mind is indirect, and that genetic differences have an important role in determining the effective psychological environment of the developing child" (Bouchard, Lykken, McGue, Segal, & Tellegen, 1990, p. 227).

This model works much like the Chomskyan model of language acquisition. The evidence strongly suggests that language acquisition is a species-specific trait that does not require formal instruction (Pinker, 1994). Children who are simply exposed to their native languages will develop the skill. In effect, acquisition of the basic trait is robust. After offering a review of a body of literature similar to that which we have just reviewed, Scarr (1992), without using language as a model, generalizes this idea to most psychological traits and the role of parenting. "Ordinary differences between families have little effect on children's development, unless the family is outside of a normal, developmental range. Good enough, ordinary parents probably have the same effects on their children's development as culturally defined super-parents" (p. 15). As Kaufman (1975) puts it, this view is

> a modification of Heinz Hartmann's famous dictum that the infant is born adapted to survive in an average expectable environment. Hartmann's statement is undoubtedly correct as far as it goes, but we need to add that in the average expectable environment of all societal species, institutions or regulatory systems have arisen that take into account the essential needs of the young, including the need to grow up to be a typical and functional member of the group. These regulatory systems provide an experiential educational process which is calculated to realize, in the young growing up, the biological predispositions evolved through natural selection. In this way one learns what comes naturally. (P. 141)

This model nicely accounts for the lack of influence of a common family environment. All that is required for normal development is an average expectable environment. We are, however, left with three large problems: the problem of specificity versus generality of mechanisms, the problem of genetic variance, and the problem of determining what the average expectable environment in which the human child evolved was like.

First, let us address the problem of specificity versus generality. EPD theory postulates multiple drives influencing the acquisition of skills by a brain that is conceptualized as a general-purpose learning mechanism. Scarr's theory does not expand on the nature or number of the underlying mechanisms beyond suggesting that human capacities may reflect the influence of structural

genes with regard to which humans do not differ. Trait variation is hypothesized to reflect regulatory genes with regard to which individuals do differ.

EPD Theory and Evolutionary Psychology

Unfortunately for EPD theory, virtually all modern theorizing, like most of the
evidence regarding the evolution of the human brain, suggests that nature
designs specific mechanisms for specific purposes. (See virtually any volume of
Behavioral and Brain Sciences published in the past ten years.) The hypothesis
of multiple drives (EPDs) is consistent with this view, but the hypothesis of a
general-purpose brain is not. Consider the example of language, a capacity
Hayes argues was simply learned by a general-purpose brain. Fodor (1980)
convincingly formulates the "modularity argument," which states that language
simply cannot reflect the general capacity of the human brain to learn; "in all
other species cognitive capacities are molded by selection pressures as Darwin
taught us to expect. A truly general intelligence (a cognitive capacity fit to
discover just any truths there are) would be a biological anomaly and an evolutionary enigma" (p. 333; see also Fodor, 1983).

This view does not necessarily imply that modules exist in specific locations in the brain. The term "modules" may be a poor characterization of this
idea because of its association with the concept of modular repair, the replacement of units in a machine. The logic underlying the modularity argument is
relatively persuasive and has been elaborated to apply to many other mechanisms (Barkow, 1989; Tooby & Cosmides, 1992; Symonds, 1979, 1987, 1989).
How does it apply to human mental ability? It certainly favors the view that
mental ability should be conceived of as a set of specialized skills, each with its
own developmental history, as opposed to a single mental ability (see Horn,
1985). No one, not even the most ardent supporters of the construct of general
cognitive ability (*g*), believes that *g* is the only mental ability. What we might
call the evolved modularity model does, however, suggest a somewhat different
way of addressing the controversy over how we should conceptualize mental
abilities. Guilford's (1967) structure-of-intellect theory with its 120 or so factors may have too many factors from a psychometric point of view (Horn &
Knapp, 1973), but does it have enough factors from an evolutionary point of
view? Do the underlying processes hypothesized by Guilford relate meaning-
fully to hypothesized selection pressures experienced by human beings during
the Pleistocene? Does it make sense to expect even rough orthogonality between ability factors, given nature's proclivity to tinker and to build on previous
structures? It seems more likely that at least some abilities would be correlated
to some degree. We believe that these kinds of questions are provocative and

may lead us to conceptualize mental abilities somewhat differently than we have in the past (see Silverman & Eals, 1992). It is still necessary to address the evidence that suggests there are individual differences in general features of the central nervous system (transmission proteins?) that have a general influence on the overall functioning of the organism. An evolutionary perspective on mental abilities gives us a great deal to think about.

EPD Theory—Revised

EPD theory as a theory of multiple drives and a single general learning capacity, although it was parsimonious in its time, is simply not consistent with current theorizing regarding the evolution of psychological mechanisms. It is also no longer consistent with known facts about the structure (Gazzaniga, 1989) and development (Thatcher, Giudice, & Walker, 1987; Hudspeth & Pribram, 1990) of the brain. Thus, we propose a significant revision we call EPD-R theory.

We suggest that what drives behavior and subsequent experience are mechanisms that involve specialized structural features of the brain, mechanisms that account for both capacity and drive. This view is consistent with the Darwinian argument that organisms are designed to do something. They are not composed of mechanisms that simply wait around to be stimulated. It is likely that these mechanisms involve sensitivity to specific features (how specific is an important question) of the environment in which the organism evolved, and that they are self-reinforcing. They are designed by natural selection to drive activity and to influence subsequent experience. In complex organisms such mechanisms do not arise out of nowhere; they must be elaborations and modifications of mechanisms previously designed for other purposes. Therefore, although they will be specialized and have the hallmarks of adaptive design (Williams, 1966), they are unlikely to be unitary or simple. Our modified theory suggests that inherited predispositions represent evolutionarily selected sensitivities to ubiquitous features of environments.[3] Exposure to these environments at the correct time in an organism's development (infancy, childhood, adolescence, sexual maturity) results in the organism's paying attention to critical features and acquiring necessary information. These evolved neural mechanisms must be motivational and must mediate the acquisition of specialized skills or abilities. It should be clear that the lack of exposure to particu-

---

3. "Predisposition" is still the most neutral term we can think of for an evolved neurological structure, with regard to which individuals may differ, that when combined with experience in development makes the organism likely to behave in a certain way under certain conditions. The concept of "instinct" carries too much baggage and tends to imply that there are no individual differences.

lar environments may result in the lack of experience by the organism and consequently retard the development of the particular ability or skill in question. A transaction with the environment is necessary for experience and the consequent growth and development of the skill, ability, or behavior pattern, however defined. The theoretical point is that the necessary environments for bringing most human traits and skills to a functional level (leaving open the possibility of exceptional skills such as those involved in ice skating, ballet, gymnastics, verbal behavior, or musical ability) are, as Scarr argues, widely present and can be readily acquired by a motivated child. We use the term "functional level" because we wish to avoid the notion that any trait is a perfect adaptation, that it cannot be refined and made more precise with further practice; in other words, we feel all traits are to some degree malleable. The degree of malleability is an empirical question.

In addition, mechanisms (traits) may be applied to entirely different problems from those they were evolved to solve. The ability to read words and numbers is an example that readily comes to mind. This skill could not have been selected for, and therefore it does not represent a natural category from the point of view of evolution. It is manifestly incorrect that the Darwinian paradigm (natural selection for characters that enhance inclusive fitness) requires perfect adaptation. It does not. The mechanism we are searching for should lead to functional errors under theoretically specified circumstances. The human proclivity discussed by social psychologists (Dawes, 1988, ch. 1; Nisbett & Ross, 1980) toward certain types of error in reasoning may reflect the influence of evolved processes designed to solve different problems. This line of thinking has been productively pursued by Cosmides and Tooby (1992). The systematic study of errors has always been of interest to psychologists. It can most usefully be employed in the context of a theoretical framework that specifies mechanisms.

How specific must these mechanisms be? Are they still in some way expressed in the traits and capacities that psychologists who specialize in individual difference tend to study? Given Fisher's fundamental theorem that natural selection for an adaptive trait causes additive variance to disappear (Fisher, 1930), our traits are not adaptive because they display too much variance and too much of it is of the additive genetic type. With respect to genetic variance, Scarr (1992) offers a clue: "Fortunately, evolution has not left development of the human species, nor any other, at the easy mercy of variations in their environments. We are robust and able to adapt to wide-ranging circumstances—a lesson that seems lost on many ethnocentric psychologists. If we were so vulnerable as to be led off the normal developmental track by slight variations in our parenting, we should not long have survived" (pp. 15–16). Scarr's model plausibly suggests that the average expected environment in which human children evolved must have been highly variable. We will return to this point in the next section.

If evolution did not leave us at the easy mercy of variations in the environment, then what did it do? It did the same thing it did with all other biological organisms: it provided us, though natural selection, with built-in mechanisms for exploiting our environment for our own benefit. We agree with Buss (1991) that the exploration of such mechanisms should be a priority in the research on individual differences in humans. This will require a different approach to studying the influence of the environment, or what Plomin calls the "nature of nurture" (Plomin, 1994, chs. 2 and 3). The implications of this viewpoint are clear:

> The next step in achieving this understanding will be the development of measurement instruments and observational methods sensitive to the individual's role in constructing experience. . . . Ultimately, our interest is in determining the extent to which experience influences human behavior. Other than to behavioral scientists, the observation that individuals somehow affect the nature of their experiences will hardly come as a major revelation. The alcoholic engages in self-destructive behavior, the sociopath surrounds himself with like tempered peers, and the extrovert seeks social stimulation. (McGue, Bouchard, Lykken, & Finkel, 1991, p. 401)

To expand our plausible conjecture, genes drive behavior and that behavior determines the environments we experience. It will also be necessary to distinguish in our models and our experiments between the objective or consensually defined environment and the subjective environment (i.e., the environment as the person actually construes and experiences it). Given the same objective environment, the genes can bias the subjective environments of different individuals, and the behaviors they call forth, in crucially diverging directions (Tellegen, 1991).

The Puzzle of Genetic Variability

As we have argued elsewhere,

> At the interface of behavioral genetics and sociobiology is the question of origin and function, if any, of the within-species variability we have been discussing. One view is that it represents evolutionary debris (Feldman & Lewontin, 1975;

Symonds, 1979) unimportant to fitness and perhaps not expressed in prehistoric environments. Another view is that variability has an adaptive function and has been selected for. Whether sociobiologists can make evolutionary sense of the varieties of human genetic variation we have discussed here remains to be seen. (Bouchard, Lykken, McGue, Segal, & Tellegen, 1990, p. 228)

Here we attempt to grapple with this problem.

The theory of natural selection has been interpreted by some sociobiologists to mean that if a character is under natural selection (if it contributes to inclusive fitness) it eventually becomes fixed (Buss, 1990, p. 4; Buss, 1991; Crawford & Anderson, 1989, p. 1453). The search for these species-specific features constitutes the quest for human nature. Tooby and Cosmides (1990), although not denying the general proposition, take a slightly different tack: "Selection, interacting with sexual recombination, tends to impose relative uniformity at the functional level in complex adaptive designs, suggesting that most heritable psychological differences are not themselves likely to be complex psychological adaptations" (p. 17). Put another way, "Human physiology is monomorphic within an integrated functional design" (p. 29). This statement simply means that everyone has one head, two arms, and so forth. These structures have the same design in each person, and they are coordinated in their functional activities. Tooby and Cosmides concede only that there is "a great deal of superficial variation." They also argue that there are "no substantive reasons to suspect that the kinds of evolutionary forces that shaped our innate psychological mechanisms are fundamentally different from those that shaped our innate physiology" (p. 30).

But most of the features of human beings that Tooby and Cosmides give as examples are also phylogenetically ancient. All are at least characteristic of the mammalian line, and many are older than that. In the time frame of evolution, human "mental organs" evolved only a short time ago. One might even speculate that most of them are in a transitional phase. Most sociobiological theorists do not even consider this possibility. If the strong selectionist argument is correct, and most observed phenotypic variance is superficial, then it is incredibly surprising to find that psychological traits (we still prefer this term to "mental organs") show a genetic variance of about the same magnitude as many physical organs that are undoubtedly adaptations.

In an interesting tour de force, Tooby expounds a theory that links sexual recombination and parasite-driven selection as an explanation of genetic diversity (Tooby & Cosmides, 1990; Tooby, 1982). Sexual recombination is thought to create an extensive biochemical diversity that protects long-lived organisms against parasites with the capacity to evolve rapidly. Although such a theory may sound absurd to psychologists, it is similar to the theory of parasite-driven HLA polymorphism (Klein & Klein, 1991). Such theories do play a role in evolutionary biology (Trivers, 1985). Tooby simply extends it from the major histocompatibility complex to the entire human genome.

Not everyone agrees with this general model. Margulis and Sagan (1986) make the case that the continued existence of sexual reproduction does not depend on parasite-driven selection. They criticize "the commonly asserted and intuitively appealing but ultimately unjustified assumption that hostile environments maintain sexuality." They also argue that "some of the most variable organisms facing continuously challenging environments are entirely asexual" (p. 208). Significantly, organisms that face continuously changing environments do display a higher degree of genetic variability than those that do not face continually changing environments. This idea has been put forward as an explanation for the maintenance of additive genetic variance, and we believe it may be possible to extend the idea in a unique manner to the human context. (See also Wilson, 1994.)

Natural Selection and the Evolution of the Human Brain

Almost everyone would agree that the human brain, which is the seat of the mental processes or "mental organs" we are discussing, has been intensely selected for in the course of evolution of the human species. Most mammals expend 3 to 4 percent of their resting metabolic energy to maintain their brains, anthropoid primates expend about 8 percent, and human beings expend 20 to 25 percent (Holliday, 1986). The human brain is large, imposes enormous energy costs, and requires a prolonged growth period (Smith, 1989). What were the driving forces that would have allowed such evolutionary extravagance? There are at least eight, and they are closely related: (a) terrestriality (Foley, 1987); (b) the emergence of hunting and gathering (Leonard & Robertson, 1992); (c) competition with other primates (australopithecines; Foley, 1987; Martin, 1989); (d) adaptation to seasonal environments (Foley, 1987; Milton, 1988); (e) glaciation (Calvin, 1990); (f) the increasing complexity of hominid social life (Alexander, 1987; Byrne & Whiten, 1988); (g) tool making (Wynn, 1988); and (h) more speculatively, autopredation (Alexander, 1979; Barkow, 1989). These processes are the explanation for the existence of numerous human skills and the evolution, among other things, of brain size. Nevertheless, head size, and consequently brain size, shows significant genetic variance (Devore, McGue, Crawford, & Lin, 1986, and references therein). Should we conclude that the human brain is not an adaptive mechanism? We think not. One need not focus on an organ as complex as the brain to make this point. There has been a major reduction in dental dimensions since the post-Pleistocene (Calcagno, 1989), but dental dimensions still show considerable genetic vari-ance, as demonstrated in our own dental studies of twins reared apart (Boraas, Messer, & Till, 1988; Michalowicz et al., 1991).

The Ubiquitousness of Additive Genetic Variance

Although we are willing to accept the evidence that suggests that evolution results in some specific mechanisms, as opposed to a few general ones (Cos-mides & Tooby, 1987; Tooby & Cosmides, 1992; Symonds, 1987; Barkow, 1989,

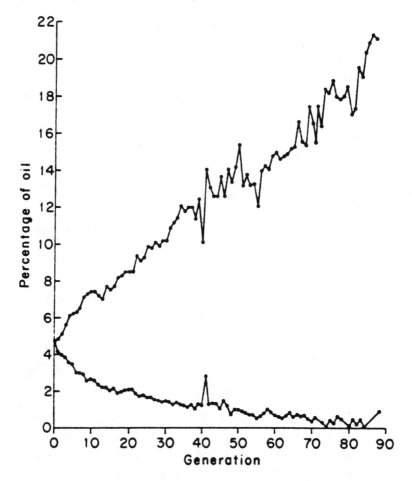

Figure 1.10. The results of nearly ninety generations of selection for high and low oil content in maize kernels.

Source: Crow (1988). Reproduced by permission.

p. 16), how much additive variance might be expected in a population is, in our opinion, an open question, one that has not been sufficiently explored. The metaphorical language of sociobiology is dramatically misleading on this point because it suggests more specificity than is intended (i.e., a gene for altruism, a gene for infidelity, and so forth). Polygenic variance is characteristic of all natural populations; the question of why natural selection has not eliminated the less fit variants (Maynard-Smith, 1989) has puzzled evolutionary theorists for years. This question is usually answered with a list all of whose items reiterate the argument that adaptation is limited by a variety of constraints (Dawkins, 1982; Foley, 1987; Maynard-Smith, 1989; Stearns, 1992). A careful reading of this literature leads to the conclusion that we simply do not know the full answer.

Two striking examples of important quantitative genetic phenomena that are not easily explained by the simple application of evolutionary reasoning (selection will wipe out genetic variance) are reported by Crow (1988) in his review of the *Proceedings of the Second International Conference on Quantitative Genetics* (Weir, Eisen, Goodman, & Namkoong, 1988). The first is a plant example involving selection for oil content in maize (see figure 1.10).

Selection, which began with only twelve ears, has been going on for ninety generations. (It began before the rediscovery of Mendel's laws.) The improvement has been twenty standard deviations above the starting value, and there is no suggestion that genetic variability is running out. Accumulating mutations may be the explanation.

The second example is milk production, which has shown improvement for many years and

> would seem an ideal candidate for a trait that is unresponsive to selection—a long history of unidirectional selection, a phenotype expressed in one sex only, and antagonisms between greater milk yielded and other desirable traits. Yet a great deal of additive genetic variance is present. That there is room for continued selective advance is illustrated dramatically by the fact that the very best cows produce about five times as much as the national average (25,000 as compared to 5,500 kilograms per lactation). (Crow, 1988, pp. 1449–1450)

The first trait (percentage of oil) does not appear to be related to fitness. Milk production, however, which reflects the cow's means of feeding her young, is unquestionably an adaptation and is related to fitness.

Constraints on Selection

Considerable genetic variance should not be a surprise even with regard to traits directly related to fitness. We do not know all the answers to the puzzle of genetic variance, but we know some of them. Consider the constraints on selection. Natural selection capitalizes on previous structures or developmental genes, and neither need be closely related to the new environmental feature or features driving selection. This is a historical constraint. Under such circumstances, adaptation could be painfully slow. Selection pressures are numerous—indeed, almost infinite—and therefore complex. Some must, therefore, conflict with others. This is the constraint of compromise, a balance of selective forces (heterosis, frequency-dependent selection, and so forth).

Allen (1970) discusses a version of this mechanism with respect to the intermediate heritability of human behavioral traits. There is often a time lag between the environmental conditions under which selection begins and current environmental conditions. The two situations may be significantly different. This is comparable to the constraint on selection for adaptation represented by the relaxation of selection pressure in a selection experiment. Such relaxation almost invariably leads to an increase in genetic variability relative to continued selection (Maynard-Smith, 1989). It is possible, for example, that selection for some component of intelligence was greater in prehistoric times than it is now, leading to greater variance in general cognitive ability among modern populations than existed in the late Pleistocene. Sometimes there is a great deal of randomness or unpredictability in the environment. Thus natural selection for some traits may be consistently erratic. If only some of these factors are at work on a trait then it is unlikely that that trait will be free of genetic variance.

If we consider the forces pursuant to which the human brain evolved—the eight items discussed earlier—two features are quite common: complexity and unpredictability. This is particularly true for the microcontext of human social interaction, both within and between families. From the point of view of the developing child, family life, and social life more generally, must appear chaotic. Indeed, many nuclear families are horrifically chaotic even from the point of view of adults. This chaos is so common that it is often imputed to be the cause of mental illness (e.g., schizophrenia). Regardless of one's position on the issue of genetic causation of schizophrenia, one must agree that most children raised by schizophrenic parents do not become mentally ill and that most schizophrenics were not raised by schizophrenic parents (Gottesman, 1991). Children's mental structures are resilient to variation in their rearing environment—not just to variation in the normal range, but also to variation well outside what the typical psychologist would consider normal (Rosenthal et al., 1975). This suggests that, from the point of view of psychological development, the average expectable environment of the human child over the course of human evolution has been far more complex and variable than our images of prehistoric life have led us to believe.

Many human psychological adaptations are probably much more flexible than evolutionary psychology would lead us to believe, and, although flexibility of behavior has not been selected for directly (few if any traits are), we suspect that it has been a concomitant feature of selection in complex social environments where there are multiple behavioral routes to the same goals: survival and reproductive fitness.

Conclusion

Modern biological thought, in the form of behavioral genetics, human ethology, evolutionary psychology, evolutionary genetics, and molecular genetics, has provided us with a richness of ideas regarding the processes and potential underlying mechanisms that drive experience and the development of behavior. These ideas require that we reexamine our cherished tools (factor analysis, within-family studies), categories (the traditional categories of personality, mental ability, psychological interests, and other variables), and beliefs (radical environmentalism) regarding the nature and nurture of human individual differences in an effort to come to a more fundamental understanding of human uniqueness.

There is no question that many human behavioral characteristics, like the characteristics of other species, are at least in part evolutionary adaptations. This view underlies the work of modern evolutionary psychology (Ridley, 1993; Wright, 1994). Although some of that work is controversial, it is now clear that the fundamental thrust is correct and that most arguments concern specific hypotheses and not the research program as a whole. We believe, for example, that for theoretical purposes (applied problems may require a different approach) the categories of ability theory, personality theory, and interest theory ought to reflect our growing understanding of our evolutionary origins.

There is every reason to believe that many of the traits we are currently studying fit into this frame of reference. Traits with important evolutionary roots should be salient and visible even if their origins are not understood (Macdonald, 1995). The personality/attitude trait of ethnocentrism immediately comes to mind. This trait goes under a wide variety of names and has been studied over the years in a wide variety of contexts. Altemeyer's (1988) Right-Wing Authoritarian (RWA) scale is a current example. It is a direct descendant of the research on the Fascism (F) scale, which contained a component scale of ethnocentrism. The California Psychological Inventory contains a reverse F scale called the Tolerance (Tol) scale. The Multidimensional Personality Questionnaire (MPQ) contains a comparable measure called the Traditionalism (Tr) scale. There is a long history of anthropological research on this trait (van den Berghe, 1981; LeVine & Campbell, 1972; Reynolds, Falger, & Vine, 1987). Our own work with twins reared apart suggests that this trait has the same type of genetic structure as ordinary personality traits. Martin et al. (1986) and Eaves, Eysenck, and Martin (1989) present compelling evidence that other attitudinal variables also show similar genetic influence.

The importance of understanding the fundamental origins of human traits and the mechanisms underlying them is not just theoretical. A reiteration of the conclusion of our presentation of some of these same facts in *Science* (Bouchard, Lykken, McGue, Segal, & Tellegen, 1990) is warranted: "Modern society not only augments the influence of genotype on behavioral variability, as we have suggested, but permits this variability to reciprocally contribute to the rapid pace of cultural change. If genetic variation was evolutionary debris at the end of the Pleistocene, it is now a salient and essential feature of the human condition" (p. 228).

Acknowledgments

This research was supported by grants from the Pioneer Fund, the Koch Charitable Foundation, and the Seaver Institute.

References

Abbe, K. M., & Gill, F. M. *Twins on twins*. New York: C. N. Potter, 1980.

Alexander, R. D. (1979). *Darwinism and human affairs*. Seattle: University of Washington Press.

Alexander, R. D. (1987). *The biology of moral systems*. New York: Aldine de Gruyter.

Allen, G. (1970). Within and between group variation expected in human behavioral characters. *Behavior Genetics* 1:175–194.

Altemeyer, B. (1988). *Enemies of freedom: Understanding right-wing authoritarianism*. San Francisco: Jossey-Bass.

Baker, L. A., Vernon, P. A., & Ho, H. (1991). The genetic correlation between intelligence and speed of information processing. *Behavior Genetics* 21:351–368.

Barkow, J. H. (1989). *Darwin, sex, and status: Biological approaches to mind and culture*. Toronto: University of Toronto Press.

Barkow, J. H., Cosmides, L., & Tooby, J. (1992). *The adapted mind*. Oxford: Oxford University Press.

Barrett, P. T., Daum, I., & Eysenck, H. (1990). Sensory nerve conductance and intelligence: A methodological study. *Journal of Psychophysiology* 4:1–13.

Bayley, N. (1970). Development of mental abilities. In P. H. Mussen (Ed.), *Carmichael's manual of child psychology* (pp. 1163–1209). New York: Wiley.

Bernhard, W., Hancke, A., Brauer, G., & Chopra, V. P. (1980). Quantitative genetical analysis of morphological characters of the human head and face. *Journal of Human Evolution* 9:621–626.

Betsworth, D. G., Bouchard, T. J., Jr., Cooper, C. R., Grotevant, H. D., Hansen, J. C., Scarr, S., &

Weinberg, R. A. (1993). Genetic and environmental influences on vocational interests assessed using adoptive and biological families and twins reared apart and together. *Journal of Vocational Behavior* 44:263–278.

Bollen, K. A. (1989). *Structural equations with latent variables.* New York: Wiley.

Boraas, J. C., Messer, L. B., & Till, M. J. (1988). A genetic contribution to dental caries, occlusions, and morphology as demonstrated by twins reared apart. *Journal of Dental Research* 67:1150–1155.

Bouchard, T. J., Jr. (1984). Twins reared together and apart: What they tell us about human diversity. In S. W. Fox (Ed.), *The chemical and biological bases of individuality* (pp. 147–178). New York: Plenum.

Bouchard, T. J., Jr. (1991). A twice-told tale: Twins reared apart. In W. Grove & D. Ciccehetti (Eds.), *Thinking clearly about psychology: Essays in honor of Paul Everett Meehl: Vol. 2. Personality and psychopathology* (pp. 188–215). Minneapolis: University of Minnesota Press.

Bouchard, T. J., Jr. (1993a). The genetic architecture of human intelligence. In P. E. Vernon (Ed.), *Biological approaches in the study of human intelligence.* New York: Plenum.

Bouchard, T. J., Jr. (1993b). Genetic and environmental influences on adult personality: Evaluating the evidence. In I. Deary & J. Hettema (Eds.), *Basic issues in personality.* Dordrecht, the Netherlands: Kluwer Academic Publishers.

Bouchard, T. J., Jr. (1994). Genes, environment, and personality. *Science* 264:1700–1701.

Bouchard, T. J., Jr. (1995). Longitudinal studies of personality and intelligence: A behavior genetic and evolutionary psychology perspective. In D. H. Saklofske & M. Zeidner (Eds.), *International handbook of personality and intelligence* (pp. 81–106). New York: Plenum.

Bouchard, T. J., Jr., Lykken, D. T., McGue, M., Segal, N. L., & Tellegen, A. (1990). Sources of human psychological differences: The Minnesota study of twins reared apart. *Science* 250:223–228.

Bouchard, T. J., Jr., & McGue, M. (1981). Familial studies of intelligence: A review. *Science* 212:1055–1059.

Bouchard, T. J., Jr., & McGue, M. (1990). Genetic and rearing environmental influences on adult personality: An analysis of adopted twins reared apart. *Journal of Personality* 58:263–292.

Bouchard, T. J., Jr., & Segal, N. L. (1985). Environment and IQ. In B. J. Wolman (Ed.), *Handbook of intelligence: Theories, measurements, and applications* (pp. 391–464). New York: Wiley.

Breland, K., & Breland, M. (1961). The misbehavior of organisms. *American Psychologist* 16:681–684.

Burks, B. S. (1938). On the relative contributions of nature and nurture to average group differences in intelligence. *Proceedings of the National Academy of Sciences* 24:276–282.

Buss, D. (1990). Towards a biologically informed psychology of personality. *Journal of Personality* 58:1–16.

Buss, D. (1991). Evolutionary personality psychology. *Annual Review of Psychology* 42:459–491.

Byrne, R. W., & Whiten, A. (Eds.). (1988). *Machiavellian intelligence.* Oxford: Clarendon.

Calcagno, J. M. (1989). *Mechanisms of human dental reduction: A case study from post-Pleistocene Nubia.* Lawrence: University of Kansas Press.

Calvin, W. H. (1990). *The ascent of mind: Ice Age climates and the evolution of intelligence.* New York: Bantam Books.

Campbell, D. T., & Stanley, J. C. (1966). *Experimental and quasi-experimental designs for research.* Chicago: Rand McNally.

Charlesworth, W. R. (1992). Darwin and developmental psychology: Past and present. *Developmental Psychology* 28:5–16.

Chipuer, H. M., Rovine, M. J., & Plomin, R. (1990). LISREL modeling: Genetic and environmental influences on IQ revisited. *Intelligence* 14:11–29.

Cosmides, L. (1989). The logic of social exchange: Has natural selection shaped how humans reason? Studies with the Wason selection task. *Cognition* 31:187–276.

Cosmides, L., & Tooby, J. (1987). From evolution to behavior: Evolutionary psychology as the missing link. In J. Dupré (Ed.), *The latest on the best: Essays on evolution and optimality* (pp. 279–306). Cambridge: MIT Press.

Cosmides, L., & Tooby, J. (1992). Cognitive adaptation for social exchange. In J. H. Barkow, L. Cosmides, & J. Tooby (Eds.), *The adapted mind: Evolutionary psychology and the generation of culture* (pp. 163–228). Oxford: Oxford University Press.

Crawford, C. B., & Anderson, J. L. (1989). Sociobiology: An environmental discipline? *American Psychologist* 44:1449–1459.

Crow, J. F. (1988). [Review of *Proceedings of the Second International Conference on Quantitative Genetics*]. *Science* 242:1449–1450.

Dawes, R. M. (1988). *Rational choice in an uncertain world*. San Diego: Harcourt Brace Jovanovich.

Dawkins, R. (1982). *The extended phenotype*. Oxford: Oxford University Press.

Deary, I. J., Langan, S. J., Graham, K. S., & Hepburn, D. (1992). Recurrent severe hypoglycemia, intelligence, and speed of information processing. *Intelligence* 16:337–360.

Degler, C. N. (1991). *In search of human nature: The decline and revival of Darwinism in American social thought*. Oxford: Oxford University Press.

Devore, E. J., McGue, M., Crawford, M. H., & Lin, P. M. (1986). Transmissible and nontransmissible components of anthropometric variation in the Alexanderwohl Mennonites: II. Resolution by path analysis. *American Journal of Physical Anthropology* 69:83–92.

Dupae, E., Defries-Gussenhoven, E., & Susanne, C. (1982). Genetic and environmental influence on body measurement of Belgian twins. *Acta Geneticae Medicae et Gemmellologiae* 31:139–144.

Eaves, L. J., Eysenck, H. J., & Martin, N. G. (1989). *Genes, culture, and personality*. New York: Academic Press.

Feldman, M. W., & Lewontin, R. C. (1975). The heritability hang-up. *Science* 190:1163–1168.

Fisher, R. (1930). *The genetical theory of natural selection*. Oxford: Clarendon Press.

Fodor, J. A. (1980). Reply to Putnam. In M. Piattelli-Palmarini (Ed.), *Language and learning: The debate between Jean Piaget and Noam Chomsky* (pp. 325–334). Cambridge: Harvard University Press.

Fodor, J. A. (1983). *The modularity of mind*. Cambridge: MIT Press.

Foley, R. (1987). *Another unique species: Patterns of human evolutionary ecology*. Burnt Mill, Harlow, England: Longman.

Galton, F. (1869). *Hereditary genius: An inquiry into its laws and consequences*. London: Macmillan.

Gazzaniga, M. S. (1989). Organization of the human brain. *Science* 245:947–952.

Gedda, L. (1961). *Twins in history and science*. Springfield, Ill.: Thomas.

Gottesman, I. I. (1991). *Schizophrenia genesis: The origins of madness*. New York: Freeman.

Gottlieb, G. (1991). Experiential canalization of behavioral development: Theory. *Developmental Psychology* 27:4–13.

Guilford, J. P. (1967). *The nature of human intelligence*. New York: McGraw-Hill.

Hansen, J. C., & Campbell, D. P. (1985). *Manual for the SVIB-SCII* (4th ed.). Palo Alto: Consulting Psychologists Press.

Hayes, C. (1951). *The ape in our house*. New York: Harper.

Hayes, K. (1962). Genes drives and intellect. *Psychological Reports* 10:299–342.

Henderson, R. W. (1981). Home environment and intellectual performance. In R. W. Henderson (Ed.), *Parent-child interaction: Theory, research, and prospects* (pp. 3–32). New York: Academic Press.

Hoffman, L. W. (1991). The influence of the family environment on personality: Accounting for sibling differences. *Psychological Bulletin* 110:187–203.

Holland, J. L. (1973). *Making vocational choices: A theory of careers*. Englewood Cliffs, N.J.: Prentice-Hall.

Holliday, M. A. (1986). Body composition and energy needs during growth. In F. Falkner & J. Tanner (Eds.), *Human growth: A comprehensive treatise* (2nd ed., Vol. 2, pp. 101–117). New York: Plenum.

Horn, J. L. (1985). Remodeling old models of intelligence. In B. J. Wolman (Ed.), *Handbook of intelligence: Theories, measurements, and applications* (pp. 267–300). New York: Wiley.

Horn, J. L., & Knapp, J. R. (1973). On the subjective character of the empirical base of Guilford's structure-of-intellect model. *Psychological Bulletin* 80:33–43.

Horn, J. M., Plomin, R., & Rosenman, R. (1976). Heritability of personality traits in adult male twins. *Behavior Genetics* 6:17–30.

Hudspeth, W. J., & Pribram, K. H. (1990). Stages of brain and cognitive maturations. *Journal of Educational Psychology* 82:881–884.

Jackson, D. N. (1977). *Jackson Vocational Interest Survey manual*. Port Huron, Mich.: Research Psychologists Press.

Jensen, A. R. (1973). *Educability and group differences*. New York: Harper & Row.

Jöreskog, K. G., & Sörbom, D. (1989). *LISREL 7: A guide to the program and applications*. Chicago: SPSS.

Kamin, L. J. (1974). *The science and politics of IQ*. Potomac, Md.: Erlbaum.

Kaufman, I. C. (1975). Learning what comes naturally: The role of life experience in the establishment of species-typical behavior. *Ethos* 3:129–142.

Keating, D. P. (1975). Possible sampling bias in genetic studies of genius. *Educational and Psychological Measurement* 35:657–662.

Klein, J., & Klein, D. (Eds.). (1991). *Molecular evolution of the MHC*. Heidelberg: Springer.

Leonard, W. R., & Robertson, M. L. (1992). Nutritional requirements and human evolution: A bioenergetics model. *American Journal of Human Biology* 4:179–195.

LeVine, R. A., & Campbell, D. T. (1972). *Ethnocentrism: Theories of conflict, ethnic attitudes, and group behavior*. New York: Wiley.

Li, C. C. (1975). *Path analysis: A primer*. Pacific Grove, Calif.: Boxwood Press.

Loehlin, J. C. (1985). Fitting heredity-environment models jointly to twin and adoption data from the California Psychological Inventory. *Behavior Genetics* 15:199–221.

Loehlin, J. C. (1989). Partitioning environmental and genetic contributions to behavioral development. *American Psychologist* 44:1285–1292.

Loehlin, J. C. (1992a). *Genes and environment in personality development*. Newbury Park, Calif.: Sage.

Loehlin, J. C. (1992b). *Latent variable models* (2nd ed.). Hillsdale, N.J.: Erlbaum.

Loehlin, J. C., & Nichols, R. C. (1976). *Heredity, environment, and personality*. Austin: University of Texas Press.

Lohman, D. F. (1994). Component scores as residual variation (or why the intercept correlates best). *Intelligence* 19:1–12.

Lykken, D. T., Bouchard, T. J., Jr., McGue, M., & Tellegen, A. (1993). Heritability of interests? A twin study. *Journal of Applied Psychology* 78:649–661.

Lytton, H. (1977). Do parents create, or respond to, differences in twins? *Developmental Psychology* 13:456–459.

Macdonald, K. (1995). Evolution, the five-factor model, and levels of personality. *Journal of Personality* 63:525–567.

Margulis, L., & Sagan, D. (1986). *Origins of sex: Three billion years of genetic recombination*. New Haven: Yale University Press.

Martin, N. G., Eaves, L. J., Heath, E. C., Jardine, R., Feingold, L. M., & Eysenck, H. J. (1986). Transmission of social attitudes. *Proceedings of the National Academy of Science* 83:4364–4368.

Martin, R. D. (1989). Evolution of the brain in early hominids. *OSSA* 14:49–62.

Maynard-Smith, J. (1989). *Evolutionary genetics*. Oxford: Oxford University Press.

McCartney, K., Harris, M. J., & Bernieri, F. (1990). Growing up and growing apart: A developmental meta-analysis of twin studies. *Psychological Bulletin* 107:226–237.

McGarry-Roberts, P. A., Stelmack, R. M., & Campbell, K. B. (1992). Intelligence, reaction time, and event-related potentials. *Intelligence* 16:289–314.

McGue, M., & Bouchard, T. J., Jr. (1989). Genetic and environmental determinants of information processing and special mental abilities: A twin analysis. In R. J. Sternberg (Ed.), *Advances in the psychology of human intelligence* (Vol. 5, pp. 264–292). Hillsdale, N.J.: Erlbaum.

McGue, M., Bouchard, T. J., Jr., Iacono, W. G., & Lykken, D. T. (1993). Behavior genetics of cognitive ability: A life-span perspective. In R. Plomin & G. E. McClearn (Eds.), *Nature, nurture, and psychology* (pp. 59–76). Washington, D.C.: American Psychological Association.

McGue, M., Bouchard, T. J., Jr., Lykken, D. T., & Finkel, D. (1991). On genes, environment, and experience. *Behavioral and Brain Sciences* 14:400–401.

Michalowicz, B. S., Aeppli, D. P., Kuba, R. K., Bereuter, J. E., Conry, J. P., Segal, N. L., Bouchard, T. J., Jr., & Pihlstrom, B. L. (1991). A twin study of genetic variation in proportional radiographic alveolar bone height. *Journal of Dental Research* 70:1431–1435.

Milton, K. (1988). Foraging behavior and the evolution of primate intelligence. In R. W. Byrne & A. Whiten (Eds.), *Machiavellian intelligence* (pp. 285–305). Oxford: Clarendon.

Moloney, D. P., Bouchard, T. J., Jr., & Segal, N. L. (1991). A genetic and environmental analysis of the vocational interests of monozygotic and dizygotic twins reared apart. *Journal of Vocational Behavior* 39:76–109.

Moos, R. H., & Moos, B. S. (1986). *Family Environmental Scale manual.* Palo Alto: Consulting Psychologists Press.

Nichols, R. C. (1978). Twin studies of ability, personality, and interests. *Homo* 29:158–173.

Nisbett, R., & Ross, L. (1980). *Human inferences: Strategies and shortcomings of social judgment.* Englewood Cliffs, N.J.: Prentice-Hall.

Oyama, S. (1985). *The ontogeny of information: Developmental systems and evolution.* Cambridge: Cambridge University Press.

Oyama, S. (1988). Populations and phenotypes: A review of development, genetics, and psychology. *Developmental Psychobiology* 21:101–105.

Pedersen, N. L., Plomin, R., Nesselroade, J. R., & McClearn, G. E. (1992). A quantitative genetic analysis of cognitive abilities during the second half of the life span. *Psychological Science* 3:346–353.

Pinker, S. (1994). *The language instinct: The new science of language and mind.* London: Penguin Books.

Plomin, R. (1988). A stake in the heart: A review of *The ontogeny of information. Developmental Psychobiology* 21:93–95.

Plomin, R. (1994). *Genetics and experience: The interplay between nature and nurture.* Thousand Oaks, Calif.: Sage Publications.

Plomin, R., DeFries, J. C., & McClearn, G. E. (1990). *Behavioral genetics: A primer* (2nd ed.). New York: Freeman.

Plomin, R., & Loehlin, J. C. (1989). Direct and indirect IQ heritability estimates. *Behavior Genetics* 19:331–342.

Plomin, R., & Thompson, R. (1987). Life-span developmental behavior genetics. In P. B. Baltes, D. L. Featherman, & R. D. Lerner (Eds.), *Life-span development and behavior* (Vol. 8, pp. 111–123). Hillsdale, N.J.: Erlbaum.

Reed, T. E. (1984). Mechanism for heritability of intelligence. *Nature* 311:417.

Reed, T. E., & Jensen, A. R. (1991). Arm nerve conduction velocity (NCV), brain NCV, reaction time, and intelligence. *Intelligence* 55:33–47.

Reed, T. E., & Jensen, A. R. (1992). Conduction velocity in a brain nerve pathway of normal adults correlates with intelligence level. *Intelligence* 16:259–272.

Reynolds, V., Falger, V., & Vine, I. (Eds.). (1987). *The sociobiology of ethnocentrism: Evolutionary dimensions of xenophobia, discrimination, racism, and nationalism.* London: Croom Helm.

Richards, R. J. (1987). *Darwin and the emergence of evolutionary theories of mind and behavior.* Chicago: University of Chicago Press.

Ridley, M. (1993). *The red queen: Sex and the evolution of human nature.* New York: Penguin Books.

Rijsdijk, F. V., Boomsma, D. I., & Vernon, P. A. (1995). Genetic analysis of peripheral nerve conduction velocity in twins. *Behavior Genetics* 25:341–348.

Rosenthal, D., Wender, P. H., Kety, S. S., Schulsinger, F., Welner, J., & Rieder, R. O. (1975). Parent-child relationships and psychopathological disorder in the child. *Archives of General Psychiatry* 32:466–476.

Rowe, D. C. (1990). As the twig is bent? The myth of child-rearing influences on personality. *Journal of Consulting and Development* 68:606–611.

Scarr, S. (1981). *Race, social class, and individual differences in IQ.* Hillsdale, N.J.: Erlbaum.

Scarr, S. (1992). Developmental theories for the 1990s: Development and individual differences. *Child Development* 63:1–19.

Scarr, S. (in press.) Behavior genetic and socialization theories of intelligence: Truce and reconciliation. In R. J. Sternberg & E. L. Grigorenko (Eds.), *Intelligence: Heredity and environment.* New York: Cambridge University Press.

Scarr, S., & McCartney, K. (1983). How people make their own environments: A theory of genotype environment effects. *Child Development* 54:424–435.

Scarr, S., Webber, P. L., Weinberg, R. A., & Wittig, M. A. (1981). Personality resemblance among adolescents and their parents in biologically related and adoptive families. *Journal of Personality and Social Psychology* 40:885–898.

Scarr, S., & Weinberg, R. A. (1978). The influence of "family background" on intellectual attainment. *American Sociological Review* 43:674–692.

Scarr, S., Weinberg, R. A., & Waldman, I. D. (1993). IQ correlations in transracial adoptive families. *Intelligence* 17:541–555.

Silverman, I., & Eals, M. (1992). Sex differences in spatial abilities: Evolutionary theory. In J. H. Barkow, L. Cosmides, & J. Tooby (Eds.), *The adapted mind: Evolutionary psychology and the generation of culture* (pp. 531–549). Oxford: Oxford University Press.

Smith, B. H. (1989). Growth and development and its significance for early hominid behavior. *OSSA* 14:63–96.

Snow, R. E. (1995). *Validity of IQ as a measure of cognitive ability.* Paper presented at the Workshop on IQ Testing and Educational Decision Making, San Diego, Calif.

Stearns, S. C. (1992). *The evolution of life histories.* Oxford: Oxford University Press.

Symonds, D. (1979). *The evolution of human sexuality.* New York: Oxford University Press.

Symonds, D. (1987). If we're all Darwinian, what's the fuss about? In C. Crawford, M. Smith, & D. Krebs (Eds.), *Sociobiology and psychology: Ideas, issues, and applications* (pp. 121–146). Hillsdale, N.J.: Erlbaum.

Symonds, D. (1989). A critique of Darwinian anthropology. *Ethology and Sociobiology* 10:131–144.

Tellegen, A. (1991). Modeling and measuring environment. *Behavioral and Brain Sciences* 14:408–409.

Tellegen, A., Lykken, D. T., Bouchard, T. J., Jr., Wilcox, K. J., Segal, N. L., & Rich, S. (1988). Personality similarity in twins reared apart and together. *Journal of Personality and Social Psychology* 54:1031–1039.

Terman, L. M., & Oden, M. H. (1959). *The gifted group at mid-life.* Stanford: Stanford University Press.

Thatcher, R. W., Giudice, S., & Walker, R. A. (1987). Human cerebral hemispheres develop at different rates and ages. *Science* 236:1110–1113.

Tomlinson-Keasey, C., & Little, T. D. (1990). Predicting educational attainment, occupational achievement, intellectual skill, and personal adjustment among gifted men and women. *Journal of Educational Psychology* 82:442–455.

Tooby, J. (1982). Pathogens, polymorphisms, and the evolution of sex. *Journal of Theoretical Biology* 97:557–576.

Tooby, J., & Cosmides, L. (1990). On the universality of human nature and the uniqueness of the individual: The role of genetics and adaptation. *Journal of Personality* 58:17–68.

Tooby, J., & Cosmides, L. (1992). The psychological foundations of culture. In J. H. Barkow, L. Cosmides, & J. Tooby (Eds.), *The adapted mind: Evolutionary psychology and the generation of culture* (pp. 19–136). Oxford: Oxford University Press.

Trivers, R. (1985). *Social evolution.* Menlo Park, Calif.: Benjamin/Cummins.

van den Berghe, P. (1981). *The ethnic phenomenon.* New York: Elsevier.

Vernon, P. A. (Ed.). (1987). *Speed of information processing and intelligence.* Norwood, N.J.: Ablex.

Vernon, P. A., & Mori, M. (1992). Intelligence, reaction time, and peripheral nerve conduction velocity. *Intelligence* 16:273–288.

Weir, G. S., Eisen, E., Goodman, M. M., & Namkoong, G. (1988). *Proceedings of the Second International Conference on Quantitative Genetics.* Sunderland, Mass.: Sinauer.

White, K. R. (1982). The relation between socioeconomic status and academic achievement. *Psychological Bulletin* 91:461–481.

Willerman, L. (1979). Effects of families on intellectual development. *American Psychologist* 34:923–929.

Williams, G. C. (1966). *Adaptation and natural selection: A critique of some current evolutionary thought.* Princeton: Princeton University Press.

Williams, R. J. (1956). *Biochemical individuality.* New York: Wiley.

Wilson, D. S. (1994). Adaptive genetic variation and human evolutionary psychology. *Ethology and Sociobiology* 15:219–235.

Wilson, R. S. (1983). The Louisville twin study: Developmental synchronies in behavior. *Child Development* 54:298–316.

Wright, R. (1994). *The moral animal: Evolutionary psychology and everyday life.* New York: Pantheon.

Wright, S. (1921). Correlation and causation. *Journal of Agricultural Research* 20:557–585.

Wright, S. (1931). Statistical methods in biology. *Journal of the American Statistical Association* 26:155–163.

Wynn, T. (1988). Tools and the evolution of human behavior. In R. W. Byrne & A. Whiten (Eds.), *Machiavellian intelligence* (pp. 271–284). Oxford: Clarendon.

2 The IQ Controversy and the Gifted

ABRAHAM J. TANNENBAUM

et me come right to the point: I count myself among my scientifically correct colleagues as a certifiable IQ basher. But I bemoan bashing below the belt. The alliteration is meant to be tongue-in-cheek, because it is hard to take the attacks too seriously. Somehow they call to mind George Bernard Shaw's social criticism—much pummeling, little pain. Either the critics do not really intend to be hurtful, or if they do, the test publishers and test users are not hurting.

Researchers investigating the nature, and educators experimenting with the nurture, of gifted children are hardly furrowing their brows over the use of IQ in designating who qualifies as "gifted." As evidence, consider the results of a simple survey I conducted of all the empirical studies published in the *Gifted Child Quarterly* over two years (1990 and 1991) that specify the criteria for defining their sample populations. Out of a total of twenty-two such reports, thirteen list IQ as the sole measure, or as prominent among several others.

My own findings that the demise of IQ testing is exaggerated confirm those of a much more elaborate study conducted by Snyderman and Rothman (1987), from which they conclude that psychologists and educators knowledgeable in areas related to intelligence testing generally agree that IQ instruments are valid and useful in measuring some of the most vital aspects of intelligence. In their subsequent book on the IQ controversy (1988), these authors place much blame on the popular media for trying to persuade the literate and informed public that most behavioral scientists judge intelligence tests to be inadequate in measuring anything related to life performance. Snyderman and Rothman were able to justify their attack on the media after carefully examining comments on the subject made in popular print and television outlets, which they compared with opinions they had previously obtained from 661 members of leading behavioral science associations. What the professionals really thought about IQ tests and the media's reports of what they thought were exact opposites. Newspapers, newsmagazines, and newscasters simply distorted reality, declaring fiction fact and fact fiction.

Sources of Concern about IQ Testing

The media have been known to falsify truths, but usually with prejudice, or because they tend to headline a few who are vocal as representing a silent many, though not a majority. This is especially true when the few are perceived by some colleagues as representing the cutting edge of thought on an issue. In this case, both conditions exist. The public to which the media caters is often suspicious of the legitimacy of any measure that purports to forecast future achievement, as if the test were controlling destiny. Reinforcing, and reinforced by, these essentially lay feelings are the assertions of some prestigious commentators who question the validity of IQ; they argue that it does not meet its prognostic or diagnostic goals.

Criticism and Defense of IQ's Legitimacy

In an open society where the Horatio Alger dream is alive and well, equal opportunity is everything, and possibly even the only thing. Belief in the mind as an open system means that everyone can capitalize on that equality in order to achieve, given the proper amount of willpower and opportunity. Unfortunately, little is known about how wide open the system is, and less is known about how to take advantage of it to the fullest extent. Do all the free and able-minded have the potential to deal with esoterica in the physical sciences or to produce an aura of artistic mystery comparable to that of the Mona Lisa? Assuming the answer is "yes," then what strategies can be used to activate that capacity in any person, *selected at random*, to measure up to the likes of a Stephen Hawking or of a Leonardo da Vinci? No one can address either question expertly at this time. However, all agree that any neglect of the mind's open system compromises democracy's open society. In other words, it is incumbent upon all of us to encourage each of us to produce or perform as well as possible and to clear away all barriers to that accomplishment.

Sound and fury. . . . Therein lies the rub. There is an undercurrent of popular feeling—which may be reflected or exploited in the media—that IQ "acts" like the hand of Fate, dictating what a person as young as age five can and cannot become in later years within not-too-broad limits. This is seen by many as an abrogation of individual freedom to control one's fate, or at least enough of an abridgment to bring us dangerously close to elitism and even racism. Others counter by arguing that if enough can be measured in human intellect to predict who does and who does not stand a chance of some day puttering around with fractals, better that it be known as early as possible in the child's life so that parents and teachers can deal with it. The debate has reduced itself to action versus polemics, with educational practitioners and researchers making use of IQ, and the media, along with many academics, decrying such use. Nobody has expressed the objection to predetermination via IQ testing better than a renowned political polemicist of another generation, Walter Lippmann, in his once-famous debate with Lewis Terman: "If . . . the impression takes root that these [IQ] tests really measure intelligence, that they constitute a sort of last judgment on the child's capacity, that they reveal 'scientifically' his predestined ability, then it would be a thousand times better if all the intelligence testers and all their questionnaires were sunk without warning in the Sargasso Sea" (Lippmann, 1976, p. 19).

In his equally acerbic riposte, Terman dubs Lippmann a jittery, head-in-the-sand alarmist who fantasizes threats to democracy. If IQ tests show that humans are not all equal, or cannot be made to become equal, in mental functioning, that's tough; that's life. That is what Terman seems to imply when he baits his adversary:

> Does not Mr. Lippmann owe it to the world to abandon his role of critic and to enter this enchanting field of research? He may safely be assured that if he unravels the secret of turning low IQs into high ones, or even into moderately higher ones, his fame and fortune are made. If he could guarantee to raise certified 100s to certified 140s, . . . nothing but premature death or the discovery and publication of his secret would keep him out of the Rockefeller-Ford class if he cared to achieve it. (Terman, 1976, p. 37)

The Lippmann-Terman debate brings to mind an age-old theological dilemma, which the faithful express as an eternal riddle: How can we retain free will while at the same time affirming God's omniscience? Agnostics turn the question around: How can God exist as an omniscient power over mortals and at the same time affirm their free will? Considering the entrenchment of opposing views on both the theological dilemma and the IQ controversy, it appears doubtful that any rapprochement can be effected in either case. Still, there would be no reason to abandon hope for resolving the IQ controversy if fears concerning its legitimacy could somehow be allayed before dealing with issues of validity.

. . . *signifying nothing*. The Lippmann-Terman debate arouses no real excitement in me, regardless of whether it is argued sarcastically or dourly, as it has been over and over again for much of this century. Each side overstates its case to the point of absurdity. There is no reason to worry that a five-year-old with an IQ of 165 is marked for life to become a brain surgeon, even if he or she aspires to be one. Nor should five-year-olds with IQs that are better (though not too much better) than average, but with superdexterous fingers and superior spatial aptitude, be ruled out as prospects if they aspire to be brain surgeons. Furthermore, a child's IQ is not chiseled in stone for his or her lifetime. If anything, evidence suggests sharp fluctuations in individual IQ scores over time when children are retested periodically (Honzik, MacFarlane, & Allen, 1948; Jackson, 1978). Even the child whose score is consistently high has no more than a better-than-average chance to earn good grades in school and to qualify someday for a prestigious occupation. The probabilities of rising to the top improve considerably only if the child also has the right kinds of special abilities, ambitions, work habits, and nurturance, and a few lucky breaks along the way. In other words, the high IQ offers a hint of how well an individual *may* fare in a variety of tasks, without guaranteeing how well he or she *will* fare, and in what specific domain of excellence. Reading grim predestination into IQ is, therefore, a bit like expecting blackjack dealers to win every game, even though the chances of winning favor dealers only moderately.

Yet, frankly, I do see a monster in IQ, not because of what it is but because of what people make of it. The Frankenstein, in this case, is not the constructor of the test; more than occasionally, it is the educator or psychologist who interprets the IQ score. The meaning of IQ has been so disfigured that it may be high time to declare a moratorium on its use until a *deus ex machina* somehow expunges superstitions about it.

One of many examples of popular distortion has to do with test norms. However we view Terman's commitment to democracy, we must acknowledge that he bequeathed to us a conviction, thus far unassailed, that all human beings are brothers and sisters under the normal curve in scholastic aptitude and performance. Accordingly, the gifted are different from their nongifted peers in degree rather than in kind. They are not a breed apart, a handful of mutants to be admired for their mental feats, yet basically freaks. Instead, their mental endowment is like that of everyone else, except that they are able to apply it at a quantifiably faster pace and higher level than can most individuals their age. Ah, that normal curve, so seductive in its symmetry, so golden in its mean, so redolent of good health and well-being—in short, of human normalcy.

But beneath the sweet aroma, it is easy to smell a rat. Through no fault of Terman's, or of any other well-intentioned psychometrician, the mean has become something of a fetish, a standard by which to judge the legitimacy of the school curriculum and of children's success in it. Clearly, schools spotlight the middle of the ability distribution, while the upper extremes remain pretty much in the dark. This pertains not only to the *level* of children's abilities targeted but also to their *nature*. If you want to know what *kinds* of skills take center stage in the curriculum, simply examine any garden-variety IQ test; not that the kinds of mental powers assessed by IQ measures are anything but the wits we need to live by these days and will need in the foreseeable future, nor are they by any means the *only* thought processes that make life possible and meaningful. What public instruction amounts to, therefore, is something akin to teaching to the test or, more precisely, to the middle range of that test.

The tyranny of the mean is not confined to IQ; it extends to standardized achievement tests as well. Whatever raw score is obtained most often by children in a particular grade or age group is the standard by which all others in that group are judged. In other words, it is "normal." But such norms represent average achievement in an imperfect world; enrich the learning conditions of that world and the norms will surely improve, too.

In a practical sense, the mean-as-ideal is used to help, or even pressure, children to come as close to it as possible. Those who fail to measure up deserve all the remediation they can get in order to be raised "to grade level" as part of their democratic birthright. However, whoever exceeds the norm for whatever reason is not just achieving better than average—she or he is ranging beyond expectation, improving on the ideal, gilding the lily, as it were. That is admirable, perhaps, but it does not commit educators to raise the standards of achievement for children who are able to measure up to higher standards. In fact, schools sometimes discourage these students from outperforming their peers by too much, lest the gifted ones become too conspicuous in the crowd and suffer its ridicule or even its hostility. So instead of stretching every student's mind as skillfully as possible in the direction of its own limits, educators allow themselves to be held captive by a golden mean, a devotion to the straight and narrow path, down the middle.

Terman and the other psychometricians never intended IQ and achievement tests to have such a straitjacketing effect on curriculum content and on standards for mastering it. Quite the contrary—they sought to highlight human diversity. Only those who put these innovations to use have turned gold (not the pure kind, but gold nonetheless) into dross. What, then, can be said about the legitimacy of IQ? Unlike other critics, I have no problems with it objectively.

I do not consider it quite so infallible as some of its protagonists do, and I do not consider it quite so blemished as its antagonists do. But there are so many all-or-nothing distortions of this kind that I am uneasy about the way it has been *used* and *abused,* rather than about its *usefulness.*

If Walter Lippmann were alive today, I wonder whether he would be more, or less, alarmed about the hand of Fate in mental testing after witnessing the proliferation of new standardized tests of academic potential that are supposed to be improvements over IQ tests in their predictive validity.

Criticism and Defense of IQ's Predictive Validity

Whereas the legitimacy issue revolves around whether it is right and proper to use IQ tests, the validity issue relates to whether these tests are useful at all for their avowed purposes. It is impossible to design such a measure to be fully legitimate *and* valid, since the two conditions counteract each other. Improve on the power of IQ (or any other test) to prophesy performance in school or to forecast occupational levels and you will arouse reactions against its allowing destiny to intrude on freedom of ambition, Horatio Alger style—reactions like Lippmann's claim that IQ is illegitimate in a democratic society. Neglect to improve on the test's predictive validity and you will encourage complaints about its failure to do what it is supposed to do. IQ can therefore be damned either way, whether or not test constructors come as near perfection as possible.

Critics assert that IQ is a poor harbinger of a child's future achievement. If true, this assertion should come as a relief to those who worry about its legitimacy. But how poor is "poor"? One person's poverty can be another's riches, as, for example, in the data of a study reported by one detractor of IQ (Feldman, 1984). He investigated nineteen men with IQs of 180 or above and compared them with a sample of fifteen men with IQs in the 150 range, all of them taken from the Terman population. Although the majority of the men in both groups pursued careers as professionals or as business executives, Feldman found that "only" four of the nineteen men with IQs of 180 or above (versus none of the men in the 150 range) could be described as "distinguished." Disappointed, he concludes that "the overall impression is one of lower achievement than the traditional view of IQ would have predicted" (p. 520).

Feldman is obviously disappointed by the fifteen "failures" in a group of nineteen; others, seeing the glass as half full, might consider four "successes" out of only nineteen cases a rousing endorsement of IQ—or, more precisely, of whatever intellective strengths IQ measures—as constituting part of the makeup of giftedness, especially since the scores were obtained some sixty years before Feldman's follow-up. So much had happened in the lives of Terman's sample over the six decades since they were first tested that one would expect these test results to be far more obsolete as predictors than Feldman found them to be. To researchers who prefer to see the IQ container as half empty rather than half full, my advice is similar to what I once suggested to a particularly demanding woman who was criticizing her child's teachers for failing to live up to her inordinately high levels of expectation: "I know of only one way you can solve your problem: lower your standards."

This suggestion to IQ critics is offered without sarcasm. To me, the failure of so many attempts to produce measures featuring perfect predictive validity, or at least better predictive validity with regard to human achievement than the conventional IQ can offer, demonstrates how futile it is to search for a more valid pencil-and-paper test of power than IQ, for two reasons. First, childhood intelligence, however it is defined, cannot be assessed directly by some kind of brain probe; all we can do is infer potential from performance on a test, which is inevitably subject to error. Second, an even more salient limitation is that intellective power is not the sole key to accomplishment in school and society. There are ancillary personal attributes and life experiences that can make or break the promise of a career, no matter what a pencil-and-paper test reveals about intelligence. I am, therefore, convinced that we have gone about as far as we can toward perfecting intelligence testing. Since such measures must fail to predict performance unerringly, it is best to accept their limitations and capitalize on whatever strengths they have rather than fulminate against them as misleading or even dangerous.

No matter how far we have gone in perfecting IQ tests, and no matter how ready we are to accept their limitations, the question of their predictive validity is a straightforward empirical one that can be asked as follows: to what extent is IQ associated with school achievement, occupational level, and advancement within a field of work? The answer is not quite so easy to come by as might be expected. The term "associated" denotes either a correlational or a categorical relationship. Unfortunately, in this case, contradictory results can be obtained depending on which empirical approach is taken. Hardly anyone would dispute that IQ is most impressive in predicting academic performance in school, provided our standards of prediction are lax enough to allow for even less accuracy than meteorologists enjoy in forecasting the weather. Correlation coefficients vary according to the kind of IQ test used, the nature and measures of criterion variables, the ages of sample groups, and the length of time between testing IQ and achievement. However, in most cases, IQ explains between 25 percent and 40 percent of the variance. Not bad, considering that this is appreciably higher than the effects of a father's education or occupation (Duncan, Featherman, & Duncan, 1973).

So much for IQ and scholastic success—except to point out that the reported coefficients are probably inflated because researchers usually do not partial out other independent variables. In a rare study where it was done, IQ by itself accounted for about 16 percent of the variance in educational achievement (Duncan, 1968)—not earthshaking, but not negligible either, since I have not found another *single* predictor to be stronger when IQ is partialed out.

Beyond school, IQ performs less well as a predictor of success, especially in the world of work. As McClelland (1976) and Wallach (1976) point out, measures of human potential have been validated for achievement in academic subjects, but scholastic records have little to do with who will qualify for what prestigious occupations and how those who manage eventually to qualify for any of them will perform in their jobs. Indeed, Duncan (1968) discovered that whereas IQ alone explained about 16 percent of the variance in school achievement, it explained only about 9 percent of the variance in occupational status. As for proficiency on the job, the picture is even less impressive, though by no means entirely clear. For example, in a review of fifty years of research involving more than ten thousand cases, Ghiselli (1966) reports a correlation of only .23 between IQ and actual success in many types of jobs. This result seems to have been confirmed in a subsequent study by Wigdor and Garner (1982), which notes that IQ explains only 4 percent of the variance in job success. But the story does not end there. Ghiselli (1966) reveals a more-impressive correlation of .4 between IQ and speed and ease of training for a variety of occupational skills. This means that the higher the IQ, the more trainable a person is for advancement in an occupation. After training, factors other than tested intelligence make the big difference between moving forward and remaining fairly stationary in career status. Considering the huge size of Ghiselli's population, McClelland (1976) observes: "It is small wonder that psychologists believe intelligence tests are valid predictors of job success. Unfortunately, [however,] it is impossible to evaluate Ghiselli's conclusion, as he does not cite his sources and he does not state exactly how job proficiency was measured for each of his correlations" (p. 49).

Meta-analytic methods such as path analysis and latent analysis have recently been used to assess the predictive power of general ability as it relates to success on the job and in job training. Most of the research has been conducted on huge samples drawn from members of the armed services with good academic credentials who are serving in military jobs at various levels of complexity.

Results of the newer research paint a sharply different picture from what has been available heretofore. For example, Ree and Earles (1992) report their own study showing an average correlation of .76 between general-ability scores and success in eighty-nine training courses for technical jobs. Tests of specific aptitudes added virtually nothing to the prediction. These researchers also found a correlation of .44 (corrected for attenuation) between general ability and job performance for air force pilots in eight areas of specialization. Again, special aptitudes added little to the prediction. These outcomes are roughly in line with others cited by Ree and Earles (1992). Perhaps McClelland's (1976) skepticism, noted earlier, can be laid to rest after all.

Categorical validations of IQ are even more compelling than prediction studies, especially at the highest extremes of the test range. Just one supportive citation is enough—Terman and Oden's Genetic Studies of Genius series—because of its huge scale and because no subsequent research of its kind has contradicted their findings. They discovered that children scoring in the highest percentile in IQ were not sickly, namby-pamby misfits whose only gift and goal in life was to get good grades in school. When they grew up, their superior academic records were matched by professional, marital, and financial success as well as adult mental health. Yes, there were underachievers in the group, which makes even high IQ fallible as a predictor of achievement. But these few failures were considered such only in comparison to the rest of the sample, judging from their better-than-average scholastic and work histories. Terman and Oden's results are impressive, even though they never controlled for the children's advantaged home environments. Nor did children qualify to join the experimental group strictly on the basis of IQ. To earn an invitation to take that test, they had to be among the youngest or in the top 10 percent of their classes. Yet the data are simply too overwhelming to be dismissed because of limitations in the study's methodology. As Oden (1968) states at the end of her long-range follow-up of Terman's men and women: "Now after forty years of careful investigation there can be no doubt that for the overwhelming majority of subjects the promise of youth has been more than fulfilled" (p. 51). It would be hard to dispute her summation of Terman's results unless one expected to find a Mozart or Shakespeare in his sample, or if one such genius were overlooked in the course of putting the sample together.

The few studies I have cited on the predictive validity of IQ probably reflect what the literature in general says about the subject. From this body of evidence, it appears that the test does identify potential high achievers, but in the process it also creates a far from piddling share of false positives and false negatives. The most likely success stories are of preschool and elementary school children whose strengths appear to be primarily in academic subjects. With all these qualifiers in place, I can appreciate the sentiments of a silent majority of practitioners who accept IQ, provided there is other confirmatory evidence to support it, while the vocal debaters in the IQ controversy tend to express either a slavish belief in IQ or a knee-jerk aversion to it.

There are reasons other than the less-than-perfect predictive validity of the IQ test that cause some people to endorse it only guardedly. They are also concerned about neglecting children who do not measure up to some fixed standard of precocity but whose performance on the test and skills at finding and solving abstract problems can be raised considerably. Feuerstein (1979, 1991) is right to criticize IQ as a static measure, a snapshot of scholastic aptitudes taken at one moment in time, without consideration of the test taker's modifiability. He argues convincingly that the human mind is an open system, amenable to change under guidance from a sensitive and trained change agent, or mediator, who helps strengthen cognitive functions, achievement motivation, self-confidence, and approach strategies in learning situations. Children with the potential to be called gifted who lack this kind of intervention may peremptorily be labeled nongifted on the basis of a static IQ score that frequently marks them for life.

No less troubling is the practice of focusing almost all the attention at school on the abilities that IQ identifies best simply *because* IQ identifies them best. Imagine a single artisan's tool, rather than a conceptual design, leading a sculptor to the realization of an artistic vision, its material and shape. It makes one wonder which is the artist and which is the tool. Too many educators have similarly capitulated to the IQ test by tailoring the curriculum to suit the abstract thinking skills that IQ taps. Even when so-called multiple criteria are used to identify precocious children, the supplemental sources of information offer further testimony on the same kinds of mental attributes revealed by IQ. This leaves other strengths largely neglected in both the identification process and the educational program. To avoid these pitfalls, I would urge practitioners to use IQ for assessing some kinds of talent in young children, but not to overlook other abilities in the identification plan. Also, we must remember that children are modifiable in test performance and in facing mental challenges successfully at school and in society, even if they do not seem to perform with distinction on an IQ test as it is conventionally administered (Feuerstein, 1979, 1980).

Criticism and Defense of IQ's Content Validity

Aside from criticism of the predictive validity of IQ testing, there have been serious reservations about the test's content and its connection to what it is supposed to measure. Indeed, parts of the battery look like gibberish, others like fun and games, still others like exercises in trivia or esoterica. As Estes (1982) suggests:

> Take for example the word-naming task, which is a subtest at year 10 of the
> Stanford-Binet Intelligence Scale. The person tested is simply required to name as

many different words as possible in one minute, without using sentences or counting. How could performance possibly reflect important aspects of intellectual ability? . . . Yet it is a well-documented fact that correlations of scores on this subtest with total test score and with criteria of validity such as school performance are of the same order of magnitude as those involving subtests with more obvious intellectual content. (Pp. 212, 213)

In view of such evidence, test users may wonder why any question is raised about test content when the score and what it implies should be the only subject of scrutiny. In other words, if a coin can occasionally be used as a screwdriver, who cares that it looks, feels, and is shaped like a coin, as long as it does the job, albeit only with certain screws? However, the doubts expressed about content validity are serious ones, not simply quibbles about irrelevancies, and they should be entertained in good faith.

Are IQ tests meant to be theory driven? It is true that the old IQ tests (which are still widely used) are based on no theory about human intelligence or about how the brain processes, stores, retrieves, and transfers learning experiences. The reason is probably more historical than conjectural. When Terman translated, adapted, and validated the Binet-Simon test, he never proposed a theory of intelligence as a rationale for his instrument. He merely intended to develop a practical device for assessing the ability to think abstractly in much the same way that an electrician tests the power of a generator without caring much how it works or how to explain the properties of electrical current.

Theory has become something of an icon in psychology—and rightly so, up to a point: it unquestionably provides enlightenment and inspires research. But it would be a bit misleading to suggest that the content validity of tests needs to be anchored in a solid corpus of theory. Nor does a wealth of theory about a particular human attribute inevitably lead to good instruments for assessing that attribute. Consider, for example, our continuing ineptitude in measuring creative potential, despite the interest countless theorists have in this subject. Unlike such phenomena as cognition and motivation, which are virtually the private preserves of psychologists and educators, creativity is a subject of speculation and investigation by professionals in other fields as well, including philosophers, historians, and critics of art, music, dance, literature, and theater, to say nothing of biographers of creative people, and the creative people themselves.

Yet despite all the well-meaning efforts to translate creativity theory into tests of creative potential, the results are disappointing. If anything, the developers of these instruments do a disservice to the concept of creativity by touting them as measures of something they, in fact, misrepresent.

To say that someone is highly creative on the basis of a score on a so-called creativity test that bears no empirical connection to any visual, auditory, or tangible manifestation of creativity is to engage in false advertising, no matter how theory-driven the test instrument claims to be. On the other hand, if an IQ score relates somehow to what many laypeople as well as educators and psychologists call "intelligent behavior," who cares that the test is not theory driven and is made up of fun-and-games exercises far removed from real-life problems? The proof of the pudding is in the eating, not in the recipe.

Should creativity tests supplement, or even replace, IQ tests? One of the fiercest and most influential attacks on IQ was lodged by Getzels and Jackson (1958, 1962); in their studies, they contend that highly creative children are excluded from the pool of gifted children when that pool is determined exclusively by IQ tests. To support their claim, they present evidence to show that highly creative, low-IQ adolescents perform as well in academic courses as do their peers with higher IQs and less creativity, and outperform them in several kinds of imaginative activity. On the basis of these findings, Getzels and Jackson plead for a broader definition of giftedness than IQ can possibly provide. Such a broadened vision would allegedly be facilitated by adding measures of creativity to the package of instruments for identifying the gifted. What do these new tests assess? Divergent thinking (i.e., generating original and multiple solutions to problems that have no single solutions), which Guilford introduced as a critical sign of creative potential in his well-known 1950 presidential address to the American Psychological Association.

Whether or not the Getzels and Jackson research stands up under close scrutiny and replication is discussed elsewhere (Tannenbaum, 1983) and is of no direct concern here. What is significant is the charge that, at best, IQ tests are designed to identify those who have it in them to qualify someday as professors in the sciences, philosophy, mathematics, art history, or literature, not as creative scientists, philosophers, mathematicians, artists, poets, playwrights, or novelists. In other words, it is seen as a test of brainpower for scholarship rather than for invention or innovation. Again, judging from the content of the IQ instrument, it is hard to see in it sensors of either a scholarly or a creative mind.

The only way to gain some clarity in the matter is to look at associations between IQ and demonstrated creativity in various domains of excellence. Unfortunately, the evidence is not abundant, and the little that exists is open to interpretation. To begin with, there is MacKinnon's 1962 study of IQs among architects, which reaches the following conclusions: "As for the relation between intelligence and creativity [as rated by peer experts], . . . we have found within our creative samples essentially a zero relationship between the two variables, and this is not due to a narrow restriction in the range of intelligence. . . . It just is not true that the more intelligent person is necessarily the more creative one" (pp. 487, 488). I wonder why MacKinnon dismisses the restricted range as irrelevant. It is hard to imagine high correlations in samples where both the independent and criterion variables are narrow in range.

Explaining some details of the relationship, Barron (1961) concludes from his own work on creative writers, along with the work of others, that the across-the-board correlations between tested intelligence and creativity ratings hover around .4—not very impressive. To make matters worse, he observes that beyond an IQ of 120, the correlation is negligible. The MacKinnon and Barron studies suggest that it would be prudent to abandon IQ and substitute a measure of divergent thinking as more relevant in its content to creative thinking. But even if you accept divergent thinking as a key to creativity, content validity is no guarantee of predictive validity. MacKinnon (1961) not only correlates IQ with creativity but also looks for a possible relationship between Guilford's divergent-thinking tests and expert ratings of architects' achievements, and the coefficients are likewise low. We are, therefore, left with the tentative impression that IQ is irrelevant to creative potential, and that so-called creativity tests are equally irrelevant.

The results yielded by MacKinnon's and Barron's research do not seem to be applicable in all domains of creativity, judging from some apparent contraindications vis-à-vis the gifted. For example, in Roe's 1953 study of distinguished scientists, she reports median IQ-equivalent scores at least 2.3 standard deviations above the mean (e.g., Verbal Subtest, 166, Spatial Subtest, 137, and Mathematical Subtest, 154). Even the lowest IQ equivalents are some 1.5 standard deviations above the mean—a far from mediocre result, considering that the scientists were selected for study on the basis of reputations for being highly creative, not highly intelligent, in their fields.

Even more impressive is Oden's (1968) follow-up survey of Terman's subjects, who had scored high in IQ during childhood and were close to age fifty in 1960. The achievements of the 759 men in this follow-up included some twenty-five hundred published papers and more than two hundred books and monographs in the sciences, arts, and humanities. "Other publications include 400 short stories, 55 essays and critiques, and a small amount of poetry and several musical compositions. Not included in the foregoing count are the professional output of editors and journalists or the many radio, TV, and motion picture scripts that have been authored" (p. 20). Also, public recognition was given to an unspecified number of architects and artists (one of whom had earned considerable distinction), and the patents issued to members of the group numbered more than 350. These figures far exceed what would be expected in a random population. Not a bad creative record for a group that was assembled nearly forty years earlier strictly on the basis of academic records and IQs during childhood. Not great either, in absolute terms, as evidenced by the size of Terman's "C" group of underachievers. Probably the only way to improve the record is to supplement IQ with other kinds of assessment, including much better measures of processes for problem finding and solving, special aptitudes, relevant personality variables, facilitative environments, and adaptive skills to help round out the picture.

As frustrating as it is to try to discern creative potential in males, it is even more difficult to discern it in females in a changing society. The level of productivity of Oden's 759 males is far more impressive than that of the 253 females maturing in an era long before the current women's movement showed signs of real strength. Despite the great gains made in equality between the sexes since Terman's sample grew into its productive years, there is still hardly reason to assume that the mental, emotional, and situational conditions conducive for creative output among females are the same as for their male counterparts. I am not aware of any major attempt to investigate these differences.

Admittedly, IQ is a poor instrument for revealing creative potential for either sex, but it cannot be discounted entirely, at least for males. In Cox's (1926) study of biographical records of 282 eminent historical figures (including only three women), all born after 1450, she estimates, on the basis of biographical information, that their IQs were exceptionally high. Walberg (1988) reports a replication of the Cox study. It produced similar results, but was updated to focus on more-recent eminent figures as well. Judging from the length of the biographical entries in two encyclopedias, one published in 1935 and the other in 1974, he noted the changes in the top-ten lists over the years. In 1903, the list included Napoleon, Voltaire, Bacon, Goethe, Luther, Burke, Newton, Milton, Pitt, and Washington. The 1935 top ten, in order of space allocation, were Samuel Johnson, Luther, Rembrandt, da Vinci, Napoleon, Washington, Lincoln, Goethe, Beethoven, and Dickens. By 1974, there was yet another change, with highest ranks going to Descartes, Napoleon, Newton, Leibniz, Luther, Hegel, Kant, Darwin, Galileo, and da Vinci, in that order. All apparently had exceptionally high estimated IQs, albeit only slightly higher than those ranking lower in eminence, and nearly every one earned his listing on the basis of creative achievement. (Note also that except for Washington and Lincoln, the lists consist of dead, white, European males—DWEMs, as they are known in modern parlance).

If anything can be learned from the few correlational, longitudinal, and historical studies of the relationship between IQ and creativity, it is that nothing definitive can be learned from them. It should come as something of a surprise to IQ watchers that high-IQ adults are so well represented among the highly creative, and vice versa, considering how little the test content represents anyone's conception of creativity. There may be something in the instrument that reflects the impulse to create, and if we ever find out what it is, we may then be closer to understanding the essences of creativity and intelligence, and the relationship between them.

And yet MacKinnon's study of top-level architects shows no correlation between IQ and creative production. Why? Possibly because IQ is a threshold variable, and beyond a certain score, its already weak correlation with creativity breaks down altogether. An IQ of 120 has been suggested as that cutoff score, not only by Barron (1969) but also by Torrance (1962) and Guilford (1968). However, this so-called fan-shaped hypothesis has not been confirmed in adolescent and adult samples (Mednick & Andrews, 1967; Dacey & Medaus, 1971). Another plausible explanation for MacKinnon's findings is that IQ is much weaker in its links with artistic talent than with creativity in science, mathematics, writing, economics, political theory, and other pursuits involving scholastic power. The latter findings are reported by Cox (1926), Oden (1968), and Walberg (1988), whose categorical methods may also account, in part at least, for the more impressive connection between IQ and creativity than is yielded by MacKinnon's correlational approach. Far more research is needed to sort out the inconsistency and to solve the mysteries in reported research outcomes. Meanwhile, it is reasonable to speculate that IQ is too narrowly conceived to identify creative potential with any degree of precision, judging from the little (probably too little) knowledge that exists on the subject, except that an alternative, more valid instrument does not exist either.

It would be unseemly for me to cite longitudinal studies pertaining to IQ without referring to the long-range predictive validity of so-called creativity tests, which are constructed around the assessment of divergent thinking. The only published study I can find is Torrance's 1981 investigation of all four hundred pupils enrolled in grades one through six in two elementary schools, who were tested on his own divergent-thinking battery from 1958 to 1964. Based on follow-up data from only 211 subjects (116 women and 95 men, ages twenty-four to thirty-two) obtained in 1979–1980, Torrance reports astonishingly impressive results. Test scores in 1958–1964 had a correlation of .46 with the number of post–high school creative achievements (.57 for males and .42 for females). The measures were even better in forecasting ratings of quality of highest creative achievement: .58 for the total group and almost the identical coefficient for each of the sexes. Most of the variance remains unexplained, but it is unlikely that scores on any other test of power administered to young children, including IQ, can produce more-dramatic results in this kind of study.

Although I occasionally find flaws in the research designs of studies reported in publications or in lectures, I almost always accept as accurate the information provided on demographics and results, especially when they are quantified. In the case of Torrance's follow-up effort, I must confess some serious skepticism because of his choice of criterion variables and how to measure them. "Number of creative achievements" implies that a single discovery of penicillin entitles the discoverer to one point, less than a songsmith earns for managing to publish more than one song, inasmuch as being prolific in creative activity is all that counts. What does "quantity" mean in these examples? Can we honestly assume that the composer who cranks out songs almost daily is more creative than the scientist who piles new idea upon new idea for years before there is an "Aha!" experience that conjures up a miracle drug? With these questions in mind it is hard to figure out how such relatively high correlations were obtained on the first criterion variable.

As for rating the quality of the highest creative achievement, those who qualified as judges by virtue of their being advanced students of creativity evaluated creative products in wide-ranging fields of specialization, as if they were equally expert in all of them. Imagine a reputable newspaper or magazine hiring a five-person squad, each member responsible for critiquing the arts, music, dance, literary publications, and scientific theory and research, when each person's only credential for taking on such an assignment was advanced study in creativity. They could not possibly be expert in all domains of creative productivity, even if they had completed advanced courses in creativity. I know, because I have been teaching graduate courses in creativity for nearly twenty years, and even the brightest of my students are not Renaissance people. How, then, can those respectable correlations between children's divergent thinking and the quality of their creative output in adulthood be explained? Could it be that the results add up to a one-in-a-million fluke? No one will ever know until a research scientist is willing to invest the necessary time, skill, and effort to replicate the study, or to design a new one that is structured more tightly.

Are IQ tests socioculturally biased? Perhaps no charge has diminished the status of IQ testing in many communities more than the argument that some minority groups are shortchanged by scores that appear unfairly deflated. Indeed, collectively, the disadvantaged do perform much less well than the advantaged in our society. This further stigmatizes the have-nots as intellectually inferior to the haves. Any test that distinguishes between individual capacities is acceptable, except to strict egalitarians; if it records differences among social, ethnic, or economic groups, it is considered prejudicial and therefore intolerable. Much of the blame for the inequality is directed at the instrument's content. Why should the lower social classes, for example, be penalized in their scores simply because they are less likely than the middle class to know the meaning of "sonata"? What does defining "sonata" have to do with reasoning power, or with any indicator of intelligent behavior, for that matter?

To illustrate the extent to which test content fosters test bias, the black social anthropologist Allison Davis reported in his 1948 Inglis lecture at Harvard that roughly 70 percent of the items in five popular group IQ measures administered to nine- and ten-year-olds discriminated between high and low socioeconomic groups. For thirteen- and fourteen-year-olds, the figure reached nearly 89 percent. To eliminate this kind of "favoritism," Davis recommended that test problems meet the following four conditions:

1. The problems must represent a reliable cross-section of the types of mental systems which normal children of all socio-economic levels exhibit in real life.

2. The problems must refer to experiences that the sociologist observes to be about equally as common in the life of one socio-economic group as in that of any other such group.

3. The problems must be expressed in symbols, in words or pictures, which the test maker has found, through his interviews with children, to be about equally familiar to, and to have common meaning for, all socio-economic groups.

4. The problems must be such as to arouse approximately equal interest, attention, and desire to achieve their solution, on the part of each socio-economic group of children. (Pp. 65–67)

With Kenneth Eells, a graduate student, Davis produced a test of general intelligence and problem-solving ability, called the "Davis-Eells Games" (1953), that follows his guidelines for making the content of the instrument equally accessible to all subcultural groups. However, I am not aware of any evidence showing that the gap in test results between minority and majority children has been closed by these so-called games.In a more recent essay on mental testing, Helms (1992) revives Davis's plea for culture-fair testing and places at the center of her argument the need to represent African American cultural components, which she lists, in the measurement instruments. According to her, it now remains the task of test constructors to produce such a test and then to determine how blacks compare to whites and whether socioeconomic status within the black community affects children's performance on the newly developed measures.

Other changes have been made in test content and scoring in order to reduce test bias. For example, Cattell's so-called culture-fair test is actually culture-free, since it consists mainly of nonsense symbols unfamiliar to any social, economic, or ethnic subgroup and is thus supposed to give everyone an equal chance to score well on the instrument. Unfortunately, social-class differences in scores persist despite this attempt to offer a level playing field for all competitors (see Tannenbaum, 1965).

Still another approach to democratizing test content is recorded by Bruch (1971), who analyzed the performance of black elementary school children on the Stanford-Binet test. Her method was to isolate those tasks the children performed best, using Guilford's structure-of-intellect model to describe these mental operations. On the basis of her findings, she developed an abbreviated form of the Stanford-Binet test that assesses only those ability areas in which blacks are proficient. The strengths turned out to be problem-solving skills with visual and auditory content, memory operations, and convergent production. The weaknesses included cognition of semantic units (i.e., vocabulary) and, surprisingly, divergent production, considering that Torrance (1975) cites several studies to show that there is no racial or socioeconomic bias in his divergent production measures. Bruch concludes that the pattern of cognitive powers revealed in this study is distinctive and indicates that cultural experiences affect the development of cognitive strengths. The educator's task is to capitalize on these strengths so that blacks may be well represented in the talent pool.

Mercer's method of eliminating test bias makes changes in scoring rather than content (Mercer & Lewis, 1977). Through her System of Multicultural Pluralistic Assessment (SOMPA), she advocates combining the formal input from measures of intelligence, perceptual-motor skills, and visual-motor gestalt with information from parents about the child's performance of various social roles, the social, cultural, and economic characteristics of the family, and health conditions that may be related to learning difficulties. Since nonintellective and environmental factors assessed through SOMPA figure prominently in the identification plan, they would account for the poor showing of socially disadvantaged children. The strategy in this kind of testing, therefore, is to obtain better evidence of "true" potential by taking into account these various sources of social handicap and eliminating them statistically when test scores are calculated.

In a powerful and persuasive critique of the assumption of "difference, ergo bias" in testing, Lorge (1953) argues that the social system rather than the test instrument is guilty of prejudice, not only against racial and socioeconomic minorities but also against groups classified by sex, age, education, geographic origin, and mental health. Test scores, including IQ, are sensitive to these differences. As such, they represent one of the consequences, not the causes, of prejudice in our society by showing that its victims are denied a fair chance to achieve excellence. In other words, the test is only a reflector of bias against minorities. Just as destroying the reflector of a flame cannot snuff out the flame, so is it naive and futile to assume that social bias can be affected by revising or eliminating the tests that reflect it.

In line with Lorge's cogent critique, what would be left of an instrument in which test items that discriminate between every conceivable subgroup were eliminated? What good does it do to doctor a test score to make up for the prejudices in our social system? Am I really as good a golfer as the pros who compete in tournaments if I keep up with them in total score after enjoying the benefits of a generous handicap? It is hard to believe that this kind of revision of test content or scoring methods can be accomplished without sacrificing the instrument's predictive validity.

Yet there is an alternative approach to dealing with bias in testing, and that is to make radical changes in the way the test is administered, as suggested by Feuerstein (1979). His Learning Potential Assessment Device (LPAD) includes actual simulations of sections in IQ instruments, but the examiner's radically changed behavior during the testing session makes all the difference. Rather than granting concessions to the child by making substitutions in test items or boosting scores artificially in direct relation to the degree of handicap, the examiner's goal is to raise the child's functional level as high as possible during the test experience. This is not a teach-to-the-test exercise. Instead, the examiner changes from being a disinterested test administrator to a participant observer, a mediator, who eliminates test bias by helping those who are disadvantaged overcome deficits that prevent them from performing at their best in testing situations. The mediator teaches the children the "name of the game" of success in the tasks at hand, helps them adopt the best possible opening gambits in approaching different kinds of test content, encourages a "can-do" attitude in dealing with intellective challenges, fosters a need and desire to achieve in complex abstract-thinking situations, and above all, repairs cognitive functions that are impaired by poor mediation in socially disadvantaged environments even if the victim is gifted.

When disadvantaged children's minds are thus stretched toward their upper limits, a new criterion for mental potential emerges. It is the child's peak performance, not the highest leveled-off or habituated competence, that denotes his or her potential. If the child has the power to show only one lightning bolt of brilliance, it is not a flash in the pan; it represents what that mind has the capacity to accomplish, again and again, given enough investment in mediation. This system of testing acknowledges the validity of cognitive operations required in conventional mental measures as keys to success in our real, though imperfect, world. Until the world changes for the better, it will be necessary to leave undoctored the existing tests that predict achievement in that world, albeit imperfectly. Mediational methods can at least give the disadvantaged a leg up in the test situation and in the real world, although both are flawed.

Should aptitude tests replace IQ tests? J. P. Guilford once wrote, "the existence of . . . *g* . . . is extremely doubtful" (1973, p. 632). A year or so before Robert L. Thorndike died, he announced to me, with what seemed to be a triumphant twinkle in his eye, "Abe, I'm a born-again *g* man!" What should we believe? Judging from professional pronouncements these days, the consensus is clearly on the side of Guilford. His own structure-of-intellect model (see Guilford, 1967), consisting of 150 separate abilities he claimed to have produced by factor analysis, is in the tradition of Thurstone's Primary Mental Abilities theory (see Thurstone, 1958). Still, it has not escaped criticism. Carroll (1968) argues that Guilford's statistical methods provide little room to reject his hypothesis. Horn and Knapp (1973) are also suspicious of the factor analysis used in generating the 150 aptitudes on grounds that it confirms hypotheses in fully 93 percent of the tests. They hasten to concede, however, that the model may have heuristic value.

In a more caustic vein, McNemar (1964) observes that fragmenting ability into what he calls "more and more factors of less and less importance" may reflect nothing more than "scatterbrainedness." In his own words, "general intelligence has not been lost in the trend to test more and more abilities; it was merely misplaced by . . . the hope that factors, when and if measured, would find great usefulness in the affairs of society. By the criterion of social usefulness, the multiple aptitude batteries have been found wanting" (pp. 875–876).

So much for factor-analytic attempts to define special aptitudes. Departing from formal, and sometimes Procrustean, methods, Gardner (1983) uses "subjective" factor analysis, which is "reminiscent more of an artistic judgment than of a scientific assessment" (p. 63), to identify separate intelligences. To qualify as an intelligence, it must satisfy eight criteria that are not coldly objective in a statistical sense and that do not spring from seat-of-the-pants cogitation. Gardner's aptitude list overlaps with those of earlier observers (e.g., De-Haan & Havighurst, 1957; Phenix, 1964; Cohn, 1981), and consists of the following seven intelligences: linguistic, logical-mathematical, spatial, bodily-kinesthetic, musical, interpersonal, and intrapersonal.

From the vantage point of those who split intelligence into special abilities, IQ has no real place in defining giftedness. As Robinson (1977) charges: "In the post-Terman era, it has indeed become possible to be a gifted individual without having any noticeable gift at all. We routinely categorize children as gifted if their IQ scores are above . . . whatever cutoff point we happen to choose, in spite of the fact that they do not do better than average work in school or demonstrate in any other fashion an exceptional degree of talent" (p. 2).

Robinson's argument is forceful and persuasive if the expectation is that every high-IQ child will perform brilliantly in a valued domain of activity. But that is no more realistic than it is to expect all children with extraordinary musical aptitude to excel at the violin or the piano. Furthermore, even child prodigies who have already performed brilliantly on the violin or on the piano often fail to blossom into mature concert artists. And yet Robinson was right to observe that it is meaningless to be gifted in IQ. In science, yes; in art, yes; in marathon running, yes. But in IQ? Absurd.

The problem is that aptitude tests do not have much of a track record, especially among young children. For adolescent and adult populations there are far more data, but even more are needed to reveal a clear picture. The work that Robinson and his staff did with toddlers and preschoolers testifies to the probability that special abilities exist in humans much earlier in life than is popularly expected (Robinson, Roedell, & Jackson, 1979). In a special elementary school for the gifted, Lesser, Davis, and Nahemow (1962) administered their science-aptitude test to children ages six to nine and ranging in IQ from 131 to 171, with a mean score of 151. The scores proved to be highly predictive of science achievement, more so than IQ. Perhaps, as in the relationship between creativity and IQ, there is a threshold level beyond which IQ fails as a predictor, and at that point measures of special ability should take over. A longitudinal study on a scale that ranged in breadth into personal, social, physical, educational, and career development, as did Terman's research on IQ, would shed some light on the efficacy of aptitude tests for children who have not yet reached their teens. Preliminary experimentation done with the Secondary School Admissions Test (SSAT) by Mills and Barnett (1992) on the verbal and quantitative aptitudes of fifth and sixth graders offers a promising beginning to a long-range investigation of precocious children identified as such by their special abilities. Similar continuous monitoring should be done of young children showing other kinds of talents as well.

For populations ranging from adolescence to adulthood there is far more evidence on the use of measures of special ability, but more is needed to ascertain their content validity and predictive validity. For example, mathematical and scientific aptitudes are sometimes seen as separable abilities. Yet Benbow and Minor (1986) seem to have discovered otherwise. In their follow-up study of 1,996 seventh and eighth graders who qualified for special acceleration programs in mathematics on the basis of their scores on the Scholastic Aptitude Test (SAT), the researchers found that the SAT mathematics scores were strongly associated with science achievement in senior high school for both sexes. Positive relationships were found also between scores on verbal tests and learning rates in mathematics among SMPY beneficiaries (Fox, 1974).

How discrete, then, are some of the so-called special-ability factors? Is it possible that Spearman (1927) and Vernon (1950) were right in postulating group factors? Is it conceivable even that g lurks in the background as some kind of common denominator, more powerful than expected, as Thurstone discovered in his PMA structure? (See Bishof, 1954.) Thorndike (1985) seems to have thought so. His cross-validation studies of three batteries of widely used aptitude tests showed that a single general-ability factor usually predicted criterion performance in each of a number of educational subjects and in job requirements at least as well as did the best single-aptitude subtest in the respective batteries. Such findings may have been enough to convert Thorndike into a "g man" late in life.

But even Thorndike admitted to me that the most recent revision of the Stanford-Binet test was standardized on a small sample, which included only a tiny group in the upper 1 percent in IQ, surely not enough to yield highly generalizable correlations with achievement within that percentile. Not only are these coefficients attenuated at the top of the range, but the reliability of scores also weakens when they deviate extremely from the norm. For the most precocious children, therefore, profitable use can be made of an SAT-type measure, an out-of-age test with a ceiling high enough to reveal how rapidly the most rapid learners are advancing in specific skill domains, which is something IQ cannot do.

In studies of successful achievement in adulthood, the use of the SAT has been only marginally helpful. Consider, for example, the Chauncey and Hilton (1965) study of SAT scores among people listed in *Who's Who*. As indicated in table 2.1, the scores were skewed toward the upper extreme, with 3.8 times as

TABLE 2.1.   *Aptitude Scores and Proportion of Individuals in* Who's Who *at Each Level of SAT College Population*

SAT Score Interval	% Expected in Each Interval	% in *Who's Who* Group (O)	O/E
696 and above	2.6	10	3.8
629–695	7.3	15	2.1
563–628	18.9	25	1.3
500–562	21.2	25	1.2
450–499	19.1	15	.8
Below 450	30.9	10	.3

Sources: Reprinted with permission from Chauncey, H., & Hilton, T. L. (1965). Are aptitude tests valid for the highly able? *Science* 148:1299. Copyright 1965, American Association for the Advancement of Science.

many people as expected earning scores of 696 and above. However, the figures also reveal that fully 25 percent of those making it to *Who's Who* scored lower than 500. Indeed, there were as many coming from the lower 50 percent as from the upper 10 percent of the SAT distribution for college students.

Since the researchers offer no clues to the careers of those constituting each stratum of the SAT range, it is impossible to know precisely the differences that must have existed between the highest and lowest quartiles. But it does not take much imagination to suspect that the upper 25 percent consisted mostly of leading scholarly professionals, while the lower 25 percent was tilted more in the direction of popular entertainers, including sports heroes, dancers, singers, movie stars, and the like. Still, it would not come as a surprise to find an impressive representation of highbrow artists, musicians, community leaders, business executives, and (even?) politicians in the bottom quartile, all in respectable domains that the SAT does not pretend to target.

If my speculations about the Chauncey and Hilton results are reasonable, they further confirm the obvious: SATs are meant to assess verbal and math-related reasoning skills exclusively, and that these limitations should be taken into account in a comprehensive talent search. My rule is that the greater the variety of reliable and valid probes sunk into an examinee's psyche and its environment, the more signs of talent potential are likely to be found, if any are there at all. Indeed, the Human Talent Project (McGuire, Hindsman, & King, 1961) demonstrated that a large and varied test package, incorporating measures of motivation and pressures to achieve, along with various assessments of ability, can explain more than 55 percent of the variance in grade point average.

From a post hoc perspective, special-aptitude tests measuring a wider range of skills than does the SAT seem to have revealed something about career potential. Among the largest-scale studies of this kind were those conducted by Thorndike and Hagen (1959), who had access to scores on the Air Force Battery of Cadet Classification Tests administered during World War II. The researchers obtained follow-up information on ten thousand individuals in 1956, approximately thirteen years after the test battery had been given. Results show that aptitude measures administered in early adulthood distinguished the successful persons in one field from those in another. However, no one could have anticipated that individuals scoring well on the tests would go on to excel in one specific occupation rather than another. There is a large difference between looking forward in anticipation and looking backward in retrospect.

What kinds of conclusions can be drawn regarding the use of special-aptitude tests to measure precocity in various disciplines? Not many, as yet. For children from preschool to the higher elementary grades, IQ is still as good a measurement of power as any. I hasten to add, however, that (1) no self-respecting educator should be bound to use it as the only measurement of power; (2) IQ is far more appropriate for measuring academic potential than for assessing social, spatial, and artistic promise; and (3) measurements of power of any kind are not the only indicators of human potential.

From the little we know about young children as potential specialists, particularly prodigies in math, music, chess, and language, I am convinced that narrowly focused abilities do exist at an early age, even if they are not prodigious, but they remain hidden because of the lack of adequate instrumentation to assess them. If, and when, such measures are developed and validated, it will be possible to check whether they can replace or supplement IQ in screening for potentially gifted children. Until then, IQ should be part of an elaborate package of instruments and other devices for recognizing precocity.

As for older children, beginning in the upper elementary grades, SAT-type tests can help identify talent in math and language reasoning, although I am not convinced that they can (yet?) distinguish the potentially creative from the "merely" proficient, the would-be mathematicians from masters of math, or literary promise from advanced skills in reading comprehension. I do not mean to slight the validity of aptitude tests, such as SATs, in identifying rapid learners in some domains of excellence. SMPY has demonstrated over and over again the benefits of academically accelerating children of junior high school age who score exceptionally high on SAT measures. My questions about SATs separating original thinkers from advanced achievers are merely attempts to clarify the precise usefulness and limitations of this battery, something that should be done with IQ tests, too, for the sake of fostering peace among believers in these respective instruments. Whatever assessments are used to identify the gifted, there is always the worrisome probability that they are guilty of producing both false positives (a minor oversight) and false negatives (a major offense) in the process. As for measuring any abilities other than verbal and mathematical ones, test users should be wary. The practiced eye or ear is the instrument of choice. A competent, experienced music teacher can still outdo any formal test in recognizing young talent by simply listening sensitively.

Should power testing give way to process testing? In recent years, behavioral scientists have tried to reach deeper into human differences by exploring what are called the processes (rather than just the surface proficiency) of cognition. My reading of the growing literature on the subject has led me to recognize processes in two contexts. One deals with the style, or the *how*, of problem finding and solving. The other, which receives far more attention from theorists and researchers, deals with a detailed amalgamation of underlying skills, or the *how well*, of problem finding and solving.

Among the rare studies in the "how" category are the systematic observations by Getzels and Csikszentmihalyi (1976) of young artists at the Chicago Arts Institute engaged in conceptualizing and producing still-life drawings, and Gruber's (1981) tracking of Darwin's thought processes as they led to the production of his famous theories. One of the few such studies dealing with young children is Kanevsky's (1992) comparison of high-IQ four- and five-year-olds with average-IQ seven- and eight-year-olds, both groups matched in Mental Age scores, on the Towers of Hanoi tasks. Kanevsky contrasted the groups on their strategic habits as well as their relative success in solving the problem and found observable differences on both criteria.

Probably the most elaborate and best-known treatment of processes as cognitive abilities is Sternberg's (1986) "triarchic theory," so named because it contains three subtheories. One of them, "componential," consists of three kinds of components involved in the performance of separate mental operations: (1) metacomponents, or the executive processes needed for planning, monitoring, and decision making in a problem-solving situation; (2) performance components, which include processes needed for executing a task; and (3) knowledge-acquisition components, which are used in selective encoding, selective combination, and selective comparison operations. Another subtheory, "experiential," incorporates the ability to deal with novelty and the ability to automatize or habituate information processing. The third subtheory, "contextual," refers to the organism's selecting, shaping, and adapting to its real-world environment.

It remains to be seen how well the triarchic theory can be translated into a viable testing operation. How, indeed, to go about measuring and validating intellectual processes of both the "how" and "how well" varieties? This is a tall order, by any estimate. Ramos-Ford and Gardner (1991) seem to have taken a stab at it, but they have a long way to go before their approach can be evaluated by psychometric standards. Still, it is worthwhile to examine the Ramos-Ford and Gardner efforts because they depart from the usual pencil-and-paper elic-itations of answers to questions or responses to examiner-initiated challenges and directives. Their assessment context is in situ instead of in sit-down, formal exchanges between test administrators and examinees. Children are monitored for their performance in learning environments that bear some resemblance to real working conditions, not to a "decontextualized setting for formal testing" (p. 59), as the authors describe scenes of conventional measurement. Children's skills are inferred from the way they deal with curricular stimuli of all varieties. Besides looking for signs of scholastic, social, and artistic proficiency, observ-ers record working styles, including degrees of engagement, persistence, and distractibility.

It is a noble and ambitious experiment, with obvious potential benefits for enlarging the talent pool while attending to ability demonstrated rather than just inferred. But I can foresee some possible difficulties. Among the most serious is that learning environments vary greatly according to how they are designed and administered. In a setting where children are taught dramaturgy, the talented playwrights among them will be spotted far more easily than in other situations where such subject matter is ignored. Anyone who has ob-served classrooms for a while knows that differences between teachers in what they teach and how well they teach are enormous. True, compared to the adaptability and flexibility of the Ramos-Ford and Gardner monitoring design, IQ testing seems positively constricted, even sclerotic. But the latter has the advantage of being standardized as well as fairly uniform in design and admin-istration, so that a score obtained by an examiner for one child can be ranked with that of another child tested elsewhere by a different examiner.

In virtually every learning environment there is a need for a talent search, and if giftedness is supposed to reveal itself in the everyday behavior of children in such a situation, then some opportunity for fast-paced or supplemental study has to be part of the experience. Otherwise, exceptional ability can go unrecognized except perhaps through traditional testing methods. I remember witnessing the experience of a six-year-old math whiz whose parents entered him into first grade without informing the school about his special talent. They simply did not want to call any attention to him for fear that it might disrupt his smooth adjustment to school. Instead, they elected to wait for the child's teacher or principal to call and share with them the great news about their brilliant young mathematician. The call never came. Finally, in midsemester, at the first parent-teacher conference, the child's father and mother breathlessly asked the teacher about their son's progress in math, and the reply was encouraging without a trace of wonderment or even enthusiasm. "Not to worry," said the teacher, "the child has progressed from counting stuffed bunnies two by two to counting by twos in the abstract." There was no doubt that the child was moving along at a normal pace without problems.

It would have taken an extremely astute observer to recognize the makings of a math prodigy in such a classroom. Is it not conceivable that a formal test such as the IQ test could "see" something special in this child that neither the teacher nor a trained monitor could discover in such a classroom? My guess is that, under the circumstances, focused observation can effectively supplement, rather than substitute for, traditional formal testing, until all teachers, not just a few, are able to activate rich, imaginative learning experiences to accommodate wide ranges of student abilities and interests.

A related caution is to avoid assuming that an enhanced learning environment automatically turns into an enriched learning experience. Feuerstein (1979, 1991) was right in inserting an instructive, supportive mediator between an organism and the external stimuli that bombards it, in order to help it sort out and interpret what is meaningful. Only in such a setting is a child's behavior amenable to analysis in situ under optimum conditions. In other words, the content validity of what Ramos-Ford and Gardner consider a contextual setting for assessing children's abilities is directly related to the quality of experiences fashioned in that setting by the mediator. Subtract the mediator, or rely on one who cannot perform that role adequately, and both learning and contextual assessment are compromised accordingly.

A Proposed Verdict on IQ and IQ Testing

It may come as a surprise to readers of this chapter that no mention is made of nature versus nurture in accounting for IQ differences among individuals and even between groups. Such puzzlement would be understandable in light of the existence of so many publications about conflicts surrounding IQ, which almost never fail to raise this topic. In one sizable book of readings on the IQ controversy (Block & Dworkin, 1976), nearly every contributor confronts the nature-nurture issue head-on, or at least sideswipes it. To me, it is a nonissue, an exercise in sophistry that has no practical meaning. Furthermore, I believe that, in general, nature-nurture debates are masquerades for political disagreements today as much as they were in 1949, when Pastore found that those who believe in the greater power of environment are liberal in their convictions whereas conservatives tend to place their bets on heredity.

Why Nature versus Nurture Is, and Should Be, a Nonissue

From a strictly social-psychological point of view, nature and nurture are like two hands working together to produce a clapping sound. What each contributes is not additive to the other's contribution; instead, the two hands work interactively, since neither can create the sound alone. Because of this interdependence, it is unimportant to ask which hand is more responsible for the loudness of the clap. Strengthen either one and the sound is sure to become louder. The same is true for the mutual reinforcement of nature and nurture in producing intelligent behavior.

The combination of art and science and a little bit of luck involved in discovering an intelligence-enhancement pill is still in its infancy, as any caretaker of a victim of Alzheimer's disease well knows. This shows that we are unfortunately a long way from enhancing intelligent behavior biologically. It is equally sad that we have made no more progress toward understanding and using our best resources for nurturing talent. Therefore, in our current state of ignorance, there is no point in musing about which of these two poorly understood forces, heredity and environment, carries greater weight in an IQ score, which is itself imperfect in its reliability and validity.

It has been suggested (Humphreys, 1992) that the nature-nurture ratio in determining human performance has practical value as a barometer of our status as an egalitarian society. Since equality of opportunity requires an optimally enriching environment for all people, the goal is to create such nurturing conditions without prejudice to any individual or subpopulation. By actualizing its democratic ideals, our society will attain a utopian condition in which no differences in the quality of the learning environment for any of its citizens will exist to account for human variability in achievement. Heredity will then explain all of the variance. Therefore, by calculating the extent to which unequal nurturance in the real world influences how well (or how poorly) people perform at school and in society, we can judge how far we have yet to progress to make that world a perfect one, from a democratic point of view. In other words, the greater the power of nature, the closer we are to reaching true democracy; conversely, the greater the influence of nurture, the clearer the signs of favorable opportunity for some and deprivation of opportunity for others, a condition that diminishes democracy.

The logic is intriguing, and it does relate to real-world matters, vital ones, in fact. But I am not persuaded enough to appreciate nature-nurture research. On the contrary, to me this is a case where a little bit of knowledge is far more dangerous than it is edifying. It conjures up images of psychologists and educators "consoling" parents of low achievers with the "assurance" that no one is to blame because the die has been cast in their children's lineage, and that, because of the powerful forces of heredity, intensive stimulation at home and teaching at school will not make a difference. Some consolation! Some assurance! This kind of advice proves only that compassion can sometimes be mean-spirited, just as humor is sometimes mean-spirited. Parents who are subjected to such gentle voices of gloom can take heart: no one knows how much so-called heredity is contaminated and enhanced by life's experiences and how much of what is thought to be environment is directed, or at least influenced, by heredity.

Worse still are the mischievous efforts of modern-style eugenicists to produce a high-IQ generation by selective breeding of high-IQ progenitors, all because research (e.g., Nichols, 1965) shows that heredity explains about 70 percent of the variance in scholastic success. I call it mischievous because it is a fairly short hop, skip, and jump from this form of managed mating to the brutal bigotry involved in liquidating the mentally handicapped and concentrating on spawning a master race. If nature-nurture research contributes, in however small a measure, to such foul play, then I say let us keep Pandora's box shut.

It is also a trifle disingenuous for members of the behavioral and social sciences to use the struggle for egalitarianism to justify nature-nurture investigations. The reason is simple: these professions, which are supposed to assume leadership in fashioning perfect conditions for learning, and assessing them via nature-nurture ratios, hardly seem to care. Is there concern about improving such environments? Yes. About optimizing them? No. In other words, there rarely exists a vision of utopian nurturance among those responsible for creating a utopia. My recall is far from encyclopedic, but the only exceptions that come to mind offhand are B. F. Skinner's baby crib, O. K. Moore's Responsive Environment, and possibly A. Machado's grand blueprint for his Ministry for Human Intelligence in Venezuela. How small-scale and short-lived these efforts were.

Furthermore, no one seems to be wondering whether the very best methods of stimulating productivity and performance are necessarily democratic. We ought to be concerned, if democracy's goal is to perfect the learning environment and thus allow heredity to account for all of the variance in human achievement. And yet I cannot help thinking about the draconian strategies used by people in power to achieve excellence. Arturo Toscanini's autocratic, intimidating style of orchestral rehearsals may have produced far better concert performances than more courteous, collaborative efforts could accomplish. It is said that he came as close as anybody could to bringing out the best in his musicians, elevating their performances close to the limits allowed by their innate potential, whatever that may have been.

If it takes such undemocratic methods to create the situations conducive to optimum learning on behalf of a society committed to equality of opportunity, are we prepared to apply these methods for the sake of reducing to zero the contribution of environment to the variance in achievement? There may well be a Hobson's choice between the preference of means and the preference of ends—a choice that advocates of a nature-nurture barometer tend to ignore.

Why IQ Testing Survives; Should It?

Despite all its imperfections, the IQ test is still very much alive in talent searches. It has the advantage of being as predictive as any measurement of power can be for success in the early years of school. None of the alternatives has either succeeded or demonstrated enough of a track record to replace IQ for children who are not yet of school age or who are in the early years of schooling. Yet there is something disturbing about the success of IQ, through no fault of those who designed it. In its long history, the test has been used to preserve several kinds of complacency in the educative process. Inasmuch as its predictive value, limited as it may be, is constantly confirmed in conditions for learning that are far from ideal, I sometimes suspect that educators would rather live with predictive validity in unchanging, and therefore predictable, learning environments than risk weakening, or even losing, IQ's validity by enriching educational environments, especially for gifted children.

A second kind of complacency has to do with the IQ test's being used to give top priority to those kinds of ability that the instrument measures while shortchanging the others, especially creative production and performance. In our schools, the tail wags the dog; there is a reluctance among educators to expand their vision to include thought processes and content areas that are timely and critical at the close of the twentieth century, even if they do not connect with performance on an IQ test.

Third, the widespread reliance on IQ testing of young children for admission to programs for the gifted seems to crowd out much serious effort to assess special abilities, which, we suspect, do exist even among preschoolers. By defining giftedness primarily in terms of IQ, we perpetuate the myth that a young child's intellect resembles a blob of general ability to be channeled later in life, presumably during adolescence, into narrow specializations. Without the omnipresence of IQ, I think there would be more activity in constructing and validating aptitude tests for young children, and that these could be used with the same kinds of success that SATs have attained with older precocious children. Perhaps such efforts could lead to significant changes away from uniform, cafeteria-style education in elementary schools toward more differentiation in the curriculum menu to accommodate individual differences.

Fourth, it is comfortable to think that an IQ score denotes fixed potential. Why invest in the much more trying effort to modify the child's potential by mediating between the child and the test? It would only upset our comfortable acceptance of a proven link between an unmediated testing experience and an unmediated environment where the child lives and learns, but almost never measures up to his or her potential. Again, laziness overrules venturesomeness.

Finally, the IQ test helps preserve our tendency to assume that demonstrated productivity or performance depends entirely on mental power and processes. Obviously, it does not. Research (see Tannenbaum, 1986) shows clearly that, in addition to general intelligence, contributors to achievement include special aptitudes, nonintellective facilitators, environmental influences, and chance, or just plain luck. Yet even critics of IQ continue to search for its replacement only in the cognitive domain. Perhaps looking beyond intellect as the only cause of gifted behavior involves assuming broader perspectives than many cognitive psychologists are prepared to consider.

In the end, IQ will continue to survive despite attacks on it, probably because it is easier to live complacently with its proven qualities than to take on the daunting responsibility of making meaningful, not merely tidy, improvements in measurement. Such an assignment is appropriate for IQ bashers, whether they (or we) aim above the belt or below.

I confess that my own brand of IQ bashing embodies the spirit of two other aggressors, albeit without their emphasis on total obliteration of their enemies from the face of the earth. One is the idol breaker who finds it easier to attack clay and wooden images than to reeducate idolators to appreciate them only as works of art. Another is the burner of lepers' clothes to prevent plague, knowing full well that the garments' contamination comes from humans, not from fabrics.

References

Barron, F. (1961). Creative vision and expression in writing and painting. In D. W. MacKinnon (Ed.), *Conference on the creative person* (pp. 237–251). Berkeley: University of California, Institute of Personality Assessment and Research.
Barron, F. (1969). *Creative person and creative process.* New York: Holt, Rinehart, & Winston.

Benbow, C. P., & Minor, L. L. (1986). Mathematically talented males and females and achievement in the high school sciences. *American Educational Research Journal* 23:425–436.

Bishof, L. J. (1954). *Intelligence: Statistical conceptions of its nature.* Garden City, N.Y.: Doubleday.

Block, N. J., & Dworkin, G. (Eds.). (1976). *The IQ controversy.* New York: Pantheon.

Bruch, C. B. (1971). Modification of procedures for identification of the disadvantaged gifted. *Gifted Child Quarterly* 15:267–272.

Carroll, J. B. (1968). [Review of *The Nature of Human Intelligence*, by J. P. Guilford]. *American Educational Research Journal* 73:105–112.

Chauncey, H., & Hilton, T. L. (1965). Are aptitude tests valid for the highly able? *Science* 148:1297–1304.

Cohn, S. J. (1981). What is giftedness? A multidimensional approach. In A. H. Kramer (Ed.), *Gifted children* (pp. 33–45). New York: Trillium Press.

Cox, C. M. (1926). *The early mental traits of three hundred geniuses.* Stanford: Stanford University Press.

Dacey, J. S., & Medaus, G. F. (1971). Relationship between creativity and intelligence. *Journal of Educational Research* 64:213–216.

Davis, A. (1948). *Social class influences upon learning.* Cambridge: Harvard University Press.

Davis, A., & Eells, K. (1953). *Davis-Eells test of general intelligence or problem-solving ability.* Yonkers-on-Hudson, N.Y.: World Book.

DeHaan, R. F., & Havighurst, R. J. (1957). *Educating gifted children.* Chicago: University of Chicago Press.

Duncan, O. D. (1968). Ability and achievement. *Eugenics Quarterly* 15:1–11.

Duncan, O. D., Featherman, D., & Duncan, B. (1973). *Socioeconomic background and achievement.* New York: Seminar Press.

Estes, W. K. (1982). Learning, memorizing, and intelligence. In R. J. Sternberg (Ed.), *Handbook of human intelligence* (pp. 170–224). Cambridge: Cambridge University Press.

Feldman, D. H. (1984). A follow-up of subjects scoring above 180 IQ in Terman's genetic studies of genius. *Exceptional Children* 50:518–523.

Feuerstein, R. (1979). *The dynamic assessment of retarded performers.* Baltimore: University Park Press.

Feuerstein, R. (1980). *Instrumental enrichment.* Baltimore: University Park Press.

Feuerstein, R. (1991). Mediated learning experience: A theoretical review. In R. Feuerstein, P. S. Klein, & A. J. Tannenbaum (Eds.), *Mediated learning experience* (pp. 3–51). London: Freund.

Fox, L. H. (1974). A mathematics program for fostering precocious achievement. In J. C. Stanley, D. P. Keating, & L. H. Fox (Eds.), *Mathematical talent: Discovery, description, and development* (pp. 101–125). Baltimore: Johns Hopkins University Press.

Gardner, H. (1983). *Frames of mind.* New York: Basic Books.

Getzels, J. W., & Csikszentmihalyi, M. (1976). *The creative vision: A longitudinal study of problem finding in art.* New York: Wiley.

Getzels, J. W., & Jackson, P. W. (1958). The meaning of "giftedness": An examination of an expanding concept. *Phi Delta Kappan* 46:75–77.

Getzels, J. W., & Jackson, P. W. (1962). *Creativity and intelligence.* New York: Wiley.

Ghiselli, E. E. (1966). *The validity of aptitude tests.* New York: Wiley.

Gruber, H. E. (1981). *Darwin on man: A psychological study of scientific creativity* (2nd ed.). Chicago: University of Chicago Press.

Guilford, J. P. (1950). Creativity. *American Psychologist* 5:444–454.

Guilford, J. P. (1967). *The nature of human intelligence.* New York: McGraw-Hill.

Guilford, J. P. (1968). *Intelligence, creativity, and their educational implications.* San Diego: Knapp.

Guilford, J. P. (1973). Theories of intelligence. In B. B. Wolman (Ed.), *Handbook of general psychology* (pp. 630–643). Englewood Cliffs, N.J.: Prentice-Hall.

Helms, J. E. (1992). Why is there no study of cultural equivalence in standardized cognitive ability testing? *American Psychologist* 47:1083–1101.

Honzik, M. P., MacFarlane, J., & Allen L. (1948). The stability of mental test performance between two and eighteen years. *Journal of Experimental Education* 4:309–324.

Horn, J. L., & Knapp, J. R. (1973). On the subjective character of the empirical base of Guilford's structure-of-intellect model. *Psychological Bulletin* 80:33–43.

Humphreys, L. G. (1992). Commentary: What both critics and users of ability tests need to know. *Psychological Science* 3:271–274.

Jackson, N. E. (1978). *Identification and description of intellectual precocity in young children.* Paper presented at the annual convention of the American Psychological Association, Toronto.

Kanevsky, L. (1992). The learning game. In P. S. Klein & A. J. Tannenbaum (Eds.), *To be young and gifted* (pp. 204–241). Norwood, N.J.: Ablex.

Lesser, G., Davis, F. B., & Nahemow, L. (1962). The identification of gifted elementary school children with exceptional scientific talent. *Educational and Psychological Measurement* 22:349–364.

Lippmann, W. (1976). The abuse of the tests. In N. J. Block & G. Dworkin (Eds.), *The IQ controversy* (pp. 18–20). New York: Pantheon.

Lorge, I. (1953). Difference or bias in tests of intelligence. In *Proceedings: Invitational conference on testing problems* (pp. 76–83). Princeton: Educational Testing Service.

MacKinnon, D. W. (1961). Creativity in architects. In D. W. MacKinnon (Ed.), *Conference on the creative person* (pp. 291–320). Berkeley: University of California, Institute of Personality Assessment and Research.

MacKinnon, D. W. (1962). The nature and nurture of creative talent. *American Psychologist* 17:484–495.

McClelland, D. C. (1976). Testing for competence rather than for "intelligence." In N. J. Block & G. Dworkin (Eds.), *The IQ controversy.* New York: Pantheon.

McGuire, C., Hindsman, E., & King, F. J. (1961). Dimensions of talented behavior. *Educational and Psychological Measurement* 21:3–38.

McNemar, Q. (1964). Lost: Our intelligence—why? *American Psychologist* 19:871–882.

Mednick, M. T., & Andrews, F. M. (1967). Creative thinking and level of intelligence. *Journal of Creative Behavior* 1:148.

Mercer, J. R., & Lewis, J. F. (1977). *System of Multicultural Pluralistic Assessment (SOMPA).* New York: Psychological Corp.

Mills, C. J., & Barnett, L. B. (1992). The use of the secondary school admission test (SSAT) to identify academically talented elementary school students. *Gifted Child Quarterly* 36:155–159.

Nichols, R. C. (1965). *The inheritance of general and specific ability* (NMSC Research Reports, Vol. 1, no. 1). Evanston, Ill.: National Merit Scholarship Corp.

Oden, M. H. (1968). The fulfillment of promise: Forty-year follow-up of the Terman gifted group. *Genetic Psychology Monographs* 77:3–93.

Pastore, N. (1949). *The nature-nurture controversy.* New York: Kings Crown Press.

Phenix, P. H. (1964). *Realms of meaning.* New York: McGraw-Hill.

Ramos-Ford, V., & Gardner H. (1991). Giftedness from a multiple intelligence perspective. In N. Colangelo & G. A. Davis (Eds.), *Handbook of gifted education* (pp. 55–64). Boston: Allyn & Bacon.

Ree, M. J., & Earles, J. A. (1992). Intelligence is the best predictor of job performance. *Current Directions in Psychological Science* 1:86–89.

Robinson, H. B. (1977). *Current myths concerning gifted children* (Gifted and Talented Brief No. 5, pp. 1–11). Ventura, Calif.: National/State Leadership Training Institute.

Robinson, H. B., Roedell, W., & Jackson, N. E. (1979). Early identification and intervention. In A. H. Passow (Ed.), *The gifted and the talented: Their education and development* (pp. 138–154). Seventy-eighth Yearbook of the National Society for the Study of Education (Part 1). Chicago: University of Chicago Press.

Roe, A. (1953). *The making of a scientist.* New York: Dodd, Mead.

Shurkin, J. N. (1992). *Terman's kids: The ground-breaking study of how the gifted grow up.* Boston: Little, Brown.

Snyderman, M., & Rothman, S. (1987). Survey of expert opinion on intelligence and aptitude testing. *American Psychologist* 42:137–144.

Snyderman, M., & Rothman, S. (1988). *The IQ controversy: The media and public policy.* New Brunswick, N.J.: Transaction Books.

Spearman, C. E. (1927). *The abilities of man.* New York: Macmillan.

Stanley, J. C. (1991). Critique of "Socioemotional adjustment of adolescent girls enrolled in a residential acceleration program." *Gifted Child Quarterly* 35:67–70.

Sternberg, R. J. (1986). A triarchic theory of intellectual giftedness. In R. J. Sternberg & J. E. Davidson (Eds.), *Conceptions of giftedness* (pp. 223–243). Cambridge: Cambridge University Press.

Tannenbaum, A. J. (1965). A review of the IPAT culture fair intelligence test. In O. K. Buros (Ed.), *Sixth mental measurement yearbook* (pp. 721–723). Highland Park, N.J.: Gryphon Press.

Tannenbaum, A. J. (1983). *Gifted children*. New York: Macmillan.

Tannenbaum, A. J. (1986). Giftedness: A psychosocial approach. In R. J. Sternberg & J. E. Davidson (Eds.), *Conceptions of giftedness* (pp. 21–52). Cambridge: Cambridge University Press.

Terman, L. M. (1976). The great conspiracy. In N. J. Block & G. Dworkin (Eds.), *The IQ controversy* (pp. 30–38). New York: Pantheon.

Thorndike, R. L. (1985). The central role of general ability in prediction. *Multivariate Behavioral Research* 20:241–254.

Thorndike, R. L., & Hagen E. (1959). *Ten thousand careers*. New York: Wiley.

Thurstone, T. G. (1958). *SRA primary mental abilities*. Chicago: Science Research Associates.

Torrance, E. P. (1962). *Guiding creative talent*. Englewood Cliffs, N.J.: Prentice-Hall.

Torrance, E. P. (1975). Creativity research in education: Still alive. In I. A. Taylor & J. W. Getzels (Eds.), *Perspectives in creativity* (pp. 278–296). Chicago: Aldine.

Torrance, E. P. (1981). Predicting the creativity of elementary school children (1958–1980)—and the teacher who made a "difference." *Gifted Child Quarterly* 25:55–61.

Vernon, P. E. (1950). *The structure of human abilities*. New York: Wiley.

Walberg, H. J. (1988). Creativity and talent as learning. In R. J. Sternberg (Ed.), *The nature of creativity: Contemporary psychological perspectives* (pp. 340–361). Cambridge: Cambridge University Press.

Wallach, M. A. (1976). Tests tell us little about talent. *American Scientist* 64:57–63.

Wigdor, A. K., & Garner, W. R. (Eds.). (1982). *Ability testing: Uses, consequences, and controversies*. Washington, D.C.: National Academy Press.

II   The Underuse of Knowledge

E very year, citizens of the United States and people across the world invest, through their taxes, millions of dollars into basic and applied research. They hope the research will lead to improvements in the overall quality of life in their society. And, indeed, much progress has been made as a result of this investment. Take the typical well-equipped university departmental office. In just the past two decades, such devices as fax machines, personal computers, laser printers, photocopiers, hand-held calculators, electronic mail, and voice mail have been introduced. They are now so much a part of our daily lives that we have trouble imagining a world without them. Similar advances can be seen in medicine and health care, with endoscopic surgical techniques and computer diagnoses.

But have the social sciences effected similar changes? Especially with regard to the identification and education of gifted children and psychometrics, what have we learned and how is it being implemented for the betterment of society? The four chapters in this section address that question; all reach the discouraging conclusion that much has been learned but not much is affecting practice in a lasting way. This seems to be particularly the case when research findings are at odds with personal or societal beliefs, a theme that also emerged in the previous section of this volume.

One of the most significant and lasting constructs in psychology is the notion of general intelligence, or g (Jensen, 1986). A major advance in practice involves the measurement of general intelligence and other specific abilities. Yet many eschew the notion of g and decry intelligence testing. Abraham Tannenbaum, as noted above, feels that its use should be curtailed. Paul Meehl captured the essence of the situation when he stated that "almost all human performance (work competence) dispositions, if carefully studied, are saturated to some extent with the general intelligence factor g, which for psychodynamic and ideological reasons has been somewhat neglected in recent years" (1990, p. 124). Perhaps this is because intelligence testing has revealed aspects of or "inequities" in our society with which we feel uncomfortable. Rather than deal with the findings, we choose to deny them by calling for the elimination of testing in schools and in employment settings. We hope, therefore, that Meehl's forecasting talents are as good as his descriptive abilities; when the statement above was made, he also predicted that g "is due for a comeback." That would certainly make social policy more consistent with what we know, and it would represent an advance. Parenthetically, we hope the same applies to work in the area of the biology of behavior, where the situation is strikingly similar, as is so eloquently documented by Thomas Bouchard, David Lykken, Auke Tellegen, and Matthew McGue in their chapter.

When topics in psychology and education are less emotionally laden (less challenging to our egalitarian views) than the above, is it easier for research findings in social science to affect practice? In the first two chapters of this section, James Gallagher and Harry Passow take a look at the literature on the educational acceleration of gifted students. This time-honored practice had its formal beginnings in the 1860s in the St. Louis school system, becoming, by the turn of this century, the most common means of meeting the educational needs of gifted students. Slowly over the twentieth century, however, the country moved away from acceleration and toward providing educational enrichment to gifted students.

The tide did not turn until the early 1970s, when Julian C. Stanley, a well-known psychometrician who was searching for work with greater meaning than that of "dry-bone methodology," entered the scene. Having carefully surveyed the literature and current practice, he decided that there was nothing more useful for him to do than to help gifted children by becoming an advocate for various forms of educational acceleration. At first he operated almost in isolation, but soon he was joined by others, many of whom have contributed chapters to this volume. Now as the century draws to a close, acceleration is widely accepted by the research community as the most effective way to provide an appropriate education that is commensurate with a gifted child's abilities. Much of this change can be credited to the dedicated work of one man, Julian Stanley, who did not mind seeming unreasonable in an unreasonable world. In honor of his efforts, he was dubbed "Mr. Acceleration" by Harry Passow. Yet is this option being implemented widely in our schools, as research suggests it should be? The simple answer is no. The goal of gaining flexibility in educational programming for gifted students through acceleration is still extremely difficult to reach in most sectors of our society.

What about the role of field research and educational improvement? Has that type of research been more successful in having its findings put into practice? Herbert Klausmeier was directly involved in field research; in his chapter he details his work with schools not only in developing and implementing Individually Guided Education (IGE) but also in demonstrating its value and usefulness. In the 1960s and early 1970s Klausmeier and his colleagues turned schools in Wisconsin and elsewhere into IGE schools. The results were positive all around. The only significant drawback was that IGE required much work up front by schools. Yet today the IGE schools have almost disappeared from the educational landscape even though many IGE principles are still in operation in some form. It seemed that as IGE schools became refined and established, people began to feel that they wanted something novel in order to demonstrate improvement. Progress seems to be judged by the number of new methods introduced rather than by the refinement of those procedures that we already know work well. This attraction to novelty seems to detract from the ability of research in the social sciences to have any lasting influence on society.

We close this section of the book with a chapter by Lloyd Humphreys and David Lubinski on the importance of spatial abilities. These authors clearly demonstrate the predictive value of such abilities for exceptional achievement in certain technical and artistic careers and suggest that we do society a great disservice by not routinely measuring them. We do a fine job of assessing abilities in the verbal and quantitative sectors of Guttman's (1954) "radex" of intellectual abilities (see Ackerman, 1987; Carroll, 1985; Humphreys, 1979; Snow, Kyllonen, & Marshalek, 1984), information from which is used to direct individuals into specific postsecondary schools. Although quantitative and verbal abilities are likely the most important, this does not detract from the potential usefulness of spatial abilities in selecting individuals for certain professions (e.g., engineering). Humphreys and Lubinski argue that the failure to assess such abilities leads to the inadequate use of a pool of talent, a large part of which comes from lower socioeconomic backgrounds, that is critically needed for our increasingly technological society. These findings regarding the importance of spatial abilities are not new; they have been around for several decades. Why are they not being implemented? Reflecting upon Benbow and Lubinski's work in the area of gender differences, we wonder if it could possibly be because certain spatial ability measures generate score distributions that separate the sexes in a manner more dramatic than that which has been encountered for quantitative abilities (See Benbow, 1988; Lubinski & Benbow, 1992; Stanley, Benbow, Brody, Dauber, & Lupkowski, 1992; Stanley, 1993). This is something that goes against America's ethos (Benbow & Stanley, in press), which militates against research findings infiltrating practice.

Clearly, the chapters in this section of the volume tell a story. They reveal how difficult it can be for work in the social sciences to effect lasting change. This is partly because we do not seem to be engaged in a cumulative science. Rather, we seem to become attracted to fads (Benbow & Stanley, in press; Dunnette, 1966). Moreover, societal values often get in the way of the acceptance of certain research findings or advances. A quotation from Getzels and Dillon provides a fitting closing: "When research findings clash with cultural values, the values are more likely to prevail" (1973, p. 717). Unfortunately, that is as true today as it was twenty years ago.

References

Ackerman, P. L. (1987). Individual differences in skill learning: An integration of psychometric and information processing perspectives. *Psychological Bulletin* 102:3–27.

Benbow, C. P. (1988). Sex differences in mathematical reasoning ability in intellectually talented preadolescents: Their nature, effects, and possible causes. *Behavioral and Brain Sciences* 11:169–232.

Benbow, C. P., & Stanley, J. C. (in press). Inequity in equity: How "equity" can lead to inequity for high-potential students. *Psychology, Public Policy, and Law.*

Carroll, J. B. (1985). Exploratory factor analysis: A tutorial. In D. K. Detterman (Ed.), *Current topics in human intelligence: Vol. 1. Research methodology* (pp. 25–58). Norwood, N.J.: Ablex.

Dunnette, M. D. (1966). Fads, fashions, and folderol in psychology. *American Psychologist* 21:343–352.

Getzels, J. W., & Dillon, J. T. (1973). The nature of giftedness and the education of the gifted. In R. M. W. Travers (Ed.), *Second handbook of research on teaching* (pp. 689–731). Chicago: Rand McNally.

Guttman, L. (1954). A new approach to factor analysis: The radex. In P. Lazarsfeld (Ed.), *Mathematical thinking in the social sciences* (pp. 258–348). Glencoe, Ill.: Free Press.

Humphreys, L. G. (1979). The construct of general intelligence. *Intelligence* 3:105–120.

Jensen, A. R. (1986). g: Artifact or reality? *Journal of Vocational Behavior* 29:301–331.

Lubinski, D., & Benbow, C. P. (1992). Gender differences in abilities and preferences among the gifted: Implications for the math-science pipeline. *Current Directions in Psychological Science* 1:61–66.

Meehl, P. E. (1990). Appraising and amending theories: The strategy of Lakostian defense and two principles that warrant it. *Psychological Inquiry* 1:108–141.

Snow, R. E., Kyllonen, P. C., & Marshalek, B. (1984). The topography of ability and learning correlations. In R. J. Sternberg (Ed.), *Advances in the psychology of human intelligence* (Vol. 1, pp. 47–104). Hillsdale, N.J.: Erlbaum.

Stanley, J. C. (1993). Boys and girls who reason well mathematically. In G. R. Bock & K. Ackrill (Eds.), *The origins and development of high ability* (pp. 119–138). New York: Wiley.

Stanley, J. C., Benbow, C. P., Brody, L. E., Dauber, S., & Lupkowski, A. E. (1992). Gender differences on eighty-six nationally standardized aptitude and achievement tests. In N. Colangelo, S. G. Assouline, & D. L. Ambroson (Eds.), *Talent development: Proceedings from the 1991 Henry B. and Jocelyn Wallace National Research Symposium on Talent Development* (pp. 42–65). Unionville, N.Y.: Trillium Press.

3   Educational Research and Educational Policy

The Strange Case of Acceleration

JAMES J. GALLAGHER

lthough the call for educational reform is hardly new, the recent
thrust seems to have been more powerful than ever, involving even
the fifty governors and the then president in a statement of national
goals for education (America 2000) and in several determined efforts
to recast the methods of program evaluation and student assessment (Gallagher, 1991). Critics have demanded to know just what we do know about
educational process, instruction, and curriculum design.

The Role of Educational Research

Such calls have raised questions about the role of educational research in the
educational enterprise. What do we really know about effective programs? Are
current educational practices following proven knowledge and data from solid
educational research efforts? If we believe the proposition that education is
being driven by research findings, there are some rather strange events to be
accounted for. (See chapter 5 below for a further discussion of this issue.)

Sometimes educational research is placed in a secondary position, where it
operates to confirm decisions already made about how to organize school
programs and practices at the local or state level. That is, research is brought in,
after the fact, to support whatever "politically correct" wisdom is abroad at the
time. Research that does not fit the current paradigm is ignored and must wait
for a more favorable political climate in order to receive appropriate attention.

The evidence related to educational acceleration is a case in point. The notion that some students need not spend the entire time allotted to each segment of the educational process (elementary school, middle school, or secondary school) is not new. Educational acceleration has been used for two major purposes.

First, it has been used to place students with advanced ability and achievement with groups of individuals similar to themselves in order to challenge them adequately. If a student is performing at the eighth-grade level while in the fifth grade, then moving him or her to the sixth grade increases the likelihood that this advanced student will have some intellectual companionship, and will make it easier for the teacher to attend to the student's educational needs.

Student acceleration is also used to reduce the amount of time a student has to spend in the educational system. Gallagher and Gallagher (1994) point out that students committed to professional or graduate training could well be thirty years old or older before completing all aspects of their formal education (see table 3.1). Therefore, one goal of student acceleration is to allow students to complete the required work at an earlier age. By the end of the sequence noted in table 3.1, a student has been physiologically mature for as many as fifteen years, and many of that student's age-mates may have been gainfully employed for ten or more years. Many gifted students, however, remain dependent intellectually and financially through the most physically vigorous part of their adult lives.

To address these needs, there are various methods of acceleration for gifted children open to the teacher and the school administrator at practically all levels of the educational program. (See table 3.2.) At the primary level, this includes admittance to kindergarten before the usual beginning age of five years. Another option at this early level is the ungraded primary program. This program enables a group of bright students to remain with one teacher, who

TABLE 3.1.   *Age of Completion of Educational Benchmarks for Medical Students*

School Program Completed	Expected Age
Elementary school	12
Middle school	15
Senior high school	18
College	22
Medical school	26
Internship	27
Residency	29–32

Source: Gallagher & Gallagher (1994).

TABLE 3.2.   *Most-Common Methods of Acceleration of Gifted Students*

Grade Level	Type of Acceleration
Primary (K–3)	1. Early admittance to school
	2. Ungraded primary
Intermediate (4–5)	1. Ungraded classes
	2. Grade skipping
Middle school	1. Three years in two
	2. Senior high classes for credit
Senior high school	1. Extra load—early graduation
	2. Advanced placement

Source: Gallagher & Gallagher (1994).

will attempt to accomplish the goals of the primary years (K-3) in less than a four-year period. This technique allows slow learners more than four years to complete the primary level, if that seems desirable.

The junior high school years can be shortened by reducing the three-year program to two years; the senior high school program can be reduced either by early admittance to college or by inclusion of seminars in various subject areas that would qualify for college credit, as in the Advanced Placement program. Even in college, the student may take tests for course credit without having to sit through the course itself; this also represents a type of acceleration.

The Effects of Acceleration on Students

Evidence concerning the effects of acceleration on students has been accumulating for more than fifty years. As early as the Terman longitudinal study (Terman & Oden, 1947), the conclusion was reached that "nearly all children of 135 IQ or higher should be promoted sufficiently to permit college entrance by the age of 17 at least, and that the majority of this group would be better off entering at 16" (p. 281).

One of the clear differences between educational policy and educational research data involves the date of entrance into school. There is no reason, based on what we know about individual differences and individual growth rates, why a single date, such as a birthday, should be chosen to determine when a person will enter the educational system.

Such a date is clearly set for administrative convenience. The provision that a child must have a birthday of October 1 or earlier is one that can be verified easily and will elicit little parental argument. However, a number of educators (see Worcester, 1956; Holson, 1963) have explored a different policy.

What would happen if youngsters deemed to be intellectually and socially mature were allowed into kindergarten or first grade within a year of the usual date? Three decades ago Reynolds, Birch, and Tuseth (1962) reviewed the research on the effects of early-admittance programs and commented: "It may be concluded from the research . . . that early admission to school of mentally advanced children who are within a year of the ordinary school entrance age and who are generally mature is to their advantage. There are few issues in education on which the research evidence now available is so clear and universally favorable to a particular solution" (p. 17).

Perhaps so, but early admittance to school is not a widespread practice, despite what the research says. The lack of availability of acceleration was pointed out in a nationwide survey (Cox, Daniel, & Boston, 1985), which found that only 28 percent of school districts offer any form of early-entrance programs. So, does this research drive educational policy? Not even around the block, in this instance.

A more recent study of early entrants into college found similar results (Brody, Assouline, & Stanley, 1990). Sixty-five students selected on the basis of Scholastic Aptitude Test scores and previous academic performance entered Johns Hopkins University two years earlier than the typical entrant. A third of these students graduated in three and a half years or less. Forty-two percent of them graduated with general honors, 35 percent with departmental honors, and 26 percent with election to Phi Beta Kappa. Eight of the sixty-five students withdrew before graduating, which is a smaller percentage than that of the entire class entering the same year; four of these students transferred to other universities, where they all graduated—one with honors. (See also Brody & Stanley, 1991.)

Concerns about Acceleration

There are legitimate concerns that teachers and parents have about the rapid acceleration of gifted students, but such results as are reported are presented as group data. Somewhere in those data there might be a boy or girl who has had a dramatically negative reaction to acceleration, and such a reaction can be vivid in the minds of those who observe it in an individual case.

Studies show that the attitude of teachers to the process of acceleration is still moderately negative. They either do not know about the research results or simply do not believe them. The teachers are still concerned that these students will have many social problems or will be subject to undue stress by such advancement. The potential gains from these programs (e.g., an extra year for the career or to start a family) are far from the immediate concerns of the teachers, who worry more about the current adjustment of the students (Southern, Jones, & Fiscus, 1989).

Weiss (1978) questioned 123 college professors who had been accelerated often through grade skipping. As a group, they said that such acceleration posed no difficulties academically, but there were social anxieties or problems noted by 40 percent of the group. The adolescent years were identified as the point of maximum social stress. Such concerns were rarely considered serious, and the majority of the professors were grateful for the time that had been saved.

The major concern of educators about the practice of educational acceleration focuses on the social and emotional development of the child. Cornell, Callahan, Bassin, and Ramsay (1991) name three reasons why educators hesitate to employ educational acceleration. First, the educators are not aware of the available research evidence; second, their policies are determined by tradition and personal sentiment; and third, they fear that the researchers may not sufficiently have taken into account the social and emotional problems that might have been experienced by the gifted students who were accelerated.

These reviewers point out that many of the studies have not done a careful analysis of the emotional and social adjustment of the accelerated students. They point to the study by the Fund for the Advancement of Education (1957), which found that the universities offering early admittance to college noted adjustment problems that they felt were minimized by the report itself. Nonetheless, apart from individual instances of poor adjustment, which may or may not have been caused by the acceleration process, there is little evidence to suggest that poor adjustment is a common finding and considerable evidence to suggest that the majority of students seem to have adjusted quite well. Although there may be concerns about the lack of hard data as opposed to subjective impressions, there is little or no doubt that the saving of a year or more represents a positive finding.

David Elkind, in his influential book *The Hurried Child* (1981), expressed his concern that acceleration would rob students of time and experience and place unwarranted stress on them at a time when they were not mature enough to react positively to it. Much of Elkind's concern seemed to stem from the school-readiness literature, which did not directly address the advanced development of gifted students. Indeed, Elkind later reversed his stand against acceleration of the gifted and is one now of its active promoters (Elkind 1988).

Other reviews of the literature investigate reasons for concern that focus on the social adjustment of the accelerated child (Daurio, 1979; Hedges, 1977; Obrzut, Nelson, & Obrzut, 1984; Pollins, 1983).

By far the most ambitious and widespread use of the process of acceleration was designed by Julian C. Stanley in his Study of Mathematically Precocious Youth (SMPY) at Johns Hopkins University. In 1971 he began a series of annual mathematics talent searches to discover how many exceptionally mathematically able students there were in a given locale. (See chapter 15 below.) A number of other universities (e.g., Duke, Northwestern, Denver) also established talent searches built on the Johns Hopkins model. By the mid-1980s, the combined searches were identifying 70,000 talented youth per year (Benbow & Stanley, 1983). Now they identify more than 140,000.

The goal of the SMPY was to provide educational opportunities to make it more likely that these gifted students would become effective, productive adults. A number of fast-paced, three-week summer classes were established in precalculus. Other such courses in calculus, chemistry, biology, and physics have shown successful outcomes (Mezynski, Stanley, & McCoart, 1983; Stanley & Stanley, 1986). Students who have done well in the fast-paced classes are apparently able to go on to the next course in the sequence without a perceptible loss.

Many fewer students have been involved in the process of *radical acceleration*, meaning that the youngsters begin full-time university work at the age of twelve, thirteen, or fourteen. These are obviously extremely unusual youngsters, chosen because of their highly advanced mastery of academic material in mathematics. This program represents an attempt on an individual basis to cope with that advanced development. The results of these experiences are usually reported in some form of case study such as the following by Robinson (1983):

> C.F.C., born in 1959, completed his doctorate in finance before his twenty-second birthday at the University of Chicago Graduate School of Business, after earning his MBA there when he was 19. C.'s father, a college graduate, is a sales manager; his mother, a high-school graduate, is an executive secretary. C [had] skipped grades seven, nine, ten, and twelve and entered Johns Hopkins with sophomore standing through Advanced Placement Program course work and college credits earned while attending the eighth and eleventh grades [graduating the month he became seventeen years old]. He held a variety of jobs while in college, including summer jobs as a staff writer on a weekly publication and a junior security analyst covering publication stocks. His hobbies include skiing, tennis, golf, horse racing, and writing. Several letters written during graduate school reflect not only the substance but also the style of a student well into his twenties. With several re-

search publications already to his credit, he joined the faculty of the Gradu-ate School of Management of Northwestern University in the fall of 1981. In 1991, at age 31, he was appointed a full professor at one of the country's leading universities.

B.J.T. was born in 1967, one of four children of the owner of a data-processing company. In May 1979, while still only 11 years old, he achieved high marks on the AP mathematics examination (Calculus Level BC) and on both of the difficult Level C AP physics examinations (Mechanics, and Electricity and Magnetism). One year later he scored extremely well on the AP chemistry examination. On the calculus examination he was, indeed, one of the highest scorers in the country. At age 10 years 7 months, he had scored 770 on the SAT-Mathematics and 590 on the SAT-Verbal tests. Later that year he took a fast-paced mathematics program at Johns Hopkins for brilliant ex-seventh-graders. B.'s family lives in New Jersey, where in the fall of 1980, shortly after his thirteenth birthday, he entered Prince-ton University as a full-time student. Princeton does not award sophomore-class standing for AP scores, and he therefore entered as a freshman but with advanced standing in mathematics, physics, and chemistry. Apparently, he is doing well ac-ademically and also from a social/emotional perspective as well. At age 16 he graduated *magna cum laude* in mathematics and Phi Beta Kappa. Within a few more years he received his Ph.D. degree in mathematics from the University of California at Berkeley and joined the faculty of the same great university at which C.F.C. teaches and where a female SMPY prodigy is an assistant professor of sta-tistics. Another SMPYer, who finished college at age 15, is a postdoctoral fellow in astrophysics there.

Such individual adjustments seem appropriate and necessary to accom-modate the special needs of specific students, but would hardly be of direct concern to educational administrators, since the odds are that children like C.F.C. and B.J.T. are not likely to appear in their schools.

Brody and Benbow (1987) tried to address the concerns of critics by following four groups of students. One group had skipped one or more grades or entered college early, a second group took AP courses in high school, another group reported taking part in special classes or accelerated course work in high school, and a final group reported no accelerative experiences. A special effort was made to check the social and emotional characteristics of the students, and no differences were found between the groups except that those who had been accelerated tended to take more risks. As the authors state, "no harmful social and emotional effects of acceleration were demonstrated" (p. 109).

The social-adjustment issue was explored further by Janos and his col-leagues (Janos et al., 1988) by following sixty-three students who had entered college at age fourteen or younger. The researchers explored particularly their patterns of friendships and whether their unique age situation created special social problems for them within the university. The findings indicated that these young students formed friendships with each other, or others of a similar chronological age, in the first two years, but broadened their base to include older students when they reached their junior and senior years. Females in the study made headway sooner and achieved higher levels of interaction and intimacy with older university students. No major instances of social isolation were discovered in this study.

An attempt has been made to synthesize all the available research results of the effects of acceleration on the performance of gifted children. Kulik and Kulik (1984) found twenty-six studies that compared students who had been accelerated for a year with comparison groups of equivalent ability. The authors came to the following conclusions: "Talented youngsters who were accelerated into higher grades performed as well as the talented older pupils already in those grades. In the subjects in which they were accelerated, talented accelerates showed almost a year's advancement over talented same-age nonaccelerates."

Discussion

It is entirely possible for acceleration to have an unhappy outcome, and there have been a number of individual cases brought forward to illustrate such unfavorable outcomes. On the other hand, there is no study of which I am aware that brings forth negative results where the subjects have been treated as a group and the data have been analyzed as a group. Certainly, many different educational strategies have received huge commitments in education (cooperative learning and site-based management, for example) with thin or nonexistent research bases compared to that of educational acceleration. We must conclude that educational decision making is influenced by many and diverse factors. How much it costs may be a more important question than how valid the research base is. How the parents feel about it may be more important than a meta-analysis of program evaluation.

The decision making can be characterized by the following formula: $D \rightarrow F(A)(B)(C)(D) \ldots (H)$, where A may be economic conditions, B may represent the political climate of the community, C may represent what we know about acceleration, and so forth. The researchers from their particular perspective must feel that all sorts of bad things are happening if their results are ignored, as they are in the case of acceleration. Until these other variables return to a favorable mode, or the research is given greater visibility and priority, we can expect that educational research may be ignored again in this as in other cases.

One prime example of the influence of a particular political climate is the death grip that has been held on the social sciences for the past three decades by the priorities assigned to the environmental approach. Bad results implied bad environments, not bad genetics. The politically correct answer was to invest in attempted massive modifications of environments in the hopes of seeing more favorable results (thus, Head Start and Title I). Now that the political force of the 1960s has diminished, there is more of a willingness to consider, once again, the possible impact of inborn characteristics on our behavior—this time, in substantial interactions with the environment (Plomin, 1989). The research has long been available, but there is now more public willingness to consider it.

In conclusion, in setting policy more than one variable (financial or philosophical or administrative convenience, for example) may drown out research findings. Indeed, that seems to be what has happened to the research on educational acceleration. We can hope for a change in some of these other factors soon so that the full use of the strategy of acceleration, which seems to have substantial merit, can be realized.

References

Benbow, C. P. (1983). Adolescence of the mathematically precocious: A five-year longitudinal study. In C. P. Benbow & J. C. Stanley (Eds.), *Academic precocity: Aspects of its development* (pp. 9–37). Baltimore: Johns Hopkins University Press.

Benbow, C. P., & Stanley, J. C. (1983). An eight-year evaluation of SMPY: What was learned? In C. P. Benbow & J. C. Stanley (Eds.), *Academic precocity: Aspects of its development* (pp. 205–214). Baltimore: Johns Hopkins University Press.

Brody, L. E., Assouline, S. G., & Stanley, J. C. (1990). Five years of early entrants: Predicting successful achievement in college. *Gifted Child Quarterly* 34:138–142.

Brody, L. E., & Benbow, C. P. (1987). Accelerative strategies: How effective are they for the gifted? *Gifted Child Quarterly* 3:105–110.

Brody, L. E., Lupkowski, A. E., & Stanley, J. C. (1988). Early entrance to college: A study of academic and social adjustment during freshman year. *College and University* 63:347–359.

Brody, L. E., & Stanley, J. C. (1991). Young college students: Assessing factors that contribute to success. In W. T. Southern & E. D. Jones (Eds.), *The academic acceleration of gifted children* (pp. 102–132). New York: Teachers College Press.

Cornell, D. G., Callahan, C. M., Bassin, L. E., & Ramsay, S. G. (1991). Affective development in accelerated students. In W. T. Southern & E. D. Jones (Eds.), *The academic acceleration of gifted children*. New York: Teachers College Press.

Cox, J., Daniel, N., & Boston, B. A. (1985). *Educating able learners: Programs and promising practices*. Austin: University of Texas Press.

Daurio, S. P. (1979). Educational enrichment versus acceleration: A review of the literature. In W. C. George, S. J. Cohn, & J. C. Stanley (Eds.), *Educating the gifted: Acceleration and enrichment* (pp. 13–63). Baltimore: Johns Hopkins University Press.

Elkind, D. (1981). *The hurried child: Growing up too fast too soon*. Newton, Mass.: Addison-Wesley.

Elkind, D. (1988). Mental acceleration. *Journal for the Education of the Gifted* 11:19–31.

Fund for the Advancement of Education. (1957). *They went to college early* (Evaluation Report No. 2). New York: Author.

Gallagher, J. J. (1991). Educational reforms, values, and gifted. *Gifted Child Quarterly* 35:12–19.

Gallagher, J. J., & Gallagher, S. (1985). *Teaching the gifted child* (4th ed.). Boston: Allyn & Bacon.

Hanson, H. P. (1980, Spring). Twenty-five years of the Advanced Placement Program: Encouraging able students. *The College Board Review*, pp. 8–13, 35.

Hedges, W. D. (1977). *At what age should children enter first grade? A comprehensive review of research*. Ann Arbor, Mich.: University Microfilms International.

Holson, J. R. (1963). High school performance of underage pupils initially admitted to kindergarten on the basis of physical and psychological examinations. *Educational and Psychological Measurement* 23:159–170.

Janos, P. M., Robinson, N. M., Carter, C., Chapel, A., Cufley, R., Curland, M., Daily, M., Guilland, M., Heinzig, M., Kehl, H., Lu, S., Sherry, D., Stoloff, J., & Wise, A. (1988). A cross-sectional developmental study of the social relations of students who enter college early. *Gifted Child Quarterly* 32:210–215.

Klausmeier, H. J. (1963). Effects of accelerating bright older elementary pupils: A follow-up. *Journal of Educational Psychology* 54:165–171.

Kulik, J. A., & Kulik, C. C. (1984). Synthesis of research on effects of accelerated instruction. *Educational Leadership* 42:84–89.

Mezynski, K., & Stanley, J. C. (1980). Advanced Placement oriented calculus for high school students. *Journal for Research in Mathematics Education* 11:347–355.

Mezynski, K., Stanley, J. C., & McCoart, R. F. (1983). Helping youths score well on AP examinations in physics, chemistry, and calculus. In C. P. Benbow & J. C. Stanley (Eds.), *Academic precocity: Aspects of its development* (pp. 86–112). Baltimore: Johns Hopkins University Press.

Obrzut, A., Nelson, R. B., & Obrzut, J. E. (1984). Early school entrance for intellectually superior children: An analysis. *Psychology in the Schools* 21:71–77.

Plomin, R. (1989). Environments and genes: Determinants of behavior. *American Psychologist* 44:105–111.

Pollins, L. D. (1983). The effects of acceleration on the social and emotional development of gifted students. In C. P. Benbow & J. C. Stanley (Eds.), *Academic precocity: Aspects of its development* (pp. 160–178). Baltimore: Johns Hopkins University Press.

Proctor, T. B., Black, K. N., & Feldhusen, J. F. (1986). Early admission of selected children to elementary school: A review of the literature. *Journal of Educational Research* 80:70–76.

Reynolds, M. C., Birch, J. W., & Tuseth, A. A. (1962). Review of research on early admissions. In M. C. Reynolds (Ed.), *Early school admission for mentally advanced children: A review of research and practice* (pp. 7–18). Reston, Va.: Council for Exceptional Children.

Robinson, H. B. (1983). A case for radical acceleration: Programs of the Johns Hopkins University and the University of Washington. In C. P. Benbow & J. C. Stanley (Eds.), *Academic precocity: Aspects of its development* (pp. 139–159). Baltimore: Johns Hopkins University Press.

Southern, W. T., Jones, E. D., & Fiscus, E. D. (1989). Practitioner objects to the academic acceleration of gifted children. *Gifted Child Quarterly* 33:29–35.

Stanley, J. C. (1991). An academic model for educating the mathematically talented. *Gifted Child Quarterly* 35:36–42.

Stanley, J. C., & Benbow, C. P. (1983). SMPY's first decade: Ten years of posing problems and solving them. *Journal of Special Education* 17:11–25.

Stanley, J. C., & Benbow, C. P. (1986). Youths who reason exceptionally well mathematically. In R. J. Sternberg & J. E. Davidson (Eds.), *Conceptions of giftedness* (pp. 361–387). Cambridge: Cambridge University Press.

Stanley, J. C., & Stanley, B. S. K. (1986). High-school biology, chemistry, or physics learned well in three weeks. *Journal of Research in Science Teaching* 23:237–250.

Terman, L. M., & Oden, M. H. (1947). *The gifted child grows up*. Stanford: Stanford University Press.

Weiss, P. (1978). *Attitudes towards gifted education*. Unpublished doctoral dissertation, University of North Carolina at Chapel Hill.

Worcester, D. A. (1956). *The education of children of above-average mentality*. Lincoln: University of Nebraska Press.

4 Acceleration over the Years

A. HARRY PASSOW

The first large-scale program of acceleration for academically able youngsters has been attributed to the efforts in 1868 of William T. Harris, superintendent of the St. Louis public schools. Under Harris's system, students were promoted first on a semiannual, then on a quarterly, and finally on a five-week basis. The strength of the short-interval promotion, Harris argues, is that it tends to "hold bright pupils up to the rate at which they are capable and keeps them from acquiring habits of carelessness and listlessness" (Henry, 1920, p. 12).

Similar administrative procedures, adapted to the learning rates of both bright and "dull" pupils, were soon established in other school systems across the country, notably in Elizabeth, New Jersey, Cambridge, Massachusetts, and Santa Barbara, California. At first, the Cambridge Double-Track Plan permitted rapid learners to complete grades three to eight in four years rather than six; later on, such learners could complete the first eight grades in six years, with special teachers assigned to work with the brighter pupils. By the turn of the century, acceleration in the form of flexible promotions characterized the provisions made for academically able students.

More than seventy years ago, the introduction to the Nineteenth Yearbook of the National Society for the Study of Education (Henry, 1920) began as follows:

> One of the most significant of modern tendencies in educational administration is revealed in the widespread attempts which are being made to adjust the subject matter and methods of the school to the varying needs and capabilities of the children whom it is the purpose of the school to serve. Instead of holding to a rigid scheme of gradation, adjusted to the theoretical "average child," to which all children must be made to conform, those who are in charge of public school systems are coming to see the advisability of making a more flexible arrangement

93

and a more careful adjustment to the varying aptitudes and capacities of the members of the school population. In other words, there is going on something which has been termed the "psychologizing" of school organization. (P. 7)

The first chapter, entitled "Flexible Promotion Schemes as Related to the School Progress of Gifted Children," provides a survey of a variety of flexible promotion procedures, including rapid promotion, double promotion, and grade skipping. Henry concludes that such provisions enable students "to do more work than ordinary pupils in the same time," "to do a different kind or type of work with no gain in time," or "to do the same work, or work differing only slightly from it, but in less time" (p. 26).

In an NSSE yearbook that was published just four years later (Whipple, 1924), a chapter is devoted to two studies: one entitled "Academic Records of Accelerated Students" and another entitled "A Study of the Subsequent Standing of Specially Promoted Pupils." Haney and Uhl (1924), the authors of the first study, begin with a quote from Lewis Terman urging early admission to university for able high school students. They define an "accelerated student" as one "who at age sixteen and one-half years has qualified fully to enter the University of Wisconsin" (p. 323). Seventy-four such students entered the College of Letters and Science of the University of Wisconsin as regular students between 1918 and 1921, and all did well academically. In the second study, "special promotion" was defined as "skipping of a half-grade of the elementary school course" (p. 333). Among children with IQs higher than 120 who had skipped two half-grades, there were no failures, leading the researcher to conclude that "continued success is almost certain to follow special promotions of pupils of very superior intelligence" (Martin, 1924, p. 351).

In their twenty-five-year follow-up of the Stanford sample, Terman and Oden devote a chapter to what they call the "problem of school acceleration":

> At one extreme is the opinion that the gifted child should be given a grade placement corresponding to his mental age; at the other extreme are those who would base promotions on the calendar without regard to mental ability. Neither of these extreme views has many advocates, though the latter is perhaps more commonly held than the former. The fact remains, however, that many educators believe considerable acceleration is desirable, whereas many others are opposed to it. (1947, p. 264)

Terman and Oden have little use for the alternative of "special classes with an enriched curriculum for the gifted," noting that "so-called enrichment often amounts to little more than a quantitative increase of work on the usual level.

This may keep the gifted child out of mischief, but it is hardly educational" (p. 264). The controversy over the pros and cons of acceleration hinges on "the relative weight that should be given to intellectual and social values in the educative process." They believe that their subjects are "caught in the lock-step and held to school work two or three full grades below the level on which they could have functioned successfully" (pp. 279–280). Terman and Oden conclude that "children of 135 IQ or higher should be promoted sufficiently to permit college entrance by the age of seventeen at the latest, and a majority in this group would be better off to enter at sixteen" (p. 281). They see acceleration as especially desirable for students who plan to go on to graduate studies for professional careers, citing studies by Keys (1939) and Pressey (1949) for additional support. In their report on the thirty-five-year follow-up, Terman and Oden (1959) reiterate their beliefs about the need for, importance of, and efficacy of acceleration.

The scholar whose name came to be synonymous with acceleration, S. L. Pressey, defines the process as "progress through an educational program at rates faster or ages younger than conventional" (1949, p. 2). In still another NSSE yearbook on the gifted, I write that "any modification of a regular program can be considered *acceleration* if it enables the student to progress more rapidly and to complete a program in less time or at an earlier age than is normal" (Passow, 1958, p. 212). Students may be accelerated as individuals or in groups: "Points of acceleration have ranged from early entrance to kindergarten through early graduation from college. Acceleration methods include: combining two years' work into one (three into two, eight into seven) either for a subject or for a grade; skipping a course or a grade; taking extra courses for additional credit; attending summer sessions to shorten time; permitting credit by examination; or allowing early admission to advanced levels" (p. 212).

Over the years, each of these acceleration practices has gone through cycles of popularity and support. For example, grade skipping was quite a common practice for many years but is currently used only rarely. Since the mid-1950s, the Advanced Placement program has grown steadily while the Early Admission to College program has tended to wane; both programs were initially sponsored by the Ford Foundation. Early entrance to kindergarten or first grade has been drastically reduced by rigid age requirements for admission. The debate about the value of acceleration has often revolved around the negative emotional and social consequences ascribed to the practice.

Lately, we have begun to sort the various means of acceleration into two overlapping categories—administrative and instructional—and begun to look at the consequences of each differently. These category labels are not exact, but they are helpful in separating the procedures. Some forms of acceleration, such as grade skipping and early admission, can be considered administrative in that they often involve no curricular changes—that is, the student experiences the usual curriculum but at an earlier age. In those settings, the gifted student may find himself or herself in a class with older children, following a lockstep curriculum at a pace geared to the older members of the class. The gifted child may engage in those experiences at an earlier age than is usual and finish them in a shorter time, but his or her needs are not necessarily being met optimally. Instructional acceleration, on the other hand, involves curricular changes— changes in the content, nature, and pace of instruction.

Historically, the curricular and instructional issues have been posed in terms of acceleration versus enrichment. Stanley (1977) writes critically of enrichment in any of four forms: "busy work, irrelevant academic, cultural, and relevant academic" (p. 90). He argues that "any kind of enrichment except perhaps the cultural sort will, without acceleration, tend to harm the brilliant student" (p. 93). What he and the staff of the Study of Mathematically Precocious Youth advocate is "a varied assortment of accelerative possibilities [from which the gifted student could] choose an optimum combination . . . to suit the individual's situation" (p. 95). Moreover, Stanley argues for homogeneously grouped, fast-paced classes in which intellectual peers can stimulate one another.

On the basis of what I see as an emerging rethinking or reconceptualization of the notions of acceleration and enrichment, I have argued for restating the perennial issue of acceleration versus enrichment instead as a question of acceleration vis-à-vis enrichment. I do not think this is simply a semantic issue. As I have argued elsewhere:

> At the simplest level, acceleration enables the student to deal with more advanced concepts at higher cognitive levels, and this represents an enriching experience. At another level, acceleration in one area provides opportunities for more advanced study in that area or for more experiences in another area or areas. Enrichment involves breadth and/or depth—learning experiences that enable the student to probe more broadly or more intensively. It uses advanced resources aimed at enabling gifted individuals to attain higher levels of insight, understanding, performance, or product development. Both enrichment and acceleration have qualitative as well as quantitative dimensions; both enable the individual to pursue differential experiences through a greater variety of opportunities and engagements.
> Given this view of acceleration and enrichment as alternative and complementary approaches to learning opportunities for the gifted, the question becomes one of *when* it is more appropriate to alter the tempo or pace of instruc-

tion and *when* it is more appropriate to alter the breadth or depth of experience. Some experiences require time for the incubation of ideas, for reflection, for "playing around" with knowledge and ideas, for pursuit in depth employing a wide range of resources if they are to result in optimal learning. Some experiences focus on the acquisition of knowledge and skills which, once mastered, are the basis for further learning. Some disciplines lend themselves to acceleration because gifted youngsters can acquire or master the knowledge and skills rapidly. Other learning must mature, and rapid acquisition is not sufficient by itself. Some disciplines, such as mathematics and foreign languages, lend themselves to acceleration, whereas other disciplines, such as literature and history, lend themselves to study in depth and breadth as well as creative reflection. (Passow, 1985, pp. 37–38)

Leaving aside the "Mickey Mouse" enrichment activities that Stanley criticized so ably, real enrichment in the sense of challenging and nurturing gifted students results from instructional acceleration, and instructional acceleration is an essential means for providing enrichment. Put another way, acceleration creates enrichment and enrichment is often best achieved through instructional acceleration.

I think Dishart (1980) puts the matter correctly and provides the appropriate challenge for curriculum designers:

There is a resultant difference between enriching or accelerating an inadequate and inappropriate curriculum and designing an adequate and appropriate curriculum in the first place. . . . An enrichment supplement does not really correct a curriculum that is weak, dull, or redundant for the learner. And such a curriculum pushed faster does not correct its faults even if the learner achieves content acceleration. There are curricula which are simplified enough and slow enough for handicapped learners. *Why not develop curricula which are enriched enough and accelerated enough for gifted learners?* (P. 26, emphasis added)

But I believe it was Marshall who once said: "If you don't like these ideas, I have others."

References

Dishart, M. (1980). [Review of *The gifted and the talented: Their education and development.*] *Educational Researcher* 9:25–26.

Haney, E. M., & Uhl, W. L. (1924). Academic records of accelerated students. In G. M. Whipple (Ed.), *The education of gifted children* (pp. 323–332). Twenty-third Yearbook of the National Society for the Study of Education (Part 1). Bloomington, Ill.: Public Schools Publishing.

Henry. T. H. (1920). *Classroom problems in the education of gifted children.* Nineteenth Yearbook of the National Society for the Study of Education (Part 2). Bloomington, Ill.: Public School Publishing.

Keys, N. (1939). *The underage student in high school and college: Educational and social adjustment.* Berkeley and Los Angeles: University of California Press.

Martin, A. H. (1924). A study of the subsequent standing of specially promoted pupils. In G. M. Whipple (Ed.), *The education of gifted children* (pp. 333–353). Twenty-third Yearbook of the National Society for the Study of Education (Part 1). Bloomington, Ill.: Public School Publishing.

Passow, A. H. (1958). Enrichment of education for the gifted. In N. B. Henry (Ed.), *Education for the gifted* (pp. 193–221). Fifty-seventh Yearbook of the National Society for the Study of Education (Part 2). Chicago: University of Chicago Press.

Passow, A. H. (1985). Intellectual development of the gifted. In F. R. Link (Ed.), *Essays on the intellect* (pp. 23–43). Alexandria, Va.: Association for Supervision and Curriculum Development.

Pressey, S. L. (1949). *Educational acceleration: Appraisals and basic problems.* Columbus: Ohio State University Press.

Stanley, J. C. (1977). Rationale of the Study of Mathematically Precocious Youth (SMPY) during its first five years of promoting educational acceleration. In J. C. Stanley, W. C. George, & C. H. Solano (Eds.), *The gifted and the creative: A fifty-year perspective* (pp. 75–112). Baltimore: Johns Hopkins University Press.

Stanley, J. C. (1978). Educational non-acceleration: An international tragedy. *Gifted Child Today* 1:2–5, 53–57, 60–63.

Stanley, J. C. (1989). A look back at "Educational non-acceleration: An international tragedy." *Gifted Child Today* 12:60–61.

Stanley, J. C. (1991). An academic model for educating the mathematically talented. *Gifted Child Quarterly* 35:36–42.

Stanley, J. C., & Benbow, C. P. (1982). Educating mathematically precocious youths: Twelve policy recommendations. *Educational Researcher* 11:4–9.

Terman, L. M., & Oden, M. (1947). *The gifted child grows up.* Stanford: Stanford University Press.

Terman, L. M., & Oden, M. H. (1959). *The gifted group at mid-life.* Stanford: Stanford University Press.

Whipple, G. M. (Ed.) (1924). *The education of gifted children.* Twenty-third Yearbook of the National Society for the Study of Education (Part 1). Bloomington, Ill.: Public School Publishing.

5

The Role of the Educational Researcher in Educational Improvement

A Retrospective Analysis

HERBERT J. KLAUSMEIER

W hat is the role of the researcher in bringing about educational improvement? What kind of research does the researcher carry out to ensure that education will be improved? By educational improvement, I mean maintaining levels of student performance (for example, in mathematics or prosocial conduct) that are already as high as can be expected while making gains in one or more areas that are below what is expected. Moreover, educational improvement for a particular group, such as the gifted or those with learning handicaps, requires not only a gain by the particular group under consideration but also no deceleration of progress by those not in the group. For example, a gain for the gifted might be defined as their completing a level of schooling more rapidly than others do, with no increase in the time it takes others to complete it.

To clarify the relationship between research and educational improvement, I discuss the kinds of scientific inquiry that potentially result in such improvement. I then draw on a report by the National Academy of Education (1991) and one by the Educational Testing Service (1990) to identify the contribution educational research made to improving the education of all children in the United States in the 1980s. In exploring the role of the individual researcher, I review two projects that extended knowledge but were not followed by implementation in schools, and two others that both improved education and extended knowledge.

99

Methods of Scientific Inquiry

Educational research can encompass any of three kinds of scientific inquiry. Knowledge-generating research is conducted to increase understanding of the phenomena associated with education—for example, student learning, curriculum, or gender. Many researchers conduct this kind of research, draw implications for practice, publish articles, and then move on to their next projects. A quick survey of the *Encyclopedia of Educational Research* (Mitzel, 1982) and the *Handbook of Research on Teaching* (Wittrock, 1986) shows that this kind of research is increasing knowledge about all aspects of education at a phenomenal rate.

The second kind of scientific inquiry involves evaluation. Practitioners and researchers evaluate an aspect of education, such as a curricular program, for the purpose of judging its quality, worth, or significance. Practitioners often make decisions and take actions based on these evaluations. Decisions that guide practice may or may not follow from evaluations conducted by researchers, however.

The third form of scientific inquiry is improvement-oriented educational research (see, e.g., Klausmeier, 1982, 1985, 1987; Klausmeier & Wisconsin Associates, 1990). Its objective is to improve student performance. Here the researcher and the school staff jointly plan the research, including the changes to be made in educational practices. The practitioners implement the planned changes as a central element of the research, and they participate in gathering data. In an iterative cycle of research, refinement of practices, and implementation, the changed practices become institutionalized. The school staff becomes increasingly independent in carrying out improvement-oriented research and the development of practices that result in progress for the students. Improvement-oriented research employs some of the same methods as those used in knowledge-generating research—for example, experimentation and longitudinal study. The knowledge gained about educational practices from this kind of research, however, can be generalized only to school settings that are similar to those in which the research is conducted.

It should be noted that these three paradigms do not necessarily yield educational improvement outside the settings in which they are employed. To result in widespread improvement, the findings must be used in either the formulation of educational policies (for example, a statewide program for educating gifted students) or the development of educational products (for example, instructional materials). To identify whether educational improvement follows, the policies and products must be implemented and the effects of the implementation on student performance must be identified. Historically, the effects—positive, neutral, or negative—have not been ascertained in the large majority of cases.

Research and Educational Improvement in the 1980s

A report published by the National Academy of Education (1991) highlighted seven areas in which research has affected practice—reading, writing, testing, cooperative learning, educating students with disabilities, student retention in grade, and school finance. Research in these areas has been conducted over a sufficient period of time that one might expect nationwide gains to have been made in student performance from the beginning to the end of the 1980s, particularly in reading and writing. Unfortunately, the report does not indicate the means by which the research made its way into practice nor its effects on student performance.

The Educational Testing Service (1990) provides some of the missing information as well as much other data on educational improvement, or the lack thereof. In the 1980s governors and state legislatures, rather than the educational research community and other broad-based education-interest groups such as schools of education, led the major reforms intended to improve education. The reforms were mandated by either state or school-district policies.

By the end of the decade forty-two states had raised standards for the type and number of courses required for high school graduation and forty-seven states had initiated statewide testing programs. Many local schools had established other policies directly related to student performance in general—for example, attendance, homework, and conduct, as well as a minimal grade point average for participation in athletics.

What were the nationwide outcomes of these policies? Surprisingly, no progress was made during the 1980s in either average reading or writing proficiency, the two subject fields that the National Academy of Education (1991) identified as the places where research affected practice (Educational Testing Service, 1990). However, there was a substantial gain in average science achievement and some gain in average mathematics achievement. But there was no change in the percentage (87%) of sixteen- and twenty-four-year-olds with high school diplomas. In passing, I note that the percentage of blacks of these ages with diplomas was nearly equal to that of whites. Relative to a goal of achieving equality in performance, some progress was made in closing the gap between the white majority and the black and Hispanic minorities—more so for the black than for the Hispanic minority. However, little progress was made in closing the gender gap in mathematics and science, in which males score higher, or in reading and writing, in which females score higher. The few small gains made from the beginning to the end of the 1980s in improving educational performance and in achieving equity suggest that the vast body of knowledge that has accrued through knowledge-generating research has not resulted in much educational improvement. My own experience supports this view.

Knowledge-Generating Research

Knowledge-generating research carried out for three years in the late 1950s yielded much new information about the learning and developmental characteristics of children of low, average, and high intelligence (Klausmeier, Feldhusen, & Check, 1959). The low-IQ children met the criteria for mental retardation and the high-IQ children met those for giftedness. School and clinical psychologists, pediatricians, radiologists, dentists, graduate research assistants, and I gathered extensive data annually on each child for three consecutive years. The developmental data included physical, mental, educational achievement, and personality measures. The learning data were drawn from individually administered arithmetic tasks. The tasks were graded in difficulty to meet each child's initial level of achievement, and each child mastered his or her tasks.

Given the same amount of time to learn counting and addition exercises, the children with average and high IQs initially completed the same number of items in counting and addition, and those with low IQs completed fewer. The median counting level for the three groups was by twos, sevens, and twelves, respectively; the highest level for a gifted student was by twenty-threes. Five weeks later the three groups performed their initial learning tasks equally well; retention was the same for all the groups (Klausmeier & Feldhusen, 1959). The gifted children, while having achieved a much higher level of proficiency in counting and addition, did not retain a higher percentage of what they had learned than the other groups. The same pattern held for subtraction exercises (Feldhusen, Check, & Klausmeier, 1961).

Having identified this pattern for quite simple tasks, we turned to problem solving (Klausmeier & Check, 1962). Each child's task, again carefully graded in difficulty, was to indicate the number of coins and bills required to make a specified sum of money. The most frequently given sum of money and number of coins and bills for the three IQ groups was 8¢ and four coins for the low-IQ group (a nickel and three pennies); 57¢ and nine coins for the average-IQ group; and $1.97 and nine coins and bills for the high-IQ group. After seven weeks, the groups did not differ either in the time required to relearn the problems or in the time required to solve different problems of the same level of difficulty.

In another problem-solving study (Klausmeier & Loughlin, 1961), the three groups again required equal amounts of time to solve their problems. However, their problem-solving behaviors differed markedly. Compared with both other groups, many fewer gifted students started with random, disconnected actions; they started with actions guided by logical reasoning. The gifted offered fewer incorrect solutions, and more often independently verified initial solutions as incorrect and a final one as correct. Many more of them also persisted until they achieved a correct solution. Thus, the gifted employed an effective metacognitive strategy. Use of this strategy, along with their higher initial levels of achievement, enabled the gifted students to solve problems of a much higher level of complexity than could the students in the other two groups.

The developmental characteristics of the children were assessed annually at ages eight, nine, and ten (Feldhusen & Klausmeier, 1959; Klausmeier, Beeman, & Lehmann, 1958; Klausmeier & Check, 1959). The gifted students at ten years of age did not differ from the other two groups on seven measures—height, weight, number of permanent teeth, ossification of the bones of the hand and wrist, emotional adjustment, expression of emotion, and behavior pattern suggestive of withdrawal-aggression (Klausmeier, Check, & Feldhusen, 1960). The gifted children scored much higher than those in the other two groups in arithmetic, reading, and language achievement, and moderately higher in achievement in relation to expectations. They scored higher than the low-IQ group and the same as the average-IQ group in integration of self-concept, handwriting speed, and strength of grip. I suspect that we would find similar developmental profiles for the three groups at the present time.

Like most researchers, we drew inferences for research and for improving educational practice (Klausmeier, Feldhusen, & Check, 1959, pp. 127–129). One inference was that the teacher should ascertain the present achievement level of each child, select a learning task at the next higher level of difficulty, and then offer individualized or small-group instruction to aid the child to master the task. Since every child would then experience success, further motivational techniques would not be needed. We hypothesized that implementing this kind of instruction would raise the average arithmetic achievement of all children one grade and that of gifted children two grades by the end of the fifth grade. We also outlined a comprehensive child-assessment program.

This project was completed at a time when research-based knowledge regarding both child development and learning in school settings was relatively meager. It provided comprehensive information about children of all levels of intelligence that schools might use in arranging a good educational program for each child. We disseminated the findings widely in journal articles and in college textbooks. However, the participating schools did not implement the suggestions, and I doubt that other schools did either.

Concept Learning and Concept Teaching

Another program of knowledge-generating research started in the late 1950s and continued into the 1990s. The first study involved ten experiments and was federally funded. It focused on strategies of concept learning and on the efficiency of concept attainment by individuals and small cooperative groups (Klausmeier, Harris, & Wiersma, 1964). Federal funding continued for years thereafter, and the scope of the research broadened.

The main outcome of the first ten years of this research was a theory of concept learning and development (CLD) and a design for teaching concepts related directly to the theory (Klausmeier, 1971, 1976a, 1976b; Klausmeier, Ghatala, & Frayer, 1974). The theory was corroborated and refined by a four-year combined cross-sectional/longitudinal study that included four cohorts of fifty boys and fifty girls each, enrolled in grades one through three, four through six, seven through nine, and ten through twelve (Klausmeier & Allen, 1978; Klausmeier & Associates, 1979; Klausmeier & Sipple, 1982). We gathered data annually on each of these two hundred boys' and two hundred girls' levels of concept attainment and their use of the concepts in understanding principles and taxonomic relations and in solving problems.

CLD theory indicates that any given concept is learned at four successively higher levels of understanding and use, and it specifies the mental processes that are necessary and sufficient for learning at each level. Thus, the theory describes concept learning and development as integrated processes. This integration permits a more accurate picture of concept development than that of Piaget's four stages (Brainerd, 1979) and a more complete explanation of concept learning than that of Rosch (1975, 1978).

The four successively higher levels of concept attainment are called concrete, identity, classificatory, and formal. Attainment of the concrete and identity levels enables a learner to use a concept only in solving simple perceptual problems. Attainment of the classificatory level enables the learner to identify some examples and nonexamples of the concept, understand some principles of which the concept is a part, understand some taxonomic and other relations involving the concept, and use the concept in solving some verbal and other problems. Attainment of the formal level results in a huge fourfold increase in performance over that of the classificatory level (Klausmeier & Associates, 1979, pp. 85–87).

The instructional design was refined and validated by a series of thirteen experiments conducted in two sets of experimental and control schools (Klausmeier & Sipple, 1980). We followed the same children for two years. The subject matter was the process concepts of science—for example, observing, inferring, and classifying. Later literature reviews led to minor refinements in the theory and design (Klausmeier, 1992a).

The instructional design provides a set of principles for teaching concepts at each of the four levels of concept attainment (Klausmeier, 1976b, 1990, 1992a). When the principles are implemented properly, students at all levels make remarkable progress—in preschool (Nelson, 1976), elementary school (Klausmeier & Sipple, 1980; McMurray, Bernard, Klausmeier, Schilling, & Feldman, 1977), high school (Bernard, 1975), and college (Wang & Horng, 1991). Three-year-olds made the most impressive gains. After sixteen minutes of one-on-one instruction, they had progressed to the level of their five-year-old controls (Nelson, 1976). In the elementary-school study, thirteen out of twenty-six comparisons favored the experimental children; no comparisons favored the controls (Klausmeier & Sipple, 1980, pp. 196–197).

The cross-sectional/longitudinal study of concept development showed that in typical schools, differences among the students in their attainment of the formal level of concepts and the uses of concepts are great. To illustrate, 3 percent of the children in grade three, those who were conceptually gifted, had attained the formal level of the concept *equilateral triangle*, but 27 percent of the students in grade twelve had not (Klausmeier & Allen, 1978, p. 187).

Many conditions accompanied the most rapid and slowest cognitive development by the time the students had reached the twelfth grade (Klausmeier & Allen, 1978, p. 201). The most-rapid developers, the top 3 percent of the total group, who might be called conceptually gifted, had higher self-esteem, achievement motivation, and self-directed behavior, and better peer relations, than the lowest 3 percent, the slowest developers. The members of this top group had more favorable attitudes toward school, the curriculum, and their parents. They were absent less often from school, took more academic subjects, were given higher grades, were involved in more school activities, and had better rapport with teachers. They also had more hobbies, read more, and watched television less often. Moreover, the socioeconomic status of the parents of this group was higher, as were the parents' expectations for the children, involvement in daily activities with the children, and supervision of the children. Finally, the intellectual climate of the homes was better. The most rapid developers did not differ from the slowest developers in participation in sports, responsibilities at home, the marital status of the parents, or the number of children in the family.

To what extent has this research influenced practice? Successive research teams presented findings in symposiums and papers at many conventions of the American Educational Research Association and the American Psychological Association. My coauthors and I reported major studies and successive versions of CLD theory and the instructional design in numerous books and chapters of edited books. I presented the theory and design at numerous national and international conventions. Researchers in the United States and abroad, as well as curriculum specialists, are conversant with the theory and design. Yet teachers are not using the theory or the instructional design to improve students' concept learning. Similarly, this research-based knowledge is not being used in developing curricular materials for students or teachers or in formulating educational policy directed toward enhancing concept learning. Instead, now as in the early 1970s, many people are pleading for the memorization of encyclopedic factual information to be replaced with an understanding and application of the main concepts of the various subject fields and for these concepts to be used in understanding principles and in solving problems (see, for example, the April 1992 issue of *Educational Leadership*).

Improvement-Oriented Research, Program Development, and Implementation

Four years of improvement-oriented research in the early 1960s and the development of related educational provisions for gifted students yielded improved education in three Wisconsin school districts (Klausmeier, 1963; Klausmeier, Mulhern, & Wakefield, 1960; Klausmeier & Ripple, 1962; Klausmeier & Teel, 1964; Klausmeier & Wiersma, 1964). We regarded giftedness as markedly and consistently superior performance in one or more subject fields, an expressive area, or leadership (Klausmeier, 1956, p. 3). The usual procedure was to develop a provision that the school personnel judged to be promising and feasible, implement it, and carry out research to determine its effects in terms of student outcomes in the cognitive and affective domains. After the fourth year, the then very large Milwaukee School District implemented a program for gifted students from kindergarten through the twelfth grade (Klausmeier & Teel, 1964). The program included districtwide procedures for identifying the gifted, psychological and guidance services that encompassed educational and vocational counseling, and the following provisions that were continuous across grade and school levels:

1. Acceleration, particularly for the children of above-average chronological age, by one or two semesters at some time between kindergarten and completion of grade four.

2. Enrichment in grade four to ensure that the children previously accelerated and the nonaccelerated gifted students in grade four were ready to enter special classes for the gifted in grade five.

3. Special classes for the gifted in grades five and six or, where there were too few gifted students, the use of an itinerant teacher.

4. Acceleration in the academic subjects in the junior high school.

5. Ninth-grade courses in the academic subjects being offered to eighth-grade students, and high school graduation credit being given for the courses.

6. Senior high school students being permitted to graduate early or to remain through grade twelve with some released time either for enrollment in university courses or for gainful employment.

7. Enrichment activities in all classes at all school levels—for example, creative projects, leadership opportunities, experimentation, club work, school and community services, and special talent activities in music, art, dramatics, dance, and athletics.

In addition to these provisions, the junior and senior high schools placed students in sections in each academic subject on the basis of the students' initial achievement levels in particular subjects. The students identified as having superior learning ability in a particular subject were placed in the highest section. Some schools called the highest section an honors section. Whether or not students continued in the same section for more than a semester depended on their performance during the semester. In the early 1960s this seemed to be a much better way to adapt schooling to individual differences than tracking across all subjects based on IQ testing. Our research showed that these provisions yielded positive results in terms of student outcomes (see, for example, Klausmeier, Mulhern, & Wakefield, 1960).

One acceleration project merits special attention (Klausmeier, 1963). Gifted second-grade children who were in the top half of their grade in chronological age were enrolled in the fourth grade after participating in a half-day, five-week summer program. Toward the end of grade five there was no difference between those who had been accelerated and their one-year-older gifted counterparts on ten out of ten tests of creativity, seven out of nine educational achievement tests, five out of six psychomotor measures, and eight out of eight measures in social, emotional, and ethical areas. The achievement areas where the older fifth-grade counterparts scored higher were word knowledge and language total; the psychomotor area was handwriting legibility. On all measures of educational achievement, those who had been accelerated were equal to or surpassed the younger gifted fifth graders who had been in school for one more year. This acceleration program cost more money to implement than most of the others because of the summer program.

These provisions for the gifted received widespread attention throughout Wisconsin. The *1990 State of the States Gifted and Talented Education Report* (Council of State Directors of Programs for the Gifted, 1991, p. 54) indicates that most if not all of the fifty states currently include these provisions, except the summer-school acceleration program, in their statewide programs.

Individually Guided Education

The provisions for gifted students discussed above were implemented in traditional schools. Even though the gifted students profited from the provisions, a few of us at the Wisconsin Center for Education Research felt that traditional schooling was incapable of providing adequately for all students, including the gifted. With cooperating practitioners, we carried out improvement-oriented research and developed replacements for traditional elementary school operations. The schools implemented the replacements. This effort led to Individually Guided Education (IGE), an alternative to traditional elementary schooling (Klausmeier, Rossmiller, & Saily, 1977). IGE is by far the most comprehensive school restructuring to come out of the federally supported Research and Development Centers Program that started in 1964. Between 1965 and 1985, 37 professors, 112 project associates, and 178 graduate students at the Wisconsin Center for Education Research participated in IGE research, development, implementation, and evaluation activities. The twenty-five-year history of IGE from 1965 to 1990 provides an informative case study of the relationship between educational research and nationwide educational improvement (Klausmeier & Wisconsin Associates, 1990; Klausmeier, 1992b).

In IGE, a nongraded instructional unit consisting of three to five teachers, a paraprofessional aide, a teacher intern, and 60 to 120 children replaces the age-graded, self-contained classroom of one teacher and 20 to 40 children. One teacher serves as the leader of the unit.

An instructional improvement committee that includes the teacher leader of each unit, the principal, the head of the instructional media center, and sometimes parents replaces the principal as the sole educational decision maker at the building level. A systemwide improvement committee composed of representative unit leaders, principals, and the superintendent replaces the superintendent as the sole educational decision maker at the district level.

By 1969 this plan for instruction and these administrative arrangements had truly revolutionized educational decision making in schools in three Wisconsin school districts. IGE teachers exercised far more control over curriculum, instruction, and student evaluation. For the first time in the history of elementary education in the United States, teachers who served as unit leaders participated in educational decision making at the building and district levels through formal, clearly defined structures and processes (Klausmeier & Pellegrin, 1971). The local schools became more autonomous. Principals became true educational leaders as they shared instructional leadership with the unit leaders; principals made school improvement a reality as they worked with a few teaching teams during school hours instead of individual teachers or the entire teaching staff before or after school. Staff development became a continuous process through the meetings of the instructional units and the instructional improvement committee.

In the IGE system, arranging an appropriate educational program for each child replaces the common assignments and whole-class instruction of the traditional elementary school. Each child's program includes one-on-one instruction, independent study, small-group activities, and large-group activities in a combination that best suits the particular child. Such individual instructional programming, in which learning activities are not based on the child's age or grade in school, ensures continuous progress in learning for every child, including the gifted. This approach to individual educational planning preceded by several years that which was incorporated in the Education for All Handicapped Children Act of 1975. Moreover, in IGE, evaluations that focus on assessing and monitoring each child's progress replace group testing directed toward comparing and grading children. Observations by the teacher, samples of students' work, and other authentic assessments supplant most pencil-and-paper testing.

In addition, traditional report cards are replaced with individual teacher-parent-child conferences; this program encourages parents to participate in planning and monitoring their children's education. To assist in this process, the program identifies exemplary communication mechanisms between the school and the community and outlines procedures for preventing problems and for resolving those that may arise between the school and the home or the community.

After 1968, the state education agency and teacher-education institutions of the states implementing IGE replaced their districtwide inservice education programs with services pinpointed to meet the needs of each IGE school. The last major element of the IGE system is a program of continuing improvement-oriented educational research and development. This program came into being in 1965 but was discontinued in 1976 when federal funding for it ceased.

I have highlighted the main IGE operations but have not attempted to show their integration into a unified system. Chase, who viewed IGE as a system, described it as having an institutional character like that of a new kind of school (1977, p. xi). He regarded it as one of the more constructive American contributions to the advancement of education. Smith (cited in Rossmiller, 1974, p. 4) perceived IGE as a breakthrough that provided a social context for enhancing student learning, classroom organization for instruction, school-wide planning, and districtwide coordination. Smith also pointed out its advantages over the traditional self-contained classroom in enabling both inservice and preservice teachers to develop teaching skills.

How did IGE implementation proceed, and what results did it achieve? Seven traditional elementary schools in Wisconsin made the changeover to IGE in 1967–68. By 1975, more than two thousand schools across the country had done so, and others were in their first year of change (Rossmiller, 1976, p. 20).

IGE schooling obtained excellent results between 1965 and 1975, as reflected in students' educational achievements, self-concepts, attitudes toward schooling, independence in decision making, responsibility for themselves, and interpersonal relations (Katzenmeyer, Ingison, Zajano, & Romaniuk, 1976, pp. 15–22). The intellectual climate was better in IGE schools, but there was also more disorder and impulsive conduct on the part of the students. Teachers had greater involvement in decision making in IGE schools, and they were more satisfied with their jobs. The teacher leaders of the units, as well as the principals, had influence in IGE schools.

Unfortunately, this momentum was lost when federal funding to the Wisconsin Center ceased in 1975 for IGE implementation, in 1976 for development, and in 1977 for IGE research (Klausmeier & Wisconsin Associates, 1990). Moreover, the IGE Teacher Education Project (Klausmeier, 1972), funded by the Sears-Roebuck Foundation, ended in 1977. The consequent loss of momentum was reflected in some schools discontinuing the more-demanding IGE practices. The overwhelming majority of the schools, however, were no longer traditional. They had broken the lockstep of age grading, common assignments, and whole-class instruction (Ironside & Conaway, 1979, pp. 93–107). Moreover, they continued to produce good results (Stewart, Klopp, & Buchanan, 1978). The mean educational achievement for the two grades tested (grades two and five) was slightly above the national mean in all areas that were tested. Yet the most positive results were to be found in the personality area. To illustrate, in grade five the average percentile scores, derived from the national standardization sample, were 62 for self-acceptance, 50 for self-security, 56 for social maturity, 59 for social confidence, 59 for school affiliation, and 57 for peer affiliation.

When funding to the IGE parent organizations ceased, they discontinued their support to the state education agencies that were leading IGE implementation. In turn, most of these agencies cut back or discontinued their support to IGE schools. Changed societal conditions also contributed to the loss of momentum. A nationwide property-tax revolt resulted in a cutback in much-needed monetary support to IGE schools for instructional aides, high-quality instructional materials, and inservice education. Also, by 1977 a back-to-basics movement was sweeping schools in the United States. The movement called for most of the school day to be devoted to the three Rs, for report cards to carry either traditional A, B, C grades or numerical values, for strict discipline (with corporal punishment an accepted method of control), and for the abandonment of all recent innovations, including the teaching of concepts (Brodinsky, 1977).

Although momentum was lost, IGE practices reemerged and were more widespread in 1989–90 than in the late 1970s, as is shown by a national survey in which officials of thirty-seven state education agencies responded to a checklist (Klausmeier, 1992b). The respondents from the huge majority of the thirty-seven states—86 percent for a certain practice to 100 percent for another practice—checked twenty-three of twenty-four key IGE practices as being implemented in one of the following: "about the same number of schools," "more schools," or "many more schools" in 1989–90 compared with the late 1970s. Moreover, nineteen of these practices were being implemented in either more or many more schools; the least frequent was implemented in 57 percent and the most frequent in 92 percent of the states. Several factors are responsible for the widespread increase. The back-to-basics movement had lost power. The effective-schools movement had taken hold nationwide. The goal of providing quality education to the individual child again received attention from many sources.

Discussion

A report published by the Educational Testing Service in 1990 indicates that there was little educational improvement from the beginning to the end of the 1980s. The many state and local educational policies of the 1980s and the huge body of research-generated knowledge together yielded only small gains in attaining a few widely accepted national educational goals. Two of my research programs—one clarifying the learning characteristics of gifted and other children, and a second one resulting in a widely disseminated theory of concept learning and development and a highly effective design for teaching concepts— show that knowledge-generating research followed only by dissemination does not lead to readily substantiated educational improvement. Many similar examples might have been drawn from the *Encyclopedia of Educational Research* (Mitzel, 1982) or the *Handbook of Research on Teaching* (Wittrock, 1986).

Although knowledge-generating research with lack of implementation holds little promise for contributing to better student performance, improvement-oriented research, with its accompanying product development and implementation, does. This is exemplified by my programs for gifted students and by Individually Guided Education. Another example is the Study of Mathematically Precocious Youth (Stanley, 1977; Stanley & Benbow, 1986; Stanley, Keating, & Fox; 1974). Stanley and his colleagues developed a program for identifying and educating mathematically precocious students of middle-school age. The early program has been greatly expanded to include precocity in many fields. Stanley and others continue to research the effectiveness of the program and to refine and extend it (Benbow, 1992; Lubinski & Benbow, 1994; see also chapter 17 below). In this study, program implementation proceeded on a relatively small scale during the early years. However, Stanley and his colleagues took steps to ensure its widespread implementation; at present, almost 150,000 new students each year enter the program (see chapter 15 below).

Instead of ensuring implementation, knowledge-generating researchers merely call for changes in the behavior and thinking of practitioners, especially teachers. The history of the lack of success in bringing about the desired changes leads one to predict that success is not likely to occur in the future. Accordingly, it would be well for knowledge-generating researchers to change their own research behavior and thinking and to start carrying on improvement-oriented research. Until this is done, their research will have little or no impact on educational practice. Federal and philanthropic support for educational research will deservedly continue to be paltry.

References

Benbow, C. P. (1992). Academic achievement in mathematics and science of students between ages thirteen and twenty-three: Are there differences among students in the top one percent of mathematical ability? *Journal of Educational Psychology* 84:51–61.
Bernard, M. E. (1975). *The effects of advance organizers and within-text questions on the learning of a*

taxonomy of concepts (Tech. Rep. No. 357). Madison: Wisconsin Center for Education Research. (ERIC Document Reproduction Service No. ED 120 625)

Brainerd, C. J. (1979). Concept learning and developmental stage. In H. J. Klausmeier & Associates, *Cognitive learning and development: Information-processing and Piagetian perspectives* (pp. 225–268). Cambridge, Mass.: Ballinger.

Brodinsky, B. (1977). Back to the basics: The movement and its meaning. *Phi Delta Kappan* 58:522–526.

Chase, F. S. (1977). IGE and education reform. In H. J. Klausmeier, R. A. Rossmiller, & M. Saily (Eds.), *Individually guided elementary education: Concepts and practices* (pp. xi-xvi). New York: Academic Press.

Council of State Directors of Programs for the Gifted. (1991). *The 1990 state of the states gifted and talented education report*. Augusta: Maine Department of Education.

Educational Testing Service. (1990). *The education reform decade*. Princeton: Policy Information Center, Educational Testing Service.

Feldhusen, J. F., Check, J., & Klausmeier, H. J. (1961). Achievement in subtraction. *Elementary School Journal* 61:322–327.

Feldhusen, J. F., & Klausmeier, H. J. (1959). Achievement in counting and addition. *Elementary School Journal* 59:388–393.

Ironside, R. A., & Conaway, L. (1979). *IGE evaluation: Phase II. On-site validation and descriptive study: Final report* (Tech. Rep. No. 499). Madison: Wisconsin Center for Education Research. (ERIC Document Reproduction Service No. ED 175 135)

Katzenmeyer, C. G., Ingison, H. J., Zajano, N. C., & Romaniuk, J. (1976). *Evaluating IGE: An initial literature review and exploratory study* (Tech. Rep. No. 404). Madison: Wisconsin Center for Education Research.

Klausmeier, H. J. (1956). America needs the gifted. *Wisconsin Journal of Education* 89:1–6.

Klausmeier, H. J. (1963). Effects of accelerating bright older elementary pupils: A follow-up. *Journal of Educational Psychology* 54:165–171.

Klausmeier, H. J. (1971). Cognitive operations in concept learning. *Educational Psychologist* 9:1–8.

Klausmeier, H. J. (1972). *An invitation to the Sears-Roebuck Foundation to improve elementary schooling through implementation, refinement, and institutionalization of IGE/MUS-E*. Madison: University of Wisconsin, School of Education.

Klausmeier, H. J. (1976a). Conceptual development during the school years. In J. R. Levin & V. L. Allen (Eds.), *Cognitive learning in children: Theories and strategies* (pp. 5–29). New York: Academic Press.

Klausmeier, H. J. (1976b). Instructional design and the teaching of concepts. In J. R. Levin & V. L. Allen (Eds.), *Cognitive learning in children: Theories and strategies* (pp. 191–217). New York: Academic Press.

Klausmeier, H. J. (1982). A research strategy for educational improvement. *Educational Researcher* 11:8–13.

Klausmeier, H. J. (1985). *Developing and institutionalizing a self-improvement capability: Structures and strategies of secondary schools*. Lanham, Md.: University Press of America.

Klausmeier, H. J. (1987). *Local school self-improvement: Processes and directions*. Bloomington, Ind.: Phi Delta Kappa.

Klausmeier, H. J. (1990). Conceptualizing. In B. F. Jones & L. Idol (Eds.), *Dimensions of thinking and cognitive instruction* (pp. 93–138). Hillsdale, N.J.: Erlbaum.

Klausmeier, H. J. (1992a). Concept learning and concept teaching. *Educational Psychologist* 27: 267–286.

Klausmeier, H. J. (1992b). Individually Guided Education: Permanent educational reform. *Education* 113:215–231.

Klausmeier, H. J., & Allen, P. (1978). *Cognitive development of children and youth: A longitudinal study*. New York: Academic Press.

Klausmeier, H. J., & Associates (1979). *Cognitive learning and development: Information-processing and Piagetian perspectives*. Cambridge, Mass.: Ballinger.

Klausmeier, H. J., Beeman, A., & Lehmann, I. H. (1958). Relationships among physical, mental, and achievement measures in children of low, average, and high intelligence. *American Journal of Mental Deficiency* 63:647–656.

Klausmeier, H. J., & Check, J. (1959). Relationships among physical, mental, and achievement measures in children of low, average, and high intelligence at 113 months of age. *American Journal of Mental Deficiency* 63:1059–1068.

Klausmeier, H. J., & Check, J. (1962). Retention and transfer in children of low, average, and high intelligence. *Journal of Educational Research* 55:319–322.

Klausmeier, H. J., Check, J., & Feldhusen, J. F. (1960). Relationships among physical, mental, achievement, and personality measures in children of low, average, and high intelligence at 125 months of age. *American Journal of Mental Deficiency* 65:69–78.

Klausmeier, H. J., & Feldhusen, J. F. (1959). Retention in arithmetic among children of low, average, and high intelligence at 117 months of age. *Journal of Educational Psychology* 50:88–92.

Klausmeier, H. J., Feldhusen, J. F., & Check, J. (1959). *An analysis of learning efficiency in arithmetic of mentally retarded children in comparison with children of average and high intelligence* (Cooperative Research Project No. 153). Madison: University of Wisconsin, School of Education.

Klausmeier, H. J., Ghatala, E. S., & Frayer, D. A. (1974). *Conceptual learning and development: A cognitive view*. New York: Academic Press.

Klausmeier, H. J., Harris, C. W., & Wiersma, W. (1964). *Strategies of learning and efficiency of concept attainment by individuals and groups* (Cooperative Research Project No. 1442). Madison: University of Wisconsin, School of Education.

Klausmeier, H. J., & Loughlin, L. J. (1961). Behaviors during problem solving among children of low, average, and high intelligence. *Journal of Educational Psychology* 52:148–152.

Klausmeier, H. J., Mulhern, J., & Wakefield, H. (1960). High school students evaluate sectioning. *Educational Leadership* 17:221–225.

Klausmeier, H. J., & Pellegrin, R. J. (1971). The multiunit school: A differential staffing approach. In D. S. Bushnell & D. Rappaport (Eds.), *Planned change in education* (pp. 107–126). New York: Harcourt, Brace, Jovanovich.

Klausmeier, H. J., & Ripple, R. E. (1962). Effects of accelerating bright older pupils from second to fourth grade. *Journal of Educational Psychology* 53:93–100.

Klausmeier, H. J., Rossmiller, R. A., & Saily, M. (Eds.). (1977). *Individually guided elementary education: Concepts and practices*. New York: Academic Press.

Klausmeier, H. J., & Sipple, T. S. (1980). *Learning and teaching process concepts: A strategy for testing applications of theory*. New York: Academic Press.

Klausmeier, H. J., & Sipple, T. S. (1982). Factor structure of the Piagetian stage of concrete operations. *Contemporary Educational Psychology* 7:161–180.

Klausmeier, H. J., & Teel, D. (1964). A research-based program for gifted children. *Education* 85:131–136.

Klausmeier, H. J., & Wiersma, W. (1964). Effects of condensing content in mathematics and science in the junior and senior high school. *School Science and Mathematics* 64:4–11.

Klausmeier, H. J., & Wisconsin Associates (1990). *The Wisconsin Center for Education Research: Twenty-five years of knowledge generation and educational improvement*. Madison: Wisconsin Center for Education Research.

Lubinski, D., & Benbow, C. P. (1994). The Study of Mathematically Precocious Youth: The first three decades of a planned fifty-year study of intellectual talent. In R. F. Subotnik & K. D. Arnold (Eds.), *Beyond Terman: Contemporary longitudinal studies of giftedness and talent* (pp. 255–281). Norwood, N.J.: Ablex.

Mitzel, H. E. (Ed.). (1982). *Encyclopedia of educational research* (5th ed.). New York: Free Press.

McMurray, N. E., Bernard, M. E., Klausmeier, H. J., Schilling, J. M., & Feldman, K. (1977). Instructional design for accelerating children's concept learning. *Journal of Educational Psychology* 69:660–667.

National Academy of Education. (1991). *Research and the renewal of education*. Stanford: Stanford University, National Academy of Education.

Nelson, G. K. (1976). Concomitant effects of visual, motor, and verbal experiences in young children's conceptual development. *Journal of Educational Psychology* 69:466–473.

Romberg, T. A. (1985). *Toward effective schooling: The IGE experience*. Lanham, Md.: University Press of America.

Rosch, E. (1975). Cognitive representations of semantic categories. *Journal of Experimental Psychology: General* 104:192–233.

Rosch, E. (1978). Principles of categorization. In E. Rosch & B. Lloyd (Eds.), *Cognition and categorization* (pp. 9–31). Hillsdale, N.J.: Erlbaum.

Rossmiller, R. A. (1976). *Evaluation, refinement, and implementation* (Technical Proposal to National Institute of Education). Madison: Wisconsin Center for Education Research.

Rossmiller, R. A. (1977). *Five-year plan of the Wisconsin Research and Development Center for Cognitive Learning.* Madison: Wisconsin Center for Education Research.

Stanley, J. C. (1977). Rationale of the Study of Mathematically Precocious Youth (SMPY) during its first five years of promoting educational acceleration. In J. C. Stanley, W. C. George, & C. H. Solano (Eds.), *The gifted and the creative: A fifty-year perspective* (pp. 75–112). Baltimore: Johns Hopkins University Press.

Stanley, J. C., & Benbow, C. P. (1986). Youths who reason exceptionally well mathematically. In R. J. Sternberg & J. E. Davidson (Eds.), *Conceptions of giftedness* (pp. 361–387). Cambridge: Cambridge University Press.

Stanley, J. C., Keating, D. P., & Fox, L. H. (Eds.). (1974). *Mathematical talent: Discovery, description, and development.* Baltimore: Johns Hopkins University Press.

Stewart, D. M., Klopp, P. M., & Buchanan, A. E. (1978). *Results of IGE evaluation: Phase I. Report 1: Descriptive statistics for staff questionnaires and student tests.* Madison: Wisconsin Center for Education Research.

Wang, C. H., & Horng, J. M. (1991). *A design for college chemistry technique instruction.* Unpublished manuscript, National Taiwan Normal University, Taipei, Taiwan.

Wittrock, M. C. (Ed.). (1986). *Handbook of research on teaching* (3rd ed.). New York: Macmillan.

6 Assessing Spatial Visualization

An Underappreciated Ability for Many School and Work Settings

LLOYD G. HUMPHREYS AND

DAVID LUBINSKI

A Brief History of Spatial-Ability Testing

Spatial Visualization in Intelligence Tests

The assessment of individual differences in spatial visualization began concomitantly with the building of early measures of general intelligence. The first Binet-Simon test (1905) contained items that today would be identified as primarily spatial in content, as did the first Stanford-Binet test (Terman, 1916). Back then, item selection was based mostly on content validity, but an empirical criterion was also consulted before an item was accepted—namely, the percentage passing with age. By the time the 1937 revision of the Stanford-Binet test appeared (Terman & Merrill, 1937), more-sophisticated techniques for item inclusion were available. Item selection depended on the percentage passing with age and on correlations between items and the total score on the test, and spatial items were still retained.

McNemar (1942) obtained item intercorrelations and computed centroid factor loadings of the items to define more clearly the number of dimensions necessary to capture their commonality. Across the many different kinds of content found in this next generation of intelligence tests, all item intercorrelations were positive. The first centroid factor, therefore, was large. Yet factors beyond the first were somewhat larger than expected for Spearman's (1904, 1914) single-factor solution, and the second and third centroids were generally interpretable. Because the item intercorrelations computed in the early days of test construction were typically tetrachorics (correlations based on dichoto-mized variables), considerable "noise" was introduced into the factor analyses by the variability in size of sampling errors as a function of variability in the percentage passing the items. Nevertheless, in McNemar's (1942) analyses, there was ample evidence to support the construct of general intelligence plus limited evidence for group factors, including spatial visualization.

Around the same time, Wechsler (1941) introduced an intelligence test that provided separate verbal and performance IQs as well as a total IQ. Spa-tial visualization contributed substantially to the variance of his performance items. This was true also of group tests of intelligence that provided both verbal and performance scores (Vernon, 1947). Moreover, regardless of the test, these separate verbal and performance IQs were not correlated with each other nearly so highly as their reliabilities would allow. Across a wide range of intellectual talent, the correlation is and always has been substantial (rs tend to be around .70 to .80). Although this supports the construct of general intelligence, neither the verbal nor the performance score alone is an adequate measure of general intelligence. In addition, the profiles of correlations of the two scores with other tests and important social criteria have not been identical. These two measures and the constructs they assess have differential validity across many different criteria commonly valued in educational and vocational contexts (Humphreys, 1962, 1986; Lubinski & Dawis, 1992). Thus performance tests of intelligence are only partial substitutes for a standard test when dealing with a person having limited proficiency in the language of the tests.

Spatial-Ability Testing in the Military

The Army Alpha and Beta tests of World War I were designed to measure general intelligence, yet they had the same limitations as Wechsler's verbal and performance IQs for assessing it. Alpha was designed for persons literate in English; Beta was designed for those who were not. Beta contained a number of spatial items, but Alpha contained few; Beta's total variance overlapped only partially with the variance of Alpha. Again, neither test alone was a comprehen-sive measure of general intelligence in the Binet tradition. However, as with Wechsler's (1941) verbal and performance IQs, aggregating these two early measures does provide a respectable index of general intelligence.

By World War II, a spatial-visualization test was in use by the military. It was included in the Army General Classification Test (AGCT). The verbal, quantitative, and spatial items were printed and administered in a quasi-random fashion and a total score was obtained. In this and similar tests, it was common for different examinees to receive the same total score based on dissimilar profiles of success in the three areas. This is not a problem with respect to the interpretation of the total score as an estimate of general intelligence. It becomes a problem, however, when quantitative-, spatial-, and verbal-ability markers of general intelligence are not given differential weights in predicting performance criteria (or group membership) for which they have differential validity (e.g., technical versus clerical occupations). This became apparent in the selection and classification of air-crew candidates. Here the military developed a special qualifying test (not designed to measure general intelligence) and then followed it with a multiple "aptitude" test battery.[1] Tests in the latter were weighted on the basis of multiple regression analyses, and separate composites were formed for each different air-crew assignment. Tests that received zero or positive weights for pilot selection, a spatially saturated occupation, are highly informative with respect to the aims of this chapter. Reading comprehension, arithmetic reasoning, and mathematics received zero weights. The positive weights for pilots were on tests measuring visual perceptual speed, spatial visualization, spatial orientation, mechanical information and comprehension, large-muscle coordination, and information about planes, flying, and pilots.

The information test, in its final form, was especially revealing psychologically, because it included a few questions involving literary and artistic information, the *wrong* answers to which were given the same positive weight as information about the P-51 airplane. By *suppressing* the variance of these specialized verbal items, the correlation between the total score on the test and performance in the air was increased. If the criterion had been performance in ground school, however, this effect, as well as the test weights, would have been reversed. That is, the suppressor emerged in the context of forecasting terminal criterion performance, but not in the context of forecasting achievement criteria that were antecedents to the terminal performance.

An experimental group that entered training without attention being paid to their test scores had a mean AGCT score of 113 and a standard deviation of 14 (in a metric with $M = 100$ and $SD = 20$). Thus, self-selection was responsible

---

1. The aptitude/achievement distinction is one of psychology's conceptual ghosts (Cleary, Humphreys, Kendrick, and Wesman, 1975). It turns out that what distinguishes "achievement" tests from "aptitude" tests is a difference in degree, along four dimensions, and not a difference in kind. In contrast to achievement tests, aptitude tests typically: sample from a broader range of content, are not tied to a specific educational curriculum, sample old learning, and are used for forecasting future performance as opposed to determining current status with respect to concurrent criterion behavior. Indeed, items from achievement and aptitude tests are often used interchangeably.

for a mean more than three-fifths of a standard deviation above the mean for the population at large. Those who also passed the qualifying test had a mean AGCT score almost one standard deviation above the overall mean. On the completion of training, the pilots were commissioned as second lieutenants. They were professionals in terms of their credentials and in terms of their levels of general intelligence, but they were *especially* gifted in spatial-visualization and mechanical-reasoning abilities. The importance of their professional status will become clearer as our discussion unfolds.

Post–World War II Military Use of Spatial-Ability Testing

The postwar Armed Forces Qualifying Test (AFQT) continued to involve the tripartite content of verbal, quantitative, and spatial items until the early 1950s, when a fourth item type, mechanical information, was introduced. One of us (Humphreys) took the lead in urging colleagues in the other services to make that addition. The demand for personnel was greater in mechanical-technical assignments than in the more academic ones, because the former were generally more critical to the military mission. Even though mechanical-information tests were already prominent and well validated in the so-called aptitude indexes used in classifying enlisted personnel, the addition of information items to an intelligence test was not accepted enthusiastically by military psychologists. Tradition required that the initial selection of military personnel be based on "aptitude." After several years of increasing somewhat the proportion of enlisted personnel who qualified for the most urgent and important assignments, mechanical information was removed from the AFQT. But it was not removed from the mechanical composite (the aptitude index), which guided the assignment of personnel to the relevant occupational specialties.

Subsequently, the spatial-visualization section of the AFQT was removed. It was also removed from the Armed Forces Aptitude Battery at the same time. Both the mechanical-information and the spatial-visualization items have an adverse impact on the scores of female applicants for military service, but perhaps lower means were more easily tolerated when they occurred on information tests than on "aptitude" tests. In any event, both these decisions were wrongheaded. Women whose scores are high with regard to their same-sex norms on mechanical and spatial tests are the ones needed by the military services to fill the increasing number of specialties open to women. At times, even psychologists forget that testing is an empirically grounded technology.

Spatial-Ability Testing in Industrial Selection

Spatial tests appeared early in the repertoire of tests used by industrial psychologists. A prominent source of training in industrial psychology and of ideas about what industrial psychologists should do was Donald G. Paterson of the University of Minnesota. Paterson also spearheaded the development of the Minnesota Paper Form Board, a well-known spatial test that is still in use (Paterson, Elliott, Anderson, & Toops, 1930). Some of the psychomotor tests used by industrial psychologists also had spatial content. Paterson, a giant in the early vocational-guidance movement (Paterson, 1938), imbued students with respect for data, and Minnesota became known as the home of "dust bowl empiricism," a term popularized by psychologists whose conception of theory was more humanistic than scientific.

The Accepted Role of Spatial Tests

Unfortunately, spatial tests became stereotyped as suitable only for personnel selection and vocational counseling in connection with occupations below the professional level. Studies of their validity were almost entirely restricted to assignments for enlisted personnel in the military and skilled technological-mechanical jobs in industry. There are few courses offered in high school, and fewer still in college, for which spatial tests will predict grades as well as verbal and quantitative tests do. Both the Scholastic Aptitude Test and the American College Test predict college grades reasonably well in light of the amount of "noise" one can expect to find in college grade point averages. These tests achieve such prediction success without spatial content. This might give the impression that there is no reason to consider spatial abilities when pursuing careers that require college credentials (but this will be refuted below).

Spatial Visualization in Factor Analysis

Spatial-visualization abilities secured a prominent place in the military and in applied-psychology circles in civilian life during both world wars; this also was true for basic psychological science. Spearman (1904) was responsible for the mathematical theory of general intelligence; later, Burt (1940) added group factors to Spearman's g. In the factor-analytic tradition in Britain, for which Spearman and Burt were largely responsible, there was no doubt about the importance of general intelligence. Nevertheless, the British recognized group factors such as verbal, numerical, and spatial abilities before Thurstone's development of centroid analysis. American users of the centroid method tended to operate at a different level of analysis, and thus were able to ignore the general factor by rotating their factors to orthogonal simple structure (that is, each variable was primarily related to only one factor, and the factors were relatively independent). American factor solutions, however, generated tests having positive intercorrelations because they possessed common general-factor variance. They were also each saturated with items whose content and nature (figures, numbers, or words) readily engendered distinct labels. Indeed, Thurstone's "Primary Mental Abilities" (1938) presented a spatial factor among the nine that he interpreted and among the seven about which he felt most confident. In addition, there were tests with spatial content waiting in the wings, in the form of one of the three additional factors that were rotated but not interpreted.

Soon thereafter, however, Thurstone started recommending and using oblique rotations. This step allowed him to factor correlations in two or more orders. It remained for Schmid and Leiman (1957) to develop a methodology that reconciled a general factor on which tests had factor loadings (the British tradition) with a general factor that hitherto could only be inferred from factor intercorrelations (the Thurstone heritage). The Schmid-Leiman methodology leads inevitably to a hierarchical model of intelligence, having a single general factor at the top of the hierarchy as long as the R-matrix is positive. Schmid and Leiman's (1957) contribution, when used on a large R-matrix, provides support for Vernon's (1950) hierarchical model. This model takes the best of what both the British and the American traditions have to offer. It recognizes the British emphasis on general intelligence (associated principally with Spearman and Burt), and the American emphasis on multiple group factors (associated principally with Thurstone).

Vernon's model provides for major group factors immediately below the general factor. The major factors break down, in turn, into minor group factors. Two major group factors in Vernon's model are verbal-numerical-educational ($v{:}ed$) and mechanical-spatial-practical ($k{:}m$). The tests used for college admission in this country measure the general factor, in part, plus the first major group factor. In contrast, the tests weighted positively for the selection of pilots in World War II measured the general factor, in part, but substituted Vernon's second major factor, $k{:}m$, for the first, $v{:}ed$. At generally lower levels of both scores and prestige, tests of the first major factor, $v{:}ed$, predict success in clerical assignments somewhat more accurately than does a test of general intelligence, while tests of the second major factor, $k{:}m$, have the same pattern for mechanical-technical assignments (Humphreys, 1986; Thorndike, 1994).

Sources of Interest in Spatial Abilities

Military experience. The manifest importance of spatial abilities was revealed in the Aviation Psychology Research Program of World War II and in postwar research on assignments of enlisted military personnel. Spatial visualization and spatial orientation were clearly distinguishable, although they just as clearly belonged to the same family, in research on air-crew assignments. A ranking of the importance of assignments of enlisted personnel to the military mission relates quite accurately to the ratio of the predictive validities of spatial to verbal tests.

It may seem strange that spatial tests given in the military are better at predicting success in military training than are such tests given in high school. The probable explanation is the availability of current military hardware for training purposes, more hands-on experience, less dependence on textbooks, and generally a greater motivation to succeed on the part of able persons who were not motivated by the high school curriculum. Military experience suggests the possibility that civilian secondary and college education is not sufficiently supportive of a society heavily dependent on technology. Is our educational system geared to the production of clerks rather than mechanics? Are we over-looking persons who are talented on Vernon's spatial (k:m) major group factor? Have we paid too much attention to an utterly false dictum concerning verbal abilities that consigns many highly able persons to second-class status in the intellectual hierarchy of occupations? The following statement is often re-peated: "If students can't write, they can't think." We believe this is nonsense.

The criterion to be predicted. One of us (Humphreys) has been interested for more than forty years in being able to predict membership in criterion groups. Professor Philip J. Rulon was fond of saying that a guidance counselor who followed the logic of multiple regression faithfully would never advise a student to consider engineering. The reason, of course, is that the chances of success as a technician are higher than those as an engineer at any score level on the predictor. The alternative to multiple regression is the multiple discrimi-nant function. The guidance counselor suggests to the examinee that the oc-cupation indicated is the one for which the examinee is close to the centroid of successful, satisfied members of an occupational group. Vocational psycholo-gists also should be interested in such persons and in those who have the highest probability of short-term success according to conventional regression forecasts.

It is reasonable to characterize regressions of proficiency measures on score distributions of predictor tests as snapshots taken at particular points in time. A recent review of the stability of criterion performance over time (Hulin, Henry, & Noon, 1990) provides a rationale for this characterization. In con-trast, group membership is a truly *cumulative* criterion. A professional engi-neer, for example, has survived numerous institutional decisions, starting with grades in high school courses, graduation, college entrance, college graduation, being hired, and being promoted. Of equal importance are the series of personal decisions about course selection, choice of college, choice of major, persistence in pursuing a degree, and staying in engineering once on the job. We were interested in examining educational and vocational tracks that might require exceptional amounts of spatial-visualization talent. This led to the research that follows.

We describe some recent research related to individual differences in spatial measures and, in turn, how these measures relate to group-membership criteria. These data also contrast other tests, such as mathematical and verbal measures, with the spatial tests in the prediction of group membership. All data were obtained from the Project Talent Data Bank (Flanagan et al., 1962; Wise, McLaughlin, & Steel, 1979).

All three of the following studies involve prediction of group membership as reported in Project Talent's eleven-year follow-up after high school graduation. The length of time following administration of the predictor tests varies from eleven to fourteen years as a function of the examinees' grade in school in 1960 (grades nine through twelve). The studies will reveal that the group-membership criterion is an important one for documenting the validity of predictor tests. Group-membership data complement conventional criteria such as individual differences in criterion performance. We offer this methodology here to supplement, not to supplant, conventional test-validation methods.

First, however, let us respond to a potential concern. Our longitudinal data were collected more than twenty years ago. It is reflexive on the part of many to dismiss the use of old data for any purpose, but a distinction between mean levels of performance and correlations (structural relations among variables) is essential. Means of psychological tests do change over time, but correlations are relatively resistant to cultural change and to cultural differences. Our interest here and in subsequent research was structural relations among variables. The problem of changes in means was met with the use of same-sex standardization scores.

Data

Self-Selection on the Spatial Dimension

A serendipitous discovery by Humphreys, Davey, and Kashima (1986) is relevant here. These authors used the extensive student information in Project Talent's tenth-grade sample to develop scoring keys to measure the construct of intellectual privilege/deprivation (P/D), a measure designed to be a salient covariant of traditional socioeconomic status (SES) measures, but whose content was restricted to environmental features thought to be especially conducive to intellectual development. In addition, these investigators formed composites of ability tests to measure Vernon's two major group factors and the general factor. Although the communality of *v:ed* and *k:m* are included in the construct of general intelligence, the composition of each of the three measures was experimentally independent of each of the others. These three composites were the criteria against which items of biographical information were validated and keyed to form three possible P/D scales.

Results on the privilege/deprivation (P/D) scales. Keys were formed for males and females separately in male and female subsamples and cross-validated in independent subsamples. The correlations of the four general-intelligence keys with the criterion of general intelligence were homogeneous about a median value of .63, which was substantially higher than the median correlation of intelligence with the measure of socioeconomic status of the student's family (.41). Thus, there is more information about family background that is associated with children's general intelligence than is available in a standard measure of SES.

There is only a little evidence to suggest that a privileged background for intelligence differs from privileged backgrounds for the major group factors. There was only a bit of differentiation between the general-intelligence key and the verbal-numerical-educational P/D key. The differentiation was so small that the authors dropped the latter P/D key from further analysis. A small amount of marginally dependable differentiation was obtained, however, for the general-intelligence P/D key and the mechanical-spatial-practical P/D key.

Results supporting self-selection. In the search for correlates of the P/D keys, data from the eleven-year follow-up also were used by Humphreys, Davey, and Kashima (1986). These data shed only a little light on the P/D keys, but postsecondary data concerning college education and occupation revealed surprising information about the ability composites. We discuss these findings in conjunction with some new data that we present here.

Humphreys, Davey, and Kashima (1986) reported mean standard scores in the metric of the follow-up sample for male and female occupational groups in the physical sciences. We supplement these earlier results here by presenting data on undergraduate majors (table 6.1). Keep in mind that these standardized

TABLE 6.1.   *Self-Selection on a Mechanical-Spatial Dimension Indicated by Means in the Standardized Metric of Unselected Tenth-Grade Students*

	General Intelligence		Mechanical-Spatial	
	Males	Females	Males	Females
Undergraduate majors				
Physics[a]	1.17	—[b]	1.28	—[b]
Engineering	.89	—[b]	.94	—[b]
All physical sciences	.88	1.05	.86	1.15
Occupations				
All physical sciences[a]	1.04	1.30	.97	1.16

[a] Includes mathematics and computer science.
[b] Sample sizes are too small for meaningful results.

scores are in the same-sex metric and were based on the entire tenth-grade sample of boys and girls.

There is relatively little difference between mean levels for both sexes on the intelligence and mechanical-spatial-practical composites in undergraduate majors and occupational groups. Moreover, there is little difference when all physical sciences are considered for both males and females. In the data for males for physics and engineering majors, however, the means for the mechanical-spatial composite are higher than the means for the intelligence composite. This points to self-selection into occupations or fields of study as a function of ability.

The argument for self-selection into the physical sciences and engineering on the spatial dimension is straightforward. The measure of general intelligence has standard content: two parts reading comprehension, one part arithmetic reasoning, and one part abstract figural reasoning. Means for general intelligence increase from high school to college and from college entrance to college graduation as functions of educational curriculum and institutional selection. The correlations of the intelligence and mechanical-practical-spatial composites are .63 and .67 in the male and female samples, respectively. If selection based on spatial ability were only incidental to selection based on general intelligence, the expected mean for the former would be no more than two-thirds the size of the intelligence mean. Yet this was not observed. Why? Explicit institutional selection would have required spatial variance in the high school grades and entrance tests used in college admission to explain the virtual equality of the means, but spatial components in these measures were lacking. Thus, this cannot explain the equality of means. That students were self-selecting engineering and the physical sciences based on their spatial-visualization abilities is most probable. This was the general conclusion of Humphreys, Davey, and Kashima (1986), which is supported by the data presented here.

A Comparison of Two Possible Selection Composites

The next research project followed up on the above serendipitous findings, and is reported more fully in Humphreys, Lubinski, and Yao (1993). Our objective here was to obtain correlates of two possible selection composites—a traditional verbal-quantitative measure and a second measure containing spatial-visualization and mechanical-reasoning variance. The latter, we suspected, would be optimal for the selection of most engineers and physical scientists. The criterion selected for the comparison, group membership, was the same one as in the serendipitous findings.

Methods and rationale. In Humphreys, Lubinski, and Yao (1993) we formed three composites from multiple short tests; each test in its own way measured verbal, mathematical, and spatial abilities or group factors. This was done separately for each sex and for each of the four high school grades. Two selection composites were then formed in each sex and in each grade from equally weighted verbal and mathematical (verbal-math) and spatial and mathematical (space-math) components. Students in the top 20 percent on either the verbal-math or the space-math composite, or both, were selected for further study. Approximately twenty-seven thousand of each sex in all grades were in the upper 20 percent on both composites, while approximately nine thousand were in the upper 20 percent on space-math only and eight thousand were at the same level on verbal-math only.

We realize that the space-math composite does not conform to the description of Vernon's second major group factor, but it seemed inconceivable to consider a selection composite for engineering that did not have a mathematical component. It was our working hypothesis that mathematical abilities are the most important abilities for securing educational credentials in engineering and the physical sciences, but that spatial abilities are also critical, and are more important than verbal abilities. In this case, the math component could not be measured with experimentally independent components. Thus, the overlap between space-math and verbal-math scores is spuriously high. Independent components would provide somewhat greater differentiation, but the potential amount is not large because all the components have substantial loadings on the general factor. The somewhat inflated correlations between the two composites are .88 in the male sample and .89 in the female sample.

Scores on the two composites for the three groups are presented in table 6.2. The upper half of the table contains data in the joint-sex metric, showing the difference in means for the two sexes that existed in 1960. The data in the

TABLE 6.2.   *Mean Ability Scores of Twelfth Graders in Three Ability Groups, Standardized in Joint-Sex and Same-Sex Distributions*

Composites	Male Groups			Female Groups		
	High Intelligence	High Space	High Verbal	High Intelligence	High Space	High Verbal
Joint-sex						
Spatial-math	1.58	1.33	.84	1.03	.70	.19
Verbal-math	1.47	.77	1.26	1.24	.44	.93
Same-sex						
Spatial-math	1.41	1.14	.61	1.58	1.17	.55
Verbal-math	1.41	.69	1.19	1.51	.59	1.15

lower half of the table are in the same-sex metric. This information is presented to undermine explicitly any assumption that means are stable over time.

Our criteria for the selection of samples resulted in approximately the same degree of superiority within sex for both boys and girls. The high intelligence group is also shown to be higher in space-math than the high space group and in verbal-math than the high verbal group. Persons in the upper 20 percent on both verbal-math and space-math are highest in general intelligence and would be expected to have many educational and vocational options open to them.

Results. Table 6.3 contains data on the largest differences in undergraduate and graduate majors for three groups of high school students: a high general-intelligence group who were in the top 20 percent on both composites, a high space-math group, and a high verbal-math group. The omitted major groups showed little effect of group membership.

For those majoring in the physical sciences, including engineering, there is little difference between the high intelligence and the high space-math group in their relatively high proportions, but there are large differences between the latter groups and the high verbal-math group. For those majoring in the humanities and social sciences, the high space-math group is low, the high intelligence group is intermediate, and the high verbal-math group is high. The principal determinants among abilities for choice of a major were the differences in levels of spatial and verbal abilities. Skill in mathematics alone does not incline students toward engineering.

Table 6.4 contains data on membership in occupational groups and on the highest educational credential earned for each of the three groups. The proportion of space-math in occupations in engineering and the physical sciences

TABLE 6.3. *Proportions in Four High School Classes of Undergraduate and Graduate Majors of Three Ability Groups*

	High Intelligence		High Space		High Verbal	
	Males	Females	Males	Females	Males	Females
Undergraduate majors						
Physical sciences, engineering	39	10	37	08	16	02
Humanities, social sciences	28	39	16	16	43	41
Arts	02	07	05	13	02	03
Graduate majors						
Physical sciences, engineering	27	07	23	02	07	01
Humanities, social sciences	31	26	16	17	46	26
Arts	02	04	08	07	03	03

Note: Decimal points omitted.

TABLE 6.4. *Proportions in Four High School Classes of Occupational Categories and Highest Educational Credentials of Three Ability Groups*

	High Intelligence		High Space		High Verbal	
	Males	Females	Males	Females	Males	Females
Occupational category						
Physical sciences, engineering	15	01	10	00	04	00
Humanities, social sciences	11	04	02	01	19	04
Arts	01	01	03	01	02	00
Artisans	14	05	28	07	12	05
Highest education credential awarded						
Ph.D.	11	02	02	00	08	01
M.A.	16	13	09	05	18	09
B.A.	34	33	25	17	34	38
H.S.	26	41	50	65	27	41

Note: Decimal points omitted.

drops relative to high intelligence, but is still well above that of verbal-math. Science-math is high, however, in the artisan category, and the explanation appears in the educational credentials earned beyond high school graduation. The space-math students had levels of credentials lower than those of the other groups.

This prompted us to go back to data obtained when the subjects were in high school to discover the kinds of persons the space-math students were. Their self-reports of grades in mathematics were similar to those in the high intelligence group, in the sciences only a little lower, but much lower in foreign languages, English, and social studies. On the other hand, their grades in vocational courses were the *highest* of the three groups. High space-math students were less likely to be in the college preparatory curriculum, had parents of somewhat lower social status, and participated more actively in hobbies. Even among the hobbies listed, there are differences. High space-math students selected hobbies that involved building and working with things: sewing, cooking, drawing, painting, and gardening. In Prediger's (1976) map of the world of work, spatially talented people tended to coalesce around the "things" sector of his fourfold Data-People-Ideas-Things model. At this point, we wondered if these observations would generalize to more-advanced educational levels, such as those found in graduate training.

Securing More-Advanced Educational Credentials: Graduate Majors

The above results encouraged further study of the possibilities of predicting group membership (Humphreys & Yao, unpublished manuscript). This time graduate majors were selected as the criteria because of the national interest in sources of scientific and engineering talent. This concern is primarily directed at the physical sciences, including engineering, and arises from several sources: the ratio of American citizens to total enrollees in these areas, and the continuously relatively low enrollment therein of majority females and of blacks and Hispanics of both sexes (see *Science*, volumes 258 [13 November 1992]; 260 [16 April 1993]; 262 [12 November 1993]; 263 [11 March 1994]).

Methods and rationale. From Project Talent, eight groups of male graduate majors were selected from the information provided by the follow-up conducted eleven years after the high school graduation of the four high school grades tested in 1960. These graduate majors were divided into the following groups: the physical sciences, the biological sciences (including medicine), the social sciences, law, engineering, humanities, education, and business. There were fewer female graduate majors, necessitating the dropping of the law and engineering female groups, and adding a small number of undergraduate majors in the physical and biological sciences to the female graduate groups to increase sample size. These latter additions did not appreciably decrease the mean level of these groups below the level of the males on the general factor. An additional group of females who had recorded an undergraduate major in business did reduce the general ability level for the business graduate major group, because these additions inadvertently included "majors" in postsecondary commercial training.

The selected predictors of graduate group membership were the individual cognitive-ability test scores, excluding composites, and the self-reported personality, interest, and background scores in Project Talent's Data Bank. The CANCOR (canonical correlation) program of SAS was used in each of the four grades for the cognitive and self-report scores separately in all but one analysis. For the ninth graders, the two sets of predictors were combined in a single discriminant analysis in order to determine whether the cognitive predictors would add accuracy to the level obtained by the self-reports alone. As it turned out, it was beneficial that most of the analyses were conducted on the separate sets of predictors. The canonical functions were more readily identified psychologically in the separate sets, presumably because of the low level of cross-correlations between sets that made almost identical discriminations among major groups. (The low cross-correlations attenuated the correlations of all predictors with the canonical functions.)

Results. The variance accounted for among males and females by four functions is presented for each in table 6.5. It can be seen that the cognitive variables accounted for more variance among males than among females. Over and beyond the larger number of male groups, boys in 1960 had wider course selection and vocational choices than girls.

The greater predictive accuracy of the self-report scores as compared to the cognitive predictors has two sources. Across all graduate major groups, both male and female, the mean level of intelligence in the ninth grade is about one standard deviation above the grade mean, and the variance is about half the variance at the same grade level. Yet the variance of the self-report scores is about as likely to be increased as it is to be decreased by the selection on the intelligence dimension. The first source, therefore, is the attenuation of predictive validities of the cognitive tests. The second source is the increment to predictive validity of the self-report measures arising from the cognitive restriction in range, which places an ability floor under the samples. Interest scores in the full range of talent are secondary or tertiary to ability in importance be-

TABLE 6.5.   *Variance Accounted for by Four Canonical Functions in Cognitive, Self-Report, and Combined Predictions*

	Cognitive		Self-Report		Combined	
Grade	Males	Females	Males	Females	Males	Females
9	.39	.32	.42	.39	.56	.51
10	.40	.36	.48	.46	—[a]	—[a]
11	.46	.38	.52	.51	—[a]	—[a]
12	.47	.42	.60	.60	—[a]	—[a]

[a] Data not obtained.

TABLE 6.6.   *Key Cognitive Predictors Defining the First Two Functions and the Principal Major Groups Contrasted*

First Canonical Function		Second Canonical Function	
Males	Females	Males	Females
Electronics	Literature	Literature	Electronics
Mechanical reasoning	Social studies	Social studies	Mechanical reasoning
Visualization-3D	Physical sciences	Bible information	Visualization-3D
Introductory math	Introductory math	Vocabulary	Introductory math
Advanced math	Advanced math	Reading comprehension	Mechanical information
Engineering, Physical sciences	All but education	Humanities, law	Physical sciences
versus	versus	versus	versus
Social sciences, humanities, education	Business	Education	Social sciences, humanities

cause so many low-ability students express interest in intellectually demanding occupations.

The increasing maturity of interests and the opportunity to select courses as students move from the ninth grade to the twelfth grade increase the validity of both sets of predictors to discriminate among group means. By the twelfth grade, an inference that the amount of variance accounted for by the combined sets of predictors would be somewhat larger than the .60 values for the self-report scores standing alone seems reasonable. Even if the gain in accuracy were smaller in the twelfth grade than in the ninth grade, this could indicate the effect of differences in cognitive profiles on the development of interests.

Table 6.6 identifies the first two discriminants among the cognitive variables. These are the data most relevant to the topic of this chapter. The first canonical function for males is defined by a combination of mathematical, spatial-visualization, and technical-information tests; verbal tests have only moderate correlations with this dimension. The first canonical function for females, in contrast, is defined primarily by verbal and mathematics tests; spatial visualization has modest negative correlations with the function. (The first component in each sex picks up the variance associated with the differences in general intelligence in addition to other differential variance.) The first female canonical function represents the ideal combination of scores for college entrance as defined by the Scholastic Aptitude Tests, but the first male canonical function is quite different.

The means of the major groups contribute to the interpretation of the first two functions. For males, engineering and the physical sciences are opposed to the social sciences, humanities, and education, with law, the biological sciences, and business being in the middle. For females, the four academic disciplines are contrasted with business, with education being intermediate.

The second male canonical function is similar to the first for females, although it appears to be even more highly verbal in content. Mathematics tests have correlations with the function of intermediate size, while those for spatial tests are close to zero. The loading of socioeconomic status is larger on the second function than on the first, even though the first function contains more variance in the general factor. Humanities and law are contrasted with education on this function.

The second female canonical function contributes less variance to differentiation, but it is still highly similar to the first function for males. Those majoring in the physical and biological sciences are contrasted with those majoring in the social sciences and humanities, with education and business majors being approximately intermediate. For females, the four academic disciplines are contrasted with business, with education being intermediate.

Discussion

Well-Supported Conclusions

The importance of spatial visualization. Spatial visualization is a more valid predictor of group membership than one would expect from its history in predicting course grades in college preparatory courses in high school, college grades in the physical sciences and engineering, and success in technical training in the military. This does not mean that spatial visualization does not show differential validity in the regression sense in several areas of such technical training. It does, but the amount is small (McHenry, Hough, Toquam, Hanson, & Ashworth, 1990). When used in civilian occupations, however, the sample size is typically too small to show a small gain. Hunter (1983) speculated that performance predictions in scientific-technical disciplines are the ones most likely to profit from spatial-visualization assessments (over and above the general factor). Our findings were consistent with this view. In our comparison of two selection composites, we showed clearly that mathematics is not sufficient for distinguishing between future engineers and future humanists. A high level of mathematics in the presence of high verbal ability and lower spatial ability led to the selection of careers in the humanities and the social sciences, while high mathematical and spatial ability combined with lower verbal ability led to highly technical scientific careers. In the prediction of male graduate majors in science and engineering, for example, the first canonical function is equally weighted by mathematics and spatial-technical-mechanical tests. Verbal ability has a positive weight, but at about the level one would expect from shared variance on the general factor of intelligence. The same pattern appears on the second canonical function for females when predicting graduate majors in the sciences. Its lower contribution to variance for females compared to males seemingly reflects the lack of attraction to the physical sciences and engineering in the occupational plans of girls in the 1960s. This is true today as well (Lubinski, Benbow, & Sanders, 1993).

Sex differences in abilities. There were large sex differences in mathematics in 1960, which were larger yet in the spatial-technical-mechanical cluster. Sex differences in means are not engraved in stone, so we consistently used same-sex norms in our analysis to allow for changes in mean levels. A good deal of not completely adequate evidence indicates that mean changes have occurred (Feingold, 1988), and there has been change in the choice of college majors and in occupational aspirations (Lubinski, Benbow, & Sanders, 1993). Nevertheless, high school girls still score lower than boys on the cluster of tests involving the physical sciences, the biological sciences, and engineering (Stanley, Benbow, Brody, Dauber, & Lupkowski, 1992).

Girls at the upper end of their same-sex distributions in mathematical-reasoning and spatial abilities are better bets for physical science and engineering majors and occupations than those with high verbal scores in joint-sex distributions, regardless of where the male and female means are at any given time. The profile of the girls' scores predicts choice and a reasonable degree of success and satisfaction. A measure of an important function should never be discarded simply because it shows a mean difference between demographic groups (Humphreys, 1988, 1991a).

Cognitive versus self-report predictors. In groups already selected to be restricted in general intelligence, self-report predictors, especially interest tests, are more valid predictors of graduate majors than are the cognitive tests. This is especially true for females, who were not so career oriented in 1960 as they are today. The difference is apparent in the ninth grade and continues to the twelfth as each set of tests becomes better at differentiating with respect to group membership. It is also clear that the cognitive set adds substantially to the predictive accuracy of self-report measures.

Not only did the restriction of range in general intelligence attenuate the predictive validity of the cognitive tests, but it also increased the validity of the self-report measures. The cross-correlations between cognitive and self-report scores are so small in the full range of high school talent that dependence solely on interest tests for predicting group membership leads to many errors. The consideration of a cognitive floor for students being counseled on undergraduate and graduate majors is, therefore, essential.

Some Cautions

Choosing criterion groups. Throughout this chapter, we have argued for the utility of predicting group membership for assessing the differential validity of contrasting ability profiles. When predicting individual membership in groups, the definition of the group is critically important. Every member does not have to be successful and satisfied, but a given group should meet those criteria on average. If one has current information concerning proficiency in performance and satisfaction for the members of a group, this information can be used to select a more homogeneous subset of the group.

Not only should the members of the groups be reasonably successful and satisfied (Dawis & Lofquist, 1984; Lofquist & Dawis, 1991), but policymakers should be satisfied with the overall performance of current groups. The discriminant methodology involves placing the persons tested in advance of the formation of the group at an estimated difference from the mean of the group. It is important to keep in mind that persons can be either too high or too low on the combination of predictors to be well suited for membership in certain groups.

The predictive design. Experience in educational or occupational groups can change mean levels of scores on both cognitive and self-report tests. The high school curriculum chosen affects test scores. Thus, at least part of the gain in predictive accuracy from the ninth grade to the twelfth grade is due to differential curriculum choice. Out-of-school learning and psychological maturation surely are also involved. Thus, the predictive design is essential. A concurrent design may be less biased when the regression methodology is used, but concurrent validation does not possess the scientific significance of predictive validation over extended periods of time.

Not-So-Firm Inferences

Spatial ability and academics. The high school grade point average reported by students in the upper 20 percent in space and math was below what one would expect from their level of general intelligence, or even their level of verbal ability. On the other hand, they reported approximately equivalent grades in math in comparison to the other two contrasted groups and were only a little below that level in science. They did, however, have the highest grades of the three groups in technical-vocational courses. Thus, generally low motivation to do well in school cannot explain these students' lower grade point average overall. What can explain it? We suggest that these students in the high space-math group may have been turned off by the verbal nature of the high school curriculum and the verbal nature of the tests used to assess achievement in school. No direct test of this hypothesis occurs to us, but some unpublished military data is suggestive. There is a modest positive correlation between scores on printed tests of proficiency in technical jobs and supervisory ratings of motivation and leadership. The latter are also correlated with the proficiency ratings of subordinates, which in turn are correlated with scores on proficiency tests. It is difficult to believe that a person can be a leader in a technical specialty without being proficient in that specialty. Thus, when test-methods scores are controlled in the proficiency tests, the correlations with the ratings increase. Similarly, when rating-methods scores are controlled in the motivation and leadership ratings, the correlations with the uncorrected proficiency tests also increase.

Changing competence in a group. The regression methodology readily allows the upgrading of competence in a group whenever there are sufficient applicants, but it also allows all too readily the selection of persons who are overqualified. This change can easily occur without planning. Upgrading the competence of a group by the discriminant methodology requires planning. It may be as simple as using current measures of proficiency and satisfaction to select the desired subsample. On the other hand, changing the nature of a group may require changing the precollege curriculum so to make it attractive to other individuals, as well as encouraging students to adopt different aspirations.

The data that we have presented may indicate the need for change in two of our groups. One group consists of the male doctorates in education; the other consists of the doctorates of both sexes in the social sciences. Both are concerned with the most important problems faced by our society. Males in the graduate education group anchored the low end of the scale on each of the first two cognitive functions. Females in education, on the other hand, had about average levels, among the graduate major groups, of abilities measured by the tests defining the functions. Yet the group of educators raised to positions of leadership has been predominantly male for many years.

Moreover, our data show that there is relatively little differentiation among students choosing law, humanities, and the social sciences when using a wide selection of cognitive and self-report scores from high school. Some would argue that future social scientists should be less similar to the other members of that cluster and more similar to biologists, or even to physical scientists and engineers.

Use in selection. Use of the discriminant methodology for the selection of personnel in education, industry, and the military is clearly in conflict with the long history and well-established place of the regression methodology in personnel selection. A proposal to use the former methodology is novel in the experience of practically all personnel psychologists, but the proposal has some important advantages. Group membership is a cumulative criterion. Also, the combination of success and satisfaction in group membership merges two criteria that are often seen as relatively independent of each other (Dawis & Lofquist, 1984). The selection of competent persons who do not quickly create vacancies by their voluntary departure is eminently desirable.

Whether or not prediction of group membership is accepted, the usefulness in educational selection of a measure of spatial visualization is clearly indicated by our data. We do not expect all involved to jump at this suggestion on the basis of our data alone. Yet we feel that we have, at a minimum, provided the foundation for a large-scale field trial of an expanded college entrance test. The criteria in a field trial must involve more than academic grades if spatial ability is to emerge as an important predictor. This idea should not simply be dismissed as impracticable. The Educational Testing Service did introduce a third score in the Graduate Record Examination (GRE) just a few years ago that adds less, based on current evidence, to the regression validities of the verbal and quantitative scores than would a measure of spatial visualization. This measure also would add much less incremental validity, if any, to the prediction of group membership in educational and occupational groups compared to spatial visualization.

In 1999, an augmented version of the GRE is scheduled to appear. A two-track package will be offered, with four tests in both packages (three of which will be identical in each package). The identical tests will be verbal reasoning, analytical reasoning, and a writing exercise. For graduate programs in the humanities and the social sciences, the first package will include a quantitative test much like the current GRE-Q. In the second package, a mathematical-reasoning test predicated on knowledge through precalculus will be recommended to graduate programs in the physical sciences, mathematics, and engineering. This advanced quantitative test was designed to forestall GRE-Q ceiling problems for the more technical disciplines. This might be an opportunity, however, for psychology to view itself as closer to the biological sciences than to the humanities, and, as such, require future graduate students to assimilate the conceptual tools of the natural science disciplines. Faculty members certainly will reveal their preferences for differential ability patterns by the tracks for which they lobby, but perhaps it would be most useful to require all psychology undergraduates to take all four tests—which is an option that would require a minimal investment of time.

It is interesting that the analytic test on the GRE is still retained, and spatial abilities are ignored; we are unaware of any evidence documenting the incremental validity of this measure over and above the information provided by the verbal and quantitative subtests for any discipline. For the departments of engineering and the physical sciences, a measure of spatial visualization would surely provide more useful information. Also, do such disciplines need two assessments of verbal ability, at the cost of not measuring spatial ability, or would one suffice?

Possible curricular changes. If some highly able students are turned off by the present high school curriculum and examining practices, as we suggest, changes are possible. For example, practically all laboratory scientists advocate more hands-on science experience from early grade school through high school. College preparatory courses in technology are possible. It is not a problem to pitch these at the level of ability required for success in college. In addition, foreign language courses that are less literary and more functional are possible. These can emphasize conversational competence, the reading of newspapers, and assignments in the foreign-language equivalent of *Scientific American*. English literature courses can be reoriented to include science fiction, biographies of scientists and mathematicians, and selected articles from *Scientific American*.

Some speculations. There are many adults who did poorly in school but were highly successful in science, technology, and business as well as many of the creative arts. Edison, Ford, and Langley may well have been spatially gifted individuals. There are probably many more such cases than there are cases of highly successful novelists, playwrights, essayists, and biographers who failed in school. It may not be necessary to invoke motivation, hard work, dependability, and other personality traits to explain such examples. Individual differences in spatial visualization may tell most of the story.

Our research suggests that the two intellectual cultures depicted by C. P.

Snow (1964) have a psychological reality. These two cultures are well established as early as the ninth grade, and the two developmental paths certainly mirror Vernon's *v:ed* and *k:m* constructs in many conspicuous ways. As children develop, differential experiences most likely augment this differentiation, but a person's pattern of abilities and preferences at age fourteen helps determine his or her subsequent experiences (Rowe, 1994; Scarr, 1992; Scarr & McCartney, 1983). It seems to us that our schools only do a good job of fostering development in one of these cultures—the more verbal one.

Conclusion

Students who are talented spatially are being overlooked by our educational system. One reason for this is the overreliance on letter grades in the highly verbal high school curriculum. A second, related reason is the overreliance on correlations between verbal and quantitative predictor tests, and the verbal and quantitative tests used to measure achievement in training and educational curricula. We suggest that educators rethink the dictum "If students can't write, they can't think." To be sure, this is true of some people, but they also tend to be low in spatial and mathematical-reasoning abilities.

Spatially talented persons prefer to solve problems involving ideation about things. They are turned off by abstract verbal subject matter. This does not mean, however, that their becoming mechanics, skilled workers, or technicians is a satisfactory solution to the career dilemma for people at all ability levels. Those students in the upper 20 percent of our space-math group were still well above average in verbal ability and should have been encouraged more strongly to prepare for professional careers. But these students are currently being excluded from the most select institutions for advanced training in engineering and the physical sciences.

Curriculum-adjustment interventions are possible ways of salvaging intellectually talented students who are not so verbally able as they are in other intellectual arenas. Precollege science should contain substantial hands-on experience. It would also be useful if engineering professionals would undertake to prepare a technological sequence for the college-preparatory curriculum in high school. Less than 200 years ago, the physical sciences entered high school and college curricula. Less than 150 years ago, agriculture, military science, and the mechanical arts entered the postsecondary curriculum through the opening created by an act of Congress. It took many more years for the land-grant colleges to become respectable in the eyes of most academics. It is past time for more change.

References

Benbow, C. P. (1988). Sex differences in mathematical reasoning ability in intellectually talented preadolescents: Their nature, effects, and possible causes. *Behavioral and Brain Sciences* 11:169–232.

Benbow, C. P. (1992). Academic achievement in mathematics and science of students between ages thirteen and twenty-three: Are there differences among students in the top one percent of mathematical ability? *Journal of Educational Psychology* 84:51–61.

Benbow, C. P., & Lubinski, D. (1994). Individual differences amongst the mathematically gifted: Their educational and vocational implications. In N. Colangelo, S. G. Assouline, & D. L. Ambroson (Eds.). *Talent development* (Vol. 2, pp. 83–100). Dayton: Ohio Psychology Press.

Benbow, C. P., & Stanley, J. C. (1982). Intellectually talented boys and girls: Educational profiles. *Gifted Child Quarterly* 26:82–88.

Benbow, C. P., & Stanley, J. C. (Eds.). (1983). *Academic precocity: Aspects of its development.* Baltimore: Johns Hopkins University Press.

Binet, A., & Simon, T. (1905). *Méthodes nouvelles pour le diagnostic du niveau intellectual des anormaux. L'année psychologique* 11:191–244.

Burt, C. (1940). *The factors of the mind.* London: University of London Press.

Cleary, T. A., Humphreys, L. G., Kendrick, S. A., & Wesman, A. (1975). Educational uses of tests with disadvantaged students. *American Psychologist* 30:15–41.

Dawis, R. V. (1991). Vocational interests, values, and preferences. In M. D. Dunnette & L. M. Hough (Eds.), *The handbook of industrial/organizational psychology* (2nd ed., Vol. 2, pp. 833–871). Palo Alto: Consulting Psychologists Press.

Dawis, R. V., & Lofquist, L. H. (1984). *A psychological theory of work adjustment.* Minneapolis: University of Minnesota Press.

Feingold, A. (1988). Cognitive gender differences are disappearing. *American Psychologist* 43:95–103.

Flanagan, J. C., Dailey, J. T., Shaycoft, M. F., Gorham, W. A., Orr, D. B., & Goldberg, I. (1962). *Design for a study of American youth.* Boston: Houghton Mifflin.

Hulin, C. L., Henry, R. A., & Noon, S. L. (1990). Adding a dimension: Time as a factor in the generalizability of predictor relationships. *Psychological Bulletin* 107:328–340.

Humphreys, L. G. (1962). The organization of human abilities. *American Psychologist* 17:475–483.

Humphreys, L. G. (1986). Commentary. *Journal of Vocational Behavior* 29:421–437.

Humphreys, L. G. (1988). Trends in levels of academic achievement of blacks and other minorities. *Intelligence* 12:231–260.

Humphreys, L. G. (1991a). Limited vision in the social sciences. *American Journal of Psychology* 104:333–353.

Humphreys, L. G. (1991b). Some unconventional analyses of resemblance coefficients for male and female monozygotic and dizygotic twins. In D. Cicchetti & W. Grove (Eds.), *Thinking clearly about psychology: Essays in honor of Paul Everett Meehl* (pp. 158–187). Minneapolis: University of Minnesota Press.

Humphreys, L. G. (1992). Commentary: What both critics and users of ability tests need to know. *Psychological Science* 3:271–274.

Humphreys, L. G., Davey, T. C., & Kashima, E. (1986). Experimental measures of cognitive privilege/deprivation and some of their correlates. *Intelligence* 10:355–370.

Humphreys, L. G., Lubinski, D., & Yao, G. (1993). Utility of predicting group membership and the role of spatial visualization in becoming an engineer, physical scientist, or artist. *Journal of Applied Psychology* 78:250–261.

Humphreys, L. G., & Yao, G. (Unpublished manuscript.) *Predicting graduate majors.* University of Illinois at Champaign.

Hunter, J. E. (1983). *Test validation for twelve thousand jobs: An application of job classification and validity generalization analysis to the General Aptitude Test Battery* (Test Res. Rep. No. 45). Washington, D.C.: Department of Labor, U.S. Employment Services.

Lofquist, L. H., & Dawis, R. V. (1991). *Essentials of person-environment-correspondence counseling.* Minneapolis: University of Minnesota Press.

Lubinski, D., & Benbow, C. P. (1992). Gender differences in abilities and preferences among the gifted: Implications for the math-science pipeline. *Current Directions in Psychological Science* 1:61–66.

Lubinski, D., & Benbow, C. P. (1994). The Study of Mathematically Precocious Youth: The first three decades of a planned fifty-year study of intellectual talent. In R. F. Subotnik & K. D. Arnold (Eds.), *Beyond Terman: Contemporary longitudinal studies of giftedness and talent* (pp. 255–281). Norwood, N.J.: Ablex.

Lubinski, D., Benbow, C. P., & Sanders, C. E. (1993). Reconceptualizing gender differences in achievement among the gifted. In K. A. Heller, F. J. Mönks, & A. H. Passow (Eds.), *International handbook of research and development of giftedness and talent* (pp. 693–707). Oxford: Pergamon Press.

Lubinski, D., & Dawis, R. V. (1992). Aptitudes, skills, and proficiencies. In M. D. Dunnette & L. M. Hough (Eds.), *The handbook of industrial/organizational psychology* (2nd ed., Vol. 3, pp. 1–59). Palo Alto: Consulting Psychologists Press.

Lubinski, D., & Humphreys, L. G. (1990a). A broadly based analysis of mathematical giftedness. *Intelligence* 14:327–355.

Lubinski, D., & Humphreys, L. G. (1990b). Assessing spurious "moderator effects": Illustrated substantively with the hypothesized ("synergistic") relation between spatial and mathematical ability. *Psychological Bulletin* 107:385–393.

McHenry, J. J., Hough, L. M., Toquam, J. L., Hanson, M. A., & Ashworth, S. A. (1990). Project A validation results: The relationship between predictor and criterion domains. *Personnel Psychology* 43:335–353.

McNemar, Q. (1942). *The revision of the Stanford-Binet scale.* Boston: Houghton Mifflin.

Paterson, D. G. (1938). The genesis of modern guidance. *Educational Record* 19:36–46.

Paterson, D. G., Elliott, R. M., Anderson, L. D., & Toops, H. A. (1930). *Minnesota mechanical ability tests.* Minneapolis: University of Minnesota Press.

Prediger, D. J. (1976). A world-of-work map for career exploration. *Vocational Guidance Quarterly* 24:198–208.

Rowe, D. C. (1994). *The limits of family influence.* New York: Guilford.

Scarr, S. (1992). Developmental theories for the 1990s: Development and individual differences. *Child Development* 63:1–19.

Scarr, S., & McCartney, K. (1983). How people make their own environments: A theory of genotype environment effects. *Child Development* 54:424–435.

Schmid, J., & Leiman, J. (1957). The development of hierarchical factor solutions. *Psychometrika* 22:53–61.

Smith, I. M. (1962). *Spatial ability: Its educational and vocational significance.* San Diego: Knapp.

Spearman, C. (1904). "General intelligence," objectively determined and measured. *American Journal of Psychology* 15:201–292.

Spearman, C. (1914). Theory of two factors. *Psychological Review* 21:101–115.

Snow, C. P. (1964). *The two cultures and a second look.* Cambridge: Cambridge University Press.

Stanley, J. C., Benbow, C. P., Brody, L. E., Dauber, S., & Lupkowski, A. E. (1992). Gender differences on eighty-six nationally standardized aptitude and achievement tests. In N. Colangelo, S. G. Assouline, & D. L. Ambroson (Eds.), *Talent development: Proceedings from the 1991 Henry B. and Jocelyn Wallace National Research Symposium on Talent Development* (pp. 42–65). Unionville, N.Y.: Trillium Press.

Terman, L. M. (1916). *The measurement of intelligence.* Boston: Houghton Mifflin.

Terman, L. M., & Merrill, M. A. (1937). *Measuring intelligence.* Boston: Houghton Mifflin.

Thorndike, R. L. (1994). g. *Intelligence* 19:145–155.

Thurstone, L. L. (1938). Primary mental abilities. *Psychometric Monographs* (No. 1). Chicago: University of Chicago Press.

Vernon, P. E. (1947). Research on personnel selection in the Royal Navy and British Army. *American Psychologist* 2:35–51.

Vernon, P. E. (1950). *The structure of human abilities.* New York: Wiley.

Wechsler, D. (1941). *The measurement of intelligence.* Baltimore: Williams and Wilkins.

Wise, L. L., McLaughlin, D. H., & Steel, L. (1979). *The Project TALENT data bank.* Palo Alto: American Institutes for Research.

III What Do We Know about Proper Provisions for the Gifted?

I n the previous section, we were left with a disappointing message: social science has produced a great deal of knowledge during its first century, but not much of this knowledge is used well. Therefore, the role that social science does and can play in the betterment of society is compromised. Indeed, if we were to decide to apply appropriately the knowledge that social science has generated, we could see a significant enhancement of societal functioning. This leads to some compelling questions: What do we know? What does work? What could we do? In this section we attempt to answer these questions as they pertain to the education of gifted children—children whose intellectual competence is so advanced for their age that the regular curriculum does not and cannot meet their educational needs.

These questions are perhaps especially critical now, because the current school-reform effort and economic considerations threaten the viability of the very programs designed to serve gifted students (Benbow & Stanley, in press). Across the country, programs for the gifted are being closed down or scaled back dramatically. This is truly a time of shrinking resources; that makes it especially important to know how to use in the most effective manner whatever resources are available. Sadly, in many programs for the gifted we have not been doing so; we have not been using our knowledge well. Such programs often have consisted of "fun and games" that could be, and often were, argued to be beneficial to all students. The programs were not designed to meet the specific educational needs of gifted students; therefore, they are difficult to justify and to defend against cuts. Consequently, school reform, which is of great concern to the gifted-education community, could be beneficial. It might force us to pause and to reflect on and evaluate our practices; it could be the stimulus for some much-needed housecleaning. For this we should be grateful. The need to meet the educational requirements of our gifted students will become appreciated again and, we hope, new programs will be built on a firmer foundation of solid empirical data, a foundation reflecting our knowledge of what works.

It may seem that the school-reform initiatives sweeping our country are all to the good. Unfortunately, this is not the case (ibid.). Not only is the housecleaning going too far in too many instances, but many of the recommendations cater to the public's attraction to fads rather than addressing the need to make practice reflect our level of knowledge. For example, most schools today are being encouraged to provide instruction in heterogeneous rather than homogeneous groups (Deutsch, 1993; see also chapter 11 below). Is this advice consistent with accumulated knowledge? No; it is in direct contrast to what research has shown to be effective. Homogeneous grouping hurts no group, and it benefits greatly those who differ from the norm (e.g., the gifted). (See Kulik & Kulik, 1992, for a review; see also chapters 7 and 11 below.) We do not seem to be using the knowledge we have gained though empirical research over the past century. If we were, however, to fashion programs for gifted students based on sound principles, empirically supported by research, rather than follow the *Zeitgeist*, of what should they consist?

Any such program should not be designed to provide the same learning experiences to everyone. To some this assertion will seem undemocratic, but that is an incorrect inference; equality is not being compromised here (Benbow & Stanley, in press). To paraphrase Thomas Jefferson, there is nothing more unequal than to treat in the same way individuals who differ. Equality involves providing equal opportunities, which entails providing equal access to appropriate (not the same) educational opportunities. The optimal use and development of talent requires responding to individual personalities—treating individuals as individuals (see Benbow & Lubinski, 1994). The gifted need to be placed in educational environments that are congruent with (and also build on) their most salient abilities and preferences. Any sound educational program must recognize and be responsive to the vast range of individual differences in the area of learning, which are evident even among the gifted. This should be our guiding premise.

With this in mind, what specifically are important constituents of a sound program serving gifted students? John Feldhusen presents a review of what we know about motivating and challenging such students, covering topics from competitions to acceleration and how important it is to provide a differentiated curriculum and an appropriate peer group for the gifted. Lynn Glass, a past president of the National Science Teachers Association, continues this theme by discussing science education and what we know is effective in challenging gifted young people in science. The importance of developing an ecology of achievement and a scientific community for these students is stressed.

This discussion is followed by two chapters focusing on acceleration, an educational resource given much support in the research literature, but one that is greatly underused. Nancy Robinson, in her eloquent chapter, discusses a highly successful program of radical acceleration at the University of Washington, where fourteen-year-olds are given the opportunity to enter college. It is one of the few such programs available in this country, even though there is much evidence to speak in its favor. This is followed by a powerful chapter by Lee Cronbach, who takes a fifty-year look at the effects of acceleration, comparing those who were accelerated and those who were not in the Terman sample. In the words of Cronbach, a participant in the Terman study himself and a college graduate at age eighteen,

> In many aspects of their adult lives those who were accelerated as a group did not differ from the roughly equated controls. Every nontrivial difference that did appear on a value-laden variable showed those who had been accelerated at an advantage. . . . Frankly, I had not expected to find effects cropping up in responses forty to fifty years after high school graduation. I expected the vicissitudes of life gradually to wash out the initial differences favoring those who had been accelerated. Instead, it appears that their personal qualities or the encouragement and tangible boost given by acceleration, or both, produced a lasting increment of momentum.

The chapter by Page and Keith follows; it presents equally stunning evidence in favor of the homogeneous grouping of students. School reformers are pushing for changes in how we deliver instruction—moving schools away from homogeneous to heterogeneous grouping. Page and Keith provide compelling data, which add to what we already know, that this movement is not in the best interests of students of any ability level; it is particularly harmful for the gifted, especially gifted students from minority groups. The message is simple: teaching children in homogeneous environments is most effective and, consequently, most defensible.

We bring this section to a close with a contribution from James Coleman. Coleman compares what is learned inside school and what is learned outside school in the verbal and mathematical domains, and finds that school has a much stronger relationship with achievement in mathematics than with success in verbal areas. This finding has many implications, one of which is relevant for the nurturing of mathematical talent. Structuring an appropriate educational environment may be critical for the achievements of the mathematically talented to be maximized. The results presented in the other chapters of this section are especially relevant when dealing with the mathematically talented, the primary focus of the Study of Mathematically Precocious Youth.

It is clear that we know much about how to respond to the advanced mastery displayed by intellectually gifted individuals and why it is important to do so. Gifted children need to be placed educationally at levels that are commensurate with their demonstrated competence. The principle of placement according to competence is as appropriate for those with academic talents as it is for those who are talented in the arts or sports, where this principle is routinely applied (see Benbow, 1991). Placement according to competence can be achieved either through homogeneous grouping or through acceleration; both options are effective and not detrimental to any group of students. Finally, students who are being challenged educationally by a differentiated curriculum need assistance in finding the places where their talents can come to fruition. In conclusion, then, if we were to use our knowledge fully, we could effect positive change in the quality of life for the gifted and, thereby, better use the talents in our midst for society as a whole. Can society afford to waste the talents of an Edison or an Einstein?

References

Benbow, C. P. (1991). Meeting the needs of gifted students through use of acceleration: An often neglected resource. In M. C. Wang, M. C. Reynolds, & H. J. Walberg (Eds.), *Handbook of special education: Vol. 4. Research and practice* (pp. 23–36). New York: Pergamon Press.

Benbow, C. P., & Lubinski, D. (1994). Individual differences amongst the mathematically gifted: Their educational and vocational implications. In N. Colangelo, S. G. Assouline, & D. L. Ambroson (Eds.). *Talent development* (Vol. 2, pp. 83–100). Dayton: Ohio Psychology Press.

Benbow, C. P., & Stanley, J. C. (in press). Inequity in equity: How "equity" can lead to inequity for high-potential students. *Psychology, Public Policy, and Law*.

Deutsch, M. (1993). Educating for a peaceful world. *American Psychologist* 48:510–517.

Kulik, J. A., & Kulik, C. C. (1992). Meta-analytic findings on grouping programs. *Gifted Child Quarterly* 36:73–77.

Lubinski, D., Benbow, C. P., & Sanders, C. E. (1993). Reconceptualizing gender differences in achievement among the gifted. In K. A. Heller, F. J. Mönks, & A. H. Passow (Eds.), *International handbook of research and development of giftedness and talent* (pp. 693–707). Oxford: Pergamon Press.

7 Motivating Academically Able Youth with Enriched and Accelerated Learning Experiences

JOHN F. FELDHUSEN

A t any age or grade level, students differ a great deal in achievement and in their ability to learn (Feldhusen & Klausmeier, 1959; Klausmeier & Feldhusen, 1959; Feldhusen, Check & Klausmeier, 1961; Dreeben, 1984). These differences have a great impact on what we teach, how we teach, and how we motivate students (see chapter 5 above). Yet it is popular now in education to attack testing and the assessment of ability (Oakes, 1985, pp. 10–12) and to argue that responding to the individual differences uncovered by testing leads to inequities in the educational treatment of students (see chapter 2 above). Nevertheless, individual differences in the ability to learn are realities that cannot be dismissed on the grounds that grouping students for instruction is ineffective, as some critics maintain. To the contrary, grouping positively affects achievement and students' motivation to achieve (Rogers, 1991; Kulik & Kulik, 1991; see also chapter 11 below).

Given the differences in students' ability to learn, how can one best bring about optimal learning for individuals in a school setting? Optimal learning occurs for all young people when the level of challenge in new material is just above their current achievement and ability levels—the optimal match. Indeed, Levin's (1987) accelerated-schools project has shown that at-risk students achieve at much higher levels and develop better motivation to learn when the level of challenge is greatly increased. An abundance of research has shown the potential value of accelerated learning for high-ability students (Benbow, 1991; Benbow & Stanley, 1983; Southern & Jones, 1991). Accelerated learning is associated not only with increased achievement but also with sustained or increased motivation to learn. Finally, enriched learning, which, if it is to be appropriate for gifted students, must also be accelerated, relates to heightened achievement and motivation. Thus, it seems that highly able students can profit greatly from an enriched curriculum delivered at an accelerated pace.

With this general principle in mind, what are the specific experiences that motivate or inspire talented youth to strive for high academic credentials and creative achievements? What operates in such young people's lives to inspire commitment to the optimal development of their abilities? Parental nurturing and school tutelage can provide impetus, but at what points and for what reasons do talented students *(a)* take charge of their own lives, *(b)* set goals to be accomplished, and *(c)* seek resources and experiences to achieve at high levels? Is the commitment to high-level achievement an evolving motivational condition? How is it sustained or even enhanced? These are crucial questions confronting all who try to nurture the development of talented youth.

The purpose of this chapter is to address these questions through an examination of the literature on motivation, grouping, acceleration, and knowledge bases. Then some educational implications of these answers are explored. First, however, the extent to which the education of gifted students falls short needs to be documented, because this provides the background for all that follows.

Problems and Needs

Sederburg and Rudman (1984) analyzed achievement-test scores in the state of Michigan and found that the greatest declines in test scores across all subjects and grade levels were among students of high ability. In a recent analysis of achievement-test results for the 1990 cohort of Indiana students in grades two through eleven, using a cognitive-skills index as a measure of ability, my colleagues and I found high levels of underachievement in reading, language, and math among high-ability boys and girls, high levels of overachievement in reading, language, and math among low-ability boys and girls, and high levels of overachievement among boys and girls in math up to grade six, but declining levels of overachievement above grade six. Girls' scores declined more severely than boys' in math overachievement, and girls showed the greatest increase in the number underachieving (Feldhusen, 1992).

A recent report from the Educational Testing Service's Policy Information

Center (1991), *Performance at the Top*, shows a severe decline from 1972 to 1990 in the number of students scoring 600 or higher on the SAT verbal test (116,630 in 1972 versus 74,836 in 1990). Happily, the number of students scoring 600 or higher on the SAT math test has remained approximately level.

The 1991 survey of high-achieving high school students, reported in *Who's Who among American High School Students* (Educational Communications, 1991), revealed that 56 percent of these top students studied seven hours or less per week, while 22 percent studied three hours or less per week. Yet these same students had quite positive views of their school situations: 68 percent felt that teachers took a personal interest in them most of the time, and 60 percent felt that their teachers enjoyed their work. On the negative side, only 22 percent judged the quality of their education as excellent, while 73 percent believed that education in the United States was weak in comparison to education in Japan. Nevertheless, many students selected mathematics (51 percent) and sciences (43 percent) as potentially useful to them; English (38 percent), computer science (20 percent), and social studies (13 percent) were seen as far less useful.

Teaching that is differentiated to meet the special needs of highly able students is limited or nonexistent. Two reports from the National Research Center on the Gifted and Talented, for example, tell us that there is practically no provision for highly able students in our schools. The first study (Archambault et al., 1993) was a nationwide survey of the classroom practices of teachers in grades three and four. The researchers concluded that few teachers modify curriculum or instruction for gifted students. Moreover, when there is a program for gifted students, regular classroom teachers rely on resource teachers to meet all the needs of the gifted students outside the classroom setting. That is, resource teachers have no impact on regular classroom offerings for the gifted. In a second study conducted by the National Research Center on the Gifted and Talented, elementary classrooms throughout the United States were observed (Westberg, Archambault, Dobyns, & Salvin, 1993). The researchers concluded that gifted students spent 79 percent of their time in heterogeneous group instruction with no differentiation of curriculum or teaching methods. Observers also noted that classroom management problems often precluded any possibility of special attention being paid to the gifted few.

Clearly, there is a problem in our schools: in American classrooms gifted and talented youth are neither served nor motivated to strive for high-level achievements that are commensurate with their abilities. Furthermore, there is a debilitating trend to abandon even special groupings for instruction in favor of mixed, heterogeneous classes, which do not serve the gifted (or anyone, for that matter); thus, the educational prospects for able youth are negative and becoming worse. This sad state of affairs is having an effect; the achievement levels of our most able young people are declining.

What Should be Done? Answers in Research

Even though not much is being done for gifted and talented students in today's schools, it is still legitimate to ask what conditions can give rise to the motivation to learn, to achieve, to strive to reach high-level educational goals. Some insights can be derived from recent research on motivation and performance among children in school. One example is the work of Dweck and her colleagues. In a series of reports, Dweck (1986), Dweck and Elliott (1983), and Dweck and Leggett (1988) discuss their research and the development of their theories about motivational processes affecting learning. They describe mastery-oriented motivation as present when students seek challenges and are persistent in efforts to learn; a helpless orientation arises when challenge is avoided and persistence is low. They also propose that the child's orientation is linked to his or her personal perception of ability as being either an entity or incremental in nature. Entity perception means the student sees ability as fixed and unchanging; incremental perception means he or she sees it as malleable and developing. Students with an entity orientation avoid challenges and seek to maintain positive views of their ability, while students who lean toward the incremental perception are mastery oriented, seek challenges, stick to tasks, and are motivated intrinsically.

It would seem, then, that for students to develop mastery-oriented motivation, they need opportunities to be challenged and to learn how to approach challenge; they need to be counseled so that they can see their abilities as emerging and developing; and they need teacher support in sticking to tasks until a mastery level of learning has been achieved. This is true for all children regardless of their abilities. Yet for the gifted, special problems arise because the regular curriculum lacks challenge. To foster their mastery orientation, curriculum modifications that challenge gifted and talented students and allow ample time for them to complete difficult learning tasks are needed.

At this point, intrinsic motivation becomes significant. Intrinsic motivation is a mastery orientation or desire to learn because of inherent interest, not for a reward or to defend one's ego. It is similar to Dweck's mastery-oriented motivation. Amabile (1983) demonstrated in a series of studies that intrinsically motivated students show enhanced capacities for learning. Moreover, although extrinsic rewards and competition may combine with intrinsic motivation in the lives of highly able learners to enhance motivation even further (Amabile, 1990), intrinsic motivation grows in students of all ability levels when tasks are interesting and challenging, when the underlying ideas are rich and complex, and when teachers' expectations are high.

But students are often bored in school. According to our own research (Feldhusen & Kroll, 1985, 1991), gifted and talented youth are as bored in school as students of low or average ability. They are, however, bored for different reasons. Children of low or average ability say schoolwork is boring because it is uninteresting and too difficult. Children of high ability, in contrast, say it is boring because it is repetitive, the tasks are too easy, and they are often taught things they have already mastered. Nonetheless, children of high ability express great interest in academic subjects. The problem seems to be that interest in and motivation for learning are present in many gifted students, but the opportunity for a challenging, differentiated learning experience is often lacking. As a result, intrinsic motivation among young people who find learning interesting and enjoyable is not fostered in contemporary schools. What can be done?

Fostering Motivation

Peers

What role do students' peers play in developing mastery-oriented motivation or intrinsic motivation? Schunk (1987) studied the effects of peer models on children's learning behavior. He specifically noted that children make judgments about their own abilities in comparison with other students, just as Nicholls and Miller (1984) demonstrated somewhat earlier. The students then emulate models who are similar in ability to themselves and who exhibit good coping behavior in school situations. Seeing others of similar ability succeed at tasks motivates students to try the tasks themselves. But, as Cohen (1984) points out, motivation is diminished when students who are judged to be smarter succeed rapidly at tasks. Thus, as Schunk (1991) concludes, "similar others offer the best basis for comparison. Observing similar peers perform a task conveys to observers [students] that they too are capable of accomplishing it" (p. 208). Schunk (1991) also reports that having challenging goals and having opportunities to set one's own goals enhances motivation to learn, and that students who have developed good learning strategies have a higher sense of efficacy in learning. The implication for gifted and talented students is that they need the opportunity to observe and to model the behavior of other highly able students who are learning within a challenging curriculum, intrinsically motivated, and sticking to tasks to achieve mastery goals.

Peer pressure also has a profound impact on students' learning behavior and motivation. Brown and Steinberg (1989) and Brown, Clasen, and Eicher (1986) conducted extensive research showing that there are a number of different peer groups—the brain crowd, nerds, loners, druggies, athletes, jocks—in a typical school setting. Students often consider bright, academically oriented students nerds, and some high achievers avoid the label "brain" through denial or even deliberate underachievement. These responses to peer pressure reflect the need among youth to conform, a need that increases from childhood through adolescence (Berndt, Laychak, & Park, 1990). Several other areas of adolescent behavior are affected by peer pressure and the need for conformity: involvement with peers, involvement with school, involvement with family, and misconduct (Clasen & Brown, 1985). Peer pressures toward peer involvement are, however, stronger than pressures toward school or family involvement. Yet Berndt, Laychak, and Park (1990) found that at times friends can have positive influences on students' academic orientation and motivation and can even counteract negative influences.

In sum, peers, especially those in a student's special crowd or group, may exert strong influences on that student's disposition, behavior, and motivation regarding school. The gifted and talented need opportunities to participate in academically oriented groups—the brain crowd—and to obtain approval for academically, intellectually, and artistically oriented motivations.

Grouping

Grouping is a major vehicle for motivating gifted students in school and in academically oriented activities. Though there is little direct research available to support the positive motivational effects of being grouped by achievement level for instruction, several studies (Moon & Feldhusen, 1994; Moon, Feldhusen, & Dillon, 1994; Feldhusen & Kennedy, 1989) report high degrees of student satisfaction with grouping. Moreover, Feldhusen and Kennedy (1989) report that 86 percent of teachers responding to a survey noted high levels of student motivation in honors classes, and Moon (1991) reports that gifted students are often motivated by the special learning activities offered in enrichment-oriented programs for the gifted. Students in the Feldhusen and Kennedy (1989) study, in their open-ended comments, frequently noted challenge and the maintenance of motivation to learn as functions of special honors classes.

By fostering the development of motivation, special classes should enhance learning. Indeed, it has been well established that gifted students learn more in special high-ability classes (Feldhusen, 1989; Gamoran, 1990; Gamoran & Mare, 1989; Kulik & Kulik, 1991; Rogers, 1991; Singhal, 1991; see also chapter 11 below), even though the results from one study suggest that such students may not profit from being in schools where the mean ability level is high (Marsh, 1991).

Special classes, therefore, should provide the challenges and the learning environments needed for students to develop a sense of efficacy and higher-level motivation. Yet the extent to which they do so is critically dependent on the curriculum and the teaching methods. If special classes offer the same curriculum as regular classes, if teachers' expectations of students are not high, and if teaching methods are slow and repetitious, the motivational benefits of special classes for high-achieving, high-ability students will not be realized.

Acceleration

A large part of the advantage of special classes may derive from accelerated instruction within those classes (see chapter 4 above). Although "acceleration" is the word commonly used to describe this form of educational intervention, it does not capture its essence. What we really do when we "accelerate" high-ability students, according to Elkind (1988), is raise the levels of the curriculum and instruction to those commensurate with students' demonstrated levels of ability and prior achievement. Acceleration yields the largest instructional benefits for gifted students (Kulik & Kulik, 1984a, 1984b). For example, in a series of studies Feldhusen and Klausmeier (1959), Klausmeier and Feldhusen (1959), and Feldhusen, Check, and Klausmeier (1961) showed that adjusting learning tasks to students' readiness levels in mathematics led to excellent learning, retention, and transfer. Children of high ability (with IQs of 120 to 140) were especially successful in learning high-level mathematical skills through this process.

The College Board Advanced Placement (AP) courses provide one form of acceleration to high-ability students. Casserly (1968) reports that 90 percent of students who had taken AP courses ranked them the most valuable educational experiences they had had in secondary school. Student comments indicated that they were motivated by the challenge of AP classes and by working with other high-ability students, but were often bored in and dissatisfied with regular non-AP classes. These students were motivated by the AP experience to work hard to achieve. The motivational power of AP classes derives from the college-level challenge, the fast pace, and the intellectual orientation of the curriculum, as well as high teacher expectations.

Another form of academic acceleration is early college admission. Brody and Stanley (1991) reviewed studies of early college admission and concluded that among the advantages is increased motivation due to the clear challenge. They also note the facilitating effect of high-ability, accelerated peers on students' motivation.

Across the age spectrum and in spite of occasional problems, acceleration leads to high-level motivation, achievement, and goal setting among students of high ability, as reviews of academic-acceleration programs have consistently shown (Daurio, 1979; Feldhusen, 1989; Feldhusen, Proctor, & Black, 1986; Kulik & Kulik, 1984a; Proctor, Feldhusen, & Black, 1988; Southern & Jones, 1991). There is always the fear of social and emotional difficulty for the accelerated student. Yet rarely is there equal concern for the social and emotional dangers to that student of remaining in the slow-paced lockstep. The potential payoffs are often worth the risks of acceleration. Furthermore, the "dumbing down" of text materials in public schools (Renzulli & Reis, 1991) has generated a great need to elevate curriculum and instruction to the readiness levels of all young people, not only the gifted, to sustain motivation and produce higher levels of achievement. Levin (1987) demonstrated in his accelerated-schools project that accelerated learning pays off for all students.

Knowledge Bases

Further insights into the motivation of gifted and talented youth can be derived from research on the role of knowledge bases and expertise in cognitive functioning. Alexander (1992) reviewed research in this area and found three conditions characterizing the expert: special strategies for solving problems, a rich, domain-specific knowledge base, and a unique set of attitudes and motivations that drive cognitive operations in the field of expertise. It is the attitudes and motivation that are especially relevant to the discussion of the education of gifted and talented youth. If gifted students are to aspire to expertise, as we surely want them to do, their educational experiences in school must include opportunities to experience the goal-setting motivations of experts. In a sense, they must become incipient experts not only by acquiring the cognitive strategies and working-knowledge bases of experts, but also by being motivated. Such experiences call for accelerated coursework with teachers and student peers who exhibit behavior that facilitates the development of expertise.

Glaser (1984) and Findlay and Lumsden (1988) elaborate more fully on the role of knowledge bases in problem solving, expertise, and creative functioning. Glaser (1984) stresses that the knowledge base is an organized body of conceptual and procedural knowledge that is usable and accessible for specific purposes and goals. Acquiring the knowledge base and learning to use it well in a domain involve the development and organization of conceptual patterns. The knowledge bases of experts and creative individuals are, by and large, conceptually well organized and efficiently accessed in relation to a problem.

The development of problem-solving, comprehension, and learning skills is a goal-driven process, however. The individual is motivated to set goals, to use knowledge bases for establishing direction in the quest for solutions, and to persist through the processes of cognition that eventually lead to solutions. Developing such motivation in students again calls for increased opportunities for them to acquire large and fluent knowledge bases, to develop skills of retrieval of information from long-term memory, and to employ problem-solving or creative-thinking strategies (Armbruster, 1989).

In addition, the gifted and talented need opportunities for active inter-action with knowledge bases in settings that involve problem finding (Getzels & Csikszentmihalyi, 1975) and creative problem solving (Isaksen & Treffinger, 1985). Glaser (1984) suggests that expert teachers use discovery methods, So-cratic inquiry, case methods, and problem solving in helping motivate students to acquire a knowledge base and expertise in a field. These are especially ef-fective methods because motivation is stimulated through mastery-oriented experiences.

Although the principles discussed above may be applicable to most stu-dents in many situations, only gifted and talented youth can operate in, learn from, and acquire well-organized knowledge bases on their way to expertise and creative functioning in cognitively complex domains and fields. Less-able students cannot. This is where a sensitivity to individual differences becomes important and distinctions in the curriculum need to be made. For example, Gallagher (1966), in reviewing research on the new curricula in science, mathe-matics, and social studies of the 1960s and 1970s, concluded that "the introduc-tion of conceptually complex material makes ability grouping almost manda-tory since so much of the current learning in those classes depends upon mastery of previous concepts. Virtually the only way a wide range of ability can be tolerated in the classroom is to teach conceptually simple materials" (p. 106). The latter approach surely cannot prepare gifted and talented youth properly for high-level careers.

Snow (1989) offers a similar conception of the problem of differentiating the curriculum: "A big part of the problem is understanding what different learners bring psychologically to the learning situation" (p. 49). He points out that high-ability learners need conceptually oriented and complex learning experiences with less structure and indirect or inductive instructional methods that are challenging and motivating to them. Less-able learners, on the other hand, need extensive scaffolding or structure. The latter, he notes, is boring for high-ability learners. He concludes: "Directive strategies that are good for less able learners are not good for able learners" (p. 39). Only through selective course taking (honors, Advanced Placement, and high-level electives) can high achievers manage to obtain high-level, conceptually complex, and challenging learning experiences in high school (Gamoran, 1987).

The enhancement of motivation in high-ability students clearly calls for instruction through courses in which cognitively complex material and large, well-organized knowledge bases are presented with extensive opportunities for students to assume dynamic, interactive, and inductive learning roles.

Educational Implications

What can schools do to motivate youth of high ability and help them develop the aspirations, the goal-setting behavior, and the persistence of experts and creators? Although the lessons from this review seem clear, an outline might best highlight the basic conditions of learning needed by high-ability and gifted and talented youth:

  I. Curriculum that is
     A. cognitively complex;
     B. high-level, advanced, accelerated;
     C. challenging to students;
     D. oriented to developing a large, conceptually well-organized knowledge base in a domain of potential expertise or creativity;
     E. oriented to strategies for problem solving and creative functioning.

 II. Teachers who
     A. have extensive command of the knowledge base of a field;
     B. model intensive interest and motivation in the domain;
     C. use inductive teaching methods;
     D. have high expectations of youth;
     E. help youth develop mastery orientation, intrinsic motivation, and an incremental sense of ability.

III. Peers who
     A. are intellectually challenging;
     B. model interest and motivation in the domain;
     C. are not anti-intellectual.

Honors classes, high-powered electives, seminars, Advanced Placement courses, mentors, internships, and college courses in high school, as well as special schools (see chapter 9 below), offer the best opportunities to create these ideal conditions for high-ability learners. Many schools with large enrollments of high-ability youth are not providing such conditions and, consequently, such students' achievements in those schools are not commensurate with the students' abilities (Marsh, 1991).

Sometimes resources outside the school structure need to be drawn on to create the necessary conditions. For example, short-term programs of classes offered on Saturdays and during summers can provide some of these conditions for high-ability youth, and can be quite effective (Feldhusen, 1991). Mentors also can be used to provide both learning experiences and motivational input for youth who have limited learning conditions in school. Counselors (Silverman, 1989, 1993) can help gifted and talented students learn to cope creatively and find alternatives to inadequate school programs. Struggling through the inadequacies and weaknesses of school programs may help some gifted and talented students develop autonomy, self-direction, and independence in their odysseys toward expertise or creativity (Betts, 1986a, 1986b). It seems preferable for the optimum development of talent, however, to use alternatives and supplements to develop good school programs for high-ability and gifted and talented youth.

References

Alexander, D. A. (1992). Domain knowledge: Evolving themes and emerging concerns. *Educational Psychologist* 27:33–51.

Amabile, T. M. (1983). *The social psychology of creativity*. New York: Springer Verlag.

Amabile, T. M. (1990). Within you, without you: The social psychology of creativity, and beyond. In M. A. Runco & R. S. Albert (Eds.), *Theories of creativity* (pp. 61–91). Newbury Park, Calif.: Sage Publications.

Archambault, F. X., Westberg, K. L., Brown, S. W., Hallmark, B. W., Zhang, W., & Emmons, C. L. (1993). Classroom practices used with gifted third- and fourth-grade students. *Journal for the Education of the Gifted* 16(2):103–119.

Armbruster, B. B. (1989). Metacognition in creativity. In J. A. Glover, R. R. Ronning, & C. R. Reynolds (Eds.), *Handbook of creativity* (pp. 177–182). New York: Plenum.

Benbow, C. P. (1991). Meeting the needs of gifted students through use of acceleration: An often neglected resource. In M. C. Wang, M. C. Reynolds, & H. J. Walberg (Eds.), *Handbook of special education: Vol. 4. Research and practice* (pp. 23–36). New York: Pergamon Press.

Benbow, C. P., & Stanley, J. C. (1983). An eight-year evaluation of SMPY: What was learned? In C. P. Benbow & J. C. Stanley (Eds.), *Academic precocity: Aspects of its development* (pp. 205–214). Baltimore: Johns Hopkins University Press.

Berndt, T. S., Laychak, A. E., & Park, K. (1990). Friends influence adolescents' academic achievement motivation: An experimental study. *Journal of Educational Study* 82:664–670.

Betts, G. T. (1986a). The autonomous learner model for the gifted and talented. In J. S. Renzulli

(Ed.), *Systems and models for developing programs for the gifted and talented* (pp. 27–36). Mansfield Center, Conn.: Creative Learning Press.

Betts, G. T. (1986b). Development of emotional and social needs of gifted individuals. *Journal of Counseling and Development* 64:587–589.

Brody, L. E., & Benbow, C. P. (1987). Accelerative strategies: How effective are they for the gifted? *Gifted Child Quarterly* 3:105–110.

Brody, L. E., & Stanley, J. C. (1991). Young college students: Assessing factors that contribute to success. In W. T. Southern & E. D. Jones (Eds.), *The academic acceleration of gifted children* (pp. 102–132). New York: Teachers College Press.

Brown, B. B., Clasen, D. R., & Eicher, S. A. (1986). Perception of peer pressure, peer conformity dispositions, and self-reported behavior among adolescents. *Developmental Psychology* 22:521–530.

Brown, B. B., & Steinberg, L. (1989). How bright students save face among peers. *Newsletter of the National Center on Effective Secondary Schools* 5(1):2–4.

Casserly, P. L. (1968). What college students say about Advanced Placement. *College Board Review* 69:1–16.

Clasen, D. R., & Brown, B. B. (1985). The multidimensionality of peer pressure in adolescence. *Journal of Youth and Adolescence* 14:451–468.

Cohen, E. (1984). Talking and working together. In P. L. Peterson, L. C. Wilkinson, & M. Hallinan (Eds.), *The social context of instruction* (pp. 171–187). New York: Academic Press.

Daurio, S. P. (1979). Educational enrichment versus acceleration. In W. C. George, S. J. Cohn, & J. C. Stanley (Eds.), *Educating the gifted: Acceleration and enrichment* (pp. 13–63). Baltimore: Johns Hopkins University Press.

Dreeben, R. (1984). First-grade reading groups: Their formation and change. In P. L. Peterson, L. C. Wilkinson, & M. Hallinan (Eds.), *The social context of instruction* (pp. 69–84). New York: Academic Press.

Dweck, C. S. (1986). Motivational processes affecting learning. *American Psychologist* 41:1040–1048.

Dweck, C. S., & Elliott, E. S. (1983). Achievement motivation. In P. H. Mussen (Ed.), *Handbook of child psychology* (4th ed., Vol. 4, pp. 643–691). New York: Wiley.

Dweck, C. S., & Leggett, E. L. (1988). A social-cognitive approach to motivation and personality. *Psychological Review* 95:256–273.

Educational Communications (1991). *The twenty-second annual survey of high achievers.* Who's Who among American High School Students. Lake Forest, Ill.: Author.

Educational Testing Service. (1991). *Performance at the top: From elementary through graduate school.* Princeton: Policy Information Center, Educational Testing Service.

Elkind, D. (1988). Acceleration. *Young Children* 43:2.

Feldhusen, J. F. (1989). Synthesis of research on gifted youth. *Educational Leadership* 46:6–11.

Feldhusen, J. F. (1991). Effects of programs for the gifted: A search for evidence. In W. T. Southern & E. D. Jones (Eds.), *The academic acceleration of gifted children* (pp. 133–147). New York: Teachers College Press.

Feldhusen, J. F. (1992). *Achievement of Indiana youth in the ISTEP testing program* (Tech. Rep.). West Lafayette, Ind.: Purdue University, Gifted Education Resource Institute.

Feldhusen, J. F., Check, J., & Klausmeier, H. J. (1961). Achievement in subtraction. *Elementary School Journal* 61:322–327.

Feldhusen, J. F., & Kennedy, D. M. (1989). Effects of honors classes on secondary students. *Roeper Review* 11:153–156.

Feldhusen, J. F., & Klausmeier, H. J. (1959). Achievement in counting and addition. *Elementary School Journal* 59:388–393.

Feldhusen, J. F., & Kroll, M. D. (1985). Parents' perceptions of gifted children's educational needs. *Roeper Review* 7:240–252.

Feldhusen, J. F., & Kroll, M. D. (1991). Boredom or challenge for the academically talented. *Gifted Education International* 7:80–81.

Feldhusen, J. F., & Moon, S. M. (1992). Grouping gifted students: Issues and concerns. *Gifted Child Quarterly* 36:63–67.

Feldhusen, J. F., Proctor, T. B., & Black, K. N. (1986). Guidelines for grade advancement of precocious children. *Roeper Review* 9:25–27.

Findlay, C. S., & Lumsden, C. J. (1988). The creative mind: Toward an evolutionary theory of discovery and innovation. *Journal of Social and Biological Structures* 11:3–55.

Gallagher, J. J. (1966). *Research summary*. Unpublished report to the Illinois Superintendent of Public Instruction.

Gamoran, A. (1987). The stratification of high school learning opportunities. *Sociology of Education* 60:135–155.

Gamoran, A. (1990). How tracking affects achievement, research, and recommendations. *Newsletter, National Center on Effective Secondary Schools* 5(1): 2–6.

Gamoran, A., & Mare, R. D. (1989). Secondary school tracking and educational inequality: Compensation, reinforcement, or neutrality? *American Journal of Sociology* 94:1146–1183.

Getzels, J. W., & Csikszentmihalyi, M. (1975). From problem solving to problem finding. In I. A. Taylor & J. W. Getzels (Eds.), *Perspectives in creativity* (pp. 90–116). Chicago: Aldine.

Glaser, R. (1984). Education and thinking: The role of knowledge. *American Psychologist* 39:93–104.

Isaksen, S. G., & Treffinger, D. J. (1985). *Creative problem solving: The basic course*. Buffalo, N.Y.: Bearly.

Klausmeier, H. J., & Feldhusen, J. F. (1959). Retention in arithmetic among children of low, average, and high intelligence at 117 months of age. *Journal of Educational Psychology* 50:88–92.

Kulik, J. A., & Kulik, C. C. (1984a). Effects of accelerated instruction on students. *Review of Educational Research* 54:409–425.

Kulik, J. A., & Kulik, C. C. (1984b). Synthesis of research on effects of accelerated instruction. *Educational Leadership* 42:84–89.

Kulik, J. A., & Kulik, C. C. (1991). Ability grouping and gifted students. In N. Colangelo & G. A. Davis (Eds.), *Handbook of gifted education* (pp. 178–196). Boston: Allyn & Bacon.

Levin, H. M. (1987). Accelerated schools for disadvantaged students. *Educational Leadership* 44:19–21.

Marsh, H. W. (1991). Failure of high-ability high schools to deliver academic benefits commensurate with their students' ability levels. *American Educational Research Journal* 28:445–480.

Moon, S. M. (1991). The PACE program: A high school follow-up study. Unpublished doctoral dissertation, Purdue University, West Lafayette, Ind.

Moon, S. M., & Feldhusen, J. F. (1994). The Program for Academic and Creative Enrichment (PACE): A follow-up study ten years later. In R. F. Subotnik & K. D. Arnold (Eds.), *Beyond Terman: Contemporary longitudinal studies of giftedness and talent* (pp. 375–400). Norwood, N.J.: Ablex.

Moon, S. M., Feldhusen, J. F., & Dillon, D. R. (1994). Long-term effects of an enrichment program based on the Purdue three-stage model. *Gifted Child Quarterly* 38:38–48.

Nicholls, J. G., & Miller, A. T. (1984). Development and its discontents: The differentiation of the concept of ability. In J. G. Nicholls & M. L. Maehr (Eds.), *The development of achievement motivation* (pp. 185–218). Greenwich, Conn.: JAI Press.

Oakes, J. (1985). *Keeping track: How schools structure inequality*. New Haven: Yale University Press.

Proctor, T. B., Feldhusen, J. F., & Black, K. N. (1988). Guidelines for early admission to elementary school. *Psychology in the Schools* 25:41–43.

Renzulli, J. S., & Reis, S. M. (1991). The reform movement and the quiet crisis in gifted education. *Gifted Child Quarterly* 35:26–35.

Rogers, K. B. (1991). *The relationship of grouping practices to the education of gifted and talented learners*. Storrs, Conn.: National Research Center on the Gifted and Talented.

Schunk, D. H. (1987). Peer models and children's behavioral change. *Review of Educational Research* 57:149–174.

Schunk, D. H. (1991). Self-efficacy and academic motivation. *Educational Psychologist* 26:207–231.

Sederburg, W. A., & Rudman, H. C. (1984). Educational reform and declining test scores. *Michigan School Board Journal* 30:8–10, 24.

Silverman, L. K. (1989). The highly gifted. In J. F. Feldhusen, J. Van Tassel-Baska, & K. Seeley (Eds.), *Excellence in educating the gifted* (pp. 71–83). Denver: Love Publishing.

Silverman, L. S. (Ed.). (1993). *Counseling the gifted and talented*. Denver: Love Publishing.

Singhal, D. J. (1991). The other crisis in American education. *Atlantic Monthly* 268:59–74.

Snow, R. E. (1989). Aptitude-treatment interaction as a framework for research on individual differences in learning. In P. L. Ackerman, R. J. Sternberg, & R. Glaser (Eds.), *Learning and individual differences* (pp. 13–59). New York: W. H. Freeman.

Southern, W. T., & Jones, E. D. (Eds.). (1991). *The academic acceleration of gifted children*. New York: Teachers College Press.

Westberg, K. L., Archambault, F. X., Dobyns, S. M., & Salvin, T. J. (1993). The classroom practices observation study. *Journal for the Education of the Gifted* 16(2): 120–146.

8   Gifted Youth

A Challenge for Science Education

LYNN W. GLASS

ardly a day goes by without either the popular press or the professional literature addressing the need to improve the quality of science education in this country. Most of the literature focuses on how American high school graduates' scores on achievement tests compare with those of students in other developed nations. According to most international studies, we are at or nearly at the bottom (Jacobson & Doran, 1991).

Many solutions have been proposed by professional educators and scientists. On most curriculum-reform points the American Association for the Advancement of Science, the National Council of Teachers of Mathematics, and the National Science Teachers Association are in agreement. Science and mathematics instruction should be developmentally appropriate for the learners, be based on real-world experiences, incorporate open-ended problem-solving activities, and include all students. A solid, world-class science curriculum can be built on these four foundation stones. I championed them throughout the United States from my position as president of the National Science Teachers Association. Each of the ideas is based solidly on research and practice.

The purpose of this chapter is to explore changes in secondary school science programs, consistent with these four agreed-upon points, that will lead to more-rigorous and more-stimulating science education for America's most highly gifted youth. Presently only 62 percent of high school graduates in the United States complete a year of geometry, 47 percent complete algebra 2, 19 percent complete trigonometry, and 6 percent complete calculus. In science the situation is no better: 88 percent of American high school graduates complete biology, 45 percent complete chemistry, and 20 percent have taken a physics course (Horizon Research Group, 1988). Mastery of the concepts, skills, and thought processes in algebra, geometry, chemistry, and physics is essential for entry into many careers. In the twenty-first century, when present graduates will be civic and scientific leaders, the need for scientific and mathematical literacy will be even greater than it is today. We must encourage and support those who are trying to raise the level of scientific and mathematical competence of all citizens.

Although much is written about the need to improve science and mathematics education for all Americans, little is written about raising the scientific competence of extremely gifted youth. Numerous research studies have indicated that these students, when properly identified and provided with appropriate experiences, enter careers in science in far greater proportions than do similar students not provided with special academic experiences (Swiatek & Benbow, 1991).

The Nature of Science

A science program designed to benefit precocious youth must reflect the nature of science. Science, as defined by George Gaylord Simpson, is the exploration of the natural universe, seeking explanations for what has been observed and testing these explanations (Simpson, 1963). To contribute to the growth of personal knowledge as well as to the growth of the shared base of scientific knowledge requires more than just reading about science or doing "cookbook" laboratory experiments. It requires that one behave as a scientist—that one do real science. How does a scientist work? Is there a scientific method? Can we teach others this method?

Scientists in the early nineteenth century thought that observations, without prejudice, were the key to science; the gathering of facts would lead to correct theories. This simplistic view may have served early scientists well. But modern science is too amorphous, diverse, and complex for humans to observe without having some idea of what is being studied (Committee on the Conduct of Science, 1989). Today we increase both personal and shared scientific knowledge through the interplay of our mental constructs and our sensory perceptions.

The concept of the hypothesis is introduced early in nearly every science course, whether in secondary school or in college. In the textbook version, the hypothesis is the starting point. What role do hypotheses play in the daily work of a scientist? Some scientists develop many hypotheses and then systematically eliminate the weaker ones until they are left with a hypothesis that cannot be eliminated. Others construct a single hypothesis and then design careful tests to corroborate or to refute it. Other scientists ask questions: "Why is it that . . . ?" "What would happen if . . . ?" Still other scientists gather a great deal of data with only a vague idea about the problem they might be attempting to solve. Scientists use methods that are particular to their work; the methods evolve over time, and they are modified to meet specific situations.

Stating a hypothesis and extracting unbiased facts from a scientific experiment are techniques that work well in the standard classroom. The hypothesis that carbon dioxide is transformed into organic compounds in green plants through a process involving light energy is tested easily in the secondary school laboratory. Students and teachers alike can state hypotheses, design experiments, make careful and appropriate observations, and reach supportable conclusions. Problems occur, however, at the edge of the personal knowledge base, where neither the problem nor the method of solution is well defined. The edge of the personal knowledge base varies with the individual; generally, a high school student's scientific knowledge base would be less well developed and sophisticated than the base of a practicing scientist. What hypothesis does one formulate when working in a biotechnology-rich plant-growth environment? How does one design an experiment to control for gene interactions? What data should be collected? How should the data be interpreted? I cannot answer these questions, for they are the very work of modern-day plant scientists. Because we have gone beyond the limits of our personal knowledge base, high school science fairs are replete with exhibits that vividly demonstrate our inability to ask appropriate questions and to make necessary observations.

Self-deception—the tendency to see what we expect to see and fail to see what we believe should not be present—cannot be corrected by using a laboratory textbook. Nor can some of the intangible qualities of scientific discovery, such as curiosity, intuition, and creativity, be taught. Nature's secrets are elusive and difficult to interpret. At the forefront of science, teams of scientists share and develop mental constructs and ways of observing to advance our knowledge of the universe. Science, as practiced today, is the interplay of many individuals and nature.

Science is a highly social activity. Individuals interact with one another to understand our natural world better. Science can be viewed as the most complex form of society, with each individual contributing what he or she is capable of contributing toward achieving a shared goal: the unlocking of nature's secrets. In 1953 Roe noted that scientists pursue their profession for the sheer joy of discovery. The human interplay involved in unlocking those secrets is a joy that our able high school students must be permitted to experience if we are to move forward as the greatest scientific nation in the world.

Gifted High School Students and Scientific Research

In the 1940s many groups sensed the need to encourage and support high school students in scientific research. The National Science Teachers Association established the Future Scientists of America program in 1946. But by the end of the 1960s, corporate support had dropped to the point where sponsorship of the program was no longer feasible. Increased interest in America's space program served as the spur for the National Science Teachers Association to develop a broad-based student research program that has the full cooperation and support of the National Aeronautics and Space Administration. The first NSTA/NASA student research projects went aloft in 1973 with the Skylab program (Carleton, 1976).

In 1946 the American Association for the Advancement of Science also initiated efforts to encourage and support research by high school students. A program was designed to bring together winners of the Westinghouse Science Talent Search, members of state Junior Academy of Science programs, and members of school science clubs for a series of papers, talks, and discussions. These meetings were held in conjunction with the annual meeting of the American Association for the Advancement of Science. Morris Meister, then president of the National Science Teachers Association and the founding principal of the Bronx High School of Science, was chairperson of the program. The spirit of this founding program is alive today in its offspring, the American Junior Academy of Science program.

The most long-lived and prestigious effort to involve high school students in scientific research is the Westinghouse Science Talent Search. The search began in 1942 with the purpose of seeking out and encouraging the scientists of the future. Each year hundreds of high school students are involved in scientific research for a long period of time. They plan, organize, conduct, and then report in writing on scientific research projects. Every year approximately seventeen hundred written scientific papers are submitted for evaluation by professional scientists. Through this process the pool of applicants is narrowed down to three hundred honors finalists and forty national winners (Phares, 1990).

The quality of work completed by students identified as national winners is of the caliber of most master's degree papers. The national winners in 1992 included:

—Cloning and Expression of Human Aldehyde Reductase Gene and Evaluation of Reductase Levels in Human Lung Tumor Cells

—Computer Assisted Space Mapping

—Effects of Expected versus Unexpected Reward on Altruism in Children

—Kinetics and Crystallization of the Enzyme 3 alpha, 20 beta-HSD in Its Inhibited Form, and Modeling of Its Catalytic Site

—Effect of Glycine and Serine Insertions in the Loop Region Linking Transmembrane Segments One and Two of the Plasma Membrane H+-ATPase of *Saccharomyces cerevisiae*

—The Tobacco Hornworm: Development as Affected by a Food Source Grown in a High Carbon Dioxide Environment. (Science Talent Search, 1992)

The forty national winners are interviewed by scientists, not so much to determine the amount of scientific knowledge they may have as to ascertain their potential for being scientists. Creativity, curiosity, intuition, and ability to think, characteristics needed to tease out the secrets of nature, are of prime importance during the interview phase. The interview process yields ten scholarship winners. Many Science Talent Search participants have gone on to illustrious careers in science; five have won Nobel Prizes in chemistry and physics, and two have won the highest award in mathematics, the Fields Medal.

The seventeen hundred annual entrants come from a broad spectrum of schools in America. A few come from tiny schools with one teacher of science; the vast majority of the entrants and winners, however, are concentrated in a relatively small number of schools. The Bronx High School of Science in New York City leads all schools with 118 national winners and nearly 1,000 honorable mentions. The efforts of Stuyvesant High School, also in New York, earn a commendable second-place rating, and in recent years Stuyvesant has surpassed Bronx Science. Ten comprehensive New York City area high schools, Evanston Township High School and Lyons Township High School in Illinois, Central High School in Philadelphia, Coral Gables Senior High School, and North Phoenix High School have all established superior records for producing Science Talent Search winners. Thirty-two schools, in a nation of sixteen thousand school districts, produce most of the winners (Brandwein, 1992). What seems to be the environment necessary to nurture and to develop such high levels of talent?

An Environment for High School Science Research

Behind every successful science student is a dedicated teacher or supportive parent, and usually both. Sister Mary Lauretta Bishop, the only science teacher in the high school in rural Marshfield, Wisconsin, produced Westinghouse Science Talent Search winners in seven of her eight years at the school. The personal attention, approval, and encouragement she gave each of her students provided the foundation on which to build successful research programs.

Dedication, support, and natural abilities are clearly important factors in determining success in science. Identifying youth with science talent is a complex task (see Brandwein, 1992, for a detailed discussion). What programmatic variables lead to greater involvement and success in scientific research on the part of high school students?

In the words of Brandwein and Passow, our schools must exhibit an ecology of achievement, where all parts of the culture interact to reach the desired end: high levels of achievement (Brandwein & Passow, 1988). There appear to be several elements of this ecology common to those schools demonstrating success in the development of high school science talent. Such success starts with shared goals: the identification of gifted, motivated students in science, and the development of these students to the point where they can carry on original, creative, independent research. Successful schools accept that for students to develop scientific talent they must have the opportunity to behave as scientists do.

Like any good high school program, a science sequence, usually three years in length, forms the foundation for the development of research talent. The approaches and strategies employed in these courses are what one would expect in a modern science-education program. A variety of "minds-on" and "hands-on" experiences with a wide array of scientific equipment and techniques is used to stimulate students to handle problems in a rational, scientific way. The outcomes are the acquisition of a body of scientific knowledge, the ability to solve complex scientific problems, and a positive attitude toward handling unforeseen difficulties.

The differences between courses in successful programs and those in less successful programs are subtle, but significant. Successful courses meet for longer periods of time, often as much as ten double periods per week. Open-ended laboratories are used where the emphasis is on recognizing problems, offering hypotheses, seeking and testing solutions to the problems, and reporting and defending appropriate conclusions. Pre- and postlaboratory discussions focus more on why rather than how or what. Recognition and analysis of problems are stressed, rather than the mastery of disjointed facts.

High school programs consistently producing research-award recipients offer a science seminar or honors science program, while less successful programs usually do not. The same ethos employed in the basic-science sequence is followed; it just goes further. Less time is devoted to discussion, less emphasis is placed on text materials, and fewer laboratory exercises are completed. Instead, readings are from scientific journals, and students formulate ongoing laboratory research experiences based on careful analysis and understanding of the current literature. A seminar or honors class will find students working in collaboration on similar or related scientific problems. These students are beginning to function in a manner consistent with the behavior of practicing scientists.

Especially strong programs, like those that develop most of the Westinghouse Science Talent Search winners, also have strong independent-research programs for students. In these programs students are given individual guidance concerning the advisability and practicality of their research proposals. They work under the close tutelage of people intimately familiar with their chosen areas of research. The ongoing nature of the research is no longer measured in terms of class weeks; these students may investigate a single problem or series of related problems year-round for three or four years. It is not uncommon for students to continue during their college years the research they started in high school.

Most high schools, even the strongest ones, do not have the resources in terms of personnel or laboratories to mentor this level of scientific research. At the Bronx High School of Science, most of the students electing to complete this level of research are matched with practicing scientists in the community. Where this model is employed successfully, the scientist mentors maintain close contact with a member of the high school science faculty.

Moreover, students must develop an appreciation for science by becoming producers of knowledge, not consumers continually engaged in presented exercises (Renzulli, 1977). These needs are met through a variety of forums. Students join their mentors in writing papers, conducting poster sessions, and presenting talks. The International Science and Engineering Fair, the U.S. Army Science and Humanities Symposium, and the American Junior Academy of Science are examples of organizations that conduct regional and national forums where students share the results of their scientific research.

Students functioning at this level truly have joined the scientific community. They are developing mental constructs to define and understand our natural world; they are learning about and expanding our ways of observing nature. And, yes, they are experiencing the joy of discovery. They are practicing scientists; they deliver papers at professional meetings and report their results in the scientific literature.

A Model to Serve Gifted Youth throughout the Nation

The foregoing discussion would seem to suggest a relatively straightforward and simple recipe for providing stimulating, enriching science experiences for precocious youth. Under our present system of education, however, the barriers are formidable. Of the sixteen thousand school districts in the United States, few have the necessary ecology of achievement and size to permit attainment of a science program that challenges, fosters, and rewards our most gifted youth. Each state, however, has the necessary resources to provide at least one program, geographically centered, for every highly able student in that state; it could be argued that the decision makers in every state have the moral responsibility to do so.

In the fall of 1980 the North Carolina School of Science and Mathematics was opened as a special environment to serve the science needs of North Carolina's highly able youth. The school, a residential program for academically talented students in grades eleven and twelve, provides a stimulating and rigorous core science curriculum, an advanced level of seminars and courses in each of the sciences, and a research mentor program at nearby universities and laboratories. Presently, similar programs are being developed in at least thirteen other states. (For some relevant considerations in founding such a school, see Stanley, 1987, and Eilber, 1987.)

Such residential programs permit each state to identify and assemble those teachers who are motivated intensely to develop and deliver science programs such as those described above. These teachers form the nucleus for an ecology of achievement, a community of individuals—teachers, parents, and students— who excite others and share with them the satisfaction of pushing the boundaries of understanding forward.

Residential programs also permit educators to assemble enough students, and hence enough teachers, to provide the diversity and depth necessary to offer advanced-level courses and seminars. Such courses and seminars require teachers well versed in their specialties. Without sufficient expertise, teachers cannot guide students in addressing significant and meaningful problems. When teachers have insufficient mastery of the subject matter, instruction often becomes burdened with disjointed facts and shallow understanding.

Even in the largest and most successful high school programs there is not sufficient depth and diversity on the faculty to provide needed expertise in all areas of potential scientific research. In metropolitan areas this need is met easily with cooperating scientists from the public and private sectors. Both the Bronx High School of Science and the North Carolina School of Science and Mathematics rely extensively on cooperating professional scientists to help their highly motivated and gifted students.

A variation on the freestanding residential high school would be the establishment of a residential high school on the campus of each land-grant university, a university that by charter is dedicated to meet the needs of the citizens of its state. By establishing residential schools for high school students gifted in science on a land-grant campus, the programmatic requirements necessary for stimulating these students to pursue high levels of achievement in the sciences could be met within each state. A basic science core, developmentally appropriate to the learner, based on real-world experiences, and incorporating open-ended problem-solving activities for all students would be the responsibility of each local school district. Exciting new models exemplifying these characteristics currently are being developed by the American Association for the Advancement of Science and the National Science Teachers Association. On completing this core and meeting certain other entrance requirements, students could be admitted for study in the residential high schools at their land-grant universities.

The honors and Advanced Placement programs in science that usually cannot be offered in the typical local high school can be offered easily on a university campus. The framework for extended laboratory periods, in-depth study, and a greater focus on current research and literature is provided presently through innovative undergraduate science instruction. Rather than using a cooperating cadre of mentors for scientific research, the university model would bring research mentors into the program as full partners. Gifted high school students would be on the same campus with their own team of senior scientists, graduate students, and technicians. Every highly gifted student in America, whether urban or rural, would have the opportunity to develop to his or her fullest with such a model. Presently, the University of North Texas is trying out such a model, the Texas Academy of Mathematics and Science (TAMS).[1]

Conclusion

Yes, there is a job to be done. Associations such as the American Association for the Advancement of Science and the National Science Teachers Association are making significant progress in creating curricular programs and delivery strategies to raise the scientific literacy of all Americans. Our job will not be done, however, until we tend to the needs of our next generation of scientists, the gifted youth of America.

---

1. See Stanley (1991). Julian Stanley is a founding member of the TAMS Advisory Board, and is the only non-Texan to serve on it. For this and other work, in 1990 he was awarded an honorary Doctor of Educational Excellence degree by the University of North Texas.

References

Aldridge, B. G. (1992). Project on scope, sequence, and coordination: A new synthesis for improving science education. *Journal of Science Education and Technology* 1:13–21.

American Association for the Advancement of Science. (1989). *Project 2061: Science for all Americans*. Washington, D.C.: Author.

Brandwein, P. F. (1992). Science talent: The play of exemplar and paradigm in the science education of science-prone young. *Science Education* 76:121–139.

Brandwein, P. F., & Passow, A. H. (Eds.). (1988). *Gifted young in science: Potential through performance*. Washington, D.C.: National Science Teachers Association.

Carleton, R. H. (1976). *The NSTA story: 1944–1974*. Washington, D.C.: National Science Teachers Association.

Commission on Standards for School Mathematics. (1989). *Curriculum and evaluation standards for school mathematics*. Reston, Va.: National Council of Teachers of Mathematics.

Committee on the Conduct of Science. (1989). *On being a scientist*. Washington, D.C.: National Academy Press.

Eilber, C. R. (1987). The North Carolina School of Science and Mathematics. *Phi Delta Kappan* 68:773–777.

Horizon Research Group. (1988). *Science and mathematics briefing book*. Chapel Hill, N.C.: Author.

Jacobson, W. J., & Doran, R. L. (1991). *Science achievement in the United States and sixteen countries: A report to the public*. New York: Columbia University, Teachers College.

Phares, T. K. (1990). *Seeking and finding talent: A fifty-year history of the Westinghouse Science Talent Search*. Pittsburgh: Westinghouse Electric Corporation.

Renzulli, J. S. (1977). *The enrichment triad model: A guide for developing defensible programs for the gifted and talented*. Mansfield, Conn.: Creative Learning Press.

Roe, A. (1953). *The making of a scientist*. New York: Dodd, Mead.

Science Talent Search. (1992). *The fifty-first annual Science Talent Search finalists*. Washington, D.C.: Science Service.

Simpson, G. G. (1963). Biology and the nature of science. *Science* 139:81–82.

Stanley, J. C. (1987). State residential high schools for mathematically talented youth. *Phi Delta Kappan* 68:770–773.

Stanley, J. C. (1991). A better model for residential high schools for talented youths. *Phi Delta Kappan* 72:471–473.

Swiatek, M. A., & Benbow, C. P. (1991). A ten-year longitudinal follow-up of participants in a fast-paced mathematics course. *Journal for Research in Mathematics Education* 22:138–150.

9   Acceleration as an Option for the Highly Gifted Adolescent

NANCY M. ROBINSON

Markedly early college entrance (and graduation) for the highly capable young student has a long and honorable history (see, e.g., Daurio, 1979). A few coherent early-entrance programs existed in the past, including one multiple-college effort funded by the Ford Foundation (Fund for the Advancement of Education, 1957; Pressey, 1967), but for the most part radical acceleration has been an individual matter, with a number of successful examples (Cox, 1926; Radford, 1990; Wiener, 1953) and a few well-publicized failures (Dear, 1984; Montour, 1977; Wallace, 1986). Today, at almost any college or university of consequence, you can find one or more young students; although only a handful of colleges actively recruit young students, most have a policy of accepting a few young full-time students who have not completed all the formal entrance requirements (Fluitt & Strickland, 1984).

Preeminent among the leaders of the movement to open early college entrance to highly qualified young students is Professor Julian Stanley. Stanley made it possible for a number of very young students to enter the Johns Hopkins University and served as their mentor during their undergraduate years and beyond. The University of Washington program described below is the direct outgrowth of Stanley's and his students' enthusiastic accounts of the exploits of exceptional students who had coped beautifully with early college entrance (e.g., Eisenberg & George, 1979; Nevin, 1977; Stanley, 1976, 1985a, 1985b; Stanley & Benbow, 1983; Stanley & McGill, 1986). Numerous students whom Stanley mentored have shown extraordinary progress: for example, Eric Jablow, a Brooklyn College graduate at age fifteen, and Colin Camerer, who by the age of seventeen was a Johns Hopkins graduate and a doctoral student at the

University of Chicago. Stanley's work left little doubt that, at least under propitious auspices, radical acceleration to college could work.

Coherent programs specifically designed for the young college entrant are still relative rarities. Professor Stanley was also instrumental in establishing one such program, the Texas Academy of Mathematics and Science at the University of North Texas, which provides completion in two years of the junior and senior years of high school and the first two years of college (Sayler & Lupkowski, 1992; Stanley, 1991a). Mary Baldwin College admits female students to a residential college setting in what would usually have been their ninth- or tenth-grade year (Callahan, Cornell, & Loyd, 1992; Cornell, Callahan, & Loyd, 1991a, 1991c); Simon's Rock Early Entrance College of Bard College and the Clarkson School of Clarkson University (Kelly, 1989) also admit young students. The Matteo Ricci program of Seattle University compresses high school and college into a six-year program, although it is not necessarily designed for gifted students.

Though the evaluative research is too sparse to be conclusive, and often lacks suitable controls and other aspects of responsible research design (Brody & Stanley, 1991; Callahan & Hunsaker, 1991; Cornell, Callahan, & Loyd, 1991c), by and large the reports from these programs are favorable (Callahan, Cornell, & Loyd, 1992; Cornell, Callahan, & Loyd, 1991a; Ingersoll & Cornell, 1995; Rogers, 1992; Sayler & Lupkowski, 1992), just as were the earlier reports of the Fund for the Advancement of Education (1953, 1957; Pressey, 1967). With the exception of one unsettling study by Cornell, Callahan, and Loyd (1991c), which found a high incidence of emotional problems, particularly depression, in a group of radically accelerated young women in a residential college, most investigators have reported no effects or mildly positive effects of acceleration on personal adjustment but strongly positive effects on academic attainment (see Kulik & Kulik, 1984; Rogers, 1992). (The Cornell, Callahan, and Loyd [1991c] study, despite having been critiqued energetically by Stanley [1991b], has served usefully to substantiate the need for care in selection of students to be accelerated [Cornell, Callahan, & Loyd, 1991b].)

These positive findings are augmented by other studies that have examined the adjustment of highly accelerated students who have not been enrolled in coherent programs (Janos, 1987; Pollins, 1983; Rogers, 1992). The weight of the evidence suggests that acceleration of this kind seems, after perhaps an initial wobble, to yield no significant positive or negative effects on adjustment, while offering students a better academic fit and golden opportunities to make use of their most creative years.

In this context, consider the University of Washington's program, which was established by my late husband, Halbert B. Robinson, in no small part as the result of his friendship with and admiration for Julian Stanley. A guiding principle in its establishment was what Hal, following the lead of J. McVicker Hunt (1961), termed the "optimal match" (Robinson, 1983; Robinson & Robinson, 1982). The notion of the match refers in Piagetian theory to the principle that learning occurs only when there is "an appropriate match between the circumstances that a child encounters and the schemata that he [or she] has already assimilated into his [or her] repertoire" (Hunt, 1961, p. 268). If one assumes, as did Hal, that learning is generally a sequential, developmental process that is relatively predictable, and that, once a learner has mastered a given stage or level of skills and conceptual understanding, it is time to proceed to the next, then it follows that readiness, challenge, and timing are of supreme importance. If moving on to the next step is delayed, boredom will ensue; if the step is reached too early or too abruptly, the learner is likely to be confused and discouraged, and find the situation aversive. (There are similarities here with what Csikszentmihalyi [Csikszentmihalyi & Larson, 1984] later termed the "flow experience.")

The optimal match has to be carefully constructed for each student, reflecting the inevitable substantial differences in rates of learning, both between and within individuals. From this point of view, one can readily see why Hal would have developed a program of (basically vertical) acceleration rather than (horizontal) enrichment to meet the needs of highly capable teenagers. For those with advancement in specific domains, Hal helped arrange appropriate coursework, but for those whose rates of development were sufficiently rapid in all the domains needed for success in college (including dealing with the broad array of courses needed to meet distribution requirements), radical acceleration to the University of Washington was possible.

Initially, Early Entrance Program students (fondly known as "EEPers") were admitted gradually—first, for a quarter or two with simultaneous enrollment in middle school and college, and then for a full-time summer program. Although support services were abundant and students were expected to meet twice a week as a group, this approach had its problems. For one thing, the simultaneous middle school–college enrollment limited the option to students who attended middle school close to the University of Washington campus. More significantly, though, students had no clear identity in either school; some needed an extra boost in math; many had poor study skills after so many years of being underchallenged; and none of them had sufficient writing experience. In 1980, Hal established a one-year Transition School, a one-room school on the campus, which, with some modifications, exists today.

Applicants are, as one might imagine, scrutinized carefully. They must be no older than fourteen and must be living with a family within commuting distance, though some have impressive distances to travel. We use for our initial screen the Washington PreCollege Test (WPCT), requiring that students, at a minimum, attain scores roughly comparable to the average scores entering University of Washington students had attained as high school seniors (85th percentile or better on either the verbal or the quantitative composite, and 55th percentile or better on the other). In Scholastic Aptitude Test (SAT) terms, this is approximately equivalent to a total of 1050, which sounds low until one remembers the students' ages. As a point of reference, combined SAT scores of 1050 or higher were earned by only about seventy-five, or fewer than 4 percent, of the nearly two thousand very bright (approximately 5 percent highest-achieving) seventh-grade students in the state of Washington who this year participated in the Johns Hopkins University Center for Talented Youth Talent Search. In addition to the WPCT, we also administer the Stanford-Binet, fourth edition (Thorndike, Hagen, & Sattler, 1986), which gives us further domain-specific information; the arithmetic subscale of the Wide Range Achievement Test, Revised (WRAT-R) (Jastak & Wilkinson, 1984); and a twenty-minute essay. Composite scores on the Stanford-Binet average, for any given year, between 145 and 155; successful applicants typically score above the twelfth-grade level on the WRAT-R. We also examine grades and past achievement tests with care, and talk at length with two or three teachers as well as the student and family. We have learned to look for students who are searching for a challenge, who have not become so negative to the educational system that they have "turned off," who read challenging material for recreation, who manage their lives efficiently and regard time as a precious resource, and who have reached for some goal of excellence—intellectual, athletic, musical, or otherwise. In addition, we have to know that this is not just the parents' idea but the student's strong commitment. Because of the likelihood that the student simply will not have enough energy to go around, we try to avoid situations in which there is intense stress at home.

Of the sixteen students we accept each year, usually all but one or two complete the intensive Transition School year, and of those who do, about 95 percent proceed to graduate with, at a minimum, a bachelor's degree. With our encouragement, many students "shop around," experiment with different majors, or even eventually obtain double majors or double degrees, so the average graduation time is in the neighborhood of five years following the Transition School year. (In-state tuition is only about two thousand dollars a year, so there is less financial pressure to graduate than there might be otherwise.) A quarter to a third join the Honors Program, which is a first-rate liberal-arts option; many others elect departmental honors options. After a year or two, about 20 percent of the students transfer to other colleges, generally highly competitive ones. As a group, the students' grades are very satisfactory, the grade point average (GPA) generally hovering around 3.5 or 3.6, in comparison with the university's average GPA of 3.0.

Contrary to stereotype, our students have chosen a wide variety of majors, displaying their diversity not only within the group but within individuals; one Caucasian student combined physics with Chinese, and another student combined molecular biology and communications. Nearly a third are in the liberal arts, about a third are in the biological sciences, and a little more than a third are in the physical sciences, mathematics, or engineering. Mightily as we seek to empower our young women (Noble & Smyth, 1995) and encourage them to consider that last group of majors, with some spectacular successes, there are the conventional gender differences in this distribution.

And how have our students fared? Very well, thank you. We have, on several occasions, compared the academic and emotional adjustment of our students with three nonaccelerated comparison groups: students who were qualified for the program but elected not to enter, nonaccelerated National Merit Scholarship finalists, and University of Washington students matched for WPCT scores before entry. The comparison with the last of these groups was not particularly interesting, so we have dropped the group from our follow-up. We soon discovered that our students were, in academic adjustment, performing very satisfactorily (Janos & Robinson, 1985; Janos, Robinson, & Lunneborg, 1989). One study of the few students with GPAs below 3.0 found that the males tended to have adjustment problems and erratic scholastic records, while the females had more salient social agendas and generally steadily rising grades (Janos, Sanfilippo, & Robinson, 1986). In social and emotional adjustment, there were practically no differences between our group and any of the comparison groups on measures such as the California Psychological Inventory (Gough, 1969), although where such differences existed, our group most closely resembled the National Merit finalists (Robinson & Janos, 1986; Janos, Robinson, & Lunneborg, 1989).

In subsequent interviews, EEPers have confirmed their feelings of alienation and difference in previous school settings, in contrast to feelings of affiliation and compatibility with fellow EEPers, their full-fledged peers (Janos, 1990). Consistent with our observations, the EEPers report close friendships with their Transition School classmates. They gradually add regular-age University of Washington students to their circles of friends, dispersing to all parts of the campus as they go along (Janos et al., 1988). Most have expressed a good deal of satisfaction with their choice to accelerate, scoffing at those who repeatedly ask, "But what about the prom?" (Noble & Drummond, 1992).

Our latest follow-up of graduates and nonaccelerated controls (Noble, Robinson, & Gunderson, 1993) yields results consistent with these. Our students proceed to the graduate schools of their choice in larger proportions than even the National Merit finalists; they generally express satisfaction with their choice to accelerate (particularly those who entered after the Transition School was established), and they continue to describe themselves—just as the National Merit finalists do—as a little more serious, introverted, and restrained than do the students who elected not to enter the program. Generally speaking, the EEPers think as well of themselves as do members of the other groups, though the qualified students who did not enter do endorse two statements, "Most times I think I am good," and "I feel I am a person of worth," more often than do EEPers or National Merit finalists. There are a few gender differences within the EEP group, but only a few: the EEP males see acceleration as having facilitated their interest in mathematics and science more than do the females who, in turn, see acceleration as having had a more favorable effect on their social lives than do the males. The students' lives seem well launched; most have been able to complete their education before marrying and having children; they are getting on with the business of adulthood.

At the same time, there are a few students who have not proceeded expeditiously to complete their education. At this point, we know of a total of fourteen students over the fifteen-year period who, having entered the full-time EEP program, have for significant, largely unplanned periods halted their college education before graduation. Of the five young women, three have completed or are currently completing their college degrees (one of them having earned an Olympic medal in the meantime, and she is currently working on another). All but one of these female students entered the EEP before the establishment of the Transition School. Of the nine young men, however, all entered via the Transition School and none, at this point, is in the process of completing a degree. Perhaps the "sink-or-swim" climate of the early phase of the program tended to discourage students with weaker motivation before they became fully identified with the program, while the Transition School may have supported some equally capable students, mostly males, who then had more difficulty with the less structured college setting.

The interested reader will compare the generally positive results of this short-term follow-up with the monumental follow-up of the accelerated students in Terman's longitudinal study (reported in chapter 10 below). Apparently, things have not changed much over the years. Indeed, given the increased opportunity, expectation, and need for extended graduate and professional education, one might predict that, in the long run, a head start will prove even more valuable in the future than it did for Terman's gifted students. We see a number of our students using their extra years to pursue additional graduate work, sometimes seizing opportunities to achieve syntheses between fields that would have been more difficult when they were older and more involved with family responsibilities (Robinson & Noble, 1992). (For example, one student is completing a law degree in the United States after having earned one in Japan, with an eye on international investment law; another, with a Ph.D. in geophysics, followed a postdoctoral academic fellowship with a congressional fellowship from the American Association for the Advancement of Science to prepare for a career in science policy; several are pursuing Ph.D.s in addition to medical degrees.) It remains to be seen, of course, what sorts of roles our EEPers eventually play as fully educated adults. Many are entering professional fields; a number are in academia, several with more than one graduate or postdoctoral degree at young ages; many show exceptional promise as creative researchers. We can only wait.

In the meantime, the comparison with the nonaccelerated groups has been reassuring to us. Whenever one of our students reports a personal difficulty, we can remind ourselves that, like other people, we sometimes have unrealistic expectations for these human beings. Indeed, such unrealistic expectations are regularly experienced as a burden by gifted young people (Delisle, 1987; Janos, 1990). Being bright does not make one immune to the problems of growing up (Noble & Drummond, 1992), but being accelerated does not necessarily create or intensify such problems, either.

The Early Entrance Program demonstrates at least two aspects of the concept of the optimal match. First, the students who chose this program option responded, among other things, to what they saw as a match for them, a challenge appropriate to the level of their mental maturity and patterns of aptitudes. Second, our experience demonstrates that the optimal match may not happen automatically; it may need a boost. Simply placing students in a more challenging environment may overstress their levels of academic preparation and study skills. An optimal match can be expedited by a coherent effort to boost students' readiness to the point where they can step easily into situations well matched to their ability levels. Our students typically report, with considerable relief, that University of Washington classes—even honors classes—are much easier for them than Transition School. Clearly, they are not only intellectually able but, at that point, well enough prepared to keep up with students who are, on average, four years older. Indeed, to judge by their GPAs, they do very well indeed.

I believe Hal would be happy with—and vindicated by—the results of the program. They tend to support his emphasis on an optimal-match approach to the education of highly capable students, and confirm the viability, and indeed the rationality, of a radical jump to college. Surely such a program does not solve everyone's problems, educational or otherwise. But apparently, neither does it create them. A program of radical acceleration to college, such as the one at the University of Washington, provides a viable alternative for adolescents with exceptionally high academic capability.

References

Brody, L. E., & Stanley, J. C. (1991). Young college students: Assessing factors that contribute to success. In W. T. Southern & E. D. Jones (Eds.), *The academic acceleration of gifted children* (pp. 102–132). New York: Teachers College Press.

Callahan, C. M., Cornell, D. G., & Loyd, B. H. (1992). The academic development and personal adjustment of high ability young women in an early college entrance program. In N. Colangelo, S. G. Assouline, & D. L. Ambroson (Eds.), *Talent development: Proceedings from the 1991 Henry B. and Jocelyn Wallace National Research Symposium on Talent Development* (pp. 248–260). Unionville, N.Y.: Trillium Press.

Callahan, C. M., & Hunsaker, S. L. (1991). Evaluation of acceleration programs. In W. T. Southern & E. D. Jones (Eds.), *The academic acceleration of gifted children* (pp. 181–206). New York: Teachers College Press.

Cornell, D. G., Callahan, C. M., & Loyd, B. H. (1991a). Personality growth of female early college entrants: A controlled, prospective study. *Gifted Child Quarterly* 35:135–143.

Cornell, D. G., Callahan, C. M., & Loyd, B. H. (1991b). Research on early college entrance: A few more adjustments are needed. *Gifted Child Quarterly* 35:71–72.

Cornell, D. G., Callahan, C. M., & Loyd, B. H. (1991c). Socioemotional adjustment of adolescent girls enrolled in a residential acceleration program. *Gifted Child Quarterly* 35:58–66.

Cox, C. M. (1926). *The early mental traits of three hundred geniuses*. Stanford: Stanford University Press.

Csikszentmihalyi, M., & Larson, R. (1984). *Being adolescent: Conflict and growth in the teenage years*. New York: Basic Books.

Daurio, S. P. (1979). Educational enrichment versus acceleration: A review of the literature. In W. C. George, S. J. Cohn, & J. C. Stanley (Eds.), *Educating the gifted: Acceleration and enrichment* (pp. 13–63). Baltimore: Johns Hopkins University Press.

Dear, W. (1984). *The dungeon master: The disappearance of James Dallas Egbert III*. Boston: Houghton Mifflin.

Delisle, J. R. (1987). *Gifted kids speak out*. Minneapolis: Free Spirit.

Eisenberg, A. R., & George, W. C. (1979). Early entrance to college: The Johns Hopkins experience. *College and University* 54:109–118.

Fluitt, J., & Strickland, S. (1984). A survey of early admissions policies. *College and University* 59:129–135.

Fund for the Advancement of Education. (1953). *Bridging the gap between school and college* (Evaluation Report No. 1). New York: Author.

Fund for the Advancement of Education. (1957). *They went to college early* (Evaluation Report No. 2). New York: Author.

Gough, H. G. (1969). *Manual for the California Psychological Inventory*. Palo Alto: Consulting Psychologists Press.

Hunt, J. M. (1961). *Intelligence and experience.* New York: Ronald Press.

Ingersoll, K. S., & Cornell, D. G. (1995). Social adjustment of female early college entrants in a residential program. *Journal for the Education of the Gifted* 19:45–62.

Janos, P. M. (1987). A fifty-year follow-up of Terman's youngest college students and IQ-matched agemates. *Gifted Child Quarterly* 31:55–58.

Janos, P. M. (1990). The self-perceptions of uncommonly bright youngsters. In R. J. Sternberg & J. Kolligian, Jr. (Eds.), *Competence considered* (pp. 98–116). New Haven: Yale University Press.

Janos, P. M., & Robinson, N. M. (1985). The performance of students in a program of radical acceleration at the university level. *Gifted Child Quarterly* 29:175–179.

Janos, P. M., Robinson, N. M., & Lunneborg, C. E. (1989). Markedly early entrance to college: A multi-year comparative study of academic performance and psychological adjustment. *Journal of Higher Education* 60:495–518.

Janos, P. M., Robinson, N. M., Carter, C., Chapel, A., Cufley, R., Curland, M., Daily, M., Guilland, M., Heinzig, M., Kehl, H., Lu, S., Sherry, D., Stoloff, J., & Wise, A. (1988). A cross-sectional developmental study of the social relations of students who enter college early. *Gifted Child Quarterly* 32:210–215.

Janos, P. M., Sanfilippo, S. M., & Robinson, N. M. (1986). "Under-achievement" among markedly accelerated college students. *Journal of Youth and Adolescence* 15:303–313.

Jastak, S., & Wilkinson, G. S. (1984). *Wide Range Achievement Test, Revised.* Wilmington, Del.: Jastak Associates.

Kelly, G. F. (1989). The Clarkson School: Talented students enter college early. In S. M. Elam (Ed.), *Prototypes: An anthology of school improvement ideas that work.* Bloomington, Ind.: Phi Delta Kappa Foundation.

Kulik, J. A., & Kulik, C. C. (1984). Effects of accelerated instruction on students. *Review of Educational Research* 54:409–425.

Montour, K. M. (1977). William James Sidis, the broken twig. *American Psychologist* 32:265–279.

Nevin, D. (1977). Young prodigies take off under special program. *Smithsonian* 8:76–82, 160.

Noble, K. D., & Drummond, J. (1992). But what about the prom? Students' perceptions of early college entrance. *Gifted Child Quarterly* 36:106–111.

Noble, K. D., Robinson, N. M., & Gunderson, S. (1993). All rivers lead to the sea: A follow-up study of gifted young adults. *Roeper Review* 15:124–130.

Noble, K. D., & Smyth, R. K. (1995). Keeping their talents alive: Young women's assessment of radical, post-secondary education. *Roeper Review* 18:49–55.

Pollins, L. D. (1983). The effects of acceleration on the social and emotional development of gifted students. In C. P. Benbow & J. C. Stanley (Eds.), *Academic precocity: Aspects of its development* (pp. 160–178). Baltimore: Johns Hopkins University Press.

Pressey, S. L. (1967). "Fordling" accelerants ten years after. *Journal of Counseling Psychology* 14:73–80.

Radford, J. (1990). *Child prodigies and exceptional early achievers.* New York: Free Press.

Robinson, H. B. (1983). A case for radical acceleration: Programs of the Johns Hopkins University and the University of Washington. In C. P. Benbow & J. C. Stanley (Eds.), *Academic precocity: Aspects of its development* (pp. 139–159). Baltimore: Johns Hopkins University Press.

Robinson, N. M., & Janos, P. M. (1986). Psychological adjustment in a college-level program of marked academic acceleration. *Journal of Youth and Adolescence* 15:51–60.

Robinson, N. M., & Noble, K. D. (1992). Radical acceleration into college: Can it work? In N. Colangelo, S. G. Assouline, & D. L. Ambroson (Eds.), *Talent development: Proceedings from the 1991 Henry B. and Jocelyn Wallace National Research Symposium on Talent Development* (pp. 267–277). Unionville, N.Y.: Trillium Press.

Robinson, N. M., & Robinson, H. B. (1982). The optimal match: Devising the best compromise for the highly gifted student. In D. H. Feldman (Ed.), *Developmental approaches to giftedness and creativity* (pp. 79–94). San Francisco: Jossey-Bass.

Robinson, N. M., & Robinson, H. B. (1992). The use of standardized tests with young gifted children. In P. S. Klein & A. J. Tannenbaum (Eds.), *To be young and gifted* (pp. 141–170). Norwood, N.J.: Ablex.

Rogers, K. B. (1992). A best-evidence synthesis of research on acceleration options for gifted students. In N. Colangelo, S. G. Assouline, & D. L. Ambroson (Eds.), *Talent development:*

Proceedings from the 1991 Henry B. and Jocelyn Wallace National Research Symposium on Talent Development. Unionville, N.Y.: Trillium Press.

Sayler, M. F., & Lupkowski, A. E. (1992, March–April). Early entrance to college: Weighing the options. *Gifted Child Today*, pp. 24–29.

Stanley, J. C. (1976). The case for extreme educational acceleration of intellectually brilliant youths. *Gifted Child Quarterly* 20:66–75.

Stanley, J. C. (1985a). How did six highly accelerated gifted students fare in graduate school? *Gifted Child Quarterly* 29:180.

Stanley, J. C. (1985b). Young entrants to college: How did they fare? *College and University* 60:219–228.

Stanley, J. C. (1991a). A better model for residential high schools for talented youths. *Phi Delta Kappan* 72:471–473.

Stanley, J. C. (1991b). Critique of "Socioemotional adjustment of adolescent girls enrolled in a residential acceleration program." *Gifted Child Quarterly* 35:67–70.

Stanley, J. C., & Benbow, C. P. (1983). Extremely young college graduates: Evidence of their success. *College and University* 58:361–371.

Stanley, J. C., & McGill, A. M. (1986). More about "Young entrants to college: How did they fare?" *Gifted Child Quarterly* 30:70–73.

Thorndike, R. L., Hagen, E. P., & Sattler, J. M. (1986). *The Stanford-Binet intelligence scale* (4th ed.). Chicago: Riverside.

Wallace, A. (1986). *The prodigy*. New York: E. P. Dutton.

Wiener, N. (1953). *Ex-prodigy: My childhood and youth*. New York: Simon and Schuster.

10   Acceleration among the Terman Males

Correlates in Midlife and After

LEE J. CRONBACH

W hen individual differences at the upper end of the ability continuum gained attention in the early decades of this century, many schools adopted such practices as allowing six-year-olds to enter at the second grade if they could read, allowing exceptional achievers to skip a semester or a year, or encouraging some to complete a four-year high school program in three years. Acceleration continues today, but with more emphasis on supplementary instruction in selected fields than on bodily transplanting the able youngster among appreciably older classmates. Acceleration has always been controversial, and many empirical studies have offered partial evaluations. A symposium volume edited by Southern and Jones (1991) offers an up-to-date review of that research and a description of many current practices. Yet a question that has not been answered is: What can be said about those who *were* markedly accelerated in schools, when we can look at nearly their whole lives?

The Terman Studies

The work of Terman has been influential both because of his advocacy of special consideration for able children and because of his unprecedented follow-up study. The remarkable standardized data collected by Terman during his lifetime were added to repeatedly, thanks to a bequest from Terman and to subsequent grants from the National Institute of Mental Health and the Spencer Foundation. This makes the file a unique resource. Findings about acceleration

179

as it was practiced before 1930 are only indirectly relevant to choices among today's diverse options for serving able pupils, but to say this is merely to recognize that findings in developmental psychology are always shaped by their historical contexts.

Terman began before 1920 to collect records on able young people, and in 1922 began a large-scale search. He asked teachers to nominate promising members of their classes, particularly those who were young for their grade, and arranged a mental test for these children. He then asked the parents of those with IQs of 135 or greater to cooperate with the study. The subjects themselves supplied some early data, but they became the main source of information only with the 1936 follow-up. The present analysis covers responses from 1950 to 1977, because the gerontological themes of the latest questionnaires seem not to fit in with my topic. A book by Holahan and Sears (1995) analyzes data through 1986, without regard to acceleration. It describes the activities, problems, and satisfactions of the later years, and characterizes the loss of cases over the decades.

The Gifted Child Grows Up (Terman & Oden, 1947) devotes a chapter to acceleration. From data collected through 1940 Terman and Oden concluded that (on average) the consequences of acceleration were consistently positive, but (not surprisingly) that acceleration seemed to work out badly for some individuals.

Acceleration is of interest only because we think it has effects. Frequency counts on those who were accelerated would be nearly meaningless by themselves, so I follow Terman and Oden in contrasting them with less-accelerated members of the group. For better comparability, I constructed a counterfactual control group, as will be seen below. My readers will know by heart the warnings of Campbell and Stanley (1963) about drawing causal inferences from nonexperimental contrasts; even so, they will not be able to absorb what I report without thinking causally. The reader risks serious error only if he or she slips into naming acceleration per se as the cause; the events that made up acceleration had their own untraceable prior causes. To avoid generalization, I have framed statements in the past tense; from the word "Go!" the Terman study has been historical research on a particular generation.

Method

The data to be analyzed come from all males having adequately complete data in the Terman file. I discarded men who did not respond at least once after 1936, and a few whose final educational level was uncertain. The cases, recruited by different methods in different years, are not a systematic sample from a definable population. Moreover, because of nonresponse and attrition, the set of cases changes from variable to variable. I therefore make no formal statistical inferences.

Even with ideal sampling, formal significance tests would be misleading because hundreds of variables are available for comparison. In fact, I discuss only about half the variables on which I made trial runs. My first step was to bring forward from each questionnaire the variables bearing on topics that seemed likely to be associated with acceleration. I set aside variables that carried little information because of small effective Ns or lack of variation, and (with exceptions) those for which distributions of accelerated students and controls were much alike. When a question had been repeated from one survey to another, I selected one response date for reporting (after confirming the consistency of the finding with findings at other dates).

The median subject finished high school at about age 17, one year ahead of the California norm. I defined accelerated students as those whose age at high school graduation (HSAGE) was 16–6 or less, and controls as those with an HSAGE of 17–6 to 18–6.[1] Note the eleven-month gap introduced to heighten the contrast. Most of the overage graduates I eliminated were born before 1905. Elder, Pavelko, and Hastings (1991) have shown that the Depression and World War II had different effects on Terman males born before 1911 and those born after 1911. The number of cases did not warrant separate reporting on those age cohorts, but with respect to many conclusions I did check that early-born and late-born subgroups showed similar trends.

The Terman-Oden categories differed from mine. Terman and Oden compared contiguous groups, taking as controls (their Group III) all persons with an HSAGE of 16–6 or more; also, they subdivided the accelerated students with a cut above 15–5. Group III included many who were appreciably past the age of 19 at graduation.

Membership in my groups defined by graduation age correlated 0.3 with IQ. The grouping had an equally strong but parabolic relation to the date of high school graduation (HSDATE). Acceleration was most frequent in the middle of the date range, probably because of the acceptance of acceleration as

---

1. Age at graduation had been written on the 1940 or 1936 blank by the Terman staff, who calculated this in each case, sometimes incorrectly and sometimes from incomplete information. Not all subjects reported month of graduation. This figure was not in the computer file. I began a trial identification of cases by computer subtraction of month and year of birth from year of graduation plus six months. (This assumes June to be the month of graduation.) I compared this first result with the age written on the blank by the staff for each case falling within six months of the cutoff ages for my groups. Ambiguous cases were resolved in the light of all information in the file.

TABLE 10.1. *Percentage Distributions of Age at High School Graduation in Two Analyses*

| | Age at Graduation | | | | | | | | | | |
Source of Data	14 to 14-5	14-6 to 14-11	15 to 15-5	15-5 to 15-11	16 to 16-5	16-6	16-6 to 16-11	17 to 17-5	17-6 to 17-11	18 to 18-5	18-6 and above
Accelerated											
This analysis (N = 195)	2	2	10	25	53	8					
Terman-Oden analysis (N = 217)	3	5	9	33	51	0					
Control											
This analysis (N = 145)							0	0	60	34	6[a]
Terman-Oden analysis (N = 568)							30	34	17	10	9

[a] These cases were at 18-6.

182

TABLE 10.2.   *Percentage of Accelerated Students in Cohorts Defined by Year of High School Graduation*

		Year of Graduation					
	1922	1923–1924	1925–1926	1927–1928	1929–1930	1931–1932	1933–1934
N accelerated	13	34	46	58	29	11	4
Percentage of accelerated students							
Before weighting	32	60	73	68	51	42	36
After weighting	51	56	67	53	40	55	47

a school policy during the 1920s. To reduce the confounding of the acceleration variable with ability and cohort, I examined the proportion of accelerated students in each region of the HSDATE-by-IQ distribution, then trimmed outlying regions where there were too few accelerated students or too few controls for a comparison. Specifically, I eliminated cases with an HSDATE before 1922 or after 1934 (nearly all of them controls) and cases with an IQ of 170 or above (nearly all of them accelerated students). A report that leaves out the brightest accelerated students may seem like *Hamlet* without Hamlet, but I could not defend a comparative analysis that averaged them in.

After these cuts my groups had the IQ distribution presented in table 10.1, which also presents the distribution for the Terman-Oden classification. Terman and Oden designated 72 percent of the subjects as controls. Because I eliminated cases with an HSAGE of 16–7 to 17–5, controls made up just 43 percent of the cases in the present analysis.

I weighted cases, with the aim of bringing the percentage of controls in each cell of the HSDATE-by-IQ plot closer to 50. Accelerated students were weighted 1. I imposed a smooth nonmonotone trend on the weights for controls and held the weights within the range of 0.3 to 3.5. For example, where the HSDATE was 1923, the weights for IQ cells had this trend: 135–139, 0.4; 145–149, 1.6; 155–169, 3.5. The mean weight was 1.18; hence weighting tended to inflate the control frequencies by about one-fifth. The percentage of controls after weighting was 47. (Fine-tuning the weights to bring this percentage to 50 would have had no consequences.) The weighting did remove the trend linking acceleration to IQ.

The weighting damped but did not remove the association of acceleration with HSDATE (see table 10.2); extremely large and small weights would have been required to eliminate the trend. Any calculation on controls from here on is weighted unless I note otherwise.

No direct adjustment was made for year of birth. The interquartile range (unweighted) was 1905–1911 for controls and 1909–1912 for accelerated students. The medians were approximately two years apart.

Results and Discussion

Education Attained

Subjects earned college degrees as late as age 54. Terman's finding of more higher education among accelerated students is confirmed in my more controlled analysis (table 10.3). Here, education is coded at six levels. Degree 2 (DG2) may be, for example, a master's degree or a professional engineering degree. Degree 3 includes all doctorates and most law degrees. (The law degree was usually a second degree, but typically represented more training than a master's degree.) Persons reaching any level are counted at all lower levels.

Transition probabilities amplify the finding. The ratios from table 10.3 generated the "completed high school" line in figure 10.1; these are ratios conditional on completing high school. Other lines are based on selected subsets of cases. The strongest finding is that, among those entering college, accelerated students were more likely to finish. Among those who completed college, accelerated students showed a slightly greater tendency to enter graduate school. Among those who entered, however, controls showed an equally good completion rate.

Educational careers depended on the time elapsed between graduation from high school and graduation from college. A lag of more than four years implies time out of school or slow college progress. Figure 10.2 is instructive. The numbers at the ends of arrows are Ns; transition percentages are also given. There is no difference between the lag distributions for the accelerated students and the controls. At the left can be seen the difference in college graduation rates already mentioned. The controls rarely went to graduate school if the first-degree lag was great, whereas the accelerated students who had experienced lags

TABLE 10.3.   *Percentages Reaching Successive Educational Levels*

| | | | Level Completed | | | |
Group	High School	Some College	College	Some Graduate School	Degree 2	Degree 3
Accelerated	100	91.8	79.5	58.5	49.8	30.8
Control	100	80.4	56.6	34.9	31.2	18.7
Ratio	1.00	1.14	1.40	1.68	1.60	1.65

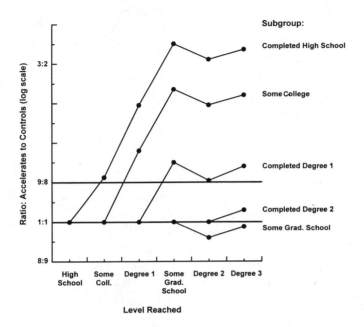

Figure 10.1. Ratio (accelerates:controls) of probabilities of achieving successive levels of education, conditional on having reached earlier stages.

Note: Departures from 1.0 that fall between the dotted lines are negligibly different from 1.

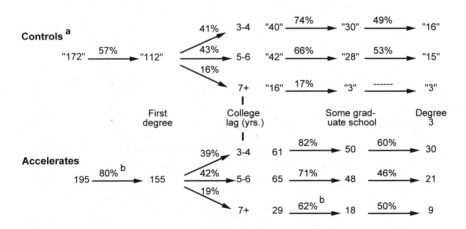

Figure 10.2. Educational progress as a function of acceleration and college lag.

Notes: [a]All control frequencies are weighted.

[b]Accelerates' transition rate differed markedly from the rate for controls.

often went on. A great lag thus did not cost accelerated students as much as it did controls, perhaps because the accelerated students, being younger, were better able to postpone full-time employment.

The undergraduate majors were diverse, and there were few appreciable differences between the groups. Here I report unweighted percentages based on cases whose majors are known. (I do not report on any major accounting for fewer than 10 percent of cases in both of my groups.) Among undergraduate accelerates ($N = 153$) and controls ($N = 91$), the respective percentages choosing engineering and the physical sciences (pooled) were 33 and 22; for the social sciences and history, the percentages were 35 and 35. At the graduate level, with 97 accelerated students and 42 controls, the respective percentages were as follows: engineering or physical science, 21 versus 12; law, 26 versus 21; medicine, 10 versus 19. The small Ns make it unlikely that the differences would have been replicated in another sample from this era. Even so, the greater appeal of engineering and the sciences to the accelerated students is intriguing. And it is surprising that medicine, with its lengthy course of study, did not attract proportionately more of the accelerated students, who had more years at their disposal.

Rated Accomplishment

To compare the groups on adult vocational accomplishment I fell back on a judgment made in 1960 by Melita Oden and Helen Marshall (Oden, 1968, p. 55). They identified as As the one hundred men they considered most successful and as Cs those who had done least well. The accelerated students differed markedly from the controls, having more A ratings and fewer Cs. Among my accelerated students 21 percent were As, but only 11 percent of the controls were (giving a ratio of 1.9:1). The effect is even stronger among persons with advanced degrees: 31 percent to 12 percent, or 2.5:1. (Cf. Oden, 1968, pp. 59–61.)

Work and Income

The extensive data on income must be pruned brutally to fit within a brief chapter. Figure 10.3 presents a summary of earnings in 1958; by then, the subjects were settled in their careers, attrition was not yet a serious problem, and no allowance for retirements was necessary. A smoothing routine has truncated the curves; nevertheless, only about ten cases determine the location for the rightmost section of each curve. The most striking finding is that in a large part of the range, the controls having no graduate degree earned less than men in other subgroups. I confirmed that difference in reports on 1949 incomes and on incomes during the 1960s.

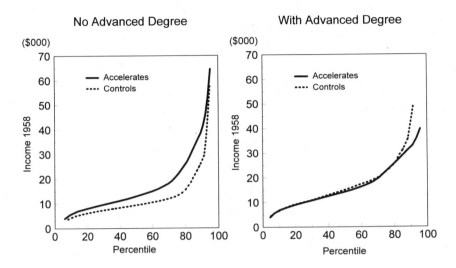

Figure 10.3. Income distributions for accelerated and control groups, subdivided by educational level.

To integrate data over these three times, I determined the median income for the accelerated students and the controls together, and also the 75th percentile. From this I obtained the rounded percentages given in table 10.4. The accelerated students with advanced degrees fared better than the other groups. None of the groups showed a steady relative improvement or decline over the three time periods.

The small numbers of cases in occupational clusters make all findings about them highly tentative. The largest groups were science-engineering (12 percent, an unweighted percentage with all cases in my contrast groups as the base), law (11 percent), and college teaching (8 percent). Upper management and second-tier management combined accounted for 13 percent. The accelerated students gravitated more toward law than toward medicine (13 percent versus 3 percent); for the controls there was no difference (8 percent in each occupation). There was no notable difference between the accelerated students and the controls in other occupations.

Examining incomes within occupations, I found that the big money was made in Hollywood and on Wall Street. Business careers tended to attract persons without advanced degrees, and it was the accelerated students among them who most often attained superior incomes in higher management (see table 10.5).

I checked on the possibility that the accelerated students, having, on aver-

TABLE 10.4. *Percentages Having Superior Incomes in Four Subgroups*

Group	Advanced Degree	Percentage in Upper Half	Percentage in Upper Quarter
Accelerated	Yes	55–65	25–35
Accelerated	No	40–50	25
Control	Yes	45–50	20–30
Control	No	30–35	15
All cases [a]		50	25

Note: Ranges are given because percentages were determined separately in income distributions from 1940 and 1953, and in a summary report of 1960–1969 income.
[a] Includes all accelerated students and all controls.

TABLE 10.5. *Occupations of Individuals Earning High 1958 Incomes as a Function of Acceleration and Education*

Income	Control without Advanced Degree	Accelerated without Advanced Degree	Control with Advanced Degree	Accelerated with Advanced Degree
ca. $600,000		Investment		
ca. $300,000	Entertainment (producer)			
ca. $150,000			Banking	
$100,000–130,000	Entertainment (producer)	Entertainment (writer) Sales management		
$60,000–80,000	Architecture Management	Investment Management		
$50,000		Management (2)	Medicine Law	Investment
$40,000–45,000		Management Law		Medicine Banking
$30,000–39,000	Management (2)	Management (3) Investment (2)	Medicine (2) Chemistry Sales management	Law (4) Medicine (2) Chemistry Engineering Management College teaching
Below $30,000	56 cases	28 cases	73 cases	57 cases

age, entered careers at an earlier age than the others, would have become satiated and retired early. A work-persistence index constructed by Sears recognizes the gradual reduction of working time between age 51 and 70 as well as outright retirement. With adjustments made for the year of birth, the distribution of this index was much the same for accelerated and control students.

Marriage

My last hard fact has to do with marriage. Terman and Oden reported that their accelerated students tended to marry a bit earlier than their controls. Looking at life histories, I found that the proportion ever divorced (an unweighted count) was higher for my controls than for my accelerated students (21 percent versus 14 percent).

Mental Health and Morale

In the early days of the study the mental health and social adjustment of accelerated students were lively concerns. Terman and Oden (1947) recognized an association of maladjustment with acceleration in some cases but concluded that generally such problems were temporary. For evaluation from a later vantage point, the best single source is a 1960 staff rating on emotional problems. Among my accelerated students, 77 percent were rated at that time as having problem-free histories, compared with 63 percent of the controls. Self-ratings at various other times are consistent with this modest positive indication. For example, in 1977, 51 percent of the accelerated students called themselves "very happy," versus 35 percent of the controls.

Satisfactions

The latter-day follow-up collected data on satisfaction, but for comparing accelerated students and controls the data are weak. The 1972 questionnaire asked, "What aspects of your work have given you the greatest satisfaction in recent years?" Because of attrition and ambiguous responses, only about one hundred codable responses per group were available. I found two suggestive differences. The unweighted percentages mentioning friendly relationships with coworkers were 15 for the controls and 5 for the accelerated students. For mentions of pleasure in competing or winning recognition, the percentages were 10 and 26.

In 1977, the project asked subjects to look back on their lives and rate the satisfaction they had found in various areas. The responses of the accelerated students were generally more positive than those of the controls.[2] (See table 10.6.) For example, the modal accelerated student reported that his work had been "highly satisfactory," whereas the modal control checked "generally satisfactory."

The accelerated students' report on the social side of life, more positive than that of the controls, is especially significant. When subjects were asked in 1940 about ways acceleration had hindered them, the only hindrance mentioned at all often was having been deprived of a normal social life in high

2. I investigated the contrasts also on a similar question asked in 1972. The two instruments offered different probes and different response scales. Perhaps because of a fault in the format, the 1972 report showed weaker trends than the ones I report from the 1977 data, but did not contradict them.

TABLE 10.6.   *Reported Lifetime Satisfaction in Seven Aspects of Life*

| | Percentage Saying Highly Satisfactory | | |
Aspect	Control	Accelerated	Ratio
Marriage (current or most recent)	74	64	.9
Your children	58	56	1.0
Cultural activities	15	15	1.0
Recreation	24	35	1.5
Community service	10	17	1.7
Friendship, social contacts	17	35	2.1
Income-producing work	28	61	2.2

school or college. As Terman and Oden predicted, abnormal experiences did not prevent the accelerated students from going on to normal or better-than-normal family and social lives. A quantitative survey cannot tell us, however, about the lasting qualitative effects that may have followed the loss of normal opportunities to learn from peers (for example, regarding gender-role behavior).

Summary

This reanalysis of the Terman files, tracing from about 1922 to 1977 a group of able persons, has compared those who finished high school at about age 15 or 16 with those who graduated near age 18. (The brightest accelerated students, lacking comparable controls, were omitted from these comparisons.) In many aspects of their adult lives those who were accelerated did not differ as a group from the roughly equated controls. Every nontrivial difference that did appear on a value-laden variable showed those who had been accelerated at an advantage. As usual, of course, variation within groups far exceeded variation between groups. Frankly, I had not expected to find effects cropping up in responses forty or fifty years after high school graduation. I expected the vicissitudes of life gradually to wash out the initial differences favoring those chosen for acceleration. Instead, it appears that their personal qualities or the encouragement and tangible boost given by acceleration, or both, produced a lasting increment of momentum.

References

Campbell, D. T., & Stanley, J. C. (1963). Experimental and quasi-experimental designs for research on teaching. In N. L. Gage (Ed.), *Handbook of research on teaching* (pp. 171–246). Chicago: Rand McNally.

Elder, G. H., Jr., Pavelko, H., & Hastings, T. H. (1991). Talent, history, and the fulfillment of promise. *Psychiatry* 54:251–267.

Holahan, C. K., & Sears, R. R. (1995). *The gifted group in later maturity*. Stanford: Stanford University Press.

Oden, M. H. (1968). The fulfillment of promise: Forty-year follow-up of the Terman gifted group. *Genetic Psychology Monographs* 77:3–93.

Southern, W. T., & Jones, E. D. (Eds.). (1991). *The academic acceleration of gifted children*. New York: Teachers College Press.

Terman, L. M., & Oden, M. H. (1947). *The gifted child grows up*. Stanford: Stanford University Press.

11   The Elephant in the Classroom

Ability Grouping and the Gifted

ELLIS B. PAGE AND TIMOTHY Z. KEITH

"Intelligence"—that quaint term—has become a source of embarrassment. There is pressure not to acknowledge that variance in human mental ability exists, a feeling that we should not mention such variance, and that if we were really virtuous we would be blind to it.

This is especially true in regard to the group with high intelligence—the gifted. Fashionable attention is aimed the other way, with extensive programs to help those of lesser ability, and these programs have led to a new vocabulary of politically correct speech. In a questionnaire sent to school principals asking how many gifted children they had in their schools, 27 percent said they had none. Because, of course, the next question might be: What are you doing for these gifted students?

The Elephant

It is as if we had an elephant in a classroom, but there were strict rules not to see it. We can imagine the teacher on the first day:

"Now class, it is common that when students first come in, they have the silly impression that there is some large, noisy, lumbering animal in this room. Don't feel embarrassed if you have the same idea [chuckle]. It's only natural.

"But, of course, we all know that there is no such animal outside of old folk tales. You have this idea just because you have been told about it.

"If you're going to do well here, you have to get rid of this idea. Let's not hear any talk about tusks, or trunks, or big gray ears, or the other things that people imagine."

Yet talent searches across the country have made it much more difficult to ignore the elephants in our classrooms. Each year, more than 140,000 twelve-year-olds take the SAT or ACT and submit their scores to talent searches and, thereby, make their talents public.

Having found these talented youngsters, what should we do with them? They require special provisions, special classes, and acceleration. Consequently, talent-search programs across the land have begun to offer work tailored for such youngsters.

So now we all recognize the elephant, yes?

No.

There are large numbers of gifted students who require special educational attention. Yet those dictating school policy, and those controlling group-think in education, often reject the very idea of the elephant. This rejection is strident, and it seems to be gaining momentum. Far from supporting the addition of new programs for the talented, the current mood reacts emotionally against the ones we have now.

Tracking

Nowhere is this trend more evident than with regard to the question of tracking or ability grouping: assigning students to different classrooms according to mental ability or subject-matter precocity. In this chapter we will treat the general question of whether students should be instructionally grouped for educational ability; we will not probe here the distinctions some make among grouping, tracking, mainstreaming, and so forth. Our interest is in a broad, psychological treatment of the current debate about instruction and student ability.

This chapter addresses the "detracking" movement in today's schools. As Passow (1988) notes, the literature on this subject ranges "from scholarly re-ports of research findings to philosophical statements to emotional polemics" (p. 205). Indeed, today the general assault typically emphasizes these polemics, with the charged word "inequality" dominating much of the language of those against ability grouping. Consider an article cowritten by Jeannie Oakes, a professor at the University of California at Los Angeles and perhaps the move-ment's most visible advocate. This article was published in the *Phi Delta Kap-pan* under the title "Detracking Schools: Early Lessons from the Field" (Oakes

& Lipton, 1992): "During the past decade, research on tracking and ability-grouped class assignments has provided striking evidence that these practices have a negative impact on most children's school opportunities and outcomes. Moreover, the negative consequences of these practices disproportionately affect *low-income, African-American, and Latino children*" (p. 448; emphasis added). "Striking evidence"? She cites works by others and herself, and two of her own titles give a sense of the movement's intention: *Keeping Track: How Schools Structure Inequality* (Oakes, 1985) and *Multiplying Inequalities: The Effects of Race, Social Class, and Tracking on Opportunities to Learn Math and Science* (Oakes, 1990).

Another writer who finds ability grouping culpable is Linda Darling-Hammond (1991): "These curricular differences explain much of the disparity between the achievement of white and minority students and between the achievement of higher- and lower-income students. . . . In this way the uses of tests have impeded rather than supported the pursuit of high and rigorous educational goals for all students." Darling-Hammond cites Lee and Bryk (1988), Oakes, and others to support her remarkable charges, which blame classroom grouping for many of the average differences between race and class groups.

Attackers of ability grouping particularly cite key articles by Robert Slavin (1987, 1988, 1990a), whose "best-evidence syntheses" are taken as the strongest scientific statements for their side.[1] On the other side, defending ability grouping, are critics of Slavin's methods and conclusions (Gamoran, 1987; Hallinan, 1990; Hiebert, 1987; Kulik, 1985; Kulik, 1991; Kulik & Kulik, 1982, 1984, 1987; Nevi, 1987; Walberg, 1988).

Although the scientific arguments seem to favor ability grouping, anyone who visits schools sees an apparently headlong movement to abandon it in practice. And American citizens, who pay for and suffer from decisions about

---

1. But see Slavin, Madden, Karweit, Livermon, & Dolan (1990) for a remarkable contradiction of the antitracking principle: in the "Success for All" program, which he reports as highly effective, primary students are put into reading groups for ninety minutes a day on the basis of reading level. Especially note the reasons Slavin and his colleagues claim for its success: "The idea behind regrouping is to allow teachers to teach the whole reading class without having to break the class into reading groups. This *greatly reduces the time needed* for seatwork and *increases direct instruction time.* . . . It does ensure that every reading class will be at *only one reading level, eliminating workbooks, dittos, or other follow-up activities* that are needed in classes with multiple reading groups" (emphasis added).

Slavin's own strategy in practice is especially notable in sweeping aside any social considerations: "a reading class might contain *first-, second-, and third-grade students* all reading at the same level" (p. 259, emphasis added). The physical and social differences between first and third grade are, of course, tremendous. And both children and their families will be well aware of these dramatic group differences.

the schools, decidedly favor the placement of "mentally handicapped" children in special classes. A recent Gallup poll shows 67 percent to 22 percent in support of such tracking (Elam, Rose, & Gallup, 1992, p. 51).

Our profession needs to respond to the claims against tracking, because if they are believed, and class assignments are reorganized without regard to mental ability, the movement away from tracking could greatly affect the future of students, especially of the most gifted students.

Problems of Evidence

The key question is: Does tracking help students or hurt them? Most educators of the gifted would probably say that it helps the abler students. Does tracking hurt other students? Many people claim that it damages poor, black, and Hispanic students, and some would agree with the statement that it destroys "high and rigorous" standards for "all students" (Darling-Hammond, 1991).

Any debate about cause and effect involves problems of evidence. Where should we look for proof? Basically, there appear to be four lines of evidence. These are:

1. Indirect argument from principles of measurement

2. Indirect argument from principles of learning

3. Direct sampling from experimental evidence

4. Direct sampling from nonexperimental data sets

Principles of Measurement

Under the principles of measurement, one of the two basic disciplines of educational psychology, ability differences are accepted by virtually all scientists as important and as strongly rooted in biology. These principles have been revealed for generations by Galton, Spearman, Binet, Terman, and many others.[2]

Almost all scientists agree that intelligence (or g) is easily found as a general or higher-order factor in virtually any set of measures of mental ability, verbal or nonverbal, "fluid" or "crystallized" (Cattell, 1987). G is also widely acknowledged as the best overall predictor of school and occupational success (Ree & Earles, 1992; Schmidt & Hunter, 1992). Indeed, g is well correlated even

2. This is not the place to argue these elementary and other principles, since they may be found in most advanced texts on measurement, learning, behavior genetics, and similar subjects.

with measures, such as nerve-response time, that are totally noncultural (see, e.g., Jensen, 1992). And the rationale for using multiple competence tests in place of intelligence tests has for the most part been set aside (see, e.g., Barrett & Depinet, 1991).

Opponents of ability grouping commonly claim that mental tests are racially biased, but testing experts are virtually in complete agreement that they are not (see Humphreys, 1992; Linn, 1982). In short, the findings of measurement indirectly support ability grouping in classes as being useful, noninjurious, and nondiscriminatory.

Principles of Learning

In educational psychology, the other major theme is that school learning acts according to certain "laws" common to most learning: principles investigated by Pavlov, Ebbinghaus, Skinner, Thorndike, and many others. Among the widely accepted principles are: working from the simple to the complex, working from the known to the unknown, and starting each lesson near each student's current level of achievement. The idea of individual "readiness" is meant to summarize such principles.

Learning is commonly taken to be individual in locus. It is exhibited in individual behavior and (biochemically) takes place within a single nervous system. Opponents of ability grouping are quite hostile to this emphasis on the individual. One opponent spoke at a session of the American Educational Research Association of the need for "less individualism and more communitarianism" (Annual Meeting of the AERA, San Francisco, April 1992). To sidestep this problem of individual differences, opponents of grouping often argue that the best instruction is through "cooperative learning" (see, e.g., Slavin, 1983). In such instruction, the huge problems of heterogeneity are obscured by many student interactions in smaller subsets (each small group having the stronger students teaching the weaker ones). In such classrooms, grades may be given for the performance of the group rather than for the performance of the individual.

Opponents of tracking must reject these established principles of measurement and learning, either by ignoring them or by attacking them (e.g., by claiming that mental tests are biased). But these two major areas of psychological theory, measurement and learning, with their mountains of cumulative evidence and reasoning, provide powerful indirect evidence in favor of grouping students for efficient instruction. And ability grouping has been strongly favored by classroom teachers, surely a sort of testimony that should be properly weighed before drastic changes are made (cf. ERIC Clearinghouse on Tests, Measurement, and Evaluation, 1988, which summarizes teachers' attitudes toward mainstreaming, and Reddick & Pearch, 1984, which reports on nearly a thousand teachers' feelings about tracking).

When researchers study applied questions, however, we commonly wish to go beyond such background principles and to study how various policies have fared in practice. Thus we consider here the two major sources of direct evidence about practices: experimentation in the schools and nonexperimental models using large data sets.

Experimental Evidence

We turn again to one of Julian Stanley's most important contributions to the social sciences: his comprehensive study of research design (see, e.g., Campbell & Stanley, 1963). If we were working in the laboratory sciences, we could perform true experiments, in which the key causal variable (here, ability grouping) would be assigned randomly to the experimental subjects (the students). Then the experimental effect might be estimated from appropriate tests taken by the students.

But in the schools, instruction must take place in classrooms. The appropriate "subjects" would properly be such classrooms, and the evidence would be classroom means on the proper tests. (These are still based on individual scores, and do not contradict the essentially private nature of learning.) In the real world, however, it is unlikely that teachers could be assigned to classrooms at random within a school. Too many other adjustments would be required in the ongoing curriculum.

The assumption behind ability grouping is that the curriculum should be adjusted to the ability levels of the students. If teachers were assigned at random, then it seems unlikely that there would be as much adjustment as when teachers are used to teaching certain defined levels of ability. It seems improbable, then, that the outcome of a random experiment would truly represent the long-term effects of such grouping.

Robert Slavin (1987, 1990b) preferred the data from "experiments," and emphasized those in his "best-evidence" summaries. Thus, for secondary schools (1990b), he reviewed six studies that were "randomized," nine that were "matched," and fourteen correlational studies. His own conclusion was that the results were sufficiently mixed as not to prove overall beneficial effects. He therefore concluded that because his research did not prove benefits in achievement, ability grouping was wrong. In sum, he was opposed to grouping for reasons other than the evidence he collected. He acknowledged, "I am *personally opposed to ability grouping*, and, particularly in the absence of any evidence of positive effects for anyone, I believe that between-class ability grouping should be greatly reduced" (1990a, p. 506, emphasis added).[3]

Thus, when Slavin's review failed to convince him of any benefits of grouping, he declared that "there [was] little reason to maintain the practice" (1990b, p. 492). He is often cited by other opponents of grouping, such as Oakes and Darling-Hammond, as if he had indeed proved harm. But this is not the case. Other scholars, frequently studying the same materials as Slavin, have reached quite different conclusions (Feldhusen, 1989, 1991; Gamoran, 1986; Gamoran & Berends, 1987; Kulik & Kulik, 1987).

In any case, the evidence from true experiments is quite thin. Little wonder; such experiments would be disruptive of the usual practices in a school or classroom, and would require much new preparation. Yet paradoxically, an experiment would be invalid if it did *not* cause school changes from one treatment to another, since it would then not represent the potential differences in curriculum and teaching made possible by grouping.

Nonexperimental Evidence

Because major experimental assignments can be so disruptive, we must look elsewhere for data to test our policies.

The good news is that the federal government has produced massive data sets of highly generalizable materials. These began with Project Talent in the 1960s (the records of which are, however, virtually unreachable by the common researcher). The 1972 National Longitudinal Study (NLS) with five follow-ups through 1986, has been made widely available on computer tapes. And in 1980 there appeared the massive High School and Beyond (HSB), the first in a series of tapes, now out on disks for personal computers. In its follow-ups (1982, 1984, and 1986), HSB also presented much information about school curricula and some aspects of tracking. Still more recent data sets now exist: the National Assessment of Educational Progress (NAEP) and the National Educational Longitudinal Study (NELS, of 1988 and after).

The bad news is this: to study the effects of ability grouping, we ideally need data about both ability and grouping. NLS and HSB are the only data sets with good ability measures—that is, test results largely independent of the

3. As the scholar can easily note, there often is a division along disciplinary lines, with sociologists usually opposed to grouping (see also Kerckhoff, 1986), and measurement specialists more often in favor of it. But there are distinguished exceptions on both sides.

achievement measures for the same students. But in these data sets the tracking practices are often difficult to identify. On the other hand, grouping practices are clearer in the more recent data sets (NAEP and NELS), but intelligence measures are nonexistent apart from those for achievement in the various subject-matter areas. In earlier data sets (Talent, NLS, and HSB), student ability was the most useful correlate, the most powerful predictor, for a host of important educational outcomes. It was far more important than income, social class, ethnicity, or school practices.

One fears that ability was too explanatory for political correctness; these nonschool, nonverbal subtests have been removed from the new data sets. Even the brief vocabulary quiz, such a quick and useful measure of general ability, has been stricken from the newer data sets. How unfortunate! And especially unfortunate are the researchers wishing to study ability grouping and its effects on achievement, who have no measures of ability not confounded with the achievement measures they are trying to explain. For this study, we have chosen High School and Beyond, with its good ability measures. (But as noted below, we have had to compromise on the estimation of ability grouping.)

There are other weaknesses in the nonexperimental data with regard to our questions. One is the assignment to classes. Rarely will this be made totally on the basis of an ability score. More often some other factor, such as past accomplishment, will influence a student's assignment to an abler or less able classroom. Such other factors may make the abler classroom appear more effective in its curriculum than it really is, and the weaker class less effective than it is. (This may often lead to a belief that ability grouping had good or bad effects, when both are illusions caused by the methods used to select the high and low groups.)

In short, when we look at the present arguments about ability grouping, we find no persuasive case for those who wish to abolish it. To the contrary, we find that the principles of both measurement and learning argue *for* ability grouping. And we find no direct evidence, whether experimental or nonexperimental, to justify wiping out ability grouping. Yet there are sources of data for analysis, and we would like, in what follows, to cast more light on such grouping than we have seen in the literature to date.

Ability Grouping or Academic Programs?

We have encountered the same difficulties as others in conducting research on the effects of ability grouping, and, as a result, our evidence about tracking is indirect. But it is also highly relevant to the debate.

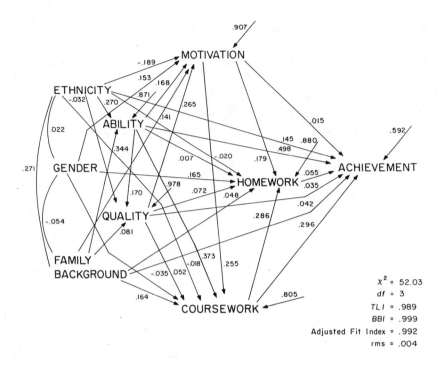

Figure 11.1. The effects of ability, quality of schooling, motivation, academic coursework, and homework on high school student achievement.

Source: Keith & Cool (1992). Copyright © 1992 by Division 16, American Psychological Association.

The difficulties in conducting research on the effects of ability grouping are magnified at the high school level because students can choose—or are assigned—different types of courses. Thus, the effects of ability grouping are confounded with those of streaming into vocational, general, and academic programs.

But what about such streams? Should they not provide us with some information about ability grouping? Our own research and that of others, for example, suggests that academic coursework is among the most powerful influences on high school students' learning (Keith & Cool, 1992; Keith & Page, 1985).

To narrow the focus: does participation in an academic program, rather than a general-education or vocational program, improve student learning? We attempt to answer that question and then look at its relevance for ability grouping.

Method

For all the analyses discussed here we have used the senior cohort of the 1980 HSB. This data set provides a nationally representative sample of more than fifty-eight thousand high school students, with twenty-eight thousand seniors. For intelligence, this cohort provides fairly robust measures, including some elementary measures little related to the high school curriculum. On the achievement side, however, the measures are of fairly basic skills rather than of the advanced abilities we would prefer to assess. Thus, we have some concerns about ceiling effects for any gifted students in the cohort.

We have conducted ordinary multiple regression analyses, which we will present as path models.

Effects of Academic Programs

Does participation in an academic track improve learning? To answer that question, we simply compared, using a dummy variable, students in an academic track (coded 1) with students in a vocational or general-education track (coded 0).

The model is presented in figure 11.2. We also controlled for students' ethnicity, family background (or socioeconomic status), and intellectual ability. The ability component included two vocabulary tests and two mosaic comparison tests—two nonverbal measures that load as well as the vocabulary tests

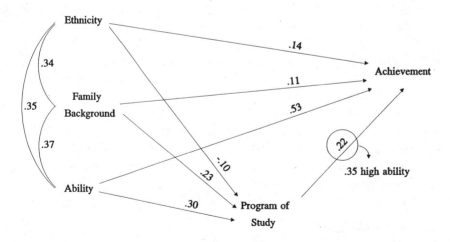

Figure 11.2. The effects of high school track—academic versus other—on student achievement.

on a general-intelligence factor. The achievement component included two mathematics tests and one reading test.

The type of program had a substantial effect on student achievement (.22). This is impressive, especially for such a grossly categorized variable as academic program; the .22 figure suggests that one's program in high school has a substantial effect on one's high school academic achievement.

Such programs, of course, are not exactly the same as ability grouping. But what is of interest is the comparison of the effect on students in general with the effect on high-ability students. We next selected only those students who scored a standard deviation or more above the mean. When we re-ran the model for these higher-ability youth, we found what can only be described as a massive .35. Thus, it appears that an academic track is even more beneficial for bright students than for others, and that abler students who are not placed in more challenging courses are being injured in their tested outcomes.

As we noted, this is indirect evidence. But it suggests that opponents of tracking may be off the mark, especially for gifted youth.

Effects of Homogeneous Grouping

The evidence for type of high school program is suggestive, but indirect. We return, then, to the central question: Is clustering by ability good or bad for gifted youth? Another way to look at this question is to ask whether students—especially gifted students—perform better in homogeneous or in heterogeneous ability groups. Refocusing the question as homogeneity versus heterogeneity gives us more flexibility in answering it. HSB does not have adequate data about grouping per se, and thus we cannot resolve this question with our data at the class level. We can, however, broaden the question and examine the effect of homogeneity versus heterogeneity at the school level.

HSB used a two-stage sampling procedure, with schools as the first level, and up to thirty-six seniors selected at random from each school. We calculated the standard deviation of the ability scores for each school and thus created a measure of the heterogeneity of ability at each of the nearly one thousand schools in HSB. Then we reversed the standard deviation of ability so that homogeneous schools received high scores and heterogeneous schools received low ones. We then used this new variable to examine the effect on student achievement of the homogeneity in ability—the underlying theme of ability grouping.

Effects on All Students

The first analysis held no surprises. Homogeneity in ability had a positive effect on achievement (see figure 11.3), but it was a small one. Indeed, even though

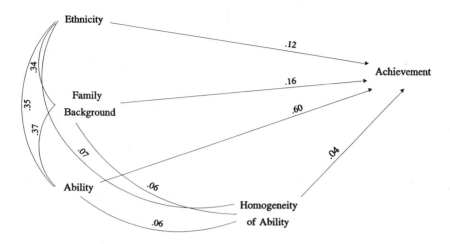

Figure 11.3. The effects of homogeneous ability grouping on high school achievement.

this effect is statistically significant, we generally do not consider paths below
.05 meaningful. This finding corresponds quite well with that of Kulik and
Kulik (1987): ability grouping shows a (rather slight) overall favorable effect on
achievement.

High-Ability Youth

But our concern in this research is primarily with gifted youth rather than
youth in general. Is homogeneous grouping helpful or harmful for brighter
students? When we selected only the top 16 percent of seniors, our analyses
painted a quite different picture. When we examined the effects of homogeneity
on high-ability students, we found a moderate influence of homogeneity on
achievement (.13; see figure 11.4). (This and subsequent figures focus only on
the effects of variability in ability; other effects are not included.)

Greater variability produces lower achievement, and greater homogeneity
produces higher achievement. That is, high-ability students perform better
when they are in a homogeneous, rather than a heterogeneous, environment.

Opponents of ability grouping may argue that these findings are well and
good, but that ability grouping is harmful for minority students. When we
examined the effect of homogeneity on high-ability *black* youth, however, we
found it had a much stronger effect on these students than on high-ability
students in general. Whereas homogeneity has a moderate positive effect on all
high-ability youth (.13), it has a very strong positive effect on high-ability black
youth (.32; see figure 11.4). This powerful effect suggests that we should oppose

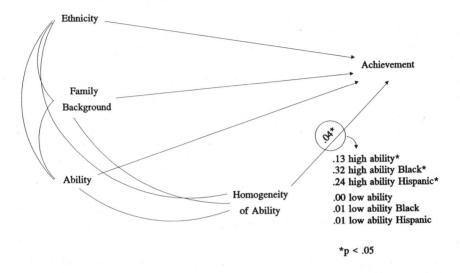

Figure 11.4. The effects of homogeneous ability grouping on high-ability, high-ability minority, and low-ability students' achievement.

heterogeneity and support grouping. Also, we found a substantial effect in favor of grouping for high-ability Hispanic youth (.24; see figure 11.4).

"Well," our hypothetical opponent of grouping might say, "grouping may be good for high-ability youth, but it undoubtedly is harmful for low-ability youth." Again our data disagree. Ability grouping had no substantive positive or negative effect on low-ability students in general (.00), on low-ability black students (.01), or on low-ability Hispanic students (.01). Contrary to current conventional wisdom, surrounding a low-ability student with a homogeneous group of students seems to have no effect. Homogeneous grouping is not apparently helpful for such students, but neither is it harmful.

Other Outcomes

Our opponent might argue (as opponents have time and again) that our analyses are too narrow because they focus only on achievement as an outcome. Does research not show that grouping is detrimental to students' self-esteem and aspirations? Such arguments rest on assumptions about the ill effects of grouping or of other systems of classification or labeling. For a deep analysis of the defects of "labeling theory," see Gordon's (1980) critique. But what of our own findings with the HSB data? Again, we could find no support for such arguments.

Educational Aspirations

We studied the effects of homogeneity in ability on students' educational aspirations: how far they and their parents want them to go in school (see figure 11.5). On students in general there were no effects of homogeneity in ability on aspirations. On high-ability students there was a small positive effect, and on high-ability Hispanic students there was a moderate positive effect. The effect on high-ability black students was insignificant.

Self-Concept

We also studied the effects of homogeneity on students based on a four-item self-concept scale in HSB (cf. Pottebaum, Keith, & Ehly, 1986). Grouping had no significant effect on students in general, on high-ability students, on high-ability black students, or on high-ability Hispanic students (see figure 11.6).

Locus of Control

Similarly, we studied the effects of homogeneity on students based on a four-item locus-of-control scale. On students in general and on high-ability students, being in a homogeneous group had a significant, but nonmeaningful, positive effect on locus of control. Homogeneous grouping had insignificant effects on the locus of control of high-ability black and Hispanic students.

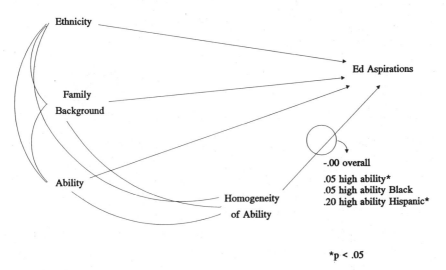

Figure 11.5. The effects of homogeneous ability grouping on students' educational aspirations.

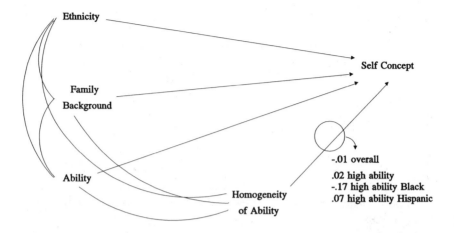

Figure 11.6. The effects of homogeneous ability grouping on students' self-concept.

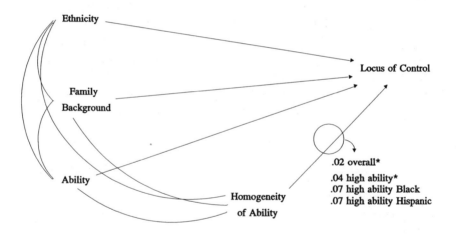

Figure 11.7. The effects of homogeneous ability grouping on students' locus of control.

In summary, we could find no evidence that grouping—attending schools with a homogeneous instead of a heterogeneous group of students, as ascertained by our ability measures—had any negative effect on these important nonacademic criteria. Indeed, the only significant effects we found are *in favor of* such grouping. Although supporting data are not presented here, there were also essentially no effects on students of low ability.

Caveats

We have already noted the problems and dangers of nonexperimental research, and we should, therefore, be cautious in our interpretation of these findings. Critics of grouping might argue that our research is flawed in other ways. Perhaps we find these effects because our ability measure is verbally weighted. Our hypothetical critic might argue that we should instead examine nonverbal ability, because it may be a "fairer" yardstick for minority youth. In fact, the effects in favor of grouping were even stronger when our examinations used the control of nonverbal ability (mosaic comparisons) alone.

Perhaps homogeneity of ability is simply a proxy for the average ability of the school. That is, is it not simply high-ability youth going to school with other high-ability youth that makes the difference? No. The addition of the mean ability of the school in our models made no substantive difference in these results.

Critics can point out that it is not really grouping we are studying. Our analyses have concerned the homogeneity of ability at the school level rather than at the classroom level. Our choice to study homogeneity was one of necessity; HSB simply had no adequate measures of grouping, unconfounded with other variables such as students' high school streams. And in some ways, homogeneity may be a preferred variable to study. It is, after all, at the heart of the controversy: Do students learn better in an environment with students similar to themselves, or with those different from themselves?

In addition, if we had been able to control for grouping at the classroom level rather than at the school level, our results—generally in favor of grouping for high-ability youth—would logically have been stronger rather than weaker. Undoubtedly some of the highly heterogeneous schools practice grouping at the classroom level, thus gaining some of the positive effects of homogeneity. Therefore, the positive effects found here may *underestimate* the true effects of grouping.

Finally, these results in favor of homogeneous schools were obtained with fairly basic measures of reading and math achievement. If the HSB tests had contained measures of advanced knowledge in these and other subject matters, our effects would again likely be stronger. Better measurement of grouping and achievement would likely result in stronger, not weaker, estimates of the positive effects of homogeneous ability groups on high-ability youth.

Summary

Schooling in a homogeneous group of students appears to have a positive effect on high-ability students' achievements, and even stronger effects on the achievements of high-ability minority youth. Grouping does not seem to affect negatively the achievements of low-ability youth. Indeed, ability grouping seems to have no consistent negative effects on any group or any outcome we studied.

Therefore, we reject the claims of opponents of ability grouping that it is harmful to students' achievements, aspirations, or self-perceptions. Instead, we assert that ability grouping may have positive effects on gifted students' learning, the most important educational outcome, and that these effects seem particularly powerful on gifted minority youth. If grouping indeed has positive effects on high-ability youth and no negative effects on low-ability youth, we can see no reason to support the current trend away from ability grouping. Talents are far too rare, and too valuable for society, to be sacrificed on an altar of blind egalitarianism.

Acknowledgments

Thanks are given to Robert Gordon, John S. Lutz, Harry Passow, and Betsy Becker for useful comments and information.

References

Barrett, G. V., & Depinet, R. L. (1991). A reconsideration of testing for competence rather than for intelligence. *American Psychologist* 46:1012–1024.

Campbell, D. T., & Stanley, J. S. (1966). *Experimental and quasi-experimental designs for research.* Chicago: Rand McNally.

Cattell, R. B. (1987). *Intelligence: Its structure, growth, and action.* New York: Elsevier.

Darling-Hammond, L. (1991). The implications of testing policy for quality and equality. *Phi Delta Kappan* 73:220–225.

Elam, S. M., Rose, L. C., & Gallup, A. M. (1992). The twenty-fourth annual Gallup–Phi Delta Kappa poll of the public's attitudes toward the public schools. *Phi Delta Kappan* 74:41–53.

ERIC Clearinghouse on Tests, Measurement, and Evaluation. (1988). *Measuring teacher attitudes toward mainstreaming.* (ERIC Document Reproduction Service No. ED 289885)

Feldhusen, J. F. (1989). Synthesis of research on gifted youth. *Educational Leadership* 46:6–11.

Feldhusen, J. F. (1991). Susan Allan sets the record straight: Response to Allan. *Educational Leadership* 48:66.

Gamoran, A. (1986). Instructional and institutional effects of ability grouping. *Sociology of Education* 59:185–198.

Gamoran, A. (1987). Organization, instruction, and the effects of ability grouping: Comment on Slavin's "best-evidence synthesis." *Review of Educational Research* 57:341–345.

Gamoran, A., & Berends, M. (1987). *The effects of stratification in secondary schools: Synthesis of survey and ethnographic research.* Madison, Wisc.: National Center on Effective Secondary Schools.

Gordon, R. A. (1980). Examining labelling theory: The case of mental retardation. In W. R. Gove (Ed.), *The labelling of deviance: Evaluating a perspective* (2nd ed., pp. 111–174). Beverly Hills, Calif.: Sage.

Hallinan, M. T. (1990). The effects of ability grouping in secondary schools: A response to Slavin's best-evidence synthesis. *Review of Educational Research* 60:501–504.

Hiebert, E. H. (1987). The context of instruction and student learning: An examination of Slavin's assumptions. *Review of Educational Research* 57:337–340.

Humphreys, L. G. (1992). Commentary: What both critics and users of ability tests need to know. *Psychological Science* 3:271–274.

Jensen, A. R. (1992). Commentary: Vehicles of g. *Psychological Science* 3:275–278.

Keith, T. Z., & Cool, V. A. (1992). Testing models of school learning: Effects of quality of instruction, motivation, academic coursework, and homework on academic achievement. *School Psychology Quarterly* 7:207–226.

Keith, T. Z., & Page, E. B. (1985). Do Catholic high schools improve minority student achievement? *American Educational Research Journal* 22:337–349.

Kerckhoff, A. C. (1986). Effects of ability grouping in British secondary schools. *American Sociological Review* 51:842–858.

Kulik, C. C. (1985). *Effects of inter-class ability grouping on achievement and self-esteem.* Paper presented at the annual convention of the American Psychological Association, Los Angeles.

Kulik, J. A. (1991). Findings on grouping are often distorted: Response to Allan. *Educational Leadership* 48:67.

Kulik, J. A., & Kulik, C. C. (1982). Effects of ability grouping on secondary students: A meta-analysis of evaluation findings. *American Educational Research Journal* 19:415–428.

Kulik, J. A., & Kulik, C. C. (1984). Synthesis of research on effects of accelerated instruction. *Educational Leadership* 42:84–89.

Kulik, J. A., & Kulik, C. C. (1987). Effects of ability grouping on school achievement. *Equity and Excellence* 23:22–30.

Lee, V., & Bryk, A. (1988). Curriculum tracking as mediating the social distribution of high school achievement. *Sociology of Education* 61:78–94.

Linn, R. L. (1982). Ability testing: Individual differences, prediction, and differential prediction. In A. K. Wigdor & W. R. Garner (Eds.), *Ability testing: Uses, consequences, and controversies* (pp. 335–388). Washington, D.C.: National Academy Press.

Nevi, C. (1987). In defense of tracking. *Educational Leadership* 44:24–26.

Oakes, J. (1985). *Keeping track: How schools structure inequality.* New Haven: Yale University Press.

Oakes, J. (1990). *Multiplying inequalities: The effects of race, social class, and tracking on opportunities to learn math and science.* Santa Monica, Calif.: RAND.

Oakes, J., & Lipton, M. (1992). Detracking schools: Early lessons from the field. *Phi Delta Kappan* 73:448–454.

Passow, A. H. (1988). Issues of access to knowledge: Group tracking. In L. N. Tanner (Ed.), *Critical issues in curriculum* (pp. 205–225). Eighty-seventh Yearbook of the National Society for the Study of Education (Part 1). Chicago: University of Chicago Press.

Pottebaum, S. M., Keith, T. Z., & Ehly, S. W. (1986). Is there a causal relation between self-concept and academic achievement? *Journal of Educational Research* 79:140–144.

Reddick, T. L., & Pearch, L. E. (1984). *Attitudes toward curriculum issues among rural educators in Tennessee.* Paper presented at the annual meeting of the Mid-South Educational Research Association, New Orleans.

Ree, M. J., & Earles, J. A. (1992). Intelligence is the best predictor of job performance. *Current Directions in Psychological Science* 1:86–89.

Schmidt, F. L., & Hunter, J. E. (1992). Development of a causal model of processes determining job performance. *Current Directions in Psychological Science* 1:89–92.

Slavin, R. E. (1983). *Cooperative learning.* New York: Longman.

Slavin, R. E. (1987). Ability grouping and student achievement in elementary schools: A best-evidence synthesis. *Review of Educational Research* 57:293–336.

Slavin, R. E. (1988). Synthesis of research on grouping in elementary and secondary schools. *Educational Leadership* 46:67–77.

Slavin, R. E. (1990a). Ability grouping in secondary schools: A response to Hallinan. *Review of Educational Research* 60:505–507.

Slavin, R. E. (1990b). *Achievement effects of ability grouping in secondary schools: A best-evidence synthesis*. Madison, Wisc.: National Center on Effective Secondary Schools.

Slavin, R. E., Madden, N. A., Karweit, N. L., Livermon, B. J., & Dolan, L. (1990). Success for all: First-year outcomes of a comprehensive plan for reforming urban education. *American Educational Research Journal* 27:255–278.

Walberg, H. J. (1988). Response to Slavin: What's the best evidence? *Educational Leadership* 46:28.

12   What Is Learned in School and What Is Learned Outside?

JAMES S. COLEMAN

n what subject areas that are covered in the curriculum does school make the most difference, and in what subject areas does it make the least difference? The question first occurred to me a number of years ago when I was reviewing results of the studies conducted by the International Association for the Evaluation of Achievement of literature, reading, and science done in the 1970s. These studies were carried out in a number of countries and at three age levels: age ten, age fourteen, and the last year of upper secondary school (age eighteen in most countries). The research was reported in three volumes, one for science, one for literature (only at ages fourteen and eighteen), and one for reading comprehension (Comber & Keeves, 1973; Purves, 1973; Thorndike, 1973). For science, the same examination was given in all countries; on the literature examination, literature in the language of the country was tested; the reading comprehension examination tested such comprehension in the language of the country. The measures of school characteristics and the measures of family-background characteristics used in the analyses were the same in the three studies.

Six countries (Chile, England, Finland, Italy, Sweden, and the United States) participated in all three studies at the age-fourteen level, and I examined results from those six at both the age-ten and age-fourteen levels. My examination consisted of a comparison of the effects of family-background characteristics as measured in the questionnaires and school characteristics, also as measured in the studies.

From the published data, it was possible to calculate certain measures of the effects of family-background and school factors. In particular, it was possible to determine the total effects of family-background characteristics and the

211

TABLE 12.1.   *Relative Amounts of Variation in Literature, Reading Comprehension, and Science Accounted for by Family and School in Studies Conducted by the International Association for the Evaluation of Achievement in Six Countries*

	Greater	Equal	Less	Greater	Age 14 Equal	Less	Greater	Equal	Less
Total family background	1	0	5	2	2	3	3	0	3
Direct school effects	6	0	0	4	1	1	2	0	4
Ratio of school to family	5	0	1	5	0	1	2	1	3

	Age 10 Science: Reading		
	Greater	Equal	Less
Total family background	2	0	4
Direct school effects	5	0	1
Ratio of school to family	5	0	1

Note: See Coleman & Hoffer (1987), chap. 8.

direct effects of school characteristics. From these results, it was possible to make several comparisons. Only two are relevant to the present volume: the total effects of family background on the subject areas and the direct effects of school characteristics on these same subject areas. Variations in reading comprehension are better accounted for by differences in family background; variations in the knowledge of literature are better accounted for by differences in school characteristics (see table 12.1). The result is that, in five countries out of six, the amount of variation in achievement accounted for by variations in school relative to that accounted for by variations in family is greater in literature than in reading comprehension. A comparison of science and reading shows much the same result, this time at both age ten and age fourteen. Variation in achievement accounted for by school relative to that accounted for by family is greater in science than in reading comprehension. Taking the eighteen family-background comparisons together (row 1 of the literature:reading comparison and the science:reading comparison) shows that reading is higher in eleven, equal in two, and lower in five. Taking the eighteen school-effect comparisons together (row 2), the literature:reading and the science:reading comparisons show that literature or science is higher in fifteen, equal in one, and lower in two. In contrast to these results, there are no consistent directions in the comparison of literature and science.

These results suggest that some subjects are learned more at school, while others are learned more outside school. However, these are only indirect indications. Accounting for variations in achievement by variations in school or family characteristics does not mean that a given subject is learned at school or at home.

This result, then, gives only a hint. The opportunity to pursue this hint came more than ten years later in an analysis of the first follow-up of the High School and Beyond tenth-grade cohort (Coleman & Hoffer, 1987). The tenth-grade cohort, interviewed and tested in the spring of 1980, was interviewed two years later, in the spring of 1982, when most of the students were in the twelfth grade. They were retested with the same tests given in tenth grade: vocabulary, reading comprehension, mathematics, science, writing, and civics. What was unique about this resurvey, however, was that a sample of students who had dropped out of school between grades ten and twelve also was located, reinterviewed, and retested. As a consequence, it is possible to compare the growth in achievement on these six tests for those who were out of school for all or some of this period. Many who dropped out did so at the end of the tenth grade because they had reached the age of sixteen, the end of compulsory education, during the tenth grade. However, information on just when they dropped out is not included in the analysis below. In this analysis, two of the tests, reading comprehension and vocabulary, have been combined into a single "verbal skills" score.

The increments in the test scores between spring of the tenth grade and two years later in the five areas tested, in a representative sample of public school students who dropped out, were compared with the increments for students from the same schools whose tenth-grade achievement levels were equal to those of the dropouts (see table 12.2). The dropouts increased 44 percent as much in verbal skills as did those with the same initial achievement who stayed in school, but only 10 percent as much in mathematics. The table indicates that

TABLE 12.2.   *Relative Achievement Growth of Dropouts and Students with the Same Initial Achievement Levels Who Remained in School*

Test (number of items)	Students in School	Dropouts	Ratio
Verbal (40)	3.68	1.63	0.44
Mathematics (38)	1.91	0.20	0.10
Science (20)	1.33	0.30	0.22
Civics (10)	1.32	0.51	0.39
Writing (17)	2.02	0.80	0.39

in verbal skills, civics, and writing skills, the ratio of what is learned outside to what is learned in school is about four times that in mathematics, and about twice that in science. By this measure, mathematics is the subject of the five for which school makes the most difference, science is next, and verbal skills, writing, and civics are the subjects for which school makes the least difference. Simplifying, and neglecting civics, we can say that more mathematics and science skills than skills related to the English language are learned in school.

What Has Been Getting Worse Faster, Families or Schools?

The differences between the locus of learning for mathematical skills and the locus of learning for verbal skills, together with trends in Scholastic Aptitude Test (SAT) scores, allows for a further inference. In the period from 1952 to 1963, before the decline in SAT scores, verbal skills averaged about 475 for all those who took the examinations, and mathematics skills averaged about 495, about 20 points higher (Murray & Herrnstein, 1992). Both underwent a decline over the next decade and a half, and then there was a slight rise and stabilization of the mathematics score and a slowed decline for the verbal score. By 1991, the verbal score stood at a little below 420, while the math score stood at about 475. The difference between the math and verbal scores approximately doubled over this period.

Two explanations of this difference in decline suggest themselves. One is that the out-of-school environment has declined more in its conduciveness to learning than has the school. The other is that changes in the population of students taking the SAT tests, together with a different mix of skills in the new components of the test-taking population, are responsible for the difference.

The principal change in the composition of those who took the SAT tests over this period was the increase in the proportion of blacks. In addition, there were small increases in the proportions of women, of Hispanics, and of immigrants taking the SAT tests. Hispanics and immigrants do less well on English verbal tests than on mathematics tests, women do better, and I know of no conclusive evidence about black students' relative performance on mathematics and verbal tests. The evidence is, I believe, insufficient to reject the possibility that the greater verbal decline is due to changes in the test-taking population.

Because the evidence is not sufficient to reject the compositional-change explanation, my conjectures about relative changes in in-school and out-of-school learning must be quite tentative. Nevertheless, the data are consistent with the conjecture that the out-of-school environment, in the family and outside, has been worsening as an environment for learning more than has the school environment. This conjecture reflects the general decline in social capital for learning in neighborhoods and families.[1] It is also consistent with a major change in school functioning, the reduction in homework assignments. Thus, although such a conjecture remains tentative, the evidence does give some indication that families and neighborhoods have declined more in their value for learning than have schools. This conjecture, if confirmed, is less encouraging than the reverse condition would be. If the school were the principal seat of the test-score decline, then public policies to reverse the decline would be closer to hand. The family and neighborhood, and the social capital for children's learning that they provide, are less amenable to change through public policy than are the schools.

Conclusion

This chapter has provided suggestive evidence that mathematics and related skills are learned less outside school, and more inside it, than are verbal skills. In addition, the greater decline in verbal SAT test scores than in mathematics tests scores suggests that the out-of-school environment in families and neighborhoods is becoming less conducive to learning than are the schools.

References

Coleman, J. S. (1975). Methods and results in the IEA studies of effects of school on learning. *Review of Educational Research* 45:335–386.

Coleman, J. S., & Hoffer, T. (1987). *Public and private high schools: The impact of communities.* New York: Basic Books.

Comber, L. C., & Keeves, J. P. (1973). *International studies in evaluation: Vol. 1. Science education in nineteen countries.* Stockholm: Almqvist and Wiksell.

Murray, C., & Herrnstein, R. J. (1992, Winter). The education impasse. *Public Interest,* No. 106, pp. 32–56.

Purves, A. C. (1973). *International studies in evaluation: Vol. 2. Literature education in ten countries.* Stockholm: Almqvist and Wiksell.

Thorndike, R. L. (1973). *International studies in evaluation: Vol. 3. Reading comprehension education in fifteen countries.* Stockholm: Almqvist and Wiksell.

1. The comparison was carried out by regressing twelfth-grade achievement on tenth-grade achievement for those students who had not dropped out, and then standardizing these results to the average tenth-grade level of achievement. That is, if $\bar{y}_{d1}$ is the average verbal test score for dropouts, and if b_0 and b_1 are the intercept and slope for the regression of the twelfth-grade verbal score on the tenth-grade verbal score for those who remained in school, then column 1 of the table is $\hat{y}_2 - \bar{y}_{d1}$, where $\hat{y}_2 = b_0 + b_1 \bar{y}_{d1}$. Column 2 of the table is simply $\bar{y}_{d2} - \bar{y}_{d1}$, where $\bar{y}_{d2}$ is the average verbal test score for dropouts two years after the tenth-grade test.

IV   The Use of Knowledge

The SMPY Project

T he six chapters contained in this section are devoted to the impact the Study of Mathematically Precocious Youth (SMPY) has had on the field of gifted education (see chapter 15, by Van Tassel-Baska) and on gifted students themselves (see chapter 17, by Benbow, Lubinski, and Suchy and chapter 16, by Brody and Blackburn). SMPY, which was founded by Julian C. Stanley in September 1971 at Johns Hopkins University with a generous grant from the Spencer Foundation, and which was initially called the Study of Mathematically and Scientifically Precocious Youth, is a fine example of when and how research can be put into practice. Evidently, this is a far too infrequent event, if we take to heart the message of the chapters in the previous section. Educational research does not seem to be a cumulative enterprise, and even well-documented findings seem to have little meaningful impact on practice. It is gratifying to see a widespread exception to this generally discouraging trend.

The practical premise guiding the work of SMPY has been to conduct research through service to intellectually gifted adolescents, with a special emphasis on the mathematically talented and the use of various forms of educational acceleration, or curricular flexibility, as the staff of SMPY would prefer to call it (Benbow & Stanley, 1983), to respond to their educational needs. (See chapter 14, by Stanley, for a brief history of SMPY.) By providing innovative and accelerated educational programs, as well as educational guidance, to those who have been identified by the SMPY talent searches (Cohn, 1991), SMPY aims to facilitate the high academic and vocational achievement of individuals who are exceptionally talented intellectually (Stanley, 1977; Stanley & Benbow, 1986; see also chapter 16 below). In the process, SMPY attempts to discover the mechanisms that promote both intellectual and social well-being among the gifted, while fostering the optimal use and development of their many talents, and then implement and disseminate its findings widely. This theme was captured by the formula $MT:D_4P_3$ developed to describe SMPY's work succinctly. (Julian Stanley was a high school chemistry teacher early in his career.) $MT:D_4P_3$ stands for

217

Mathematical Talent: Discovery, Description, Development, and Dissemination of its Principles, Practices, and Procedures.

To help meet this goal, SMPY established a fifty-year longitudinal study, which currently includes about five thousand talented individuals identified over a twenty-year period (Lubinski & Benbow, 1994). Through this study, which is being carried out by Camilla Persson Benbow and David Lubinski at Iowa State University, SMPY is trying to develop a better and more refined understanding of the process whereby precocious forms of intellectual talent, identified during childhood, develop into noteworthy adult achievement and creativity. Additionally, the SMPY longitudinal study provides the critical element for programmatic work—long-term evaluation. The chapter by Benbow, Lubinski, and Suchy is one example of such work. It is devoted to documenting how the participants themselves view the role that SMPY played in their lives or, more specifically, in their educational development. To get the flavor of SMPY's more basic and current work, the interested reader might wish to consult Benbow (1988, 1992b), Lubinski and Benbow (1992, 1994), and Lubinski, Benbow, and Sanders (1993). SMPY's *Studies of Intellectual Precocity* series, listed at the front of this book and of which this book is the most recent volume, is the first resource for anyone interested in SMPY's programmatic or basic work and its evolution since 1971.

The SMPY philosophy, which has been implemented at several university-based centers across the United States (e.g., the Center for Talented Youth at Johns Hopkins and on half a dozen college campuses across the nation, the Talent Identification Program at Duke, the Office of Precollegiate Programs for Talented and Gifted at Iowa State, the Center for Talent Development at Northwestern, and the Rocky Mountain Talent Search at the University of Denver) and in other administrative structures, is directly affecting the lives of approximately 150,000 gifted students on an annual basis. It also has grown from being purely a secondary school model, focusing exclusively on the mathematically talented, to one that now serves upper elementary students and the verbally talented as well (see Mills & Barnett, 1992; see also chapter 16 below). In terms of current impact, the SMPY model (Benbow, 1986), as implemented in its various forms, is probably the most influential and far-reaching. It clearly has affected educational practice over the past two decades. Thus, it is timely to determine how well SMPY has fared and how well we can expect its findings to apply generally (see chapter 18, by Snow and Ennis). SMPY seems to have fared well (in addition to the chapters in this section, see also Benbow, 1992a, 1992b; Benbow & Arjmand, 1990; Lubinski & Benbow, 1994; Swiatek & Benbow,

1991a, 1991b; and Richardson & Benbow, 1990), and the findings are likely to be applicable generally (compare the findings in chapters 16 and 18 below).

We begin with an essay by Arnold Ross, a mathematician widely esteemed for his many years of work dedicated to the teaching of pure mathematics to extremely talented high school students for eight weeks every summer at Ohio State University. In his chapter, Ross reveals the wisdom of his age and presents a philosophical argument about the societal importance of work in the area of exceptional abilities. He provides a rich context in which to interpret that which follows. After all, the essence of SMPY's work, scholarly and programmatic, is the optimal development and use of talent.

References

Benbow, C. P. (1986). SMPY's model for teaching mathematically precocious students. In J. S. Renzulli (Ed.), *Systems and models for developing programs for the gifted and talented* (pp. 1–25). Mansfield Center, Conn.: Creative Learning Press.

Benbow, C. P. (1988). Sex differences in mathematical reasoning ability in intellectually talented preadolescents: Their nature, effects, and possible causes. *Behavioral and Brain Sciences* 11:169–232.

Benbow, C. P. (1992a). Academic achievement in mathematics and science of students between ages thirteen and twenty-three: Are there differences among students in the top one percent of mathematical ability? *Journal of Educational Psychology* 84:51–61.

Benbow, C. P. (1992b). Mathematical talent: Its origins and consequences. In N. Colangelo, S. G. Assouline, & D. L. Ambroson (Eds.), *Talent development: Proceedings from the 1991 Henry B. and Jocelyn Wallace National Research Symposium on Talent Development* (pp. 95–123). Unionville, N.Y.: Trillium Press.

Benbow, C. P., & Arjmand, O. (1990). Predictors of high academic achievement in mathematics and science by mathematically talented students: A longitudinal study. *Journal of Educational Psychology* 82:430–441.

Benbow, C. P., & Stanley, J. C. (1983). Constructing educational bridges between high school and college. *Gifted Child Quarterly* 27:111–113.

Cohn, S. J. (1991). Talent searches. In N. Colangelo & G. A. Davis (Eds.), *Handbook of gifted education* (pp. 166–177). Needham Heights, Mass.: Allyn & Bacon.

Lubinski, D., & Benbow, C. P. (1992). Gender differences in abilities and preferences among the gifted: Implications for the math-science pipeline. *Current Directions in Psychological Science* 1:61–66.

Lubinski, D., & Benbow, C. P. (1994). The Study of Mathematically Precocious Youth: The first three decades of a planned fifty-year study of intellectual talent. In R. F. Subotnik & K. D. Arnold (Eds.), *Beyond Terman: Contemporary longitudinal studies of giftedness and talent* (pp. 255–281). Norwood, N.J.: Ablex.

Lubinski, D., Benbow, C. P., & Sanders, C. E. (1993). Reconceptualizing gender differences in achievement among the gifted. In K. A. Heller, F. J. Mönks, & A. H. Passow (Eds.), *International handbook of research and development of giftedness and talent* (pp. 693–707). Oxford: Pergamon Press.

Mills, C. J., & Barnett, L. B. (1992). The use of the secondary school admission test (SSAT) to identify academically talented elementary school students. *Gifted Child Quarterly* 36:155–159.

Richardson, T. M., & Benbow, C. P. (1990). Long-term effects of acceleration on the social-emotional adjustment of mathematically precocious youth. *Journal of Educational Psychology* 82:464–470.

Stanley, J. C. (1977). Rationale of the Study of Mathematically Precocious Youth (SMPY) during its first five years of promoting educational acceleration. In J. C. Stanley, W. C. George, & C. H. Solano (Eds.), *The gifted and the creative: A fifty-year perspective* (pp. 75–112). Baltimore: Johns Hopkins University Press.

Stanley, J. C., & Benbow, C. P. (1986). Youths who reason exceptionally well mathematically. In R. J. Sternberg & J. E. Davidson (Eds.), *Conceptions of giftedness* (pp. 361–387). Cambridge: Cambridge University Press.

Swiatek, M. A., & Benbow, C. P. (1991a). A ten-year longitudinal follow-up of ability-matched accelerated and unaccelerated gifted students. *Journal of Educational Psychology* 83:528–538.

Swiatek, M. A., & Benbow, C. P. (1991b). A ten-year longitudinal follow-up of participants in a fast-paced mathematics course. *Journal for Research in Mathematics Education* 22:138–150.

13   *Quo Vadis* America?

ARNOLD E. ROSS

> America is sauntering through her resources and through the mazes of her politics with an easy nonchalance; but presently there will come a time when she will be surprised to find herself grown old—a country crowded, strained, perplexed,—when she will be obliged to pull herself together, husband her resources, concentrate her strength, steady her methods, sober her views, restrict her vagaries, *trust her best not her average members*. That will be the time of change.
>
> Woodrow Wilson, 1889

The emphasis in the epigraph above is mine; in my view, the time to trust America's best has come. Who are they? How do they appear in our midst? Do they arrive through a concatenation of random happy events, or is the process of renewal of our reservoir of America's best complex in structure and sensitive and responsive to wise (or sadly enough, to unwise) policies?

Creativity is one of the happy attributes of humans. In their maturity humans display this trait to varying degrees of fulfillment. We do not understand what in human nature assures its presence. We have conflicting ideas about whether nature or nurture is responsible for its flowering (Ross, 1990–1991). Yet the creativity of its citizens is vital to the well-being of every nation, and this is true more than ever in our contemporary technological society, where change and tradition are intertwined in a more dramatic and fluid manner than ever before.

A high measure of vitality seems to be a quality inescapably associated with creativity. Yet what are its first manifestations? The early acquisition of unusual competence in the traditionally taught basic skills is one such promising initial indicator. Unlike creativity, this competence can be measured by accepted standardized tests, taken by a large number of pupils early in their school careers. One example is the College Board Scholastic Aptitude Test (SAT). This testing instrument has been adopted by national talent-search programs, which administer it to many youngsters long before it is usually given (as a preamble to college entrance). The use of the SAT in this manner allows the identification of those who exhibit an early acquisition of unusual competence in the traditionally taught basic skills, particularly in mathematics. It is significant that Julian Stanley's effort to identify the reservoir of mathematical talent at age thirteen and to gain concomitant statistical insights about the individuals included therein (Stanley, 1977) became only the first step in the subsequent process of sifting for significant talent and the work of nurturing this talent to its full fruition. Helping the "discovered" youngsters move rapidly through the traditionally stagnant middle school years was the next step. These youngsters were given an opportunity to acquire rapidly the basic skills typically imparted during the four years of high school. For some, this led to an early move to college. The goal of this work was to make optimal use of, and to conserve, the talents within our society.

When we focus our attention on the rich details of individual achievement that are possible among the talented when they are given the opportunity to bring their talents to fruition, we cannot help being impressed by their diversity of interests and differences of temperament. The talented are not a homogeneous group. Individual differences are as vast among them as among students with abilities that are in the more typical range. We often tend to overlook this point. Let me illustrate by giving a few examples drawn from my pure-math program for talented high school students.

Example 1

This youngster did extremely well in the accelerated summer program at Johns Hopkins. His teacher's recommendation added to high praise a warning that he was habitually distracting in the classroom. He came to us as one of the youngest participants in our summer program. When his performance rather quickly placed him in the top third of our able participant group, he began to live up to his teacher's warning. We had to provide a special challenge, after which he had to work intensively to maintain his standing as one of the top five performers. He came to the program every summer until his early admission to the Massachusetts Institute of Technology. His thirst for knowledge was unusual. He was graduated from MIT at age twenty with four degrees and is doing graduate work in engineering there.

Example 2

This young man was a junior at fourteen in a fine liberal arts college, and came with high recommendations. He performed extraordinarily well in his studies in our program. He was unusually mature and thoughtful, and returned as a counselor the following summer. At sixteen he went to graduate school at a great state university to study particle physics. In 1992 he received his Ph.D. degree at age twenty.

Example 3

This girl came to us at fourteen. Quiet and thoughtful and with a deep interest in ideas, she excelled in her studies. She returned to us for a number of summers, first as an advanced participant and then as a counselor. At sixteen she went to Harvard. She was elected to membership in Phi Beta Kappa her second year there and went on to win the Fay Prize, the highest academic award at graduation. Five years later she received her Ph.D. in physics from the University of California at Berkeley.

Example 4

This youngster came to us right after he earned a score of 800 on the SAT-M at the age of twelve. In the program, for the first time in his life, he had to compete with other very able youngsters. This shook his confidence in himself. Fortunately, his father, a schoolteacher, was studying the same range of mathematical ideas and through thoughtful and tactful collaboration restored his son's confidence. The youngster continued to work in the program, first as an advanced participant and then as a counselor for a number of years in spite of a trying interlude in which he had a kidney transplant. At MIT he majored in mathematics and computer science. MIT's mathematics department gave him its special award for excellence upon his graduation. He is doing graduate work at the University of California at Berkeley.

The above is only a small sample of young people. Yet these case histories amply illustrate the uniqueness of the talented, as well as an aspect shared by all—how the quality of their lives was enriched by the search for and nurturing of America's best. Does this preoccupation with the nurturing of human talent, as heartwarming as it is, serve only to satisfy our aesthetic sensibilities? It does that, but I believe it does much more.

The increasing complexity of most occupations forming the infrastructure of our technological society compels us to look closely at the way we bring up our youth (Ross, 1992). On the one hand, we need to upgrade the quality of experience of our whole work force. If we do not act promptly and if we do not bring the needed resourcefulness and imagination to bear on this task, we shall find that the demands of society's growing complexity will make a large number of our fellow citizens not only unemployed but unemployable. The tragic consequences of the continuing neglect of issues vital to our competitiveness, and hence essential to our economic well-being, have been stressed dramatically in recent years. To date, in spite of the expenditure of public and private treasure, we have not faced up to this problem effectively.

At its best, the upgrading of our work force aims to develop only the supporting staff for our laboratories and our industry. In addition to this, however, the pressures of competitiveness demand that we should have cadres of able people capable of imaginative innovation who can provide the needed leadership. These people make up our critically needed scientific and professional elite. Neglecting either the task of developing the needed cadres of the creative elite or the task of upgrading the quality of our general work force would spell disaster for our society.

At present our nation's material resources are used almost exclusively for the work of upgrading the basic competence of our work force. The importance of the discovery and development of our native talent is downgraded by the use of the term "the elite" as an aspersion. It is, therefore, critically important to display individual initiative in the work that can be described as paying imaginative attention to our young talent.

References

Ross, A. E. (1990–1991). Creativity: Nature or nurture. *Conference Board of the Mathematical Sciences Issues in Mathematics Education* 2:39–84.

Ross, A. E. (1992). Talent search and development: A clinical approach. In N. Colangelo, S. G. Assouline, & D. L. Ambroson (Eds.), *Talent development: Proceedings from the 1991 Henry B. and Jocelyn Wallace National Research Symposium on Talent Development* (pp. 348–352). Unionville, N.Y.: Trillium Press.

Stanley, J. C. (1977). Rationale of the Study of Mathematically Precocious Youth (SMPY) during its first five years of promoting educational acceleration. In J. C. Stanley, W. C. George, & C. H. Solano (Eds.), *The gifted and the creative: A fifty-year perspective* (pp. 75–112). Baltimore: Johns Hopkins University Press.

14   In the Beginning

The Study of Mathematically Precocious Youth

JULIAN C. STANLEY

T he Study of Mathematically Precocious Youth (SMPY) began on September 1, 1971, as the result of a serendipitous occurrence almost three years earlier. An eighth grader named Joseph Louis Bates had been observed during the summer of 1968 by a Towson State University computer science instructor, Doris K. Lidtke, who was helping with a summer computer science program for local students at Johns Hopkins University. She called his extreme intellectual precocity to my attention and sought my assistance. I was somewhat hesitant and perhaps even reluctant at first to get involved; there were too many other pressing duties. But I did, and my life and career were never to be the same.

In January 1969, then, I was faced with the challenge of Joe and how to help him. I had little knowledge to draw on, since until that time most of my work was limited to measurement and statistical issues. I let my interest and expertise in measurement guide me. I felt that I needed to know more about Joe. I decided to administer to him the College Board Scholastic Aptitude Test (SAT), several College Board achievement tests, and some other standardized exams. It seemed to many then, including me, that this was a bold move. After all, Joe was only thirteen years old. At the same time, he was taking college courses. I reasoned that, if he could handle college-level material, then why not college-level tests?

My hunches, fortunately, did not lead me astray. His scores were startlingly high. This sparked my interest and commitment. I began casting around for high schools, public or private, that would allow him to take mainly eleventh- and twelfth-grade Advanced Placement (AP) or honors courses. Principals and headmasters thought this a ridiculous suggestion (probably as ridiculous as taking college-level tests!). So, quite reluctantly, Joe, his parents, and I decided to let him try being a regular student at Johns Hopkins—seemingly an even more ridiculous suggestion. We feared that he would find the courses that seemed best for him initially (calculus, computer science, and physics) too difficult, but our options were severely limited. Yet, to our great surprise and pleasure, Joe thrived and went on to receive his B.A. and master's degrees in computer science at age seventeen. Then, still seventeen, he became a doctoral student at Cornell University. Today, more than twenty-five years later, Dr. Bates is an outstanding research professor, striving at Carnegie Mellon University to bring drama to "virtual reality" (see Peterson, 1992).

Joe's success as a freshman started me thinking, but I remembered the old proverb, "One swallow does not make a spring." Fortunately, Jonathan Middleton Edwards and his mother entered the scene, having heard of Joe. They insisted that the thirteen-year-old Jonathan be given the same opportunities Joe had received. I was skeptical at first, but extensive testing and summer courses taken in 1970 by Jonathan convinced me that he was as academically promising as Joe. Jonathan, too, earned excellent grades. He majored in computer science, and in 1974 became an independent computer consultant. Today he is the technical wizard of a large computer software company he helped found.

The success of Joe and Jonathan encouraged me to embark on a new line of scientific inquiry.

The Founding of SMPY

These experiences, together with my longstanding but almost latent interest in intellectually talented youths (see, e.g., Stanley, 1954), made me receptive in 1970 to a call for grant proposals from the newly formed Spencer Foundation. It had plenty of money but no established list of grant seekers; I had some tentative ideas about how to find "youths who reason exceptionally well mathematically" and to provide them the special, supplemental, accelerative educational opportunities they sorely need and, in my opinion, richly deserve for their own development and the good of society. My four-and-a-half-page, double-spaced proposal won a $266,100 five-year grant, which ended in 1976. Generously, the Spencer Foundation renewed its support until 1984, at lower levels. With that the Study of Mathematically and Scientifically Precocious Youth was born. (Shortly thereafter, the "and Scientifically" was dropped, because mathematical reasoning ability is a prerequisite for most scientific achievement nowadays.)

From the pool of applicants for graduate study in the Department of Psychology at Johns Hopkins in 1971 I recruited two outstanding doctoral aspirants, Lynn H. Fox and Daniel P. Keating. Both earned their Ph.D. degrees in three years while spending an enormous amount of time and high-level effort developing SMPY (see, e.g., Keating & Stanley, 1972; Stanley, Keating, & Fox, 1974; Keating, 1976; and Fox, Brody, & Tobin, 1980).

For a while, during the fall of 1971, we located math-talented boys and girls through local publicity. Then, in March 1972, Dan, Lynn, and I conducted a mathematics and science talent search involving 450 youths (seventh and eighth graders) in the upper 5 percent of ability in the Greater Baltimore area. Its success was much more extensive than any of us anticipated, and we became committed to the talent search concept. The mathematical part of the SAT, used in an out-of-level testing format, became the basic instrument of our search. In the 1973 search we added the verbal part of the SAT, because we realized that mathematical reasoning ability is mediated by verbal reasoning ability, which the SAT-V measures. From this rather humble beginning the talent-search concept began to grow and blossom, and its influence spread (see chapter 15 below).

Over the next two decades the talent search was to become the most frequently used identification procedure for gifted students in the United States. Student participation grew from 450 to about 200,000 students annually, with the geographic area covered expanding greatly. Now the whole nation and some foreign countries are participating. Moreover, to date, nearly all academic talent searches in the United States and elsewhere rely heavily on our choice of instrument, the SAT (since April 1995, the SAT-I), or, in some searches, the American College Testing Program. Even the definition of a mathematically precocious youth (a boy or girl who scores at least 500 on the SAT-M before age thirteen) has been adopted widely, as has the definition of a verbally precocious youth (one who, before age thirteen, scores at least 430 on the SAT-V or at least 510 on the recentered SAT-I V). Each of those two scores defines at least the top 1 percent of that age group. But I have gotten ahead of my story.

Early Offshoots of SMPY

At first, verbally talented individuals were not served by SMPY. This was an omission about which we felt uncomfortable. Thus, we helped form at Johns Hopkins another group, the Study of Verbally Gifted Youth, to serve such students. Soon, it won a large grant from the Spencer Foundation to study youths who reason exceptionally well verbally. That lasted from 1972 until

1977, at which time the grant was not renewed (see McGinn, 1976; Stanley, George, & Solano, 1977). A few years later, after a stopgap arrangement, interest in serving the verbally precocious manifested itself fully again, but now in a different organization, a sequel that searches for both mathematically and verbally talented boys and girls. I shall return to that story later.

The Intellectually Gifted Child Study Group (IGCSG), created by Lynn Fox in 1975, also was an outgrowth of SMPY and is an integral part of its early story. It flourished for several years with Spencer Foundation support, focusing its work on gifted females and then also on learning-disabled gifted students (see, e.g., Fox, 1976; Fox, Benbow, & Perkins, 1983; Fox, Brody, & Tobin, 1980, 1983). IGCSG closed its doors upon Fox's departure from Johns Hopkins in 1982, but its legacy has continued.

Educational Intervention: The Evolution of Fast-Paced Classes

Identification and description are insufficient if we are to help precocious youth optimally develop their abilities. Identified students need to be served; they require some form of educational intervention, not unlike students at the other end of the ability continuum. This leads to another strand of the story, a strand that developed in tandem with identification and became an integral part of the fabric known as SMPY.

By June 1972, less than a year since SMPY had begun, on September 1, 1971, it had become clear that we needed to do something for the children identified as mathematically precocious. In haste, we decided to create a special, fast-paced mathematics class for the most mathematically able young students we had found. Joe Bates's chief mentor in the seventh and eighth grades, Paul R. Binder, was to teach this, but he brought in Joseph R. Wolfson to take over. Wolfson, a physicist by training who after obtaining his master's degree from the University of Chicago discovered that he preferred to teach mathematics, worked expertly with about twenty boys and girls, most of whom had just completed the sixth grade. All were in the top 1 percent of ability in mathematical and also in verbal or nonverbal reasoning. The class was a huge success (Benbow, Perkins, & Stanley, 1983; Fox, 1974; Swiatek & Benbow, 1991b) and was followed by a string of successful classes. Wolfson went on to become a mathematics teacher at the prestigious Phillips Exeter Academy in New Hampshire.

As we continued to conduct talent searches for ever-larger numbers in 1973, 1974, 1976, 1978, and 1979, we experimented incessantly with many different ways of speeding up the learning of mathematics from algebra through calculus at the Advanced Placement program level (two semesters of college credit), as well as the learning of biology, chemistry, and physics (Benbow & Stanley, 1983a; Fox, 1974; George, Cohn, & Stanley, 1979; George & Denham, 1976; Stanley, 1976, 1990, 1993; Stanley & Benbow, 1986; Stanley & Stanley, 1986). This led to refinement and extension of our procedures. We also experimented with other forms of acceleration, or curricular flexibility (which came to be our preferred term), to develop what we called the SMPY smorgasbord of accelerative opportunities (Stanley & Benbow, 1982).

The Large-Scale Spread and Extension of the SMPY Model

My wife of thirty-two years died in late 1978. She had been ill with metastatic breast cancer for nearly six years. I was exhausted from teaching my university classes, looking after her, expanding SMPY, and developing the SMPY model. In 1979, I went to President Steven Muller of Johns Hopkins and, in fifteen minutes, arranged to create at Johns Hopkins, independent of SMPY, the Office of Talent Identification and Development (OTID) to take over the operational aspects of the program. Its first director was William C. George, a longtime staff member of SMPY. Later, OTID was renamed the Center for the Advancement of Academically Talented Youth (CTY) and the directorship was turned over to William G. Durden (its current director). Starting in the fall of 1979, OTID took off like a rocket with an expanded talent search, now including both verbal and mathematical ability. The first residential program of fast-paced courses followed that summer. CTY has expanded ever since, now serving about eighty thousand young boys and girls each year in its talent searches and about five thousand in its summer programs, which offer a great variety of courses.

Soon thereafter, SMPY helped other regional talent searches get started at Duke University, Northwestern University, and the University of Denver. Also, it helped create programs in Arizona, California, Georgia, Illinois, Indiana, Iowa, Minnesota, North Carolina, Pennsylvania, Texas, Washington, Wisconsin, Australia, China, Costa Rica, and Spain. SMPY continued its programmatic work, chiefly on behalf of youths who before age thirteen score extremely high on the SAT-M (700 or higher): one in ten thousand of their age group. This came to occupy much of my time and continues to do so.

There are two establishments, created rather late in SMPY's evolution, that need to be singled out and noted at this point. They are the ones that will continue SMPY's work and move it into the next century. SMPY at Iowa State University was established in 1986 when my longtime student and colleague Camilla Persson Benbow moved there. Not only does SMPY at Iowa State University conduct, through the Office of Precollegiate Programs for Talented and Gifted, a talent search and educational programs based on the SMPY model, but it is also carrying out the SMPY longitudinal research program. The vast SMPY database, currently with a total of five thousand participants, is located there and being augmented annually (see the description provided in chapter 17 below, and Lubinski & Benbow, 1994). This longitudinal study is the largest of its kind in the world, greatly exceeding Lewis M. Terman's classic Genetic Studies of Genius (e.g., Oden, 1968; Holahan & Sears, 1995). It provides much of what we know about the characteristics of gifted students today, their needs, and their development. Finally, Linda Brody established the Study of Exceptional Talent in 1991 at Johns Hopkins's CTY. As described in chapter 16 below, counseling and facilitation of this country's most mathematically and verbally able youth, done in an individualized manner, is being continued there.

Some of SMPY's Chief Principles

It might be profitable at this time to step back and reflect on SMPY's accomplishments. SMPY's work has now spanned more than two decades, and its influence is widespread. During this time we have learned much about mathematically precocious youth and how to help them. What are some of the most important principles derived from SMPY's work?

1. It is crucial to find—via systematic, objective, well-focused procedures—youths who *reason* exceptionally well in the content domain of a specific interest. For SMPY, this was mathematics. The annual talent search among members of a given age group, such as seventh graders (in whom SMPY specializes), seems essential. Yet with their exclusive use of a mathematics and a verbal test, the talent searches miss a group of talented students crucial for the continued progress of this nation. This is the spatially gifted (those who can mentally rotate objects in space; see chapter 6 above, and Stanley, 1994). This omission needs to be addressed. Nonetheless, the principle remains the same: if you want to make rabbit stew, first catch a rabbit. Otherwise, you'll have squirrel stew, skunk stew, or no stew (see Wallach 1978).

2. Thus far, SAT-M, augmented by SAT-V, has provided the most secure, appropriately difficult way to assess the quantitative aptitude of twelve-year-olds in the upper 5 percent of ability. CTY and others (see, e.g., Lupkowski & Aussoline, 1992) are using the Secondary School Admissions Test and other above-grade-level exams for younger students (Mills, Ablard, & Stumpf, 1993). Moreover, spatial ability is currently assessed in already-identified mathematically talented students (those with SAT-M scores of 500 or higher), and its predictive value above SAT-V is being determined (Benbow &

Lubinski, 1994). It will be interesting to learn how useful these approaches will be.

3. In addition to the test-based systematic talent search, wherein each student's abilities are carefully assessed, a distinctive feature of SMPY has been its emphases on subject-matter acceleration in its many forms and on fast-paced academic courses. In the latter, students are individually, rigorously, and quickly paced by a mentor through a standard high school subject, such as first-year algebra, biology, chemistry, or physics (see Stanley & Stanley, 1986; Lynch, 1992). Appropriately gifted students can master a whole year of high school subject matter in three intensive summer weeks. Of course, it is essential that this involves appropriate articulation of out-of-school academic experiences with the relevant in-school courses. For example, the student who masters algebra 1 in three summer weeks should move into algebra 2 that fall. Those who master first-year high school biology should move into AP biology that fall to work for college credit or into some other advanced science experience.

4. SMPY emphasizes subject-matter acceleration more than grade skipping. Yet these are only two of at least twenty major ways to accelerate educational progress. Various kinds of curricular flexibility are encouraged (see, e.g., Southern, Jones, & Stanley, 1993) and now have gained wide acceptance in the educational community. Actually, the change in the acceptance of acceleration by the educational community from 1971, when SMPY started, to the present day is one of SMPY's major accomplishments. In 1971 acceleration was anathema to most educators. Today it is endorsed by the National Association for Gifted Children. It also has been shown to have a positive relationship with academic achievement up to ten years after implementation (Swiatek & Benbow, 1991a; Charlton, Marolf, & Stanley, 1994).

5. SMPY's DT-PI model, involving diagnostic testing followed by prescribed instruction, enables students in fast-paced academic situations to concentrate on just what they do not yet know, rather than being forced to work through a textbook from page 1 onward (see Benbow, 1986). It is an effective means of putting challenge back into instruction for gifted students and has long-term positive outcomes (Swiatek & Benbow, 1991b).

6. Comprehensive newsletters aimed directly at the talented students themselves are a prime way to help large groups across the country acquire information about special opportunities and show each other how much can be done by the well motivated (see chapters 16 and 17 below).

7. Long-term longitudinal follow-ups of the youths who reason extremely well mathematically (and verbally) are highly important. Camilla Persson Benbow, Distinguished Professor and Chair of the Department of Psychology at Iowa State University in Ames, Iowa, and her close colleague, David Lubinski, are conducting such studies of SMPY's excellent scorers from 1972 to 1982 and of Midwestern students more recently identified by them from 1987 to

the present. This study, which includes five thousand gifted individuals grouped into five cohorts of students, is planned to continue for at least fifty years (see Lubinski & Benbow, 1994). To date, data have been or are being collected via comprehensive questionnaires on individuals considered gifted using SMPY's criteria at ages thirteen, eighteen, twenty-three, and thirty-three. This is truly a modern-day extension of Terman's classic longitudinal follow-up study from 1921 to the present (e.g., Oden, 1968; Holahan & Sears, 1995).

8. University programs that cover grades eleven through fourteen in two years via college courses have been one of my hobbies (see Stanley, 1991). They are among the most effective means of meeting the educational and social needs of gifted students in the last years of secondary school. An excellent recent example is the unique Advanced Academy of the State University of West Georgia (Stanley, 1995).

9. In a fax message dated March 11, 1993, Daniel P. Keating emphasized to me that "one of the important principles advanced (in theory, research, and practice) by SMPY is a workable model of educating for individual development, as opposed to categorical placement approaches that dominate most of contemporary education. I think this is a potentially generalizable way of dealing with developmental diversity. Folks who are interested in a wide range of educational issues could learn from the SMPY experience."

10. Benbow and Stanley (1980, 1981, 1982, 1983b) helped start a strong, continuing debate about gender differences on cognitive tests. For their later work on this topic, see Benbow (1988) (and the critiques that follow it), Benbow (1990), Stanley, Benbow, Brody, Dauber, and Lupkowski (1992), Lubinski and Benbow (1992), Stanley (1993), Lubinski, Benbow, and Sanders (1993), and Stumpf and Stanley (1996).

Conclusion

I have been amazed at how quickly and well SMPY's principles, practices, and techniques caught on and spread (see chapter 15 below). The growth and rate of adoption of the SMPY model have increased exponentially since its modest beginnings in 1972, when SMPY conducted a 450-person talent search and a 20-person fast-paced math class. All over the United States and in some foreign countries, many thousands of intellectually highly talented children have been recognized and helped educationally; far more than a million have been touched by SMPY's work. Quite a few schools and school systems have been encouraged or even forced to adopt more flexible ways to accommodate those of their students certified by the talent searches as being excellent reasoners mathematically or verbally. This increasing acceptance of several types of acceleration has been gratifying to observe.

And yet, the impact of these ideas on national educational policy has been less than we had hoped. Perhaps this is due to our approach. Mostly, we have "burrowed under" a particular school in what I, coining an oxymoron, term a "benignly insidious" manner. SMPY and its sequels send SAT scores directly to the young examinees, who then can work with their parents within their local schools and communities to secure needed curricular adjustments and other opportunities to move ahead faster in the academic areas of their greatest precocity. SMPY has almost never tackled school boards directly. There are too many, and it is extremely difficult to effect long-term changes in their stated policies. Benbow and Stanley (in press) have tried to highlight policy issues.

It would be inappropriate, however, to bring this chapter to a close without mentioning that the accomplishments of many of the mathematically precocious students have been superb and continue to be so. That is a story that Benbow and Lubinski are developing through their longitudinal research (see Lubinski & Benbow, 1994). Perhaps at some future time I shall supplement their reports, Charlton, Marolf, and Stanley (1994), and Plotinck, Cargain, and Chambers (1995) with case studies of highly successful and less successful SMPYers. (Those who cannot wait may want to consult the two case histories provided by Gallagher; see chapter 3 above.) Mathematical precocity is an intriguing topic; it certainly captured my interest back in January 1969 when I first met Joe Bates, and continues to do so.

Acknowledgments

I thank Camilla Persson Benbow, Carol Blackburn, Linda Brody, Susan Hellerman, Daniel Keating, David Lubinski, and Barbara Stanley for their helpful comments.

References

Benbow, C. P. (1986). SMPY's model for teaching mathematically precocious students. In J. S. Renzulli (Ed.), *Systems and models for developing programs for the gifted and talented* (pp. 1–25). Mansfield Center, Conn.: Creative Learning Press.

Benbow, C. P. (1988). Sex differences in mathematical reasoning ability in intellectually talented preadolescents: Their nature, effects, and possible causes. *Behavioral and Brain Sciences* 11:169–232.

Benbow, C. P. (1990). Sex differences in mathematical reasoning ability among the intellectually talented: Further thoughts. *Behavioral and Brain Sciences* 13:196–198.

Benbow, C. P., & Lubinski, D. (1994). Individual differences amongst the mathematically gifted: Their educational and vocational implications. In N. Colangelo, S. G. Assouline, & D. L. Ambroson (Eds.). *Talent development* (Vol. 2, pp. 83–100). Dayton: Ohio Psychology Press.

Benbow, C. P., Perkins, S., & Stanley, J. C. (1983). Mathematics taught at a fast pace: A longitudinal evaluation of SMPY's first class. In C. P. Benbow & J. C. Stanley (Eds.), *Academic precocity: Aspects of its development* (pp. 51–78). Baltimore: Johns Hopkins University Press.

Benbow, C. P., & Stanley, J. C. (1980). Sex differences in mathematical ability: Fact or artifact? *Science* 210:1262–1264.

Benbow, C. P., & Stanley, J. C. (1981). Mathematical ability: Is sex a factor? *Science* 212:114–121.

Benbow, C. P., & Stanley, J. C. (1982). Consequences in high school and college of sex differences in mathematical reasoning ability: A longitudinal perspective. *American Educational Research Journal* 19:598–622.

Benbow, C. P., & Stanley, J. C. (Eds.). (1983a). *Academic precocity: Aspects of its development.* Baltimore: Johns Hopkins University Press.

Benbow, C. P., & Stanley, J. C. (1983b). Sex differences in mathematical reasoning ability: More facts. *Science* 222:1029–1031.

Benbow, C. P., & Stanley, J. C. (in press). Inequity in equity: How "equity" can lead to inequity for high-potential students. *Psychology, Public Policy, and Law.*

Charlton, J. C., Marolf, D. M., & Stanley, J. C. (1994). Follow-up insights on rapid educational acceleration. *Roeper Review* 17:123–130.

Fox, L. H. (1974). A mathematics program for fostering precocious achievement. In J. C. Stanley, D. P. Keating, & L. H. Fox (Eds.), *Mathematical talent: Discovery, description, and development* (pp. 101–125). Baltimore: Johns Hopkins University Press.

Fox, L. H. (1976). Sex differences in mathematical precocity: Bridging the gap. In D. P. Keating (Ed.), *Intellectual talent: Research and development* (pp. 183–214). Baltimore: Johns Hopkins University Press.

Fox, L. H., Benbow, C. P., & Perkins, S. (1983). An accelerated mathematics program for girls: A longitudinal evaluation. In C. P. Benbow & J. C. Stanley (Eds.), *Academic precocity: Aspects of its development* (pp. 113–118). Baltimore: Johns Hopkins University Press.

Fox, L. H., Brody, L. E., & Tobin, D. (Eds.). (1980). *Women and the mathematical mystique.* Baltimore: Johns Hopkins University Press.

Fox, L. H., Brody, L. E., & Tobin, D. (Eds.). (1983). *Learning-disabled/gifted children: Identification and programming.* Baltimore: University Park Press.

George, W. C., Cohn, S. J., & Stanley, J. C. (Eds.). (1979). *Educating the gifted: Acceleration and enrichment.* Baltimore: Johns Hopkins University Press.

George, W. C., & Denham, S. A. (1976). Curriculum experimentation for the mathematically talented. In D. P. Keating (Ed.), *Intellectual talent: Research and development* (pp. 103–131). Baltimore: Johns Hopkins University Press.

Holahan, C. K., & Sears, R. R. (1995). *The gifted group in later maturity.* Stanford: Stanford University Press.

Keating, D. P. (Ed.). (1976). *Intellectual talent: Research and development.* Baltimore: Johns Hopkins University Press.

Keating, D. P., & Stanley, J. C. (1972). Extreme measures for the exceptionally gifted in mathematics and science. *Educational Researcher* 1:3–7.

Lubinski, D., & Benbow, C. P. (1992). Gender differences in abilities and preferences among the gifted: Implications for the math-science pipeline. *Current Directions in Psychological Science* 1:61–66.

Lubinski, D., & Benbow, C. P. (1994). The Study of Mathematically Precocious Youth: The first three decades of a planned fifty-year study of intellectual talent. In R. F. Subotnik & K. D. Arnold (Eds.), *Beyond Terman: Contemporary longitudinal studies of giftedness and talent* (pp. 255–281). Norwood, N.J.: Ablex.

Lubinski, D., Benbow, C. P., & Sanders, C. E. (1993). Reconceptualizing gender differences in achievement among the gifted. In K. A. Heller, F. J. Mönks, & A. H. Passow (Eds.), *International handbook of research and development of giftedness and talent* (pp. 693–707). Oxford: Pergamon Press.

Lupkowski, A. E., & Assouline, S. G. (1992). *Jane and Johnny love math: Recognizing and encouraging mathematical talent in elementary students.* Unionville, N.Y.: Trillium Press.

Lynch, S. J. (1992). Fast-paced high school science for the academically talented. *Gifted Child Quarterly* 36:147–154.

McGinn, P. V. (1976). Verbally talented youth: Selection and description. In D. P. Keating (Ed.), *Intellectual talent: Research and development* (pp. 160–182). Baltimore: Johns Hopkins University Press.

Mills, C. J., Ablard, K. E., & Stumpf, H. (1993). Gender differences in academically talented young students' mathematical reasoning: Patterns across age and subskills. *Journal of Educational Psychology* 85:340–346.

Oden, M. H. (1968). The fulfillment of promise: Forty-year follow-up of the Terman gifted group. *Genetic Psychology Monographs* 77:3–93.

Peterson, I. (1992). Wizard of Oz: Bringing drama to virtual reality. *Science News* 142:440–441.

Plotinck, A., Cargain, M. J., & Chambers, V. (1995). *CHI News* (London) 3:15–20.

Southern, W. T., Jones, E. D., & Stanley, J. C. (1993). Acceleration and enrichment: The context and development of program options. In K. A. Heller, F. J. Mönks, & A. H. Passow (Eds.), *International handbook of research and development of giftedness and talent* (pp. 387–409). Oxford: Pergamon Press.

Stanley, J. C. (1954). Identification of superior learners in grades ten through fourteen. In H. Robinson (Ed.), *Promoting maximal reading growth among able learners* (Supplementary Educational Monographs No. 81, pp. 31–34). Chicago: University of Chicago Press.

Stanley, J. C. (1976). Special fast-mathematics classes taught by college professors to fourth- through twelfth-graders. In D. P. Keating (Ed.), *Intellectual talent: Research and development* (pp. 132–159). Baltimore: Johns Hopkins University Press.

Stanley, J. C. (1990). *My many years of working with the gifted: An academic approach.* Williamsburg, Va.: College of William and Mary, School of Education.

Stanley, J. C. (1991). A better model for residential high schools for talented youths. *Phi Delta Kappan* 72:471–473.

Stanley, J. C. (1993). Boys and girls who reason well mathematically. In G. R. Bock & K. Ackrill (Eds.), *The origins and development of high ability* (pp. 119–138). New York: Wiley.

Stanley, J. C. (1994). Mechanical aptitude: Neglected undergirding of technological expertise. *Illinois Association for Gifted Children Journal Portfolio*, article 7, pp. 1–3.

Stanley, J. C. (1995). Three or four years of schooling in two. *World Business Review* 5:41.

Stanley, J. C., & Benbow, C. P. (1982). Educating mathematically precocious youths: Twelve policy recommendations. *Educational Researcher* 11:4–9.

Stanley, J. C., & Benbow, C. P. (1986). Youths who reason exceptionally well mathematically. In R. J. Sternberg & J. E. Davidson (Eds.), *Conceptions of giftedness* (pp. 361–387). Cambridge: Cambridge University Press.

Stanley, J. C., Benbow, C. P., Brody, L. E., Dauber, S., & Lupkowski, A. E. (1992). Gender differences on eighty-six nationally standardized aptitude and achievement tests. In N. Colangelo, S. G. Assouline, & D. L. Ambroson (Eds.), *Talent development: Proceedings from the 1991 Henry B. and Jocelyn Wallace National Research Symposium on Talent Development* (pp. 42–65). Unionville, N.Y.: Trillium Press.

Stanley, J. C., George, W. C., & Solano, C. H. (Eds.). (1977). *The gifted and the creative: A fifty-year perspective.* Baltimore: Johns Hopkins University Press.

Stanley, J. C., Keating, D. P., & Fox, L. H. (Eds.). (1974). *Mathematical talent: Discovery, description, and development.* Baltimore: Johns Hopkins University Press.

Stanley, J. C., & Stanley, B. S. K. (1986). High-school biology, chemistry, or physics learned well in three weeks. *Journal of Research in Science Teaching* 23:237–250.

Stumpf, H., & Stanley, J. C. (1996). Gender-related differences on the College Board's Advanced Placement and Achievement Tests, 1982–1992. *Journal of Educational Psychology* 88:353–364.

Swiatek, M. A., & Benbow, C. P. (1991a). A ten-year longitudinal follow-up of ability-matched accelerated and unaccelerated gifted students. *Journal of Educational Psychology* 83:528–538.

Swiatek, M. A., & Benbow, C. P. (1991b). A ten-year longitudinal follow-up of participants in a fast-paced mathematics course. *Journal for Research in Mathematics Education* 22:138–150.

Wallach, M. A. (1978). Care and feeding of the gifted. *Contemporary Psychology* 23:616–617.

15   Contributions of the Talent-Search Concept to Gifted Education

JOYCE VAN TASSEL-BASKA

The Status of Gifted Education

In the early 1970s, gifted education was beginning to experience its greatest period of growth and even some degree of popularity at the grass-roots level. Buttressed by the 1972 Marland report on the status of gifted and talented education in the nation, and incipient federal legislation, which was accompanied by funding, the field began the training of educators who would secure leadership roles at both state and local levels. These short-term training efforts were targeted on one goal: to train state teams to develop plans that would lead to state and local policies for educating gifted students. Led by Teachers College of Columbia University, more substantive university training programs also were fostered to develop leaders at the national and collegiate levels. Because the field of gifted education was focused on training and the multiplier effect that could accrue from it in policy development, less attention was paid to serious program development practices that were grounded in research and pilot-tested in schools. Moreover, there were no dollars allocated to research and development in this nascent field.

As a consequence of these trends and directions, most local programs in the 1970s might be characterized as:

—Programs grounded in identification practices based on group IQ scores and teacher nominations

—Enrichment-oriented programs defined by their organizational approach, typically a resource-room model of fewer than one hundred minutes per week

236

—Programs with a content-free (and frequently insubstantial) curriculum, activity based and strategy driven, and totally separate from the traditional subject matters of school by both organizational and curricular design

Julian Stanley's founding of the Study of Mathematically Precocious Youth (SMPY) in 1971 and the development of the talent search during this period signaled, however, the beginning of change even in these confused areas of identification, programming, and curriculum and instruction (Keating & Stanley, 1972; Stanley, Keating, & Fox, 1974). The impact this work has had on gifted education is the focus of this chapter.

Identification

The development of the talent-search identification model in 1971 was the catalyst for all that was to follow. The simple but elegant idea was to administer a more difficult test, one normed on older children, to a younger but highly able group (the top 2 percent to 5 percent on standardized achievement tests, such as the Iowa Test of Basic Skills). Specifically, the College Board Scholastic Aptitude Test (SAT) was used to find precocious seventh- and eighth-grade students. The efficiency of this approach is now legendary. Currently, more than 140,000 students at the sixth-, seventh-, and eighth-grade levels are tested annually using this procedure, both nationally and internationally, in university-based programs at Johns Hopkins, Duke, Northwestern, Arizona State, Iowa State, Denver, and elsewhere. Through this process, information becomes available that allows talent to be differentiated by degree and type (verbal, math, or both).

What is a talent search? The talent-search model employs a two-step testing protocol. In step one, all students who score in the top few percentiles on their in-grade standardized achievement test batteries, in mathematical or verbal areas or overall, are sought. In step two, this academically able population is administered the SAT, a test designed for above-average high school students. This results in a wide dispersion of scores on the SAT; there is no longer a ceiling effect for the talented youth tested. Consequently, educators can better discern the potential of these students of junior high school age at this critical stage of their development in key academic areas (verbal and math). Furthermore, because such younger students usually have not had advanced coursework in mathematics or verbal subjects, the scores are more representative of their reasoning power than of their achievement (Benbow & Stanley, 1981, 1983).

What important implications does aptitude testing using the SAT have for identification policies in gifted education? The identification policies in the talent-search model have been employed, first of all, within school districts to identify those students most in need of a differentiated program, namely the highly gifted. Two specific principles embodied in the talent search model have had an even more powerful effect on local gifted education practices.

One of these is the principle of above-level testing (Stanley, 1990). The talent-search model has demonstrated that true potential for specific academic work in mathematics and verbal areas can be discerned better by administering an above-level test, standardized on older populations, than by arbitrarily using cutoff points within a narrow band of ability on in-grade measures, calling those above the cutoff "gifted" and those below "not gifted." Because scores in the top range are difficult to interpret and cannot be differentiated, such cutoffs at the highest range produced many false positives and false negatives. Most serious in this regard were the false negatives—the many students who could have performed well on a second-level testing who were eliminated from further consideration through a faulty screening mechanism. They were prevented from showing their true capabilities on a more difficult measure. Local school districts now apply this principle of above-level testing in their identification practices to help avoid such problems.

A second principle of the talent search identification model that has had a significant impact on local educational practices is the testing of specific areas of aptitude rather than tapping only global intelligence. (With regard to the latter, see chapter 2 above.) Indeed, in support of this practice, current theoretical work in gifted education suggests a conception of multiple intelligences (Gardner, 1983) displayed in domain-specific contexts (Feldman, 1980). Moreover, studies of predictive validity have demonstrated the effectiveness of the SAT in finding students who can profit from advanced coursework in specific aptitude areas (Benbow, 1992; Keating, 1976; Stanley & Benbow, 1981; Van Tassel-Baska, 1983).

But even if theory and research did not support SMPY's innovations regarding identification, the talent search approach would still represent a practical course for local school districts that program for gifted learners within a limited time frame and, therefore, frequently are not able to meet all of the educational needs of this population. It allows school personnel to focus more of their attention on matters other than identification. Furthermore, targeting individual aptitude areas has political benefits: it allows for a larger number of students to be identified and served, and thereby dispels the notion that the gifted program is serving only high-IQ students. Diversification of program options, based on differences in aptitude, is possible at higher socioeconomic levels in suburban school districts where many bright students may be found. This allows for differentiated programming even among the gifted. Yet the benefits can be made equally apparent for those at the other end of the socioeconomic continuum. Approximately 14 percent of the talent-search students identified annually through either mathematical or verbal scores in the Midwest, for example, are from low socioeconomic backgrounds (Van Tassel-Baska & Chepko-Sade, 1985).

Finally, the talent search concept has provided a systematic approach to identification that recognizes four distinct aspects of the process: screening, identification, program planning, and validation of selection criteria. This systematic work has positively affected identification policy at both state and local levels and for all stages of student development.

Programming

The talent search concept has deeply affected our ideas about appropriate programming for gifted and talented learners. Educational interventions need to be talent specific and responsive to individual needs. If students are verbally able, they need high-powered verbal programs that test their limits. If students are mathematically precocious, programs should be geared to address that strength directly. The true beauty of aptitude testing, such as that done through the talent search, is that it provides administrators with important diagnostic information for curriculum planning. One could even argue that a cursory content analysis of the test would yield curricular implications that might be translated into classroom instruction. Based on the types of items contained in the SAT-V, for example, one could begin to develop a strong verbal-arts curriculum that focused on critical reading, deductive reasoning, vocabulary development, and the use of analogies, all valid curriculum emphases within a rigorous English program. It needs to be noted, however, that this approach is different from the misguided practice of having standardized testing drive the curriculum (see chapter 2 above). Here it represents an effort to build on strengths.

The summer programs associated with each talent search have demonstrated the effectiveness of matching talent systematically to a core curriculum offering. In such programs, students with high math talent, for example, are given the opportunity to choose from developmentally appropriate coursework in math and the sciences. Consistently, the students have performed well in such courses, which usually involve three weeks of instruction totaling seventy-

TABLE 15.1.   *Program Options for Performance Ranges on the SAT*

SAT-V/SAT-M Range			
200–390	400–520	530–590	600–800
Honors-level work in the content area of qualification Enrichment seminars Academic counseling	Fast-paced, advanced coursework during the academic year in area of strength (e.g., algebra, Latin) Academic counseling University summer programs	Individualized programs of study: diagnostic-prescriptive approach in area of strength University programs that employ fast-paced model Academic counseling Early access to AP Grade acceleration	Individualized programs of study: diagnostic-prescriptive approach in area of strength University programs that employ fast-paced model Academic counseling Early access to AP Grade acceleration Advanced standing at college entrance; early admissions Mentorships Career counseling

five to ninety-nine hours of classroom time; at the end of the courses they have scored at or above the mean for college-bound high school seniors on the College Board achievement tests in the appropriate subject areas (see, e.g., Stanley & Stanley, 1986). Data from three consecutive years of the Northwestern University summer programs illustrate well the utility of this "matching" phenomenon. In both aptitude and achievement testing situations, students of junior high school age, after three weeks of intensive instruction, consistently have performed at levels comparable to students four to six years older than they are (Van Tassel-Baska & Strykowski, 1986).

Beyond issues of optimal match by content area lie other important considerations for programming alternatives. The talent search model has demonstrated two important general programming principles regarding the range of abilities tapped by SAT testing. First, the more gifted the student, the greater the need for intensification of services, such as compressed summer programs, correspondence study, and mentorships. Second, the more gifted the student, the greater the need for extension of services—providing an array of options that are simultaneously accelerated, enriched, and personalized (see table 15.1). Thus, the treatment of students by level of aptitude has provided important insights as well for program planning in gifted education.

The one approach to programming that can be considered the essence of the talent search model is acceleration. It might even be said that SMPY single-handedly revived this once time-honored practice. In the 1970s acceleration was rarely used; now it is used more widely but still not as much as is desirable (see chapter 3 above).

Acceleration of the gifted fits well with our understanding of learning and with current developmental theories and research. (See the spring 1992 special issue of *Gifted Child Quarterly* on the topic, as well as chapter 7 above). For example, Csikszentmihalyi (1988) found that high-IQ students were able to handle about twice as many challenging tasks as average-IQ students, just as Leta Hollingworth claimed more than fifty years ago. Bloom (1985) observed that the development of high-level talent in any domain is carefully nurtured through exposure to progressively more complex tasks in a prestructured continuum of learning experiences based on mastery and readiness. Dweck and Elliott (1983) also demonstrated the positive relationship between achievement motivation and task difficulty set at a challenging level; such challenges for the gifted are provided through acceleration. Thus, acceleration that is flexible, based on individual students' needs, and carefully organized over the years in school is a necessary aspect of gifted programming (see chapter 7 above).

Reviews of the literature on acceleration have appeared with some regularity over the past twenty-five years (Benbow, 1991; Daurio, 1979; Gallagher, 1969; Kulik & Kulik, 1984; Reynolds, Birch, & Tuseth, 1962; Van Tassel-Baska, 1986), and each review has carefully noted the overall positive effects of acceleration on students at various stages of their lives (see chapter 10 above). Recent studies, moreover, continue to show positive results in cognitive development, and no negative effects in social emotional development, from acceleration. For example, researchers have reported no harmful effects of various forms of acceleration, including grade skipping and the taking of advanced courses, among students subsequent to high school graduation (Brody & Benbow, 1987; Swiatek & Benbow, 1991a). Accelerated students generally earn more honors and attend more-prestigious colleges, with the best predictor of college achievement being early and continued Advanced Placement (AP) course taking. Swiatek and Benbow suggest that advanced and challenging work on an ongoing basis is a powerful spur to achievement at later levels (see chapter 7 above).

Richardson and Benbow (1990) and Swiatek and Benbow (1991a), moreover, have reported no harmful effects of acceleration on social and emotional development subsequent to college graduation (see also Brody, Assouline, & Stanley, 1990). In studies done by researchers at the University of Washington, no detrimental effects of early entrance to college (as early as age fourteen) were reported; the adjustment of early entrants was comparable to that of members of three equally able nonaccelerated groups (Janos et al., 1988; Robinson & Janos, 1986).

Curriculum and Instruction

The talent search concept has done more than affect identification, programming, and accelerative practices, however. It also has had an important impact on practices in the areas of curriculum and instruction. The renewed emphasis on accelerating traditional content has been accompanied by a resurgence of interest in subjects such as Latin, Greek, philosophy, German, and rhetoric, which had been dropped from school curricula or disregarded in favor of more modern options. An interest also developed in the more rigorous treatment of standard courses such as English, literary analysis, and expository writing, rather than more creative forms of expression. The resurgence of such curriculum options has created a new appreciation for the serious study of such subjects even prior to high school.

The use of diagnostic-prescriptive approaches to ensure instructional progress at an appropriate rate evolved into a staple of well-run, fast-paced programs for highly talented students. Also heralded as a technique to counter repetition of material already learned and the resulting lack of motivation on the part of the gifted, these procedures became fundamental to the effort to modify instruction for them. The teachers of the resulting fast-paced classes became facilitators of small-group and individual learning, as well as the providers of direct instruction. Frequently instruction in as many as three courses in mathematics, for example, would be taking place in the same classroom, thus highlighting the individualized nature of the instructional process and the wide range of abilities even among the highly gifted.

Finally, curricula that emphasized the core disciplines became more acceptable as a result of the talent-search model. Advanced Placement coursework, which provided many key features of excellent curricula, was restored for the gifted; many school-based programs for the gifted also began to modify traditional content rather than develop curricula outside traditional boundaries.

The Impact on Higher Education

The talent search concept has had a great impact on the landscape of higher education as well. Several university centers have been developed at key institutions as a direct result of the model. Each of these centers provides a broad-based set of services: the administration of SAT testing (and now ACT testing as well) to thousands of junior high school students; the offering of precollegiate learner programs during the academic year and in the summer; and research-and-development initiatives that provide a greater basis for understanding gifted students, their families, and the institutions with which they interact. Beyond these centers, precollegiate learner programs have been developed at hundreds of other campuses, sponsored as a result of the talent-search model. In the Midwest, for example, when the talent search began, there was only a handful of university-based programs for these students. Within one year, there were twenty-four; by 1987 there were sixty-six. Today approximately eighty institutions of higher education provide programming in the eight-state region served by the Midwest talent search.

Clearly, there is an element of self-interest for these institutions: they are concerned with the recruitment of high-level talent. However, the direct benefits to students as a result of these programs are enormous: (1) they can earn advanced high school and even college credit in an economical manner, (2) they can associate for the first time with an equally able peer group, (3) they can develop the habits of mind associated with serious study on a college campus, and (4) they can gain a sense of academic competence by being challenged to learn more-difficult material. This list does not mention the enormous personal gains in the area of social and emotional development that these students seem to experience, as judged by anecdotal reports.

In addition to finding and serving academic talent, however, most of the universities with precollegiate programs have developed an ongoing research agenda to learn more about these students and the talent-development process itself. Graduate programs also have emerged that provide for the education of teachers and other professionals in gifted education.

The Implications of Mentoring

Another area of emphasis that the talent search concept has affected is the art of mentoring. We owe our conception of mentoring in the university to the Greeks, but much of the best mentoring I have seen take place in the field of gifted education comes directly from Julian Stanley's approach with his SMPY students and their families. Through personal correspondence, a fine and comprehensive newsletter, and frequent personal contacts, SMPY has fostered the development of many individual students and placed them on the path to educational and career success. The focus for SMPY's mentoring is always on educational opportunities for which students are ready, coupled with sound advice for future possibilities that they should be considering. Mentoring then becomes more than just the establishment of a one-to-one relationship with a well-chosen adult; it allows access to a network of options available through a carefully constructed talent search system. The sole objective of Linda Brody's Study of Exceptional Talent at Johns Hopkins University is to carry out this form of mentoring.

Conclusion

Through the talent search concept, SMPY has opened debate and dialogue in the field about viable alternatives to enrichment. SMPY has restored a long tradition of emphasis on the highly gifted, begun by Terman and Hollingworth, by developing a systematic approach to finding and serving such students. SMPY also has shifted the conception of what giftedness is, from an emphasis on global ability to an emphasis on talent. SMPY, moreover, has affected school-based programs by providing a research and developmental base for content and other forms of acceleration. It has stimulated institutions of higher education to undertake precollegiate learner programs that develop the specific talents of young people, provide links to university-level resources, and contribute to the educational enrichment of thousands of students nationwide. And through personal mentoring, the lives of many of this country's and other countries' best young minds have been directly affected.

References

Benbow, C. P. (1991). Meeting the needs of gifted students through use of acceleration: An often neglected resource. In M. C. Wang, M. C. Reynolds, & H. J. Walberg (Eds.), *Handbook of special education: Vol. 4. Research and practice* (pp. 23–36). New York: Pergamon Press.

Benbow, C. P. (1992). Academic achievement in mathematics and science of students between ages thirteen and twenty-three: Are there differences among students in the top one percent of mathematical ability? *Journal of Educational Psychology* 84:51–61.

Benbow, C. P., & Stanley, J. C. (1981). The devil's advocate: Sex differences in mathematical reasoning ability. *Journal for the Education of the Gifted* 4:169–243.

Benbow, C. P., & Stanley, J. C. (Eds.). (1983). *Academic precocity: Aspects of its development.* Baltimore: Johns Hopkins University Press.

Bloom, B. (1985). *Developing talent in young people.* New York: Ballantine Books.

Brody, L. E., & Benbow, C. P. (1987). Accelerative strategies: How effective are they for the gifted? *Gifted Child Quarterly* 3:105–110.

Brody, L. E., Assouline, S. G., & Stanley, J. C. (1990). Five years of early entrants: Predicting successful achievement in college. *Gifted Child Quarterly* 34:138–142.

Csikszentmihalyi, M. (Ed.). (1988). *Optimal experience.* New York: Cambridge University Press.

Daurio, S. P. (1979). Educational enrichment versus acceleration: A review of the literature. In W. C. George, S. J. Cohn, & J. C. Stanley (Eds.), *Educating the gifted: Acceleration and enrichment* (pp. 13–63). Baltimore: Johns Hopkins University Press.

Dweck, C. S., & Elliott, E. S. (1983). Achievement motivation. In P. H. Mussen (Ed.), *Handbook of child psychology* (4th ed., Vol. 4, pp. 643–691). New York: Wiley.

Feldman, D. H. (1980). *Beyond universals in cognitive development.* Norwood, N.J.: Ablex.

Gallagher, J. J. (1969). Gifted children. In R. L. Ebel (Ed.), *Encyclopedia of educational research* (4th ed., pp. 537–544). New York: Macmillan.

Gardner, H. (1983). *Frames of mind.* New York: Basic Books.

Janos, P. M., Robinson, N. M., Carter, C., Chapel, A., Cufley, R., Curland, M., Daily, M., Guilland, M., Heinzig, M., Kehl, H., Lu, S., Sherry, D., Stoloff, J., & Wise, A. (1988). A cross-sectional developmental study of the social relations of students who enter college early. *Gifted Child Quarterly* 32:210–215.

Keating, D. P. (Ed.). (1976). *Intellectual talent: Research and development.* Baltimore: Johns Hopkins University Press.

Keating, D. P., & Stanley, J. C. (1972). *From eighth grade to selective college in one jump: Case studies in radical acceleration.* (ERIC Document Reproduction Service No. ED 061 679)

Kulik, J. A., & Kulik, C. C. (1984). Synthesis of research on effects of accelerated instruction. *Educational Leadership* 42:84–89.

Reynolds, M. C., Birch, J. W., & Tuseth, A. A. (1962). Review of research on early admissions. In M. C. Reynolds (Ed.), *Early school admission for mentally advanced children: A review of research and practice* (pp. 7–18). Reston, Va.: Council for Exceptional Children.

Richardson, T. M., & Benbow, C. P. (1990). Long-term effects of acceleration on the social-emotional adjustment of mathematically precocious youth. *Journal of Educational Psychology* 82:464–470.

Robinson, N. M., & Janos, P. M. (1986). Psychological adjustment in a college-level program of marked academic acceleration. *Journal of Youth and Adolescence* 15:51–60.

Stanley, J. C. (1990). Leta Hollingworth's contributions to above-level testing of the gifted. *Roeper Review* 12:166–171.

Stanley, J. C., & Benbow, C. P. (1981–1982). Using the SAT to find intellectually talented seventh graders. *College Board Review* 122:3–27.

Stanley, J. C., Keating, D. P., & Fox, L. H. (Eds.). (1974). *Mathematical talent: Discovery, description, and development.* Baltimore: Johns Hopkins University Press.

Stanley, J. C., & Stanley, B. S. K. (1986). High-school biology, chemistry, or physics learned well in three weeks. *Journal of Research in Science Teaching* 23:237–250.

Swiatek, M. A., & Benbow, C. P. (1991a). A ten-year longitudinal follow-up of ability-matched accelerated and unaccelerated gifted students. *Journal of Educational Psychology* 83:528–538.

Swiatek, M. A., & Benbow, C. P. (1991b). A ten-year longitudinal follow-up of participants in a fast-paced mathematics course. *Journal for Research in Mathematics Education* 22:138–150.

Van Tassel-Baska, J. L. (1983). Statewide replication of the Johns Hopkins Study of Mathematically Precocious Youth. In C. P. Benbow & J. C. Stanley (Eds.), *Academic precocity: Aspects of its development* (pp. 179–191). Baltimore: Johns Hopkins University Press.

Van Tassel-Baska, J. L. (1986). The case for acceleration. In J. Maker (Ed.), *Critical issues in gifted education* (pp. 148–161). Rockville, Md.: Aspen Systems.

Van Tassel-Baska, J. L., & Chepko-Sade, D. (1985). *An incidence study of disadvantaged gifted students in the Midwest.* Evanston, Ill.: Northwestern University, Center for Talent Development.

Van Tassel-Baska, J. L., & Strykowski, B. (1986). *An identification resource guide on the gifted and talented.* Evanston, Ill.: Northwestern University, Center for Talent Development.

16   Nurturing Exceptional Talent

SET as a Legacy of SMPY

LINDA E. BRODY AND

CAROL C. BLACKBURN

ollege-bound high school seniors who earn a standard score of at least 700 out of a possible 800 on either the mathematical or the verbal portion of the SAT-I (formerly the Scholastic Aptitude Test, or SAT) are usually extremely pleased by their performance. Such a score may be given considerable weight in competitive college admissions. However, when a student scores this high at a much younger age, such as eleven or twelve, suggesting exceptional precocity in mathematical or verbal reasoning,[1] initial pride and pleasure often take a back seat to concern about meeting the educational needs of the student until he or she is academically, socially, and emotionally ready to enter college full time. Helping extremely talented students develop appropriate educational plans and locate challenging supplemental opportunities has been a major focus of the Study of Mathematically Precocious Youth (SMPY) and is now the primary mission of the Study of Exceptional Talent (SET).

SMPY and the "700–800 on SAT-M before Age 13 Group"

SMPY was founded by Julian C. Stanley at Johns Hopkins University in 1971 to identify, study, and facilitate the education of youths who reason extremely well mathematically (Stanley, Keating, & Fox, 1974; see also chapters 14 and 17 herein). SMPY pioneered the use of above-level testing to identify precocious mathematical or verbal reasoning ability and designed rigorous academic

---

1. We estimate that students who score at this level represent approximately the top one in ten thousand of their age group in mathematical or verbal reasoning ability.

coursework to challenge high-scoring students. The SAT, a test designed to predict success in college among high school seniors, was administered to seventh graders. The concept of systematic talent searches expanded rather rapidly; today approximately 150,000 students participate annually in regional, state, or local talent searches (Cohn, 1991).[2]

Prompted by great concern for the needs of the most academically talented students among those identified in the talent searches, and wishing to direct his primary efforts toward those students, Julian Stanley made arrangements in 1979 for the creation of a separate organization, now the Center for Talented Youth (CTY) of the Institute for the Academic Advancement of Youth (IAAY), to conduct the Johns Hopkins Talent Search and academic summer programs. In 1980, SMPY announced a search for students throughout the country who had scored between 700 and 800 on the SAT-M before age thirteen.

Stanley's purpose in founding the "700–800 on SAT-M before Age 13 Group" echoed SMPY's original goals: to identify students who reason extremely well mathematically, to facilitate the further development of their talent, and to study their progress (Stanley, 1988). However, the highly selective nature of the 700M criterion kept the size of the group small enough that individual counseling could be offered. This individualized approach was considered important in meeting the needs of these extremely talented students, who come from a variety of home and school environments and differ greatly from most of their agemates in cognitive abilities. The students' progress was tracked so that the effectiveness of programmatic options could be evaluated.

The Study of Exceptional Talent

In 1991, SMPY's work on behalf of students who reason extremely well mathematically moved to IAAY as a department devoted to exceptional talent. Renamed the Study of Exceptional Talent in recognition of an expanded interest in high verbal as well as high mathematical talent, SET's mission is to continue the service efforts developed by SMPY and to study the progress of the students.

Although SET is based at IAAY, its efforts are national in orientation, and students are recruited from all talent searches or may take the SAT on their own.[3] Eligibility for SET is consistent with the standards established by SMPY:

2. Regional talent searches are conducted by Johns Hopkins, Northwestern, Duke, and the University of Denver. There are also several state and local talent searches, such as those conducted by Iowa State University and California State University at Sacramento. Some talent searches accept either the ACT or the SAT-I.
3. We thank the directors of the regional, state, and local talent searches who have supplied SMPY and SET with the names of qualifying students.

students must score between 700 and 800 on the mathematics portion of the SAT-I before age thirteen. To qualify on the verbal portion of the SAT, students must score between 700 and 800 on the recentered SAT-I, or have scored between 630 and 800 prior to recentering in 1995.[4]

Once eligibility is determined, students join SET by completing background questionnaires. Brief annual questionnaires provide updated information about students' activities, and in-depth surveys are administered periodically for specific research studies. SET members are also encouraged to call or write to SET's staff at any time with their questions and concerns regarding educational decisions, or to visit in person if that is feasible. Of course, some students seek SET's counseling and others do not. All SET members do, however, receive newsletters that provide information about opportunities to accelerate or supplement their school programs. The newsletters also include news about the students themselves. It is hoped that the students serve as role models for each other, stimulating and supporting high achievement.

Indeed, engendering the feeling of a peer group among SET members is an important component of the intervention. Students who are so highly able and who need a special educational program sometimes feel different from and uncomfortable with other students their age. The knowledge that there are students like themselves, their true intellectual peers, even if they never meet (although many do meet each other in academic summer programs and competitive events), can be an important source of comfort and support. (See chapter 17 below.)

Characteristics of SET Members

From 1980 through 1992, 1,132 students joined SMPY or SET by scoring between 700 and 800 on the SAT-M, between 630 and 800 on the SAT-V, or both. The data summarized below refer to this population.

Students typically qualify for SMPY or SET in the seventh grade, when they participate in one of the talent searches, although they may qualify at any time if they meet the age and score eligibility requirements. Thus, 3 members qualified for SET at age eight, 4 at age nine, 21 at age ten, 134 at age eleven, 796 at age twelve, and 174 at age thirteen.

Of this group, 76.1 percent ($N = 861$) are male and 23.9 percent ($N = 271$) are female; 76.0 percent ($N = 860$) qualified on the SAT-M, 11.3 percent ($N =$

4. Students tested after their thirteenth birthday are eligible for SMPY/SET if they score a minimum of ten additional points for each additional month or fraction of a month of age.

128) on the SAT-V, and 12.7 percent ($N = 144$) on both. Females are more heavily represented among the verbal qualifiers, with 55.5 percent of verbal qualifiers being female, compared to only 18.9 percent of the math qualifiers and 25.7 percent of the double qualifiers. SET members represent forty-two states, the District of Columbia, and several foreign countries.

These SET members include recently identified students who are between eight and thirteen years old, and students in their mid-twenties who were identified in the early 1980s and are now in graduate school or the work force. During the 1992–1993 school year, 3 SET members were still in elementary school (1 in grade four and 2 in grade five), 166 students were in middle school (grades six through eight), 413 were in high school (grades nine through twelve), 237 were in college, and 276 were college graduates and were attending graduate school, working, or both. (We do not have post–high school follow-up data on 37 members.)

A summary of additional selected characteristics of the SET members is presented below. Background information about students' families was obtained from questionnaires completed when students joined SMPY or SET, typically in the seventh grade.[5] Information that relates to students' behavior after that time was obtained from follow-up questionnaires.

Family Characteristics

Ethnic background. The representation of Asian Americans in the SET membership is much greater than in the general population for this age group.[6] Of the students who qualified for SET, 66.1 percent ($N = 748$) are Caucasian; 31.8 percent ($N = 360$) are Asian American; 0.8 percent ($N = 9$) are of mixed Asian American and Caucasian background; and 1.3 percent ($N = 15$) are African American, Hispanic, or a mixture that includes one of these backgrounds. (In subsequent statistics the 9 Asian American–Caucasian students are included in the Asian American population.) In contrast, the ethnic composition of all American students enrolled in colleges in the United States in 1991 was as follows: 78.8 percent Caucasian; 4.6 percent Asian American; and 16.6 percent African American, Hispanic, and Native American ("1991 Enrollment," 1991).

The Asian American representation is greater among the students who qualified for SET on the basis of their scores on the SAT-M than among those

5. Portions of this section appear in Blackburn & Brody (1994).
6. See Moore & Stanley (1988) for an earlier review of the ethnic backgrounds of a subset of this population.

who qualified on the SAT-V. Of the math qualifiers,[7] 63.4 percent ($N = 637$) are Caucasian, 35.3 percent ($N = 354$) are Asian American, and 1.3 percent ($N = 13$) are African American or Hispanic. In contrast, 80.1 percent ($N = 218$) of the verbal qualifiers are Caucasian, 19.1 percent ($N = 52$) are Asian American, and 0.7 percent ($N = 2$) are African American or Hispanic.

Asian American representation is also greater among the female SET members than among the male members: 29.3 percent ($N = 252$) of the males and 43.2 percent ($N = 117$) of the females are Asian American. Within the group of students who qualified on the SAT-M, 55.0 percent ($N = 110$) of the females are Asian American, while 30.3 percent ($N = 244$) of the males are Asian American. Among the verbal qualifiers, on the other hand, Caucasians make up approximately 80 percent of both gender subpopulations: 79.3 percent ($N = 130$) of the males and 81.5 percent ($N = 88$) of the females are Caucasian.

There is a striking difference in the immigration histories of the Asian American and Caucasian SET members. Of the members for whom we have relevant data, less than 6 percent ($N = 79$) of the fathers and mothers of the Caucasian members were educated in a country other than the United States (data are available for 1,349 out of a total of 1,505 Caucasian parents). In contrast, over 80 percent ($N = 550$) of the Asian American members' parents were educated (at least through the bachelor's degree level) in Asian countries (data available for 682 out of a total of 729 Asian American parents). The countries where the largest numbers of Asian American SET parents were educated are Taiwan (33.7 percent; $N = 230$), India and Sri Lanka (16.6 percent; $N = 113$), Korea (14.1 percent; $N = 96$), and the People's Republic of China (8.4 percent; $N = 57$). The remaining 8.1 percent of the Asian-educated parents were educated in Japan, the Philippines, Thailand, Pakistan, Bangladesh, Malaysia, Vietnam, and Burma.

The first-generation-immigrant status of such a large majority of the parents of Asian American SET members raises interesting research questions. Immigrant status alone, and the drive to succeed in America, cannot fully explain the high representation of Asian Americans in the SET population. It is likely that well-educated immigrant parents from such socially stable and technologically advanced countries as Taiwan and Korea are in a better position to take advantage of the opportunities America has to offer than are poorly educated immigrant parents from such less stable and technologically developed countries as Vietnam and Cambodia, and the backgrounds of the Asian Ameri-

7. This group includes individuals who qualified on both math and verbal scores.

can SET members reflect these social and economic factors. However, other stable and technologically advanced regions of the world from which well-educated people emigrate to the United States are not so heavily represented in the SET membership. For example, the total number of people who immigrated to the United States in 1991 from China and Taiwan is one-sixth the number who immigrated from Europe, yet children of first-generation European immigrants are not prevalent in the SET population. The relationship between ethnic background and talent development will be explored further in future studies of SET members.

Family demographics. SET members tend to come from small families: 13.8 percent are only children, 53.4 percent have one sibling, 24.4 percent have two siblings, 6.7 percent have three siblings, 8.4 percent have four or more siblings, and 2.5 percent have stepsiblings. Of those with siblings, 60.2 percent are the oldest child, 31.8 percent are the second child, 7.2 percent are the third child, and 0.8 percent have a twin. These percentages are approximately the same for males and females in the group. The percentage who are only or oldest children is higher in the Caucasian (69.6 percent only or oldest) than in the Asian American (57.6 percent) subpopulation ($\chi^2 = 14.9$; $p < .001$).

These students live overwhelmingly in intact biological families (based on responses at the time the student qualified for SMPY or SET membership, typically age twelve to thirteen); 93.3 percent ($N = 1,057$) of SET members live with both biological parents. Of the remainder, 1.9 percent ($N = 21$) live with one biological parent and one stepparent; 2.1 percent ($N = 24$) live with one biological parent only; 0.8 percent ($N = 9$) were adopted; and our data are incomplete for the remaining 1.9 percent ($N = 22$) of the members.

These results portray students who come from stable home environments, with over 90 percent living in intact families with both biological parents. Small families are also common, with two-thirds of the SET members living in families with two or fewer children. In addition, two-thirds of the SET members are only or oldest children. The latter finding is compatible with other reports of gifted and talented students (e.g., Hollingworth, 1942; Terman & Oden, 1925; Van Tassel-Baska & Olszewski-Kubilius, 1989) that note a predominance of oldest children among the subjects studied.

Education and occupation of parents. The parents of these students are, as a group, extremely well educated. Approximately 75 percent of the fathers and 49 percent of the mothers have completed graduate degrees, and 49 percent of the fathers and 16 percent of the mothers have completed a doctoral-level degree.

TABLE 16.1.   *Parents' Occupations (Expressed as Percentages within Each Row)*

Parent	Math/ Engineering	Medicine/ Biology	Business/ Law	Humanities	Blue Collar	Full-time Homemaker
Fathers						
Caucasian ($N = 707$)	28.0	12.3	36.8	17.0	5.9	0.0
Asian American ($N = 339$)	47.2	27.4	13.0	10.6	1.8	0.0
All ($N = 1,058$)	34.2	17.0	29.2	15.0	4.6	0.0
Mothers						
Caucasian ($N = 704$)	8.0	3.1	12.4	42.8	0.7	33.1
Asian American ($N = 325$)	15.7	10.2	15.7	21.9	1.8	34.8
All ($N = 1,042$)	10.6	5.3	13.3	36.5	1.0	33.3

The following are the highest levels of education completed by members' fathers (data available for $N = 1,102$): 7.3 percent have less than a B.A.; 17.7 percent have a B.A. or B.S.; 25.4 percent have a master's degree; and 49.6 percent have a Ph.D., M.D., J.D., or other doctoral degree. There are significant differences in the percentages computed for subpopulations as functions of gender and ethnicity: 58.1 percent of female SET members' fathers have completed doctoral-level degrees, as compared to 47.0 percent of male SET members' fathers ($\chi^2 = 9.6$; $p < .01$); and 66.6 percent of the Asian American fathers have completed doctoral-level degrees, as compared to 41.7 percent of the Caucasian fathers ($\chi^2 = 58.9$; $p < .0001$).

The highest levels of education completed by members' mothers (data available for $N = 1,101$) are as follows: 14.2 percent have less than a B.A.; 36.4 percent have a B.A. or B.S.; 33.5 percent have a master's degree; and 15.9 percent have a Ph.D., M.D., J.D., or other doctoral degree. A significantly higher percentage of Asian American mothers have completed doctoral-level degrees (20.7 percent, as compared to 13.2 percent of Caucasian mothers; $\chi^2 = 9.7$; $p < .01$). There are no other significant differences in mothers' education as functions of either gender or ethnicity.

The occupations of the parents of SMPY or SET members are outlined in table 16.1.[8] The general breakdowns of parental occupations are approximately the same when computed for subpopulations as a function of students' gender.

8. For this study, parents' occupations were divided into the following categories: Math/Engineering, including mathematics, computer science, engineering, physics, and chemistry; MD/Biology, including medicine and the biological sciences; Business/Law, including law, politics, and all types of business; Humanities, including not only the academic humanities disciplines but also social service professions such as clinical psychology, social work, nursing, elementary or secondary education, library work, and secretarial work; Blue Collar; and Full-time Homemaker, for a parent who does not work outside the home. We do not have data on the occupations of 6.5 percent of the fathers and 7.9 percent of the mothers.

However, a much higher percentage of Asian American than Caucasian parents work in mathematical or scientific professions. Table 16.1 lists the breakdown of parents' occupations for the entire population and for the Caucasian and Asian American subpopulations (excluding the parents whose occupations we do not know). Thus, the percentage of Asian American parents who work in mathematical or scientific professions is approximately double that of Caucasian parents in both cases: 74.6 percent of the Asian American fathers (as compared to 40.3 percent of the Caucasian fathers) and 25.8 percent of the Asian American mothers (as compared to 11.1 percent of the Caucasian mothers). The relatively high percentage of mothers who do not work outside the home is essentially identical in the Asian American and Caucasian subpopulations.

Career Interests of SET Members

The career goals of SET members are heavily weighted toward math and science. At the time they first joined SMPY or SET, 81.5 percent of students indicated career goals. Of these members, 50.9 percent indicated that they planned to go into careers in math, computer science, the physical sciences, or engineering; 24.9 percent planned to go into medicine or the biological sciences; 11.3 percent planned to go into law or business; and 12.7 percent planned to go into the humanities.

There are marked gender differences in the career goals of SET members. For the purposes of this comparison, we looked separately at math and verbal qualifiers, since the career goals of the individuals in those two high-ability groups might understandably be quite different. Furthermore, in this analysis, we excluded those students who qualified on both math and verbal scores; thus "math" refers to students who qualified only on the basis of their SAT-M scores, and "verbal" to students who qualified only on the basis of their SAT-V scores.

Among males with high math ability, career goals in math and the physical sciences were indicated three times more often (63.8 percent) than career goals in medicine and the biological sciences (20.4 percent); indeed, among these males, careers in medicine and biology were indicated only slightly more often than careers in law, business, and the humanities (15.8 percent). (See table 16.2.) The females with high math ability, on the other hand, most frequently indicated career goals in medicine and biology (43.1 percent). It is noteworthy that, compared to the boys' career goals, the career goals of the girls with high math ability were somewhat more evenly split among the biological sciences (43.1 percent), math and the physical sciences (30.9 percent), and the humanities (26.0 percent, including law and business). The students with high verbal ability also exhibited gender differences in their early career preferences: the

TABLE 16.2.   *Students' Career Goals in Seventh Grade (Expressed as Percentages within Each Row)*

	Math/ Engineering	Medicine/ Biology	Business/ Law	Humanities
Math				
Males ($N = 564$)	63.8	20.4	9.2	6.6
Females ($N = 123$)	30.9	43.1	13.0	13.0
Verbal				
Males ($N = 48$)	33.3	25.0	18.8	22.9
Females ($N = 58$)	13.8	15.5	13.8	56.9

majority of the boys indicated career goals in the sciences (58.3 percent), while the majority of the girls indicated career goals in business, law, and the humanities (70.7 percent).

SMPY and SET began identifying extremely able twelve-year-olds in 1980; many members are now college age or older. Thus, we can examine the college majors of SET members as an indication of their interests as they have grown older. Since all these early members were identified on the basis of math ability, a prevalence of majors in mathematics and the physical sciences is not surprising. The gender differences noted earlier in the group with high math ability persist, however. Among all SET members in college (including double qualifiers),[9] 69.4 percent of males ($N = 408$) and 33.0 percent of females ($N = 80$) chose math or a physical science field as their major. The biological sciences were chosen by 5.9 percent of males and 26.2 percent of females, and the humanities were chosen by 13.5 percent of males and 26.2 percent of females. (The remaining students are majoring in at least two areas.)

We can compare the career goals indicated by SET members at the age of twelve or thirteen with the majors these same students chose in college. The percentage of students whose field of interest stayed the same or changed between seventh grade and college is set forth in table 16.3. In contrast to other studies that have found the career interests of mathematically talented males to be more stable over time than those of mathematically talented females (e.g., Tobin, 1985), the interests of male and female SET members changed little during the intervening years. In particular, few males or females changed from having an interest in mathematics or the physical sciences to majoring in the

9. There is little change in the percentages presented here when double qualifiers are excluded from this group of highly able math reasoners. When double qualifiers are excluded, 70.7 percent of males ($N = 341$) and 38.1 percent of females ($N = 63$) chose math or a physical science field as their major. Among females, the percentage choosing the humanities is smaller when double qualifiers are excluded.

biological sciences or the humanities. In fact, for both genders, the percentage of students moving from the humanities to math or engineering is greater than the movement from math or engineering to the humanities. (Note that premedical students need not major in the biological sciences. Indeed, several SET members who majored in math or the physical sciences have gone on to medical school.)

Type of School Attended

At the time the students were identified for SMPY or SET (in seventh grade, in most cases), 75.8 percent of them attended public schools, 3.6 percent attended magnet schools or schools for the gifted and talented, 16.0 percent attended independent schools, and 4.0 percent attended parochial schools. Thus, the majority of SET members attend public schools, at least through the middle school years.

Although we do not have complete data on the high schools of which SET members are graduates, the majority attend neighborhood public high schools. After middle school, a few SET members have enrolled in private high schools, while several others have attended state magnet high schools, such as the North Carolina School of Science and Mathematics. However, boarding-school attendance is rare in this group. Most students have chosen to stay in their community public schools, using flexibility, acceleration, and supplemental opportunities to augment the school program. (See the discussion of options below.)

Postsecondary SET Members

By the fall of 1992, 547 SET members had entered college or were college graduates. Although SET members are or have been represented at approx-

TABLE 16.3.   *Individual SET Members' Career Goals in Seventh Grade and College Majors (Expressed as Percentages within Each Column)*

Career Goal	College Major	Males (N = 338)	Females (N = 65)
No change in career goal			
Math/engineering	Math/engineering	60.0	18.5
Medicine/biology	Medicine/biology	4.7	33.9
Business/law/humanities	Business/law/humanities	6.5	20.0
Change in career goal			
Math/engineering	Medicine/biology	3.0	1.5
Math/engineering	Business/law/humanities	5.3	3.1
Medicine/biology	Math/engineering	9.7	7.7
Business/law/humanities	Math/engineering	7.7	10.8

imately one hundred colleges or universities, the majority have attended highly selective institutions. Ninety-three SET members attend or have attended Harvard. Next in frequency of attendance are Princeton (47 students), the Massachusetts Institute of Technology (43), Stanford (38), the University of California at Berkeley (24), Yale (18), the University of Chicago (15), the California Institute of Technology (12), Johns Hopkins (11), Carnegie Mellon (10), Cornell (9), the University of Michigan (9), Brown (8), Duke (8), Rice (8), the University of Maryland (8), the University of Pennsylvania (8), the University of Washington (8), Northwestern (7), Washington University (7), Case Western (6), Harvey Mudd (6), and the University of Wisconsin (6). The remaining institutions had 5 or fewer SET members in attendance. It appears that many SET members have been accepted to the colleges of their choice. When a less selective college is chosen, it is often a state university or a college that offers merit-based financial aid and is chosen for financial reasons.

A subset of the group described above has graduated from college ($N = 276$). The paths these students pursued upon graduation were as follows: 43.5 percent ($N = 120$) entered graduate school, 5.4 percent ($N = 15$) entered medical school, an additional 2.9 percent ($N = 8$) enrolled in an M.D./Ph.D. program, 2.9 percent ($N = 8$) went to law school, 1.1 percent ($N = 3$) enrolled in business school, and 19.6 percent ($N = 54$) entered the work force, although some have indicated that they might return to graduate school in the future. Unfortunately, we lack updated information for 68 of the postcollege members. Nonetheless, the majority have chosen to continue their education beyond the baccalaureate, most in graduate or medical school.

Like the array of undergraduate colleges and universities chosen by SET members, the list of graduate schools SET members are attending or have attended is extremely impressive. As of the 1992–1993 academic year, SET members were pursuing graduate programs at the following institutions: Stanford (22 students), the University of California at Berkeley (17), Harvard (14), the Massachusetts Institute of Technology (12), the University of Chicago (5), the University of Michigan (5), the University of Pennsylvania (5), the University of Washington (5), the California Institute of Technology (4), Princeton (4), the University of California at Los Angeles (4), the University of Illinois (4), Carnegie Mellon (3), Columbia (3), Cornell (3), Duke (3), Johns Hopkins (3), and the University of Wisconsin (3). (Other universities had fewer than 3 SET members enrolled as graduate students.) Acceptance at such institutions is indicative of students' having accumulated excellent undergraduate academic records.

Only a few SET members are old enough to have completed their graduate studies yet. Thus, it will be some time before we can assess many of their career achievements. We will continue to observe these students as they embark on their career paths; meanwhile, the academic achievements of the group to date are outstanding.

Programmatic Options for Challenging SET Members

The primary purpose of SET is to provide information to students about opportunities to accelerate, enrich, or supplement their school programs so that they are stimulated and challenged. Our goal is for students to achieve an optimal match between their interests and abilities and their educational programming, through the use of curricular flexibility and an expanded view of learning that includes opportunities outside the classroom.

Students are encouraged to look beyond the lockstep curriculum, to identify appropriate courses and learning experiences in their schools and communities, and to design a program that meets their needs. Highly individualized programs are necessary, and flexibility on the part of schools is required. Some of the options students might consider in developing a program are listed below.[10]

Subject-Matter Acceleration

SET member Jonah took high school math in the sixth, seventh, and eighth grades, Matthew took physics courses at a local university while in ninth grade, and David studied calculus with a tutor provided by his school while in the fifth grade. Because of their exceptional mathematical reasoning abilities, these students needed to move more rapidly than their agemates through the mathematics curriculum and related subjects, but chose not to skip grades in the process. For social reasons they preferred to remain with their agemates for most of the school day; they felt they were adequately challenged in their verbal subjects, so moving ahead in grade placement to the level of their mathematics ability was neither necessary nor desirable. Moving ahead in mathematics was important, however, if they were to be adequately challenged.

Subject-matter acceleration permits students to progress in one or more subjects without regard to age or grade placement. It may involve students' taking classes with older students (e.g., SET members in junior high often take

10. See also Benbow (1986), Brody & Stanley (1991), and Southern, Jones, & Stanley (1993).

courses in high school, and high school students take college courses on a part-time basis), working with a tutor, studying independently, or taking courses in a summer program, such as the accelerated courses offered by the talent searches. However, it is essential that schools recognize such experiences and grant appropriate credit or placement so that students do not have to repeat coursework taken for the purpose of acceleration. (See Kolitch & Brody, 1992, for a summary of SET members' experiences with regard to acceleration in mathematics.)

Grade Skipping

Students who need greater challenges in several subject areas than a typical school program provides and who are willing to leave their agemates may want to skip one or more grades so that they can take all of their classes with older students. For example, SET member Lisa, precocious in reading and mathematics at a young age, entered kindergarten at age four. James completed first and second grade in one year. Kurt, already accelerated in mathematics and bored with middle school, skipped the eighth grade and entered high school a year early. Nancy attended the Early Entrance Program at the University of Washington in lieu of high school. Daniel left high school after the ninth grade and enrolled full time in a local university. Pamela skipped the twelfth grade to enter college a year early.

Students contemplating skipping one or more grades will want to consider the impact of such a decision on their social and emotional development. Academically, they will need to consider whether there will be gaps in content that should be filled, even though their mental age suggests that placement with older students is appropriate. If early entrance to college is contemplated, students should be aware that most colleges do not make special provisions to assist young students; however, some programs, such as the Early Entrance Program at the University of Washington, offer much support to such students (Brody & Stanley, 1991; Janos & Robinson, 1985). Although caution and planning are advised for students who wish to skip grades, the procedure has been a useful mechanism for selected SET members seeking escape from a curriculum that lacks challenge.

Independent Study and Correspondence Courses

Independent study can be used as a vehicle for accelerating in a subject or for exploring subject material that is outside the regular school curriculum. SET member Sophia studied geometry and precalculus independently in the eighth grade, while Michael opted to complete his high school mathematics curriculum through a university correspondence course while in the ninth grade. Johanna studied independently to take the Advanced Placement music examination. As a fourth grader, David studied high school chemistry with his mother; he will want to work with the school system to avoid repeating this material later in a formal class in high school. His scoring well on the College Board chemistry exam may help convince the relevant educators.

Provision for independent study and access to correspondence courses can greatly expand the academic offerings a school is able to make available to an individual student. The logistical and social concerns about placing young students with older students also can be avoided in this manner. However, access to a tutor or mentor is desirable, and it is important that arrangements be made for appropriate credit or placement as a result of the experience.

Mentorships and Internships

Mentorships allow students to work under the direction of a knowledgeable individual; an internship is similar but may not provide the same one-on-one interaction. An internship typically provides an experience in an office or laboratory, and it may or may not be supervised by someone who acts as a mentor. A mentorship might involve completing regular coursework under the mentor's direction or being exposed to material outside the school curriculum.

SET member Stephanie did a mentorship in aerospace engineering through a summer program. Thomas worked with a scientist at the Mayo Clinic, while Erik's mentor was a professional writer who critiqued his writing. Emily did an eight-week internship with the American Heart Association. Stephen attended the prestigious Research Science Institute, a summer program that pairs talented young people with professional scientists as mentors. Such arrangements provide opportunities for access to role models and real-world experiences, as well as for expanding content knowledge.

Extracurricular Activities

One should not overlook the value of extracurricular activities as learning experiences. For example, academic competitions can extend learning in a particular subject area far beyond the school curriculum. Winners earn much recognition as well. SET member Jonathan enjoys the challenge of competitions, and he qualified to attend the training camps for the U.S. International Mathematical, Physics, and Chemistry Olympiad teams. Ashley earned first place in the Westinghouse Science Talent Search Competition. In general, SET members are well represented in mathematics and science competitions and do extremely well.[11] The participation of SET members in humanities competitions in such areas as foreign languages, geography, and spelling is increasing dramatically.

Students also may use extracurricular activities to gain experience in the arts, athletics, leadership, and public service, fields that are outside the scope of most school programs and yet should be part of a well-educated person's background. SET members participate in a wide variety of pursuits: Mark's many activities included working with a church group; Jennifer volunteered at a hospital and tutored inner-city students; Chris was on his high school tennis team; Jim played in his school orchestra.

Making it clear that extracurricular activities offer opportunities for learning also imparts the message to students that learning should be lifelong and without boundaries; it is not something that occurs only in school. Appropriate use of leisure time will be important to students' achieving their full potential.

Academic Summer Programs

The message that learning should extend beyond school boundaries recognizes that it should also extend into the summer. Summers offer time for enrichment such as travel, music and athletic camps, internships, and a host of other options. However, students seeking academic courses at younger-than-typical ages or courses not offered in their schools can turn to an increasing network of opportunities to take academic courses in the summer.

CTY and the other talent searches offer a variety of accelerated and enriched courses in residential summer programs for students who meet the eligibility requirements. SET students have participated widely in these programs. For example, SET member Patrick took writing at CTY, while Jennifer took calculus and physics. Peter took astronomy at Duke's Talent Identification Program. Other SET members have attended similar programs at Northwestern, the University of Denver, Iowa State, Arizona State, and other universities.

While the talent-search model offers one option, numerous other summer programs that emphasize academic content have been developed for the pre-college population. SET members have been particularly well represented at institutes devoted to mathematics. For example, Jacob attended Dr. Arnold Ross's summer program at Ohio State University (see chapter 13 above), while

11. For example, in the 1993 Putnam Competition (in college-level mathematics), Harvard's team was number one in the United States and Canada; all three of its team members are in SET's 700-M group.

Anita chose to attend the Program in Mathematics for Young Scientists at Boston University.

High school students can also consider regular college summer school courses. Partly as a recruiting tool, many colleges have opened their summer school courses to high-achieving high school juniors and seniors (College Board, 1995). These courses have the advantage of offering college credit. For example, during the summer between her junior and senior years of high school, SET member Kathleen took psychology for credit at a college near her home.

Study and Travel Abroad

Foreign travel and studies abroad also offer unlimited opportunities for learning. SET member Kevin lived in Europe for several years with his family while he attended high school. Several SET members, such as Amit, who has relatives in India, have traveled to visit family members who live in other countries. Other students have traveled as tourists; one summer, David spent a month visiting Spain, France, and Germany with his family.

SET members have also participated in organized programs abroad. Irwin attended a six-week summer course in Taiwan in Chinese language and culture, and Margaret attended a five-week exchange program in Spain. Ashley participated in a program, organized by the American Regions Mathematics League, that gives high school students the opportunity to study mathematics in Russia for several weeks in the summer. Rebecca spent her high school junior year as an exchange student in Denmark, living with a Danish family and attending school.

Study abroad can be useful to supplement accelerative practices for students who hesitate to move ahead too quickly. For example, SET member Tui was a high school graduate at age fifteen; she then postponed college for a year while she studied in Europe. Besides the obvious benefits such an opportunity provided, it enabled her to be closer in age to the typical college student when she enrolled in college.

Optimal Use of Leisure Time

Many of the examples above include organized activities, whether they take place in or out of school. Students' free, unorganized time should also be recognized as providing opportunities for learning. Reading, writing, doing independent research, visiting museums, socializing with friends, and participating in athletics are just a few examples of activities that contribute to learning and to the development of the whole person. Parents and educators should be aware of the value of leisure activities when planning a child's education. Much that a child does on his or her own can supplement school.

SET members participate in a great many leisure activities. For example, Heather has enjoyed essay and poetry writing, sketching and painting, gardening, and coin collecting. Jim participated in a computer bulletin board, and Jennifer has spent time playing the piano and violin, doing crafts, and reading. These and similar activities develop important skills and interests.

Using Programmatic Options to Meet Individual Needs

The typical SET member employs not just one but many of the above options in an effort to develop an appropriate educational plan. There is much variation in the patterns selected by students because their interests, abilities, needs, and opportunities differ. There is also variation in parents' abilities to intervene and schools' willingness to respond to requests. In addition, continuous reevaluation and planning are necessary as a child progresses through school because needs and opportunities change. Aided by advice and suggestions from SMPY and SET, many students have been quite successful in making the system work for them, in requesting opportunities to be academically challenged. The precollege educational experiences of one SET member, Chris, are summarized below.

Chris grew up in a community that is not known for its progressive schools. However, the town is the home of a university, and the local schools responded with a willingness to be flexible in their attempts to meet Chris's educational needs. Chris's parents played an active role in requesting appropriate placement for him. As a result, the unique educational plan that Chris pursued met his needs quite well and helped him achieve at a high level.

Chris's precocity in mathematics was noticed early. From the second through the fourth grade, he received tutoring in algebra outside school from a graduate student at the local university. This tutor remained a mentor to Chris throughout his precollege years. In fifth grade, he took geometry at the local high school, but he was unhappy with the education he was receiving in the fifth-grade classroom. The decision was made that he would study at home, using a home-schooling correspondence program. During what would have been his sixth-grade year, he completed the seventh-grade correspondence curriculum. He also took algebra 2 at the high school, followed by precalculus in CTY's summer program. After one year of education via correspondence courses, he chose to return to the school system. His progress in all subjects allowed him to reenter school as a ninth grader. In ninth grade, he took Advanced Placement calculus, earning the maximum score of 5 on the AP examination. Throughout the rest of high school, he took mathematics at the local university, successfully completing such courses as multivariate calculus, differential equations, and topology. He graduated from high school two years earlier than is typical, having skipped the sixth and eighth grades. He was also highly accelerated in mathematics, having completed almost enough college mathematics to graduate as a mathematics major.

Throughout high school, he was active in mathematics competitions and was chosen to represent his state at the national level. He participated in other school activities as well, music being one of his major interests. Chris has a warm personality and feels comfortable with himself; he managed to maintain friendships with his agemates as well as make friends among his classmates, who were two years older than he. The social and emotional concerns that are paramount among many critics of acceleration were not an issue for Chris, though this is not true for all SET members.

Chris is not the most famous or illustrious student who has qualified for SMPY or SET. Some students earned higher scores on the SAT at younger ages, while others earned top prizes in national or international competitions. Some SET members chose more radical paths of acceleration. However, he is an example of a student whose exceptional abilities required atypical educational experiences and who succeeded in getting them.[12]

Chris spent most of his school years in a fairly average school environment, as have most SET members. By using accelerative opportunities, a summer program, a correspondence program, a mentor, extracurricular activities, and university courses to supplement the high school program, Chris succeeded in creating an educational environment that met his needs better than any one program possibly could. By finding ways to challenge himself, he kept his interest in mathematics alive, and he entered college full-time with a strong love of mathematics and much motivation to learn, as well as much subject-matter knowledge. He is a model for students everywhere, not only the highly able, whose needs do not quite fit the mold that schools offer.

Conclusion

The SMPY/SET population is a unique and comparatively large national sample of students who reason extremely well mathematically, verbally, or both.

12. For other examples, see Durden & Tangherlini (1993).

There are few such students in any given school or community; thus, typical school programs are unlikely to meet their needs. SMPY and SET have encouraged these students to choose from a variety of educational options, both in and out of school, to develop individualized educational plans that are uniquely suited to their abilities and interests. An ideal plan should provide for maximum challenge in the student's areas of strength, and also expose the student to the broad spectrum of a strong liberal arts curriculum as well as the arts, athletics, travel, and other activities.

The typical SET member has made use of a variety of accelerative and supplemental options in an effort to obtain a challenging precollegiate education. As a group, these students have achieved at extremely high levels. They have been well represented at prestigious academic competitions and in competitive summer programs; they have won numerous awards, honors, and fellowships; and they have gained acceptance to our nation's most selective universities and graduate schools.

Data on SET members' backgrounds suggest that they are likely to have well-educated and high-achieving parents; it is likely that such parents value education and do whatever they can to help their children attain the best education possible. Such family support is a great asset, and it has been supplemented with support and information provided by SMPY and SET. However, students at this level have educational needs that are most at variance with a typical school's offerings; they are also at risk for social and emotional problems because they differ so much from their agemates in their cognitive abilities. If we can help students at this level succeed in the system, it should be a less formidable task to help less able students develop a program that truly meets their needs as well.

SET will continue to monitor the progress of its members as they mature and as more students are added to the group in an effort to identify the educational options and other experiences that facilitate high achievement among academically talented individuals. We will also explore the contribution of such factors as family background, personality, motivation, and interests in promoting optimal talent development.

Although nature and nurture have both undoubtedly contributed to the exceptional abilities exhibited by the SET members, appropriately challenging educational experiences are vital to the full use and further development of those abilities and to stimulating a love of learning and an interest in high achievement. These students need and deserve the chance to reach their full potential, and our country cannot afford to lose the contributions that such highly able youths can make.

Acknowledgments

We acknowledge the great contribution of Julian Stanley in establishing the principles and mission that guide SET today and in providing continuing advice and direction. We also thank him, as well as Susan Hellerman and Lois Sandhofer, for helpful comments on this manuscript.

References

Benbow, C. P. (1986). SMPY's model for teaching mathematically precocious students. In J. S. Renzulli (Ed.), *Systems and models for developing programs for the gifted and talented* (pp. 1–25). Mansfield Center, Conn.: Creative Learning Press.

Blackburn, C. C., & Brody, L. E. (1994). Family background characteristics of students who reason extremely well mathematically and/or verbally. In N. Colangelo, S. G. Assouline, & D. L. Ambroson (Eds.). *Talent development* (Vol. 2, pp. 439–444). Dayton: Ohio Psychology Press.

Brody, L. E., & Stanley, J. C. (1991). Young college students: Assessing factors that contribute to success. In W. T. Southern & E. D. Jones (Eds.), *The academic acceleration of gifted children* (pp. 102–132). New York: Teachers College Press.

Cohn, S. J. (1991). Talent searches. In N. Colangelo & G. A. Davis (Eds.), *Handbook of gifted education* (pp. 166–177). Needham Heights, Mass.: Allyn & Bacon.

College Board. (1995). *Summer on campus*. New York: Author.

Durden, W. G., & Tangherlini, A. E. (1993). *Smart kids*. Seattle: Hogrefe & Huber.

Hollingworth, L. S. (1942). *Children above 180 IQ*. New York: World Book.

Janos, P. M., & Robinson, N. M. (1985). The performance of students in a program of radical acceleration at the university level. *Gifted Child Quarterly* 29:175–179.

Kolitch, E. R., & Brody, L. E. (1992). Mathematics acceleration of highly talented students: An evaluation. *Gifted Child Quarterly* 36:78–86.

Moore, S. D., & Stanley, J. C. (1988). Family backgrounds of young Asian Americans who reason extremely well mathematically. *Journal of the Illinois Council for the Gifted* 7:11–14.

1991 enrollment by race at 3,100 institutions of higher education. (1991, March 3). *The Chronicle of Higher Education*, p. A31.

Southern, W. T., Jones, E. D., & Stanley, J. C. (1993). Acceleration and enrichment: The context and development of program options. In K. A. Heller, F. J. Mönks, & A. H. Passow (Eds.), *International handbook of research and development on giftedness and talent* (pp. 387–409). Oxford: Pergamon Press.

Stanley, J. C. (1988). Some characteristics of SMPY's "700–800 on SAT-M before age 13 group": Youths who reason *extremely* well mathematically. *Gifted Child Quarterly* 32:205–209.

Stanley, J. C., Keating, D. P., & Fox, L. H. (Eds.). (1974). *Mathematical talent: Discovery, description, and development*. Baltimore: Johns Hopkins University Press.

Terman, L. M., & Oden, M. H. (1925). *Mental and physical traits of a thousand gifted children*. Stanford: Stanford University Press.

Tobin, D. (1985). A longitudinal study of values and career interests of mathematically gifted students. Unpublished doctoral dissertation, Johns Hopkins University, Baltimore, Md.

Van Tassel-Baska, J. L., & Olszewski-Kubilius, P. (1989). *Patterns of influence on gifted learners*. New York: Teachers College Press.

17 The Impact of SMPY's Educational Programs from the Perspective of the Participant

CAMILLA PERSSON BENBOW,

DAVID LUBINSKI, AND BABETTE SUCHY

T he Study of Mathematically Precocious Youth (SMPY) was founded by Julian C. Stanley in September 1971 at Johns Hopkins University. Its work has now spanned more than two decades and it has been adopted at several universities (principally Iowa State University). SMPY is concerned with the optimal development of intellectually precocious youth (particularly adolescents identified by age thirteen), and its empirical investigations are predicated on conducting research through service to intellectually gifted adolescents (see chapter 14 above). SMPY's aim is to help individual students fulfill their academic potential by developing and providing innovative educational programs and educational counseling (see chapter 16 above; see also Stanley, 1977; Stanley & Benbow, 1986). In the process, it attempts to discover those mechanisms that promote both intellectual and social well-being among the gifted. Those mechanisms have now become established in the form of a model, the SMPY model (Benbow, 1986; Stanley & Benbow, 1986).

The SMPY Model: MT:D_4P_3

The educational philosophy guiding SMPY's activities over the past two decades can be captured in a pseudochemical formula devised by Stanley: MT:D_4P_3. This stands for Mathematical Talent: Discovery, Description, Development, and Dissemination of its Principles, Practices, and Procedures (Stanley, Keating, & Fox, 1974). SMPY's focus is on the individual student, and its first step is to understand that student. This is accomplished in the identification (through participation in a talent search; see below) and characterization phases of its model (i.e., the first two Ds), where students come to learn about their distinct profiles of abilities and preferences. Once a student's ability and preference profile is known, he or she is encouraged to devise an educational program to create an appropriate learning environment, an environment commensurate with and responsive to his or her unique constellation of abilities and preferences (the third D, Development). This is accomplished through acceleration— that is, following the principle of placement according to competence. Students are prompted, through personal correspondence, newsletters, and other means, to look at the entire curriculum available to them (and this includes the postsecondary curriculum as well) in order to locate where in each subject they might be appropriately placed according to their demonstrated competence rather than their chronological age. Then they are encouraged and supported in their attempts to gain access to appropriate curricula or educational experiences (such as the MathCounts competition) that may or may not be available within the schools.

In essence, SMPY promotes competence rather than age as the main criterion to be used in determining who obtains access to what curricula and opportunities, and at what time. The goal is to develop a combination of accelerative options that reflect the best possible alternative for educating a specific child. It uses available resources to meet the needs of gifted children. This approach has been termed curricular flexibility. The various options SMPY has developed, experimented with, and offered to students seeking to add challenge to their education have been grouped together and called a smorgasbord of educationally accelerative opportunities (Benbow, 1986; Benbow & Lubinski, 1994; Southern, Jones, & Stanley, 1993). Such opportunities include: grade skipping, entering a course a year or more early, taking college courses while in high school, enrolling in Advanced Placement classes and taking their examinations, graduating from high school early or entering an early-entrance college program, mentoring, and taking fast-paced classes. (It should be noted that the last is an innovation of SMPY and does not reflect an already available resource; it is described in more detail below.) Through the use of curricular flexibility and relevant out-of-school experiences, an individual program is tailored to meet the needs of each intellectually gifted child, and the program is periodically monitored and updated. This in essence is the SMPY model for educating intellectually talented children.

In less than two decades, Stanley and his colleagues worked out and refined this model for identifying and serving mathematically and verbally gifted youth. Concurrently, they marshaled empirical support for this model through multiple studies conducted in many different settings (see, e.g., Benbow, 1992; Benbow & Stanley, 1983a). As a result of their efforts, the model has probably become the dominant one in the field—certainly if measured by the number of lives touched.

Talent Search: The Identification Phase

Through the talent search, the first component to be developed (it was begun in March 1972 with 450 students from the Greater Baltimore area) and the first component experienced by students (Keating & Stanley, 1972), many more than one million students from across the nation have been identified as exceptionally talented, mathematically or verbally (or both). Today, approximately 150,000 students participate in talent searches on an annual basis. All of these students, who are already known to be in the top 3 percent on age-appropriate standardized achievement tests typically administered by our nation's schools (e.g., the Iowa Test of Basic Skills), take the College Board Scholastic Aptitude Test (SAT).[1] Through this out-of-level testing they are able to learn about their relative strengths and weaknesses with respect to the two most critical intellectual attributes for academic excellence, verbal and mathematical reasoning abilities.

For gifted adolescents, the SAT enables a precise assessment of the nature and relative strengths of their intellectual gifts, because these students are all bumping their heads on the ceiling of conventional ability instruments (designed for their age-equivalent peers). By circumventing the ceiling problem attendant with conventional age-appropriate assessment tools, the SAT indexes the full scope of their academic potential along two dimensions, mathematical and verbal reasoning, allowing for more-precise differentiation of the exceptionally able from the able, along with providing each student's intraindividual pattern (see figure 17.1). (Students who receive high scores on the SAT also are given the opportunity to learn about some of their other abilities, principally spatial ability, and their educational and vocational preferences are assessed with questionnaires initially designed for young adults.)

The predictive value of the SAT for gifted thirteen-year-olds has been

---

1. In some geographic areas the ACT Assessment also has become an option for talent-search participants.

Differentiation of Talent

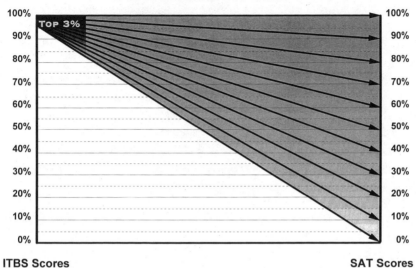

ITBS Scores   SAT Scores

Figure 17.1. Differentiation of talent.

demonstrated by Benbow (1992), who underscores the importance of assessing individual differences within the top 1 percent of intellectual talent (viz., IQs ranging from approximately 137 to beyond 200). Benbow (1992) shows that over ten-year time frames, between ages thirteen and twenty-three, the academic accomplishments of those individuals in the *top quarter of the top 1 percent* in mathematical ability were much more impressive than the accomplishments of those in the *bottom quarter of the top 1 percent* (who were, nonetheless, themselves high achievers). An additional conclusion drawn from this study, as well as others, is that SMPY can identify early those individuals who have the potential to become our nation's great scientific achievers. What has not been demonstrated, however, is how useful the students themselves consider this process of learning about their abilities through the talent search.

Educational Facilitation

SMPY has never favored identification solely for the sake of learning about students' ability profiles—that is, their relative strengths in mathematical, spatial, and verbal reasoning abilities, which are the intellectual abilities known to have differential validity for competence in contrasting educational and vocational tracks (Humphreys, Lubinski, & Yao, 1993; Lubinski & Dawis, 1992). Ideally, identification should be followed by services for the identified students (Stanley, 1977; Stanley & Benbow, 1982). The purpose of identification, in SMPY's view, is to help assess what educational interventions and services are essential for the students.

In 1971, when SMPY began, it was not clear what was appropriate for facilitating the education of intellectually precocious youth. It did appear, however, that acceleration, although rarely used, seemed the method with the most empirical support (see chapters 3 and 4 above). SMPY began experimenting with various educational innovations, based on the principle of acceleration, in the hope of uncovering better ways to provide academic challenges to the gifted students following their identification. Through this work, the concept of acceleration in its many forms was developed and given further empirical support; it also became more widely accepted by the educational community (Stanley, 1978).

In conjunction with the above work, SMPY developed fast-paced mathematics and science classes, where students have the opportunity to (and do!) master one full year of high school subject matter in just three intensive weeks during the summer. This effort began in 1972 with a mathematics class of some thirty students, called Wolfson I in honor of its capable instructor (Fox, 1974). Today, more than seven thousand students across the country are served annually by such classes, which are offered in verbal, mathematical, and scientific areas (from philosophy to physics). Also, SMPY began experimenting with radically accelerating highly precocious adolescents, with several students entering college before age sixteen (some even at ten) and succeeding beyond Stanley's or anyone else's expectations (see also chapter 9 above). Now, in the mid-1990s, entering college a year early has become fairly commonplace, an event not worthy of note even in local papers.

How have these programmatic innovations fared when evaluated? Quite well indeed. Results of evaluation studies have been uniformly positive (see Bartkovich & Mezynski, 1981; Benbow & Stanley, 1983a; Brody & Benbow, 1987; Kolitch & Brody, 1992; Mezynski & Stanley, 1980; Richardson & Benbow, 1990; Stanley & Benbow, 1983; Stanley & McGill, 1986; Stanley & Stanley, 1986; Swiatek & Benbow, 1991a, 1991b, 1992). Although multiple longitudinal studies have been conducted on a variety of acceleration options, we can summarize the results quite succinctly: when differences are found, they tend to favor those who had been accelerated over those who had not, irrespective of the mode of acceleration (see, e.g., Swiatek & Benbow, 1991a, 1991b). This is precisely what Cronbach reports for the Terman subjects (see chapter 10 above), who were identified in the early 1920s and have been studied longitudinally for more than seventy years. Moreover, we know that students are satisfied with their acceleration in both the short and the long term (Richardson & Benbow, 1990; Swiatek & Benbow, 1992).

What has not previously been explored, however, is how SMPY's services and programs are viewed several years later by the participants themselves. Is SMPY still seen as beneficial by students when, for example, they have graduated from high school or college? Do they feel that having been SMPY participants was useful to them? What components of the SMPY model are viewed as most useful in the long term? How many students actually followed some of SMPY's advice that was delivered either personally or through its various newsletters and booklets? The purpose of this chapter is to provide answers to these questions and others like them.

The Purpose of the Current Study

This chapter, then, is the complement to chapter 15 above, in which the impact SMPY has had on the field of education, particularly on gifted education, was revealed. This chapter documents the impact that SMPY has had on the students it has served, not in terms of their eventual academic achievements, as that has already been documented (see, e.g., Benbow, 1983, 1992; Benbow & Arjmand, 1990; Swiatek & Benbow, 1991a, 1991b), but in terms of their subjective impressions of their participation and its influence on their development. Our evaluation will focus on students identified by SMPY, regardless of whether or not they received any assistance beyond the basics provided through the talent search. This makes the analysis comparable to that of Van Tassel-Baska in chapter 15, who did not limit her analysis to schools that had worked closely with SMPY.

This evaluation will draw on the vast amount of data collected by SMPY at Iowa State University through its longitudinal study. This longitudinal study, originally begun at Johns Hopkins, is in its third decade. The study currently includes about five thousand mathematically and verbally talented individuals identified over a twenty-year period and grouped into five cohorts, each separated by a few years.

The SMPY Longitudinal Study

The SMPY longitudinal study is primarily designed to develop a better understanding of the processes whereby precocious forms of intellectual talent, identified before age thirteen, result in noteworthy adult achievements and creative products.

Design

A description of the longitudinal study is provided in figure 17.2. There are five cohorts in all (see Lubinski & Benbow, 1994). Four were assembled through talent searches; a fifth cohort is composed of graduate students in engineering, mathematics, and physical science departments at top universities in the United States. (Each cohort is separated by a few years.) Combined, the cohorts span twenty years, with findings from each of the first four cohorts being able to replicate analyses conducted in other time frames. In addition, because the students in the first four cohorts were identified over a twenty-year period using the same criteria and are studied at the same junctures, the study allows for a reasonable assessment of historical effects and also for some degree of control of historical influences.

Another unique aspect of this study is the ability to modify and add new assessment materials. Cohort 4 grows by approximately four hundred partici-

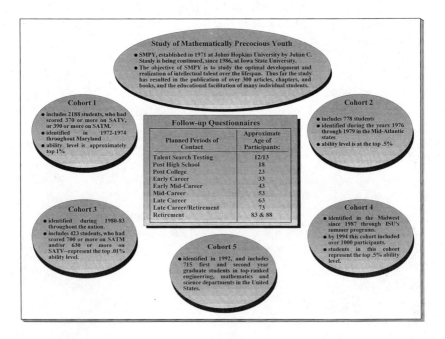

Figure 17.2. SMPY longitudinal study.

pants each year, allowing us to ask questions not pertinent to participants in 1972. The currency of the study is, therefore, maintained. Finally, the retrospective but also longitudinal study of cohort 5, graduate students in this nation's top engineering, mathematics, and physical science departments, has been initiated to ascertain whether such students differ in experiential or psychological ways from students identified in conventional talent searches. Data from cohort 5 will help assess how well SMPY's findings based on students identified by the SAT at age thirteen can be generalized to other groups of gifted individuals (see also chapter 18 below).

The Cohorts

The first four SMPY cohorts were formed using different ability cutoffs on the SAT. The first three cohorts are successively more able, while the fourth, consisting primarily of Midwestern residents who are being identified through the Office of Precollegiate Programs for Talented and Gifted (OPPTAG) at Iowa State University, represents the same ability level as cohort 2. A detailing of each cohort outlined in figure 17.2 is given in Table 17.1.

Cohort 1 was identified in SMPY's March 1972, January 1973, and January 1974 talent searches as seventh or eighth graders scoring 390 or higher on the SAT-M or 370 or higher on the SAT-V (Benbow, 1983, 1992; Benbow & Arjmand, 1990). Those cutoff scores were selected because they represented the average performance of a random sample of high school females on the SAT at that time. The approximately two thousand students were drawn primarily from the state of Maryland, with a heavy concentration from the Greater Baltimore area. Cohort 2 is composed of at least the top third of seventh-grade students from SMPY's December 1976, January 1978, and January 1979 talent searches (using cutoff scores at or above the top 0.5 percent in general intellectual ability). These nearly eight hundred students were drawn from the Middle Atlantic states and were studied by Brody and Benbow (1987). It should be noted that these first two cohorts are separated by at least three years. About 60 percent of the participants are male.

Cohort 3 is composed of three groups and is national in its representation (see chapter 16 above for a more comprehensive description of cohort 3). It consists of approximately three hundred students who scored at least 700 on the SAT-M before age thirteen between November 1980 and November 1983 (700Ms). It also includes more than 150 students scoring at or above 630 on the SAT-V before age thirteen (630Vs). (These scores represent the top one in ten thousand for mathematical and verbal reasoning abilities, respectively.) Finally, for comparison purposes, cohort 3 includes one hundred seventh-grade stu-

TABLE 17.1.   *Cohorts of SMPY's Longitudinal Study*

Cohort	N	When Identified	Age at Identification	Criteria	Ability Level
1	2,188	1972–1974	12–13	SAT-M ≥ 390 or SAT-V ≥ 370	Top 1%
2	778	1976–1979	12	Top third of talent-search participants	Top 0.5%
3	423	1980–1983		SAT-M ≥ 700 or SAT-V ≥ 630	Top 0.01%
Comparison groups	150	1983 1982	12 12	SAT-M + SAT-V ≤ 540 SAT-M 500–590 SAT-M 600–690	Top 5%
4 >	1,000	1987–	12	SAT-M ≥ 500 or SAT-V ≥ 430	Top 0.5% Top 0.5%
5	715	1992	23	Graduate students in top-ranked engineering, math, and science departments in the United States	

dents scoring nearly at chance on the SAT (i.e., SAT-M + SAT-V 540) in the 1983 talent search conducted by the Center for Talented Youth (CTY) at Johns Hopkins University. Because chance performance tends to imply low ability, it is important to keep in mind that this last group's ability level is still in the top 5 percent on national norms (only students scoring in the top 3 percent in ability can enter a talent search); thus, by most definitions they too would be considered at least modestly gifted.

Cohort 4 consists of one thousand students, primarily Midwesterners, scoring before age thirteen at least 500 on the SAT-M, 430 on the SAT-V, 930 on the SAT-M plus the SAT-V, or 20 on an ACT subtest composite. Like cohort 2, they represent the top 0.5 percent in ability. Students in cohort 4 had enrolled in Iowa State's summer program for intellectually talented youth (see Lubinski & Benbow, 1992, for a profile of their abilities and values), which is based purely on the SMPY model. Several comparison groups also are being formed from the Iowa Talent Search, which screens students with abilities in the top 3 percent in the nation, as well as from students in the normative ability range.

Finally, cohort 5 contains more than 715 individuals who are currently enrolled in top graduate programs. Approximately 50 percent of the sample members are female. This sample was surveyed in the spring of 1992, with a response rate of 93 percent. Some of the findings from this survey are reported in Lubinski, Benbow, Eftekhari-Sanjani, and Jensen (in preparation).

Collectively, the five cohorts of SMPY comprise approximately five thousand highly able students. This number will soon increase to about six thousand. All of the students in the five cohorts are being surveyed at critical junctures throughout their youth and adult lives, as can be seen in figure 17.2. Each cohort, moreover, will be surveyed at the same ages to ensure comparability of findings across cohorts.

The Status of the Longitudinal Study

To date, we have surveyed cohort 1 at ages thirteen, eighteen, twenty-three, and thirty-three (in progress). Cohort 2 also has been surveyed at ages thirteen, eighteen, and twenty-three; their age thirty-three survey will be mailed to them over the next three years. Cohort 3 has been surveyed at ages thirteen, eighteen, and twenty-three (in progress). Cohort 4 has been surveyed at ages thirteen and eighteen (in progress). Cohort 5 has been surveyed at age twenty-three only, but that survey included much retrospective information. Response rates to our several follow-up surveys range from 75 percent to well over 90 percent. Respondents did not differ significantly from nonrespondents on key variables including ability, family background, and college attendance (Benbow & Arjmand, 1990; Benbow & Stanley, 1982).

Plan of Analysis

In this chapter, we present data on the SMPY participants' subjective impressions of SMPY's programs and services. Longitudinal data with any reasonable sample size is available only for cohorts 1, 2, and 3. Thus, our analysis will be restricted to those cohorts, except in a few instances where preliminary data from cohort 4's survey at age eighteen will be presented. The total N across cohorts approximates thirty-five hundred. Further, for cohorts 1 and 2 we have data on students at ages eighteen and twenty-three. Because the survey at age twenty-three is in progress for cohort 3, preliminary analyses were conducted only for a few specific, but highly relevant, questions in that survey. Thus, for the most part, data on cohort 3 are limited to those obtained at age eighteen.

The two primary groups of cohort 3 will be isolated for analysis, the 700Ms (the extremely talented mathematically, who represent the top one in ten thousand) and 630Vs (the extremely talented verbally, who represent the top one in ten thousand). The 700Ms, as a group, received intensive exposure to the SMPY model; they could choose to receive much assistance from SMPY throughout their high school years. The 630Vs, for reasons beyond the scope of this chapter, had access to relatively little additional assistance beyond that provided by the talent-search program, which was not directly operated by SMPY at the time of their identification (see chapter 14 above).[2] Those who met the criteria for inclusion in both groups were included with the 700Ms for the purposes of this evaluation, since they could choose to partake of intensive treatment interventions.

Cohort 3 received the most-intensive treatment with the SMPY model, followed by cohort 2. Cohort 1 received the least amount of assistance from SMPY, as its members were identified when SMPY was working out its procedures (the talent search, fast-paced programs, and so forth). Thus, the later cohorts not only received much more assistance from SMPY, they also benefited from the experience gained with the earlier cohorts. Finally, each cohort is successively more able. It is, therefore, difficult to separate out and evaluate these confounding influences.

Data from all relevant questions in our various surveys at ages eighteen and twenty-three will be presented. All analyses were performed separately by sex, but findings are discussed collapsed across sex unless there were meaningful gender differences. Any important differences between cohorts, the two sexes, or other variables are evaluated by means of an effect size (Cohen, 1988), because almost any difference is bound to be statistically significant with the large sample sizes in this study. For means, the effect size is d; $d = [X_1 - X_2]/SD$ (where the standard deviation is pooled across both genders). Differences between proportions are represented by the effect size, h (computed by performing an arc sine transformation of each proportion and then calculating the difference, following Cohen, 1988).

The various cohorts did not necessarily respond to the same questions, nor were the same questions necessarily asked at ages eighteen and twenty-three. Also, the actual number of students responding to any one question tended to vary within a cohort. With these caveats in mind, comparisons of students' perceptions of SMPY's usefulness were made across time and across cohorts.

We start off with a presentation of these students' SAT scores at age thirteen and at the end of high school, their educational aspirations, the extent to which they were accelerated (following SMPY's advice), and how they were accelerated. We then present data on how students who had been accelerated

2. Those who qualify for the 630V group now do have access to services similar to those offered to individuals meeting the criteria for the 700M group (see chapter 16 above). This expansion of services from the mathematics domain to other domains reflects well how SMPY has operated all along. SMPY first focuses its efforts on mathematics and related disciplines. When those programs are in place, the focus expands to accommodate other forms of talent and the disciplines in which they are applied and needed.

viewed their acceleration and how those who had not viewed their lack of acceleration. This naturally leads to the students' perceptions of SMPY and its various components, the primary focus of our chapter.

Results and Discussion

SAT Scores

In table 17.2 we present mean SAT scores, separately for students in each of cohorts 1 through 3 and by sex, at the time of the talent search (age twelve to thirteen, or seventh grade) and at the end of high school (approximately age seventeen). The differences in degree of giftedness among the cohorts is clearly evident, even though all three groups must be viewed as highly gifted. In addition, the usefulness of assessing these students' abilities with the SAT at age thirteen rather than at the typical age of seventeen is illustrated in table 17.2. This is because there are clear ceiling effects evident in the data from age seventeen for students in all three cohorts, but especially for students in cohort 3. The ceiling effects for cohort 3 are so marked that, if you looked only at their high school SAT scores, it would be difficult to differentiate between those whose talents lie primarily in verbal areas and those whose talents are primarily mathematical (i.e., 630Vs versus 700Ms). Yet the SAT scores at age thirteen bring out those differences beautifully; if an SAT with a ceiling of 1,100 were designed, profile differences would reemerge.

TABLE 17.2.   *Talent Search and High School SAT Means and Standard Deviations for Cohorts 1-3, by Sex*

	T.S. SAT-M		T.S. SAT-V		H.S. SAT-M		H.S. SAT-V	
	Mean	(SD)	Mean	(SD)	Mean	(SD)	Mean	(SD)
Cohort 1								
Males	535	(77)	429	(81)	694	(69)	593	(86)
Females	502	(61)	456	(86)	649	(68)	598	(86)
Cohort 2								
Males	569	(70)	456	(76)	747	(43)	660	(74)
Females	522	(60)	471	(72)	705	(58)	674	(67)
Cohort 3								
700M								
Males	729	(27)	494	(75)	781	(22)	692	(60)
Females	725	(19)	505	(85)	773	(31)	701	(52)
630V								
Males	593	(69)	665	(31)	741	(49)	756	(29)
Females	535	(82)	656	(25)	680	(79)	740	(40)

TABLE 17.3.   *Educational Aspirations of Cohorts 1–3, by Sex*

| | Highest Degree Planned For | | | |
	Less than Bachelor's (%)	Bachelor's (%)	Master's (%)	Doctorate (%)
Cohort 1				
Males	4	16	36	44
Females	6	24	34	36
Cohort 2				
Males	1	1	37	62
Females	2	1	33	64
Cohort 3				
700M				
Males	1	12	20	68
Females	0	6	18	77
630V				
Males	0	17	6	79
Females	0	17	25	58
College freshmen, 1992				
Males	0	31	36	23
Females	0	28	38	24

Source: Chronicle of Higher Education (1992).

The SAT scores increase by about 150 to 200 points over the high school years, excluding consideration of those scores that are so affected by insufficient ceilings that growth is impossible to assess with the SAT (e.g., the SAT-M scores of the 700Ms). Preliminary analyses of the SAT growth curves for these students indicate that most of the growth in SAT scores is complete by the end of the tenth grade. Finally, the well-documented and much-discussed gender differences in SAT-M scores also are apparent (see Benbow, 1988; Benbow & Stanley, 1980, 1981, 1983b; Lubinski & Benbow, 1992). These differences are comparable to those observed by other investigators using different instruments in other samples (Lubinski & Humphreys, 1990a, 1990b; Stanley, Benbow, Brody, Dauber, & Lupkowski, 1992).

Educational Aspirations

Table 17.3 contains relevant data for the first three cohorts, for the highest degree the students hope to earn. The degree most frequently aspired to, across all cohorts and both genders, is a doctorate. This is particularly so for cohorts 2 and 3, where 60 percent to well over 70 percent of the students in any of the groups hope to earn doctoral degrees. Compare these numbers to that obtained for college freshmen in the fall of 1990 (Chronicle of Higher Education, 1992), where 23 percent aspired to a doctorate and the most common aspiration was a master's degree (37 percent).

Acceleration

Grade acceleration. We will first consider grade skipping. Table 17.4 gives the proportion of students who skipped a grade before the talent search (i.e., in elementary school, where this option tends to be more appropriate) and after participation in the talent search, when some students would have been advised by SMPY to consider this form of acceleration. The overall proportion of students skipping a grade, from kindergarten through twelfth grade, also is reported. The greatest amount of grade skipping was reported by cohort 3, the group for whom this option would have been most appropriate. For all groups but one in cohort 3, over 50 percent skipped a grade. The exception was the 630V females, only 19 percent of whom skipped a grade. Somewhat unanticipated was that the majority in cohort 3 who skipped did so before seventh grade. In cohorts 1 and 2, 14 percent and 28 percent, respectively, skipped at least one grade, but here the majority were accelerated after their participation in the talent search.

A couple of conclusions can be drawn. First, the more able the group, the more frequently its members skipped a grade. Second, the influence of SMPY's

TABLE 17.4.   *Percentage of Cohorts 1–3 Skipping at Least One Grade, by Sex*

	Skipped Grade		
	Before Talent Search (%)	After Talent Search (%)	Total (%)
Cohort 1			
Males	8	10	14
Females	6	11	15
Cohort 2			
Males	16	26	29
Females	17	24	28
Cohort 3			
700M			
Males	36	18	52
Females	39	24	57
630V			
Males	23	29	50
Females	19	6	19

advice is suggested for at least cohorts 1 and 2, who skipped at a higher rate after their identification by SMPY. The data for cohort 3 did not show this trend, but this finding is difficult to interpret. Many of the students in that cohort were brought to SMPY's attention at ages younger than twelve. Also, their degree of precocity would make the need for grade skipping much more apparent to all involved. Finally, by the 1980s acceleration was becoming increasingly accepted by the educational community, especially for exceptional children like those in cohort 3.

Content acceleration. For many SMPY participants, grade skipping is not warranted but subject-matter acceleration would be beneficial. In table 17.5 we present data on how frequently this option was used by students. In cohorts 1, 2, and 3, respectively, approximately 85 percent, 86 percent, and 92 percent took advantage of at least one form of subject-matter acceleration. In cohort 2, the students used subject-matter acceleration more frequently after their participation in the talent search than before. For cohort 3 the data are less clear-cut, potentially for the same reasons as noted for grade acceleration. (For cohort 1 this breakdown could not be done; data were not collected in a form that would allow such an analysis.)

We can clarify the picture, however, if we consider the various forms of acceleration used by individuals in cohorts 2 and 3 (see table 17.6). Excluding the generic (and uninterpretable) category of acceleration in subject matter, the most common forms of content acceleration are, in order of frequency: receiving college credit through examination (e.g., Advanced Placement coursework

TABLE 17.5. *Percentage of Cohorts 1–3 Using Content Acceleration, by Sex*

	Before Talent Search	After Talent Search	Total
Cohort 1			
Males	–	–	87
Females	–	–	81
Cohort 2			
Males	55	69	88
Females	54	62	81
Cohort 3			
700M			
Males	82	82	96
Females	83	89	94
630V			
Males	63	77	96
Females	69	64	89

TABLE 17.6.   *Percentage of Cohorts 2 and 3 Using Acceleration, by Sex*

| | Cohort 2 | | Cohort 3 | | | |
| | | | 700M | | 630V | |
	Males	Females	Males	Females	Males	Females
Credit by exam (e.g., AP)	68	63	84	89	61	76
Subject matter	80	73	85	91	75	70
College courses in high school	39	31	61	46	36	38
Special classes	32	23	44	46	33	38
Tutor	9	6	28	37	8	11
Early graduation (no grade skipping)	2	4	9	3	6	3
Early college entrance	11	9	22	26	17	3

and exams), taking college courses while in high school, and participating in special classes (e.g., SMPY's fast-paced mathematics class). These are the very options of which SMPY is a strong advocate; they also tend to be used in secondary schools, after the students would have participated in the talent search. The comparison of the results from the 700Ms and the 630Vs also is helpful here. More of the 700Ms elected to use content acceleration than the 630Vs. In combination, these results would seem to indicate that students and their parents were heeding SMPY's advice to speed up their educational progress.

Students' perceptions of their acceleration. At ages eighteen and twenty-three, the individuals in cohort 1 were asked to rate how their acceleration had affected them educationally as well as socially and emotionally (Benbow, 1983; Richardson & Benbow, 1990). The overall conclusion gleaned from these data, as reported by Benbow (1983) and Richardson and Benbow (1990), was that acceleration helped educationally while not detracting from their social and emotional development. For example, at age eighteen, 68 percent felt that acceleration had affected them for the better or much better, and less than 1 percent felt it had affected them significantly for the worse. By age twenty-three the negative effects noted at age eighteen seemed to have faded (Richardson & Benbow, 1990).

Recently, more-extensive data became available at both ages eighteen and twenty-three for cohorts 3 and 2, respectively. At the end of high school, for example, those who had been accelerated were asked to rate on a five-point scale how acceleration had affected them in sixteen different areas. The mean for each of these sixteen individual items consistently exceeded the midpoint of the scale, which was labeled "no effect." There was only one exception, where the mean for the item did not quite reach 3 (the midpoint): ability to get along

TABLE 17.7. *Students' Perception of the Effect of Acceleration for Cohorts 1–3, by Sex*

	Age 18						Age 23					
	General Academic Progress		Interest in Learning		Social		General Academic Progress		Interest in Learning		Social	
	Mean	(SD)	Mean	(SD)	Mean	(SD)	Mean	(SD)	Mean	(SD)	Mean	(SD)
Cohort 1												
Males	–		–		–		3.8	(.76)	3.7	(.59)	3.4	(.60)
Females	–		–		–		3.9	(.75)	3.7	(.59)	3.6	(.65)
Cohort 2												
Males	3.9	(.73)	3.8	(.62)	3.4	(.57)	3.7	(.76)	3.6	(.55)	3.4	(.50)
Females	3.9	(.71)	3.8	(.60)	3.6	(.58)	3.7	(.72)	3.6	(.59)	3.4	(.60)
Cohort 3												
700M												
Males	4.0	(.68)	3.9	(.58)	3.4	(.62)	–		–		–	
Females	4.1	(.68)	3.9	(.65)	3.6	(.64)	–		–		–	
630V												
Males	4.1	(.80)	3.9	(.62)	3.5	(.70)	–		–		–	
Females	3.8	(.86)	3.8	(.53)	3.5	(.43)	–		–		–	

Note: Students rated the effect of acceleration using a five-point scale, where 1 = strongly unfavorable and 5 = strongly favorable effect. Dashes indicate that data are not available in the proper form.

282

with agemates (it was 2.9 for cohorts 2 and 3). We then grouped for analysis the sixteen item responses into three categories: those that assessed general academic progress (two items), those that assessed interest in learning (six items), and those that assessed social influence (eight items); means were computed (see table 17.7). Although these aggregates are somewhat encumbered by ceiling effects, it appears that the most positive effects are found for general academic progress and interest in learning for both cohorts. In the social area, positive effects were nonetheless apparent, with acceleration being seen as most beneficial for acceptance of one's abilities and the ability to get along with peers at comparable mental ages.

The same sixteen questions were again posed to the participants at the end of college, but this time to cohorts 1 and 2. The evaluation of acceleration in the three different areas was surprisingly similar across cohorts and across time (i.e., from high school to college).

As for the students' views, at the end of high school and college, about their acceleration or nonacceleration, the vast majority (over 70 percent) were satisfied with their choices, with approximately 15 percent (ranging from 12.1 percent to 23.7 percent) wishing they had been accelerated or had been accelerated more. Few, in retrospect, wished they had been accelerated less (the proportions ranged from 1.5 percent to 8.9 percent). Again the three cohorts varied surprisingly little, and views were stable over time.

Overall, then, these numbers justify the conclusion that students view the effects of acceleration positively, mostly educationally but socially as well. This finding was replicated across the three cohorts and over time. The consistency of these results reinforces findings of earlier evaluations of acceleration. (See chapters 3, 4, and 10 above.)

The Perceived Influence of SMPY

Up to this point we have not directly assessed students' perceptions of SMPY and the SMPY model; we have considered them only indirectly, through the assessment of the students' use of and views on acceleration—the program option that SMPY advocates and the one for which it is noted. In this section, we provide data on SMPY's influence from the perspective of the participants. First, however, reemphasizing the treatment differences among the cohorts will facilitate the interpretation of what follows. Not only did the SMPY model for serving gifted students emerge through direct, hands-on work with intellectually precocious students, which meant that later cohorts benefited from the experience SMPY gained from working with the earlier cohorts (particularly cohort 1), but the model was delivered in a more vigorous manner to students in the later cohorts. Thus, few of the participants in cohort 1 (less than 5 percent) had the opportunity to participate in any special classes or programs; their SMPY involvement primarily was limited to the talent search itself and its monthly newsletter (the *Intellectually Talented Youth Bulletin*, or *ITYB*), the vehicle through which SMPY delivered its educational advice. (And both of those evolved through experimentation with students in cohort 1.) Cohorts 2 and 3 benefited from SMPY's increasing experience and ability to offer more services, especially in the form of programs. The 700Ms in cohort 3 also could choose to receive especially intensive treatment with the SMPY model. Much individualized assistance was provided and many program options were offered (e.g., summer classes, precalculus mathematics by mail, educational counseling, special recognition of their talent, scholarships) to all willing takers (see chapter 16 above). Because the 630Vs were not given this opportunity but are contemporaries of the 700Ms, they offer an interesting contrast for this evaluation. The students in cohort 4, from whom preliminary data at age eighteen is used for certain critical variables, were exposed only to SMPY's fast-paced classes and the concomitant educational advice. Thus, one should anticipate that the most positive evaluation or view of SMPY would come from the 700Ms in cohort 3, followed by cohort 2, the 630Vs in cohort 3, cohort 4, and, finally, cohort 1.

Overview

At age eighteen, the members of cohort 1 were simply asked to rate how SMPY had helped them educationally, socially, and emotionally. Over 60 percent of the participants felt that SMPY had been of some help to them educationally, with very few (about 1 percent) feeling it had hurt them (Benbow, 1983). Benefits from SMPY in the social and emotional arenas were seen as negligible, with about 80 percent reporting no influence (Benbow, 1983). Means and standard deviations can be found in table 17.8.

At age eighteen, the members of cohorts 2 and 4, and at age twenty-three, those of cohorts 1 and 3, were asked to rate, on a five-point scale (from greatly hindered to greatly helped), how being SMPY participants had affected them educationally and, separately, emotionally (see table 17.8)—very similar questions to the ones posed to cohort 1 at age eighteen (discussed above).[3] Individ-

3. The actual questions responded to by the four cohorts differed somewhat in wording but not substantively. Cohort 2 at age eighteen and cohort 1 at age twenty-three responded to the exact same question, however.

TABLE 17.8. *Effect of Participation in SMPY on Cohorts 1–4, by Sex*

	Educationally			Emotionally		
	N	Mean	(SD)	N	Mean	(SD)
Cohort 1 (age 18)						
Males	1,215	2.9	(.85)	1,210	3.3	(.70)
Females	761	2.7	(.78)	760	3.3	(.67)
Cohort 1 (age 18) in SMPY classes						
Males	222	3.1	(.97)	222	3.4	(.74)
Females	80	3.0	(.91)	103	3.4	(.72)
Cohort 1 (age 23)						
Males	776	3.6	(.69)	739	3.6	(.69)
Females	450	3.6	(.66)	438	3.7	(.72)
Cohort 1 (age 23) in SMPY classes						
Males	213	3.7	(.76)	195	3.5	(.67)
Females	95	3.7	(.77)	89	3.8	(.81)
Cohort 2 (age 18)						
Males	385	3.9	(.76)	365	3.7	(.76)
Females	166	3.9	(.74)	167	3.9	(.78)
Cohort 2 (age 18) in SMPY classes						
Males	110	4.1	(.73)	105	3.7	(.78)
Females	35	4.1	(.72)	35	4.3	(.65)
Cohort 3 (age 23)						
700M						
Males	22	4.1	(.98)	21	3.3	(.86)
Females	1	4.5	(0)	1	4.5	(0)
630V						
Males	3	3.7	(.86)	3	3.3	(.58)
Females	10	3.7	(.82)	10	3.7	(.82)
Cohort 4 (age 18)						
Males	41	4.2	(.80)	30	3.8	(1.07)
Females	29	4.2	(.75)	29	4.3	(.86)

Note: Except for the educational rating of cohort 1 at age eighteen, the five-point scale used was: 1 = greatly hindered, 3 = neither hindered nor helped, 5 = greatly helped; or 1 = strongly negatively, 3 = no effect, 5 = strongly positively. At age eighteen for cohort 1, the five-point scale used to rate educational influence was: 1 = it has hurt me educationally, 2 = none, 3 = a little, 4 = considerably, 5 = much.

uals in all four cohorts felt that SMPY had benefited them at least somewhat. The more recent cohorts, who had benefited from SMPY's increased experience and had been worked with more intensively, had the more positive ratings of SMPY's educational influence (the effect ranged from .14 to .72). No such pattern was detected for ratings of SMPY's influence on emotional development, however.

There is another way to look at the data from cohorts 1 and 2 at ages twenty-three and eighteen, respectively. This is by considering the proportion who found at least one component of the model helpful either educationally or emotionally (table 17.9). Our conclusions remain unaltered using this strategy. Most individuals found at least one aspect useful to them (69 percent to 93 percent), and few could think of anything that hindered them.

The 700Ms, along with their verbally talented counterparts, were given four open-ended items at age eighteen, where they were asked to report what aspects of SMPY had helped or hindered them educationally or emotionally. Thus, the questions answered by cohort 3 at age eighteen are much different from the ones given to cohort 1 and those to which cohort 2 responded at age eighteen. Yet this was the very same set of questions that cohort 2 responded to at age twenty-three. The data for both cohorts are presented in table 17.10. In both cohorts, most students reported at least one component of the SMPY model to be helpful either educationally or emotionally; most could find no component that had hindered them, even though they had been specifically prompted to provide a response. The picture is most positive for the 700Ms, as had been anticipated. Indeed, when asked to report any person or group having a helpful influence on their educational development, 19 percent of the 700Ms who answered the question spontaneously listed SMPY. The most frequent response went to the students' parents (41 percent).

Overall, then, at the end of high school and college the participants in all four cohorts had primarily a positive global view of SMPY and its services. Several trends are worth commenting on, however. First, the participants found greater educational benefits than emotional ones from the various components of the SMPY model (and this makes sense, given SMPY's primary objectives). Moreover, males and females responded in a similar fashion; there were no gender differences in perceptions of SMPY's usefulness. Finally, the refinements of the SMPY model and the greater possibilities for involvement with SMPY over time apparently were both positively received by the participants. The most positive reports came from individuals in later cohorts and those who had

TABLE 17.9.   *Percentage of Individuals in Cohorts 1 and 2 Finding at Least One Component of the SMPY Model Helpful or Harmful, by Sex*

	Educationally		Emotionally	
	Helpful	Harmful	Helpful	Harmful
Cohort 1 (age 23)				
Males	75	4	69	7
Females	75	3	76	8
Cohort 2 (age 18)				
Males	90	8	83	13
Females	92	3	93	12

TABLE 17.10.   *Percentage of Individuals in Cohorts 2 and 3 Finding at Least One Component of SMPY Helpful or that Nothing Had Hindered Them, by Sex*

	Educationally		Emotionally	
	Helpful	Nothing Hindered	Helpful	Nothing Hindered
Cohort 2 (age 23)				
Males	74	65	50	83
Females	76	79	51	73
Cohort 3 (age 18)				
700M				
Males	89	83	68	77
Females	91	73	78	76
630V				
Males	79	93	66	89
Females	76	87	81	83
Cohort 4 (age 18)				
Males	88	78	71	71
Females	93	69	87	56

Note: Individuals were asked to specify what helped them and what hindered them.

received the strongest exposure to the SMPY model. This pattern is critical if one is to suggest that the SMPY model, as it has evolved, is a good one from the subjective view of the participants.

The Most Beneficial Aspects of SMPY

When we looked at the various components of the SMPY model to determine what aspects the participants actually found most beneficial educationally, the top three responses that emerged for cohort 1 (at age twenty-three) and cohort 2 (at age eighteen) were, in order: taking the SAT, acknowledgment of their ability, and special classes (see table 17.11). In table 17.12 we provide data for emotional rather than educational influences. The two sets of data in tables 17.11 and 17.12 are strikingly similar. They also reveal one of the few gender differences in perceptions of SMPY. Females consistently tended to feel that they benefited more than males from the acknowledgment of their abilities, although the differences tended to be small (but the largest effect size was .38). Consistent with the above, SMPY's newsletter (the *ITYB*) was seen as *not* helpful by a full 40 percent in cohort 1 or 2. Most were uncertain about its influence.

We also obtained findings for cohort 2 at age twenty-three on four open-ended questions that limited the individual to just one response. The greatest benefits educationally were said to be acceleration and the special fast-paced classes (29 percent and 22 percent of males and females, respectively, of those

TABLE 17.11. *Views of Cohorts 1 and 2 of How Much Specific Components of SMPY Helped Them Educationally, by Sex*

| | Cohort 2 (Age 18) | | | | | | Cohort 1 (Age 23) | | | | | |
| | Males | | | Females | | | Males | | | Females | | |
	N	Mean	(SD)	N	Mean	(SD)	N	Mean	(SD)	N	Mean	(SD)
Taking SAT	380	4.0	(.72)	167	3.9	(.75)	673	3.7	(.71)	395	3.7	(.69)
Newsletter	360	3.3	(.49)	162	3.4	(.53)	660	3.2	(.43)	389	3.2	(.45)
Special classes	217	4.0	(.87)	73	4.0	(.83)	218	3.6	(.84)	98	3.5	(.83)
Peer contact	262	3.4	(.65)	116	3.6	(.70)	303	3.4	(.62)	130	3.4	(.65)
Acknowledgment of ability	369	4.0	(.76)	165	4.2	(.69)	562	3.8	(.70)	346	3.9	(.73)
Counseling	185	3.3	(.57)	46	3.6	(.80)	194	3.2	(.62)	70	3.2	(.51)
Personal contact	234	3.5	(.70)	83	3.7	(.75)	245	3.3	(.60)	105	3.2	(.58)

Note: Responses were to be provided only if the respondent had experienced the component (e.g., he or she was a participant in a special class). Responses also were made on a five-point scale, where 1 = greatly hindered and 5 = greatly helped.

TABLE 17.12. Views of Cohorts 1 and 2 of How Much Specific Components of SMPY Helped Them Emotionally, by Sex

| | Cohort 2 (Age 18) | | | | | | Cohort 1 (Age 23) | | | | | |
| | Males | | | Females | | | Males | | | Females | | |
	N	Mean	(SD)	N	Mean	(SD)	N	Mean	(SD)	N	Mean	(SD)
Taking SAT	376	3.8	(.75)	166	3.9	(.78)	647	3.6	(.73)	380	3.7	(.77)
Newsletter	351	3.1	(.44)	156	3.3	(.55)	636	3.1	(.46)	369	3.3	(.53)
Special classes	216	3.3	(.74)	75	3.6	(.87)	202	3.3	(.70)	90	3.4	(.87)
Peer contact	263	3.5	(.70)	113	3.7	(.80)	286	3.3	(.65)	121	3.4	(.82)
Acknowledgment of ability	357	3.9	(.80)	167	4.2	(.78)	540	3.9	(.74)	341	4.0	(.77)
Counseling	192	3.2	(.51)	48	3.4	(.65)	191	3.2	(.54)	70	3.1	(.50)
Personal contact	240	3.3	(.65)	81	3.6	(.73)	231	3.2	(.60)	97	3.3	(.63)

responding), followed by acknowledgment of ability and increased confidence (22 percent and 30 percent of the males and females, respectively, who responded). The greatest emotional benefit was said to be acknowledgment of abilities and increased confidence (36 percent and 46 percent of the males and females, respectively, who responded).

Similar findings were obtained for cohort 3 at age eighteen, who responded to the same open-ended questions to which cohort 2 responded at age twenty-three. The educational and social experiences obtained in SMPY's special classes were again highly valued and these classes were the benefit most frequently noted (36 percent), even though most participants had not enrolled in such a class.[4] For the 700Ms, the second most valued service was the extensive newsletter (25 percent), which only cohort 3 received. (This shows that a newsletter can be effective.) This latter finding was the only exception, however, to the general pattern noted for cohorts 1 and 2.

Students were also asked what hindered them the most, either educationally or emotionally. That few (6 percent to 20 percent) provided any response was the only consistent finding across time, gender, and the cohorts. We elaborate on this point further in the qualitative analysis section below.

Specific Evaluation of Services

In addition to noting how helpful (or unhelpful) various aspects of SMPY were, the students in the various cohorts were asked to respond to more-specific questions regarding SMPY and how it influenced them. Participants in cohorts 2 and 3 were asked to report how helpful talent-search SAT scores were in being accelerated or in their overall development (see table 17.13). The scores were seen as quite helpful by both cohorts. Students also were asked if they would have been accelerated as much without SMPY's help. Data are available only for cohorts 1 and 2, where 28 percent of cohort 1 at age twenty-three and 44 percent of cohort 2 at age eighteen reported that they would not have been accelerated so much.

An important part of the services provided by SMPY, hardly touched on so far, is the enhancement of students' awareness of various educational oppor-

---

4. Students in cohort 3 did not enroll in classes that were directly sponsored by SMPY. At that time the fast-paced classes offered as part of summer programs were conducted by organizations fully independent of SMPY (e.g., Johns Hopkins's CTY or Duke's Talent Identification Program). They were, however, entirely based on the SMPY model. The staff of SMPY strongly encouraged students in cohort 3 to enroll in these classes and even offered scholarships as a further inducement. We cannot know, therefore, what proportion of students did not associate the fast-paced classes with SMPY and did not report them as a benefit. We believe the proportion is relatively small, since many students could not take these classes due to cost and other considerations.

TABLE 17.13. *Percentage of Individuals in Cohorts 2 and 3 at Age 18 Finding that Talent Search SAT Scores Were Helpful, by Sex*

	Overall Educational Development	Becoming Accelerated[a]	
		Grade	Subject Matter
Cohort 2			
Males	51	48	50
Females	57	52	42
Cohort 3			
700M			
Males	66	85	77
Females	58	63	75
630V			
Males	65	80	67
Females	56	0	71

[a] Only those who were actually accelerated were included.

tunities. This is accomplished though educational opportunities guides, mailings, personal correspondence, career days, and, most importantly, newsletters. In this domain, the staff of SMPY certainly felt that it became more effective with time, to the benefit of the later participants. How well did SMPY succeed (and improve) from the participants' point of view? Cohort 1 was asked this question only at age twenty-three, when somewhat less than 40 percent felt SMPY had enhanced somewhat or greatly their awareness of educational opportunities. For cohort 2, who responded at age eighteen, 63 percent responded similarly. In cohort 3 at age eighteen the respective percentage for the 700Ms was 75 percent and for the 630Vs somewhat less than 40 percent. The latter is an especially interesting difference for this evaluation, since this service was especially targeted at the 700Ms through an extensive newsletter; the treatment provided to the 630Vs in this regard was similar to that given to cohort 1 and cannot be seen as comparable to that provided for their mathematically talented counterparts.

Complementing the above statistics are the data on whether the participants thought they would have accomplished as much educationally without SMPY's help. As a group, most participants in cohort 1 (78 percent) felt, at age twenty-three, that they would have. The remainder either said no or were uncertain. Given that few students received personal attention in those days, this perception is probably realistic. Yet this does not imply that the SMPY model was ineffective by any means. The model as it was being developed in the early 1970s reached few students. When we look at the responses from cohort 2, however, the picture becomes more favorable for SMPY. At age eighteen, only

TABLE 17.14.   *Percentage of Individuals across Cohorts 1–4 Finding that SMPY Participation Helped Intra- and Interpersonally, by Sex*

	Helped Them Accept Their Giftedness	Positively Changed Others' Attitudes
Cohort 1 (age 23)		
Males	36	19
Females	35	18
Cohort 2 (age 18)		
Males	97	94
Females	98	96
Cohort 3 (age 18)		
700M		
Males	55	24
Females	59	28
630V		
Males	41	28
Females	47	38
Cohort 4 (age 18)		
Males	58	–
Females	63	–

Note: Proportions reported are for those finding that SMPY participation had a small or large favorable effect.

50 percent felt that they would have accomplished as much without SMPY's help. (No such question was posed to cohort 3, unfortunately.)

The final two questions to be considered here concern social and emotional arenas, and query students on how and to what extent SMPY helped them accept their giftedness and how others' attitudes toward them changed subsequent to their SMPY experience. The ratings, made on a five-point scale, from all four cohorts are presented in table 17.14; data on cohort 1 were obtained at age twenty-three and for the other three cohorts at age eighteen. For all four cohorts the results are again positive, especially for cohort 2, 90 percent of whose members felt that SMPY had helped them accept their giftedness and that SMPY participation changed others' attitudes toward them in a positive fashion.

One might have thought (as we did) that cohort 3, particularly the 700Ms, would have been the ones to respond the most positively to these last two questions. They did not, however. Three possible explanations come to mind. First, given their degree of precocity and how students became part of cohort 3 (many took the SAT on their own, not through the formal mechanism of a talent search), many people, including the students themselves, were probably well aware of their talents. Thus, perhaps not much change could be effected. Second, it might be harder to accept one's giftedness if it is extreme. Third, it might simply be the case that SMPY was less effective in this domain with cohort 3. It is difficult to know.

Gender Differences

For almost all parameters studied, we detected no substantively significant gender differences. The only domain in which they emerged was in the acknowledgment of the students' own abilities and talents, which led to greater confidence in and acceptance of themselves. Females seemed to have benefited somewhat more from this than did the males. There was an interesting trend across the comparisons, however. Males and females made a total of twenty-nine ratings on how certain aspects of SMPY had affected them emotionally. For twenty-six of those ratings, females acknowledged greater emotional benefits than did the males, with two comparisons exhibiting no differences, and one comparison favoring the males ($X^2 = 3.3$, $p < .07$). Although it is not statistically significant, there is a trend in which gifted females express a greater need for and feel they receive more benefits from the social support gained through their SMPY participation (or participation in any program for the gifted) than gifted males do. This finding is consistent with expectations gleaned from their interest (Lubinski, Benbow, & Ryan, 1995) and values (Lubinski, Schmidt, & Benbow, 1996) profiles (see Achter, Lubinski, & Benbow, 1996).

A Qualitative Analysis

The quantitative analyses provided above help us understand how and in what ways SMPY participation affected the individuals involved. Yet they lack the flavor that emerges when one reads the expressed thoughts of the participants. To allow a fuller appreciation of the above statistics, we quote some subjects from cohorts 2 and 3. Our selected items are composed of those statements that seemed most effectively to capture the spirit of what a significant proportion of the students communicated to us.

— SMPY helped me feel less alone as a woman who was good in math and science. It provided a support network.

— Seeing so many other people like me . . . it helped me gain confidence in who and what I am.

— Enabled me to meet 3 other women who were gifted and whose achievements continue to encourage me in terms of my future.

— It's made me realize that I'm not alone. Through SMPY, I've met others to talk to and to share experiences with.

— Creating a 3–6 week haven for gifted to learn with and from one another.

—Making me aware of opportunities I didn't know existed.

—The newsletters helped me a lot—I saw what others had done, which assured me that I could do it too.

—Dr. Stanley's persistent attentiveness to my needs encouraged me to think about my future, even before it was obligatory.

—Finally, the chance to learn at the pace and intensity I had always longed for.

Of course, not all students were so positive about their experiences with SMPY as the students quoted above, and even they found things that affected them in a negative manner. We were interested in those views as well, especially since the quantitative analyses of the data from cohort 2 (at age twenty-three) and cohort 3 (at age eighteen) were not especially revealing in this regard. That is, as noted above, most of the students had provided no responses to code or reported that nothing had hindered them educationally or socially and emotionally. Moreover, those who did respond varied widely in their perceptions. What was seen as a benefit by some (e.g., increased confidence—35 percent of cohort 2 who responded at age twenty-three) was viewed as a detriment by others (10 percent). This gave us a greater appreciation of the individual differences among the participants and the need to be sensitive to them (see Benbow & Lubinski, 1994). It also helped clarify further how no one program or intervention will be responded to by all individuals in precisely the same fashion (Scarr, 1992). No single model can serve each member of a group of students equally well. We need to be flexible in our approach to meet the educational needs of gifted children (Feldhusen & Robinson, 1986). The following quotes, when considered in conjunction with the earlier set of testimonials, bring out this sentiment nicely. At the same time, they reveal clearly the individuals' feelings about how SMPY participation can become a negative experience for some.

—Too many opportunities that I felt guilty about not following up.

—Tendency to over focus on one specific ability.

—The special network of SMPY sometimes made me feel more different from my peers in school.

—I fell behind socially and as a result disliked my high school experience.

—Put me in math classes which had no social peers in it.

—I learned too much too quickly.

—It was one more way of being labeled a "brain" and being set apart socially.

—Overemphasis on acceleration as a goal in itself, and on curriculum as a means to acceleration, rather than curriculum as an education in itself.

—I ran out of math classes in high school.

—Reading about things "other" SMPY students were doing made me feel like I was wasting my talents.

Summary of Findings on SMPY Influence

It seems safe to conclude, on the basis of the findings presented above, that SMPY participation was seen by most students as beneficial not only educationally but also socially, particularly in dealing with and accepting their precocious talents. SMPY was viewed as helpful emotionally, especially by females, even though the interventions provided by SMPY were exclusively educational in nature. Perhaps just meeting and realizing that there are others like oneself has a soothing influence. It certainly seemed to increase confidence and reduce the sense of isolation that some gifted adolescents report.

These findings also might support a broader interpretation of what happens when we provide an optimal educational environment to gifted children. Perhaps arranging an appropriate and challenging educational environment also enhances the probability that the attendant social environment becomes more suitable for the individual as well (Lubinski, Benbow, & Sanders, 1993, p. 705, n. 3). This hypothesis was prompted initially when we were faced with the overwhelmingly positive consumer evaluations of classes and programs based on the SMPY model (see table 17.15). In our programs at Iowa State, we

TABLE 17.15.   *Evaluation Data from CY-TAG Programs Conducted in 1989 and 1991 at Iowa State University*

	1989		1991
	Parents	Students	Students
Enhanced student's social growth (% yes)	98	73	87
Enhanced motivation to learn (% yes)	—	69	76
Most important way changed due to CY-TAG (% yes)			
More confident	—	—	23
More comfortable with self	—	—	7
Increased maturity	—	—	5
Fun learning	—	—	5
Made friends	—	—	4
Overall CY-TAG rating (scale 1–10)	—	—	8.9

Students' open-ended responses to "The three best things about CY-TAG are:"

Most frequent response	Friends	Social activities
Second most frequent response	Social activities	Friends
Third most frequent response	College-level material	Classes/challenges

Note: CY-TAG is a program at Iowa State University in which fast-paced academic classes, based on the SMPY model, are offered in a variety of disciplines to students in the top 0.5 percent in ability.

find that the social benefits of these classes are as highly valued as the educational ones, whether we ask students or parents to judge. For example, one parent noted that "the academic challenges provided our daughter helped her grow in self-confidence and dramatically increased her desire to learn." Another concluded that Challenges for Youth—Talented and Gifted (CY-TAG), Iowa State's program built on the SMPY model, "is a growing experience that takes your child where he or she is emotionally, academically, and socially and allows personal growth under watchful guidance." Many of our CY-TAG students, like the individuals in cohorts 2 and 3 who were participants in SMPY programs more than ten years ago, spontaneously report to us as well that this is the first time they have been able to interact with individuals who are like themselves and that this "inoculates" them. As one student put it, "I now have more faith in myself, and I am more daring." Other programs based on the SMPY model across the country have collected similar testimonials.

Summary and Conclusion

Since SMPY's founding, its work has focused on the optimal development of intellectual talent. Through a programmatic research agenda, it systematically developed an identification procedure based on out-of-level testing (i.e., the talent search; see Cohn, 1991), which had diagnostic value for gifted individuals, and provided predictive validity for this procedure over a ten-year interval (Benbow, 1992). We know, through SMPY's research, that the future pool of truly exceptional scientists and engineers will consist mostly of individuals who could be identified by a talent search—specifically, those displaying mathematical giftedness by age thirteen (Benbow & Arjmand, 1990). Moreover, through its programmatic work, SMPY experimented to find the best ways to provide an education that is commensurate with gifted students' advanced abilities. Acceleration in its many variants seemed to be the procedure of choice, and indeed it was. Those who were accelerated performed better academically than those who were not (see, e.g., Swiatek & Benbow, 1991a, 1991b). Moreover, fast-paced classes not only are invigorating intellectually but also appear to be advantageous socially and emotionally. In these classes students are challenged for the first time in their lives; they also meet a large group of their intellectual peers for the first time—those who are like them and whom many had believed did not exist. Previous research has indeed shown that SMPY's procedures are effective. It is no wonder that the SMPY model has had the effect it has had on education, particularly the education of the gifted, as documented by Van Tassel-Baska (see chapter 15 above).

What we did not know until now was how the students themselves subjectively perceived SMPY's work. We knew that they tended to be high achievers (Benbow, 1983; Benbow & Arjmand, 1990), but we did not know how useful SMPY they felt had been to them in that regard. The ultimate aim of SMPY is, after all, to help gifted children make the most of their abilities and to enhance their intellectual, but also their emotional, well-being. It thus seemed appropriate to ask the gifted students themselves for an evaluation of SMPY.

How successful was SMPY in meeting its objective from the participants' perspective? Overall, the data collected from the SMPY participants at age eighteen and again at age twenty-three in the first four cohorts of SMPY's longitudinal study lead to the conclusion that SMPY did a fairly good job, especially with later participants who benefited from the experience SMPY gathered from the work with the earlier ones and who received more-intensive treatment. On the whole, they valued SMPY participation on both educational and emotional grounds.

Beyond this positive and global view of SMPY, we learned that the participants felt that SMPY had done a fairly good job of enhancing their awareness of the educational opportunities available to them—a service consistently offered to all students, but in varying degrees of intensity. A majority of the SMPY participants did accelerate their education, which SMPY had advocated, and they felt good about their acceleration (see also Swiatek & Benbow, 1992). Its greatest benefits were educational, but some positive reactions also were noted in the social and emotional arenas. SMPY was seen as having a positive influence on the lives it touched, beyond helping students accelerate their education and making them aware of educational opportunities. Some of the greatest benefits noted by the participants were that it helped them learn about and accept their abilities and that its special classes not only challenged them educationally but also allowed them contact with their intellectual peers.[5] It enhanced their confidence in themselves. Yet the most telling finding was perhaps that many students felt they would not have achieved so much academically without SMPY. Many indeed felt that SMPY had enhanced their academic success in lasting and meaningful ways. Thus, the model for serving gifted students that SMPY has developed over the past two decades does seem worthy of its widespread implementation and recognition.

By and large, this evaluation of the SMPY model from the students' perspective was positive across all four (talent search–identified) cohorts. Many

5. Those who received SMPY's extensive newsletter (i.e., the 700Ms) saw that as one of the primary benefits of their participation; it was exceeded only by SMPY's special fast-paced classes.

students were not served directly, especially in the early years when the model was being developed through hands-on work with the students. Nonetheless, the services and information provided seemed to help the participants educationally and in dealing with and accepting their abilities. The most positively perceived benefits were to be found among those who received the most services or the most intensive treatment, which we interpret as evidence of the utility of the SMPY model for helping students bring their talents to fruition in an emotionally supportive environment composed of their intellectual peers.

References

Achter, J. A., Lubinski, D., & Benbow, C. P. (1996). Multipotentiality among intellectually gifted: "It was never there and already it's vanishing." *Journal of Counseling Psychology* 43: 65–76.

Bartkovich, K. G., & Mezynski, K. (1981). Fast-paced precalculus mathematics for talented junior-high students: Two recent SMPY programs. *Gifted Child Quarterly* 25:73–80.

Benbow, C. P. (1983). Adolescence of the mathematically precocious: A five-year longitudinal study. In C. P. Benbow & J. C. Stanley (Eds.), *Academic precocity: Aspects of its development* (pp. 9–37). Baltimore: Johns Hopkins University Press.

Benbow, C. P. (1986). SMPY's model for teaching mathematically precocious students. In J. S. Renzulli (Ed.), *Systems and models for developing programs for the gifted and talented* (pp. 1–25). Mansfield Center, Conn.: Creative Learning Press.

Benbow, C. P. (1988). Sex differences in mathematical reasoning ability in intellectually talented preadolescents: Their nature, effects, and possible causes. *Behavioral and Brain Sciences* 11:169–232.

Benbow, C. P. (1992). Academic achievement in mathematics and science of students between ages thirteen and twenty-three: Are there differences among students in the top one percent of mathematical ability? *Journal of Educational Psychology* 84:51–61.

Benbow, C. P., & Arjmand, O. (1990). Predictors of high academic achievement in mathematics and science by mathematically talented students: A longitudinal study. *Journal of Educational Psychology* 82:430–441.

Benbow, C. P., & Lubinski, D. (1994). Individual differences amongst the mathematically gifted: Their educational and vocational implications. In N. Colangelo, S. G. Assouline, & D. L. Ambroson (Eds.). *Talent development* (Vol. 2, pp. 83–100). Dayton: Ohio Psychology Press.

Benbow, C. P., & Stanley, J. C. (1980). Sex differences in mathematical ability: Fact or artifact? *Science* 210:1262–1264.

Benbow, C. P., & Stanley, J. C. (1981). Mathematical ability: Is sex a factor? *Science* 212:114–121.

Benbow, C. P., & Stanley, J. C. (1982). Consequences in high school and college of sex differences in mathematical reasoning ability: A longitudinal perspective. *American Educational Research Journal* 19:598–622.

Benbow, C. P., & Stanley, J. C. (1983a). An eight-year evaluation of SMPY: What was learned? In C. P. Benbow & J. C. Stanley (Eds.), *Academic precocity: Aspects of its development* (pp. 205–214). Baltimore: Johns Hopkins University Press.

Benbow, C. P., & Stanley, J. C. (1983b). Sex differences in mathematical reasoning ability: More facts. *Science* 222:1029–1031.

Brody, L. E., & Benbow, C. P. (1987). Accelerative strategies: How effective are they for the gifted? *Gifted Child Quarterly* 31:105–110.

Chronicle of Higher Education. (1992). *Almanac of higher education*. Chicago: University of Chicago Press.

Cohen, J. (1988). *Statistical power analysis for the behavioral sciences* (2nd ed.). Hillsdale, N.J.: Erlbaum.

Cohn, S. J. (1991). Talent searches. In N. Colangelo & G. A. Davis (Eds.), *Handbook of gifted education* (pp. 166–177). Needham Heights, Mass.: Allyn & Bacon.

Feldhusen, J., & Robinson, A. (1986). The Purdue secondary model for gifted and talented youth. In J. S. Renzulli (Ed.), *Systems and models for developing programs for the gifted and talented* (pp. 155–178). Mansfield Center, Conn.: Creative Learning Press.

Fox, L. H. (1974). A mathematics program for fostering precocious achievement. In J. C. Stanley, D. P. Keating, & L. H. Fox (Eds.), *Mathematical talent: Discovery, description, and development* (pp. 101–125). Baltimore: Johns Hopkins University Press.

Humphreys, L. G., Lubinski, D., & Yao, G. (1993). Utility of predicting group membership: Exemplified by the role of spatial visualization in becoming an engineer, physical scientist, or artist. *Journal of Applied Psychology* 78:250–261.

Keating, D. P., & Stanley, J. C. (1972). Extreme measures for the exceptionally gifted in mathematics and science. *Educational Researcher* 1:3–7.

Kolitch, E. R., & Brody, L. E. (1992). Mathematics acceleration of highly talented students: An evaluation. *Gifted Child Quarterly* 36:78–86.

Lubinski, D., & Benbow, C. P. (1992). Gender differences in abilities and preferences among the gifted: Implications for the math-science pipeline. *Current Directions in Psychological Science* 1:61–66.

Lubinski, D., & Benbow, C. P. (1994). The Study of Mathematically Precocious Youth: The first three decades of a planned fifty-year study of intellectual talent. In R. F. Subotnik & K. D. Arnold (Eds.), *Beyond Terman: Contemporary longitudinal studies of giftedness and talent* (pp. 255–281). Norwood, N.J.: Ablex.

Lubinski, D., Benbow, C. P., Eftekhari-Sanjani, H., & Jensen, M. B. (in preparation). The psychological profile of our future scientific leaders.

Lubinski, D., Benbow, C. P., & Ryan, J. (1995). Stability of vocational interests among the intellectually gifted: A fifteen-year longitudinal study. *Journal of Applied Psychology* 80:90–94.

Lubinski, D., Benbow, C. P., & Sanders, C. E. (1993). Reconceptualizing gender differences in achievement among the gifted. In K. A. Heller, F. J. Mönks, & A. H. Passow (Eds.), *International handbook of research and development of giftedness and talent* (pp. 693–707). Oxford: Pergamon Press.

Lubinski, D., & Dawis, R. V. (1992). Aptitudes, skills, and proficiencies. In M. D. Dunnette & L. M. Hough (Eds.), *The handbook of industrial/organizational psychology* (2nd ed., Vol. 3, pp. 1–59). Palo Alto: Consulting Psychologists Press.

Lubinski, D., & Humphreys, L. G. (1990a). Assessing spurious "moderator effects," illustrated substantively with the hypothesized ("synergistic") relation between spatial and mathematical ability. *Psychological Bulletin* 107:385–393.

Lubinski, D., & Humphreys, L. G. (1990b). A broadly based analysis of mathematical giftedness. *Intelligence* 14:327–355.

Lubinski, D., Schmidt, D. B., & Benbow, C. P. (1996). A 20-year stability analysis of the Study of Values for intellectually gifted individuals from adolescence to adulthood. *Journal of Applied Psychology* 81: 443–451.

Mezynski, K., & Stanley, J. C. (1980). Advanced Placement oriented calculus for high school students. *Journal for Research in Mathematics Education* 11:347–355.

Richardson, T. M., & Benbow, C. P. (1990). Long-term effects of acceleration on the social-emotional adjustment of mathematically precocious youth. *Journal of Educational Psychology* 82:464–470.

Scarr, S. (1992). Developmental theories for the 1990s: Development and individual differences. *Child Development* 63:1–19.

Southern, W. T., Jones, E. D., & Stanley, J. C. (1993). Acceleration and enrichment: The context and development of program options. In K. A. Heller, F. J. Mönks, & A. H. Passow (Eds.), *International handbook of research and development of giftedness and talent* (pp. 387–409). Oxford: Pergamon Press.

Stanley, J. C. (1977). Rationale of the Study of Mathematically Precocious Youth (SMPY) during its first five years of promoting educational acceleration. In J. C. Stanley, W. C. George, & C. H.

Solano (Eds.), *The gifted and the creative: A fifty-year perspective* (pp. 75–112). Baltimore: Johns Hopkins University Press.

Stanley, J. C. (1978). SMPY's DT-PI model: Diagnostic testing followed by prescriptive instruction. *Intellectually Talented Youth Bulletin* 4:7–8.

Stanley, J. C., & Benbow, C. P. (1982). Educating mathematically precocious youths: Twelve policy recommendations. *Educational Researcher* 11:4–9.

Stanley, J. C., & Benbow, C. P. (1983). Extremely young college graduates: Evidence of their success. *College and University* 58:361–371.

Stanley, J. C., & Benbow, C. P. (1986). Youths who reason exceptionally well mathematically. In R. J. Sternberg & J. E. Davidson (Eds.), *Conceptions of giftedness* (pp. 361–387). Cambridge: Cambridge University Press.

Stanley, J. C., Benbow, C. P., Brody, L. E., Dauber, S., & Lupkowski, A. E. (1992). Gender differences on eighty-six nationally standardized aptitude and achievement tests. In N. Colangelo, S. G. Assouline, & D. L. Ambroson (Eds.), *Talent development: Proceedings from the 1991 Henry B. and Jocelyn Wallace National Research Symposium on Talent Development* (pp. 42–65). Unionville, N.Y.: Trillium Press.

Stanley, J. C., Keating, D. P., & Fox, L. H. (Eds.). (1974). *Mathematical talent: Discovery, description, and development.* Baltimore: Johns Hopkins University Press.

Stanley, J. C., & McGill, A. M. (1986). More about "Young entrants to college: How did they fare?" *Gifted Child Quarterly* 30:70–73.

Stanley, J. C., & Stanley, B. S. K. (1986). High-school biology, chemistry, or physics learned well in three weeks. *Journal of Research in Science Teaching* 23:237–250.

Swiatek, M. A., & Benbow, C. P. (1991a). A ten-year longitudinal follow-up of ability-matched accelerated and unaccelerated gifted students. *Journal of Educational Psychology* 83:528–538.

Swiatek, M. A., & Benbow, C. P. (1991b). A ten-year longitudinal follow-up of participants in a fast-paced mathematics course. *Journal for Research in Mathematics Education* 22:138–150.

Swiatek, M. A., & Benbow, C. P. (1992). Nonintellectual correlates of satisfaction with acceleration: A longitudinal study. *Journal of Youth and Adolescence* 21:699–723.

18 Correlates of High Mathematical Ability in a National Sample of Eighth Graders

RICHARD E. SNOW AND MICHELE ENNIS

J ulian Stanley's programmatic research on the identification and nurturance of mathematical talent is a landmark contribution to both education and psychology. As a small addition to that work, we offer here an exploratory analysis of data on the characteristics of students showing high mathematical ability in a national sample of eighth graders. The results represent only a progress report, not a comprehensive analysis, in our continuing study of individual differences in achievement in mathematics and science. We will not take space here to relate our preliminary findings to the significant body of other evidence that may point in similar directions (see, e.g., Benbow, 1992).

Our research is part of a larger project conducted at the Center for Research on the Context of Secondary School Teaching at Stanford University. The purpose of that project is to evaluate the potential and the limits of the National Educational Longitudinal Study of 1988 (NELS:88) for assessing teaching and learning in high school English, history, mathematics, and science. NELS:88 is the latest of three national longitudinal surveys conducted by the United States Department of Education, and it focuses more than its predecessors did on measuring classroom instructional practices and cognitive outcomes in the four core subject areas. It began in the spring of 1988 with a national survey and testing of eighth-grade students; the first follow-up was conducted in the spring of 1990, with a second follow-up in the spring of 1992. National survey data analyzed so far in our project are from the eighth-grade base year only; data from the follow-up years are being added to the analysis as they become available. The project combines analyses of NELS:88 data with our own small-scale studies that include the same tests and questionnaires. The aim is to devise more-refined and sensitive measures of student achievement and attitudes, classroom instructional variables, and their interrelationships than are typical of test and questionnaire instruments conventionally used in national assessments. For a first progress report from this project, see Ennis, Kerkhoven, and Snow (1993).

Characteristics of the NELS:88 Base-Year Tests

Rock, Pollack, Owings, and Hafner (1990) provided a detailed psychometric report for the NELS:88 base-year test battery, so details need not be given here. In brief, they produced four tests that fit into one and a half hours of testing time and yet were sufficiently reliable to justify IRT (item response theory) scoring. The tests were designed to allow adaptive testing in the tenth and twelfth grades, vertical scaling to study individual student gains across the three testing sessions, and cross-sectional trend comparisons with the gains made between the tenth and twelfth grades from 1980 to 1982 in the High School and Beyond study. The tests were shown to be relatively unspeeded and free of gender and ethnic bias. Beyond the unidimensional total score, Rock, Pollack, Owings, and Hafner (1990) provided for diagnostic interpretation, as far as was possible within practical limits. They formed content testlets to allow subscores for specific content areas within subject-matter domains, and for reading and math they designed proficiency-level subscores to track progress over the years in more detail.

Our purpose is to investigate subscoring further, to determine whether richer cognitive interpretations might be gotten from the tests and the questionnaires. Although performances on achievement tests may be treated as unidimensional for some purposes, they are clearly complex psychologically. Interpretations of student achievement should attempt to go beneath such molar constructs as "the amount of science knowledge possessed" or "the level of mathematical ability reached." Thus, we hope to produce subscores that distinguish different kinds of knowledge and reasoning even within these conventional mathematics and science achievement tests. In turn, this work should suggest improvements in test and questionnaire design that may provide richer cognitive descriptions and diagnoses in other assessment devices. Eventually, we hope to help build an improved cognitive psychology of achievement assessment.

Method

Sample

The analyses reported here are based on those eighth graders in the NELS:88 sample whose data include teacher questionnaires from both a math and an English teacher, as well as math, science, reading, and history test scores, and student, parent, and school questionnaires. This subsample of 6,022 students (3,016 females and 3,006 males) is regarded as representative of the NELS:88 total sample, which was designed to be a nationally representative sample of eighth graders. For purposes of the larger project we have used students with science teachers' and English teachers' reports; the NELS:88 design did not permit both math teachers' and science teachers' reports for the same students. Our analyses do not use the national probability weights; here we treat each student's data as representing one individual only.

Other Measures

The teacher, student, parent, and school questionnaires include a range of items on students' perceptions and attitudes about themselves and their schools, parental expectations, teaching practices, and various aspects of the schools' instructional and social contexts. The present report concentrates for the most part on the students' characteristics.

Analysis

The present analysis explores correlates of mathematics achievement mainly across high levels of total scores in math. That is, we are particularly interested in the students' characteristics that distinguish the highest scorers in math from high and moderate scorers. We have divided the total score distribution into 5 percent intervals, or twentieths; following the Latin *vigesimus*, these are referred to here as "vigentiles." Then the high vigentiles have been contrasted with respect to various other characteristics of the students, using only simple descriptive statistics. Because gender differences in mathematics have been a major concern in the literature (see, e.g., Benbow, 1992; Chipman, 1988; Hyde, Fennema, & Lamon, 1990), we have routinely divided vigentiles by sex. In order not to misrepresent the data, we have included the full distribution of all vigentiles in most data displays. It is our purpose here to do preliminary detective work, not to build detailed multivariate models to account for differences in achievement or gender. As we increase our understanding of the structure of these data and as data for tenth- and twelfth-grade students are included, more-comprehensive analyses can be planned and conducted.

Results

Total Score Distributions

Figure 18.1 gives the distribution of total scores in math separately for males and females; the abscissa shows the midpoints of the intervals of IRT estimated formula scores, not of vigentiles. It is noteworthy that more males than females appear in both the high and low tails of the distribution. There has been some controversy about the analysis and interpretation of this oft-noted trend, partly because it must be considered in relation to other features of each distribution (see, e.g., Feingold, 1993; Hedges & Friedman, 1993a, 1993b). In the present data for males the mean is 17.31 with a standard deviation of 11.66; for females the mean is 16.26 with a standard deviation of 11.11. These are hardly important differences. However, more males appear in the upper half of the distribution and more females appear in the lower half, except in the tails. Note that both tails in figure 18.1 appear somewhat truncated. There are thus floor and ceiling effects in the present math test that limit differentiation in the highest and lowest vigentiles, so these regions are likely to be more heterogeneous in mathematical ability than are adjacent vigentiles, and also than are the high and low tails of distributions on other tests.

Figure 18.2 shows the distributions of IRT total scores in reading, separated by math vigentile and gender. Median reading scores for females are higher than reading medians for males throughout the math-score range, including in the highest vigentiles. However, the distributions vary. More high-math males than females have medium or low reading scores. In other words, among high-math students, males show more variance in reading ability than do females. In the total distribution, the reading-math total score correlation is .71 for both males and females. Thus, many high-math students are also high in other complementary abilities, such as reading comprehension. Yet despite the high correlation, different students show different mixes of these abilities, and this finding may be associated with other characteristics as well as gender. It is clearly wrong to make simple generalizations about such persons that connect other characteristics with high ability in math alone; abilities commingle.

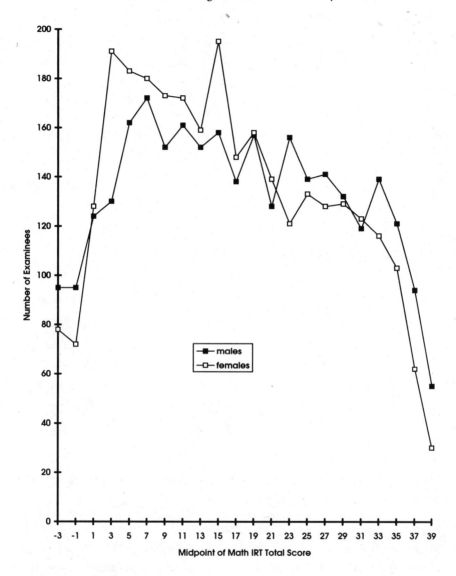

Figure 18.1. Distributions of male and female math IRT total scores, plotted at midpoints of score intervals.

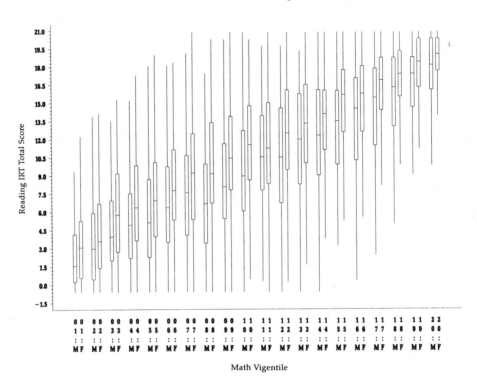

Figure 18.2. Distributions of male and female reading IRT total scores, plotted separately for math total score vigentiles.

Math and Science Subscores

As noted above, one aim of our project is to distinguish math and science subscores that reflect different aspects of cognitive knowledge and performance. Using factor analysis, nonmetric multidimensional scaling, and interviews of student performers, we have provisionally identified five subscores for the eighth-grade math test and six subscores for the eighth-grade science test (see Ennis, Kerkhoven, & Snow, 1993). There is some doubt that all these subscores should be retained; some rest on very few items and some appear to be mainly difficulty factors. For the math test, however, at least three subscores seem to have substantive interpretations. These are: Advanced Knowledge and Computation; Inferential Reasoning; and Basic Facts and Computation. For the science test, subscores distinguishing everyday science knowledge from formal, school-based achievement can be justified, and each of these categories seems to have two levels, so there are four subscores. However, the items that make up some of these scores refer to different science content. We identify the science subscores with general labels here but note the content emphases in parentheses. They are: Everyday Knowledge (with an emphasis on astronomy); Elementary Knowledge with Reasoning (with an emphasis on biology); Basic Formal Achievement (with an emphasis on chemistry and physics); and Advanced Formal Achievement. In subsequent analyses, we have used simple number-correct scores in each set of items, rather than factor scores.

Figures 18.3, 18.4, and 18.5 show the means for the three math subscores, separated by vigentile and gender. Advanced Knowledge and Computation approximates the first principal component of the total score in math; in figure 18.3, it shows a steep relation to math vigentile and no important gender differences. Figure 18.4 gives the trend for Inferential Reasoning, where averages for males are seen to be higher than averages for females throughout most of the total score range; this difference disappears in the highest vigentile, however. Figure 18.5 offers data that suggest that averages for females for Basic Facts Computation are higher than those for males in the lower half of the total score distribution, but not in the upper half as performance tends toward the maximum in both groups.

Figures 18.6 through 18.9 give the average trends across math vigentiles by gender for the four science subscores. In figure 18.6, males average higher than females on Everyday Knowledge of science (especially astronomy) through most of the upper math range, although in the highest vigentile the difference is relatively small. For Elementary Knowledge and Reasoning in science (especially biology), the average for females is higher through most of the range in Figure 18.7, although the difference disappears at the highest level. Figures 18.8 and 18.9 give the trends for Basic and Advanced Formal Achievement, respectively. In both, there are mostly small and inconsistent differences in averages, usually favoring males. Only perhaps for Advanced Formal Achievement is this difference appreciable at the highest levels of scores in math.

The two math and two science subscores that are not pictured in figures 18.3 through 18.9 appear to reflect difficulty or item-format factors. All show markedly high performance in the highest vigentile. Only one shows an appreciable gender difference; females do much better than males in the highest vigentile on two items involving difficult abstract reasoning in biology.

To probe these differences further, we have computed correlations among the math and science subscores and between them and the total reading-comprehension score, separately for males and females, within just the subsample comprising the highest five vigentiles ($N = 769$ males and 672 females). A gender difference appears in the correlation of math reasoning with reading

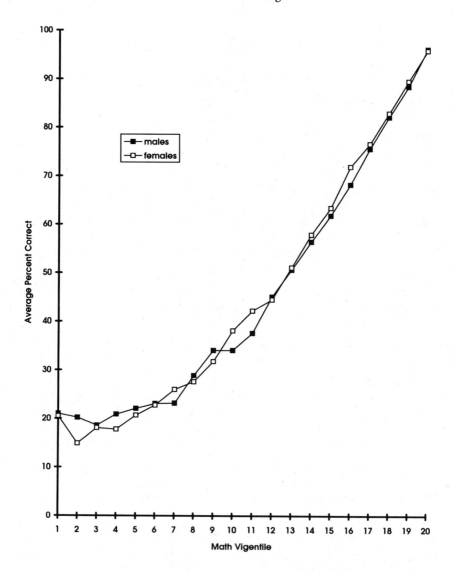

Figure 18.3. Average percentage correct on advanced knowledge and computation subscore on math tests for males and females in different math total score vigentiles.

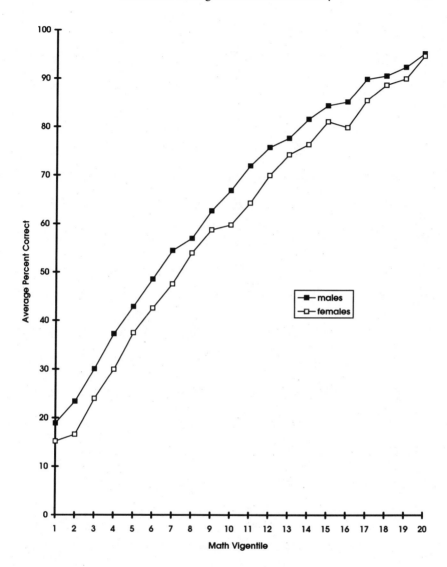

Figure 18.4. Average percentage correct on inferential reasoning subscore on math tests for males and females in different math total score vigentiles.

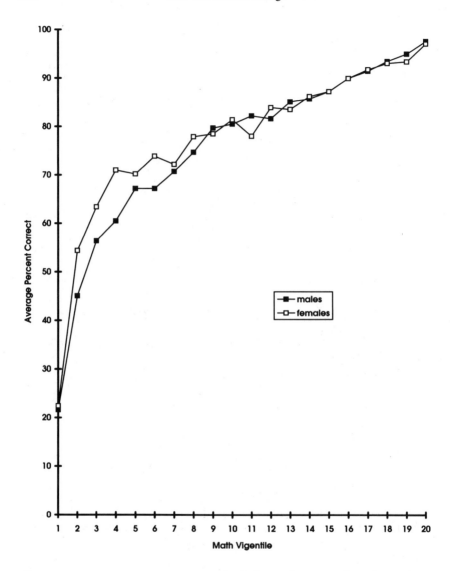

Figure 18.5. Average percentage correct on basic facts and computation subscore on math tests for males and females in different math total score vigentiles.

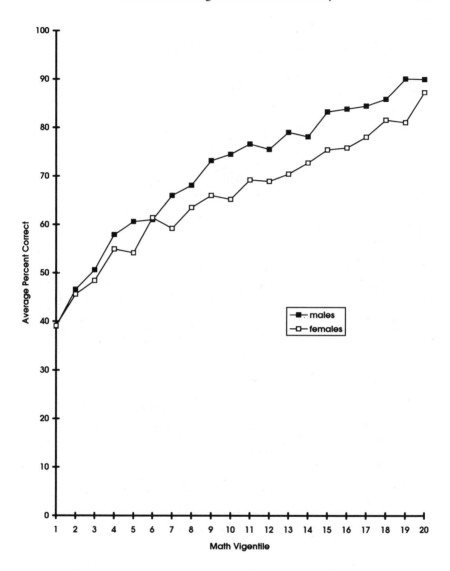

Figure 18.6. Average percentage correct on everyday knowledge subscore on science tests for males and females in different math total score vigentiles.

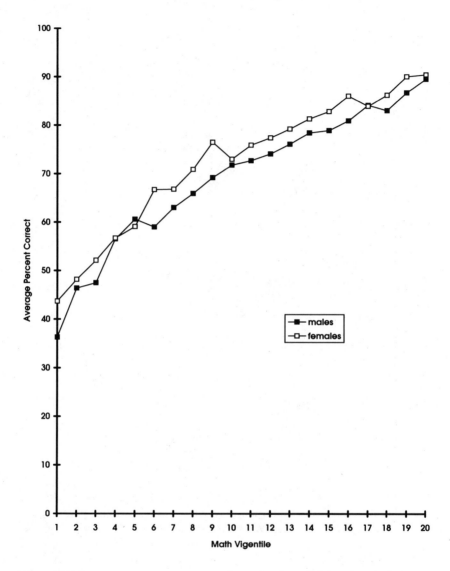

Figure 18.7. Average percentage correct on elementary knowledge and reasoning subscore on science tests for males and females in different math total score vigentiles.

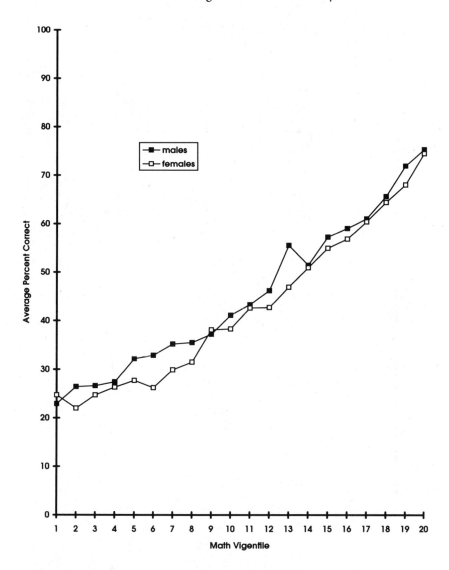

Figure 18.8. Average percentage correct on basic formal knowledge subscore on science tests for males and females in different math total score vigentiles.

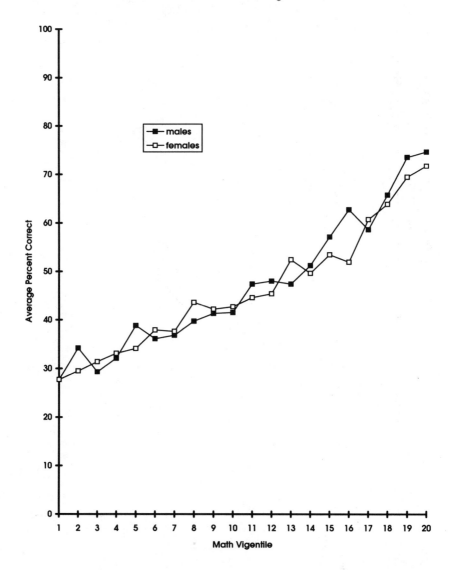

Figure 18.9. Average percentage correct on advanced formal knowledge subscore on science tests for males and females in different math total score vigentiles.

(male $r = .09$; female $r = .21$), and in the first and fourth science subscores (male $r = .08, .08$; female $r = .19, .17$). Both gender groups show many strong correlations of reading with science subscores ($.21 \ r < .40$). These high-math males seem to show more intercorrelations among science subscores than do the high-math females, particularly for those correlations involving Elementary Knowledge and Reasoning (male $r = .30, .24, .24$; female $r = .15, .14, .12$). The correlation comparisons do not appear to be differentially affected by floor or ceiling effects.

Student Grades and Learning Activities

Students were asked about their previous grades in English, math, and science. Figure 18.10 gives the percent per math vigentile that reports receiving mostly As in English since sixth grade. The average difference favoring females is quite marked and increases in higher-math vigentiles. In contrast, for math and science since sixth grade, differences in reports of A grades often also favor females over males but exceed a 10 percent difference only in a few high-math vigentiles; at the twentieth math vigentile and also from the middle of the range down, gender differences appear to be trivial. In the highest math vigentiles, very high percentages of both gender groups report taking algebra or advanced math; much lower proportions of both groups report taking advanced English or science courses.

In the twentieth vigentile, 60 percent of males and 63 percent of females report being included in a program for the gifted and talented, whereas the comparable reports from parents are 50 percent and 53 percent, respectively; this discrepancy has not yet been investigated. There is a rapid drop-off in reports of programs for the gifted and talented below this highest vigentile. Also, the parents of these highest-vigentile students emphasize the importance of programs for the gifted for encouraging intellectual challenge and deeper understanding; they do not see them as facilitating the early completion of school. Parents of female students emphasize the development of musical or artistic abilities more than do parents of male students (55 percent versus 26 percent).

A higher percentage of females than males reports studying music or dance outside school; the music percentages are shown in figure 18.11. The gender difference increases with each higher math vigentile. On the other hand, more males than females in the high-math vigentiles have access to computers for educational use in the home (fig. 18.12). More males than females study computer science outside school, although this difference does not appear in some high vigentiles, most notably the twentieth.

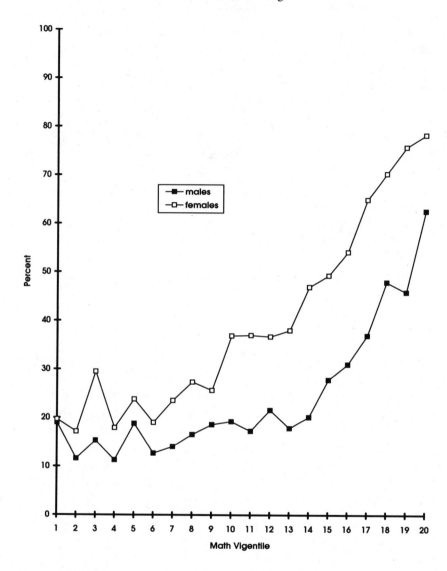

Figure 18.10. Percentage of males and females in different math total score vigentiles reporting "mostly A grades in English since the sixth grade."

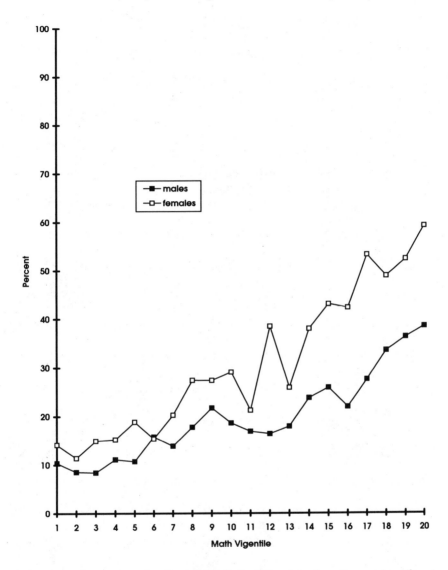

Figure 18.11. Percentage of males and females in different math total score vigentiles reporting studying music outside school.

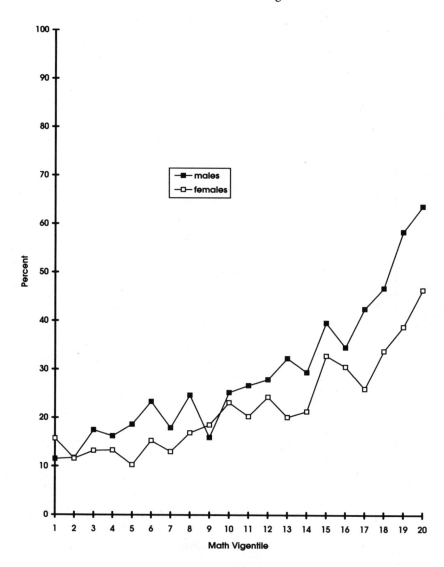

Figure 18.12. Percentage of males and females in different math total score vigentiles reporting having access to a computer for educational purposes at home.

Students' Attitudes about Themselves and Their Schools

The NELS:88 student survey asked students about their attitudes toward school subjects (e.g., "I am afraid to ask questions in math class;" "I look forward to science class") and toward themselves (e.g., "At times I think I am no good at all"; "I feel useless at times"). Males appear to have a more positive attitude toward math and science than do females, on average. The difference is notable in high-math vigentiles, but also in several other regions of the math distribution. The average anxiety with respect to math class is systematically lower for males than for females, especially in the higher half of the math-score distribution. The average agreement with statements of feeling "no good" or "useless" is markedly higher for females than for males on these items throughout most of the math-score range, including the highest vigentile. An example of these differences is given in figure 18.13.

Students' and Parents' Expectations

Other contrasts involve the expectations students and parents have about higher education. Parental educational level is closely related to student math vigentile even in the highest range; those in the twentieth vigentile are more likely to have parents with advanced degrees, those in the nineteenth vigentile are more likely to have parents who are college graduates, and so forth (fig. 18.14). In figures 18.15 through 18.17, three sets of expectations for higher education are given. Figure 18.15 shows students' plans for college graduation versus the obtaining of advanced degrees, separated by vigentile and gender. Vigentile has a marked effect on students' plans to obtain advanced degrees, and females plan for advanced degrees more than males within each vigentile, especially the highest. Figure 18.16 shows parents' expectations for students' college graduation versus the obtaining of advanced degrees, by vigentile and gender. Again, vigentile has a marked effect on expectations for advanced degrees, but here male students are thought by parents to be more likely than females to reach this level, at least in the top three vigentiles. Figure 18.17 gives students' beliefs about their parents' expectations for them. It is striking that, on average, female students in the highest vigentile correctly perceive parental expectations for their advanced-degree work, and these are consistent with their own expectations, whereas males significantly underestimate their parents' expectations. Both gender groups in the nineteenth vigentile underestimate their parents' expectations somewhat. These differences disappear at lower vigentiles.

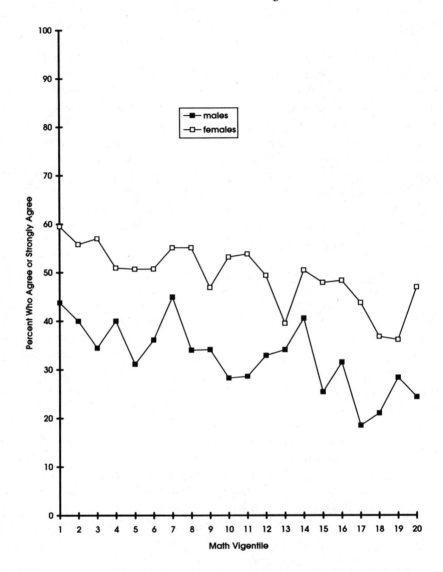

Figure 18.13. Percentage of males and females in different math total score vigentiles agreeing or strongly agreeing with the statement: "At times I think I am no good at all."

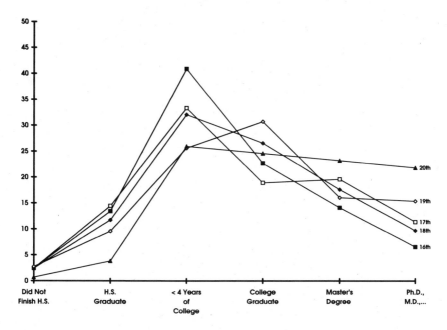

Figure 18.14. Distributions of parental educational levels for students scoring in the top five math total score vigentiles.

In keeping with their high expectations, parents of students in the twentieth and nineteenth vigentiles report more contact with schools than do parents of students in the eighteenth and lower vigentiles. These contacts primarily concern academic choices, programs, and performance. However, a significant number of contacts concern problems with behavior and schoolwork, and these are higher for males (26 percent) than for females (11 percent).

Other Characteristics of Students

Certain other characteristics and activities of students deserve attention alone or in interaction with the variables discussed above. For example, it was noted at the outset that more males than females achieve the highest math scores; among students in the highest vigentile in math, 39 percent are female and 61 percent are male. However, among these females 75 percent are Caucasian and 20 percent are Asian; the comparable percentages for males are 82 percent and 11 percent. In other high vigentiles, Asian males and females each constitute about 8 to 10 percent of the group. In the total NELS:88 sample, it should be possible to examine students' and parents' characteristics in interaction with gender and ethnicity simultaneously.

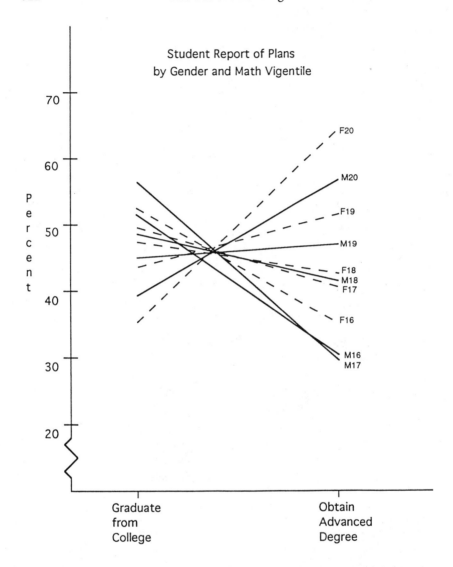

Figure 18.15. Percentages of male and female students scoring in the top five math total score vigentiles who plan to graduate from college versus obtain more advanced academic degrees.

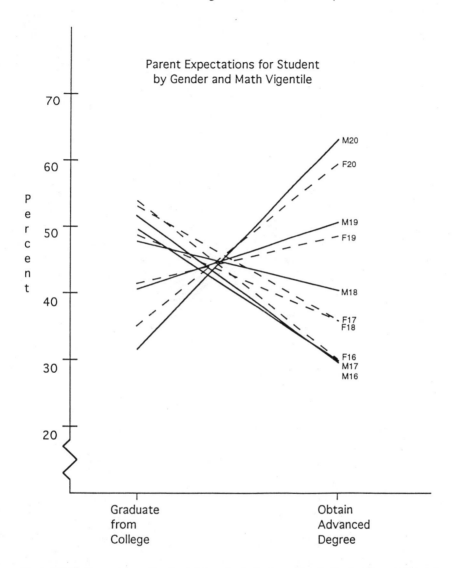

Figure 18.16. Percentages of male and female students scoring in the top five math total score vigentiles whose parents expect them to graduate from college versus obtain advanced degrees.

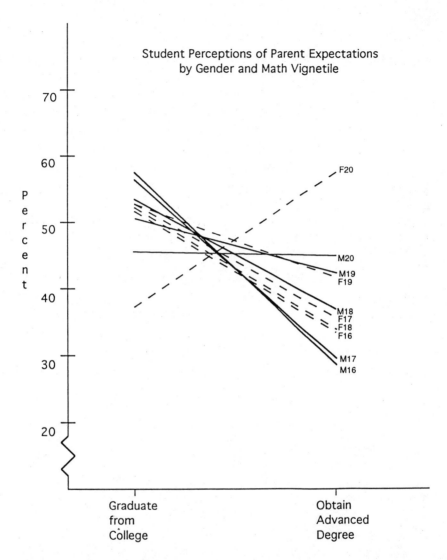

Figure 18.17. Percentages of male and female students scoring in the top five math total score vigentiles who perceive their parents as expecting them to graduate from college versus obtain advanced degrees.

Several variables also imply daily or weekly time trade-offs for students and should thus be considered in combination. Time spent on music rather than on computer lessons is one such combination suggested by the separate results reported above. Other examples come from considering the reports of time spent working for pay and the trade-off between home reading and television viewing. In the highest vigentile, 61 percent of the females but only 47 percent of the males report working for pay up to ten hours per week; 34 percent of females and 43 percent of males report never having worked for pay. In the immediately lower vigentiles, the average number of hours worked by males and females is similar, and higher percentages of females report never having worked for pay. It is not clear why this gender difference should be reversed at the highest level of math performance; unfortunately, the questionnaire did not ask the students to specify the type of work done.

Considering the trade-off between reading and television viewing, males report reading less and watching television more than do females, on average, in all high vigentiles, including the highest. Stepping down the range of vigentiles, reading time is seen to decrease as television viewing time increases in both gender groups. Within each high vigentile, the correlation between reading time and television viewing time is zero or negative. The highest correlation ($r = -.31$) occurs among twentieth-vigentile females; males show somewhat stronger negative correlations than do females in other vigentiles. In many high vigentiles, for both males and females, reading ability correlates positively with reading time and negatively with television viewing time. It is noteworthy that many parents report having rules regarding television viewing days and times, but the highest vigentiles show relatively less emphasis on rules. The important question of what kinds of reading and viewing content receive attention at different achievement levels was not addressed by the survey.

Discussion

Important further steps can now be taken to examine in multivariate analyses the leads identified in this initial exploration. Even within the limits of the NELS:88 eighth-grade tests and questionnaires, there are many opportunities for rich descriptions of individual differences in mathematics (and science) achievement. As data for tenth- and twelfth-grade students are included, the achievement subscores can be represented as growth functions rather than as single points in time, and the variables on the survey questionnaires can be substantially elaborated as well.

For the present, our focus has been on the correlates of high mathematical ability at the eighth-grade level alone. The initial findings and implications regarding this question can be summarized as follows:

1. The overall mathematical-ability distribution is highly correlated with distributions for other abilities, such as reading comprehension and various components of science achievement. Yet at the highest levels of mathematics performance, there remain substantial individual differences in these other abilities. It is not the case that very high achievers in mathematics are as a group homogeneous in other respects. On the other hand, they are not on average radically different from those in other nearby math strata.

2. Overall mathematics performance can be divided into advanced knowledge, basic skills, and reasoning. Although they are correlated, these dimensions provide profile differences that relate to other characteristics of students.

3. A major correlate of high mathematical ability is gender; more males than females appear at the highest (and also the lowest) score levels. However, there are no average gender differences within these high strata on scores reflecting advanced math knowledge or basic skills. Males show higher averages than do females on scores reflecting reasoning at all strata except the highest. Females show higher averages on scores for basic skills, but only in the lowest third of the overall math distribution. Clearly, further research designed to investigate gender differences more deeply will need to distinguish these components of mathematical ability. Further research on mathematical ability will need to include gender as an interacting variable throughout its distribution. The interaction of gender with race and ethnicity may be worth investigation, because Asians appear as a disproportionately large subgroup among the highest-scoring females in our data.

4. Some components of science knowledge show average gender differences favoring males (e.g., everyday knowledge of astronomy) and some show differences favoring females (e.g., elementary knowledge and reasoning in biology). Except for some aspects of advanced science knowledge, these differences are small at the highest level of math scores. Among high achievers in math, correlations among math reasoning, science, and reading scores appear stronger for females, whereas the males show stronger intercorrelations among science scores. Both groups display strong correlations between science and reading. The implied qualitative differences in ability structure for different student groups deserve deeper study.

5. Females show higher average reading scores and grades in English courses than do males throughout the math-score range; this difference implies stronger verbal abilities in general for females. Males appear more heterogeneous than females in English-language abilities even at high levels of math scores. Females also get higher average grades than males in math and science courses, but these differences are small at high levels of math.

6. On average, high-math females are more likely to study music outside school, less likely to study computers, and less likely to have computers at home for educational use than are males. They are also likely to show more anxiety about math and less-positive attitudes about math and science and about their own self-worth. On the other hand, many of the highest scorers in math expect to reach high educational levels, and females plan for advanced degrees more than do males. They more accurately perceive their parents' high expectations for their advanced academic work than do males. They also work more often for pay, read more, and view television less than their male counterparts.

Deeper analyses of the differences in math scores and gender will need to study the intersections of all these personal variables and trade-offs of time. We are pursuing several lines of further work toward this end.

References

Benbow, C. P. (1992). Mathematical talent: Its origins and consequences. In N. Colangelo, S. G. Assouline, & D. L. Ambroson (Eds.), *Talent development: Proceedings from the 1991 Henry B. and Jocelyn Wallace National Research Symposium on Talent Development* (pp. 95–123). Unionville, N.Y.: Trillium Press.

Chipman, S. F. (1988). Far too sexy a topic. *Educational Researcher* 17:46–49.

Ennis, M. M., Kerkhoven, J. I. M., & Snow, R. E. (1993). *Enhancing the validity and usefulness of large-scale assessments* (Paper No. 93–151). Stanford: Stanford University, Center for Research on the Context of Secondary School Teaching.

Feingold, A. (1993). Joint effects of gender differences in central tendency and gender differences in variability. *Review of Educational Research* 63:106–109.

Hedges, L. V., & Friedman, L. (1993a). Computing gender difference effects in tails of distributions: The consequences of differences in tail size, effect size, and variance ratio. *Review of Educational Research* 63:110–112.

Hedges, L. V., & Friedman, L. (1993b). Gender differences in variability and intellectual abilities: A reanalysis of Feingold's results. *Review of Educational Research* 63:94–105.

Hyde, J. S., Fennema, E., & Lamon, S. J. (1990). Gender differences in mathematical performance: A meta-analysis. *Psychological Bulletin* 107:139–155.

Rock, D. A., Pollack, J. M., Owings, J., & Hafner, A. (1990). *Psychometric report for the NELS:88 base year test battery* (Contractor Report No. NCES 91–467). Washington, D.C.: U.S. Department of Education.

V   Psychometrics

Generality and Specificity

O ne theme running through this volume is that of resistance to the profound implications of findings documenting individual differences in human abilities, particularly when these findings are applied in educational and work settings. When such differences are revealed, their implications are at odds with the prevailing ideological-political *Zeitgeist*; attention then seems to turn naturally to the properties of the measuring instruments carrying the bad news (Cronbach, 1975). Many people maintain that the differences between groups that are observed when conventional measures of ability are used are the result of the assessment tools themselves and hence can be ignored justifiably. Such assertions persist even though evidence is lacking for the predictive bias of conventional assessment tools (Cleary, Humphreys, Kendrick, & Wesman, 1975; Linn, 1982).

The first two contributions in this section take a look at this issue within a population of gifted students, students who in the seventh grade were selected to take the College Board Scholastic Aptitude Test in an out-of-level format (through the talent search originated in 1972 by Stanley). This population was chosen because of the persistent gender differences in mathematical reasoning ability found therein (Benbow, 1988). Benbow and Wolins, followed by Minor and Benbow, analyze the internal psychometric properties of the SAT-M (the measure of mathematical reasoning ability) at the item and scale levels, respectively. These treatments compare the item-level response pattern (Benbow and Wolins) and the factorial structure (Minor and Benbow) of the SAT-M across gifted thirteen-year-olds and college-bound high school students. Essentially, both populations appear to respond to the SAT-M in a similar manner, as do both sexes. Yet the age differences are of much greater magnitude than the gender differences, which are best described as minuscule. These internal analyses support the integrity of the SAT-M for gifted seventh graders, as well as for males and females. Moreover, they are complemented by documentation of the SAT-M's external validity for mathematically gifted thirteen-year-olds. Benbow (1992) reveals that the SAT-M achieves impressive predictive validity coeffi-

329

cients (from age thirteen to age twenty-three) for a variety of standardized achievement criteria as well as secured educational credentials.

By and large, then, these analyses demonstrate that the SAT-M is indexing "real" individual differences in abilities that are developed earlier and are capable of being developed more fully in this gifted population than in the typical college-bound high school student. For gifted thirteen-year-olds and for high school students, whether male or female, the SAT-M systematically differentiates comparable gradations of individual differences in mathematical reasoning ability.

The analyses of the SAT-M are followed by a contribution from Becker. Her chapter is not only relevant to investigators interested in assessing intellectual talent but also of general interest to those in the field of psychometrics. Becker's chapter provides a useful technical treatment of how ability parameters are best estimated through aggregation, an aggregation based on Cronbach's generalizability theory. She draws on the domain of cognitive abilities to illustrate her points and highlights, in an innovative fashion, how the concept of aggregation (the basis for computing effect sizes in meta-analytic reviews) is also advantageous for gaining a better purchase on constructs in psychological science.

The final two contributions in this section address basic conceptual questions regarding the developmental (and even philosophical) framework undergirding opinions and research on individual differences in talent. Gage's discussion touches on a number of different philosophical arguments frequently generated by those who recoil from attempts to (*a*) index extreme levels of individual differences in intellectual talent and (*b*) respond to those differences with special educational interventions. Objectifying human behavior with quantitative tools has historically tended to be distasteful to many, especially those within the humanistic sphere of C. P. Snow's (1964) two cultures. Perhaps Gage is right in maintaining that to ignore such critics is foolish. It might behoove investigators studying individual differences in intellectual talent to point out more routinely the implications of their findings, as some have done so well. Some critics may be surprised to learn, for example, that:

—A society in which the heritabilities of intellectual talent are decreasing reflects a culture whose resources are allocated on the basis of privilege as opposed to talent. (Humphreys, 1992)

—If test scores and grades were judiciously employed to allocate educational resources and for personnel selection, there would be one-third more variance between reared-in and achieved socioeconomic status. (Jencks et al., 1972)

—If intellectual giftedness is defined as the top 1 percent on tests of general intelligence (z-score 2.3), half of the students surpassing this cutoff score will be found in homes *below* the 84th percentile in socioeconomic status (and less than 9 percent will be found in commensurably privileged homes—within the top 1 percent in socioeconomic status)

We also need to be alert to Bereiter's (1976) argument that, given the amount of regression toward the mean (observed from highly able parents and their children), perhaps part of the resistance to standardized testing comes from an attempt to *preserve* the status quo.

References

Benbow, C. P. (1988). Sex differences in mathematical reasoning ability in intellectually talented preadolescents: Their nature, effects, and possible causes. *Behavioral and Brain Sciences* 11:169–232.

Benbow, C. P. (1992). Academic achievement in mathematics and science of students between ages thirteen and twenty-three: Are there differences among students in the top one percent of mathematical ability? *Journal of Educational Psychology* 84:51–61.

Bereiter, C. (1976). IQ and elitism. *Interchange* 7:36–44.

Cleary, T. A., Humphreys, L. G., Kendrick, S. A., & Wesman, A. (1975). Educational uses of tests with disadvantaged students. *American Psychologist* 30:15–41.

Cronbach, L. J. (1975). Five decades of public controversy over mental testing. *American Psychologist* 30:1–14.

Humphreys, L. G. (1992). Commentary: What both critics and users of ability tests need to know. *Psychological Science* 3:271–274.

Jencks, C., Smith, M., Acland, H., Bane, M. J., Cohen, D., Gintis, H., Heyns, B., & Michelson, S. (1972). *Inequality: A reassessment of the effect of family and schooling in America*. New York: Basic Books.

Linn, R. L. (1982). Ability testing: Individual differences, prediction, and differential prediction. In A. K. Wigdor & W. R. Garner (Eds.), *Ability testing: Uses, consequences, and controversies* (pp. 335–388). Washington, D.C.: National Academy Press.

Snow, C. P. (1964). *The two cultures and a second look*. Cambridge: Cambridge University Press.

19

The Utility of Out-of-Level Testing for Gifted Seventh and Eighth Graders Using the SAT-M

An Examination of Item Bias

CAMILLA PERSSON BENBOW AND

LEROY WOLINS

For more than twenty years the Study of Mathematically Precocious Youth (SMPY) and its various offshoots have been identifying gifted seventh and eighth graders using the College Board Scholastic Aptitude Test (SAT) (Cohn, 1991; Keating & Stanley, 1972). This instrument has proven to be an invaluable tool for assessing meaningful individual differences among gifted seventh and eighth graders (i.e., students scoring in the top 2 to 5 percent on conventional, grade-appropriate, standardized achievement tests). When these students are given the SAT-M, for example, they generate score distributions that mirror those generated by high school students (Benbow, 1988). Further, their SAT-M scores have demonstrated predictive validity, as a recent study underscored. Among students in the top 1 percent of mathematical ability, individual differences assessed by the SAT-M when the students were thirteen years old have generated meaningful correlates across a variety of important academic and vocational criteria that follow temporal gaps of up to ten years (Benbow, 1992). Moreover, the average effect size of the difference in the academic achievement variables, primarily in the areas of math and science, between the top quarter of the top 1 percent and the bottom quarter of the top 1 percent was .80 for the continuous variables and .46 for the categorical variables. These differences were greater than the much discussed gender differences on the same math and science achievement variables (for which the effect sizes were .57 and .34, respectively). Thus, without question, this instrument reveals useful information about gifted populations, making it clear why it currently is used with almost 150,000 students annually in talent searches across the country.

One of the more robust findings stemming from SMPY's research on preadolescent samples, however, has been the consistent and stubborn gender differences favoring males on the SAT-M (Benbow, 1988; Benbow & Stanley, 1980, 1981, 1983; Lubinski & Benbow, 1992). These differences have been examined in a variety of validation studies, with gender differences in test scores typically translating into pronounced gender differences across a host of academic and vocational criteria (Benbow, 1988, 1992; Benbow & Arjmand, 1990). An explanation for the gender differences in SAT-M scores at age thirteen remains to be offered (Benbow, 1988).

Despite the substantial amount of longitudinal data gathered in support of the predictive validity of the SAT-M for both genders in this special population, to our knowledge no one to date has systematically examined the item characteristics generated by gifted adolescents, or even compared them to those manifested by high school students, for whom the test was designed. That was the purpose of our investigation. Specifically, we were interested in ascertaining whether the items found on the SAT-M have comparable properties for high school students and gifted seventh graders; we were especially interested in determining if the item characteristics generated by this instrument are moderated by gender.

Various factors could bias the results obtained from the SAT. The manner in which the items that make up the test are worded, for example, has been studied for some time with respect to the items' relationship to gender differences. Some researchers have found support for the notion that references to male or female characters, pronoun usage, and stereotypical gender content are related to gender differences in performance (Boldt, 1983; Donlon, Ekstrom, Harris, & Lockheed, 1977; Donlon, Ekstrom, & Lockheed, 1979; Diamond & Tittle, 1985), while others (Rowell & Hennen, 1978; Strassberg-Rosenberg & Donlon, 1975) have not. More recently, McLarty, Noble, and Huntley (1989), Chipman, Marshall, and Scott (1991), and Sappington, Larsen, Martin, and Murphy (1991) have found that mathematical performances by males and females did not vary as a function of gender content or gender-familiar wording. Males performed better even on ostensibly "female" items.

Another possibility is that subject-matter content, format, or even the placement of a question within a test could result in different performances by males and females or by seventh and twelfth graders. These possibilities have been studied with respect to gender differences. Mundy (1982), Donlon (1973), and Sweeney (1953) have found that certain items, particularly those requiring spatial ability or cognitive restructuring, did favor males. McGee (1979), Burnett, Lane, and Dratt (1979), and Battista (1990), among others, have reported that gender differences in mathematical ability can be accounted for by gender differences in spatial ability. It should be noted, however, that several studies, including one by Lubinski and Humphreys (1990a), have disputed the latter result. Lubinski and Humphreys label the hypothesized synergistic relationship between mathematical and spatial ability "spurious." Using a sample of gifted students, Becker (1978) also did not find that the visuospatial content of SAT-M items was related to gender differences on the SAT. Rather, Becker (1990) reported that algebra items were more difficult for females than for males, with the opposite pattern for miscellaneous items.

There is some evidence to justify the view that the nature of a test item might differentially relate to the test performances of males and females. The issue of the differences between seventh graders and high school students has not been addressed. We assessed whether and the extent to which the robust gender differences in SAT-M scores among gifted seventh and eighth graders could be due to bias at the item level. Investigation of item bias was limited to item difficulty and the differential rate of omitting items, however. We compared differences related to gender with developmental differences—those produced by age (seventh versus twelfth grade). The following three questions were posed: (1) Is the precision with which the SAT-M measures meaningful individual differences comparable for seventh graders and high school students? (2) Is there gender bias at the item level? and (3) Is gender bias more pronounced than age bias?

Method

Subjects

SAT-M item responses for a sample of gifted seventh graders and for high school students were provided by the Educational Testing Service from the January 1981 SAT testing. To be eligible to take the SAT in the seventh grade, students must have scored at least at the 97th percentile on a nationally normed achievement test, such as the Iowa Test of Basic Skills. Although the high school students were not selected on the basis of ability, most high school students who take the SAT are college bound. Thus, they represent academically able high school students. Because both groups of students chose to take the SAT and did so for potentially different reasons, our interpretation of the findings was limited to the extent to which such self-selection affected the results.

Subjects were placed in groups on the basis of grade and within grade by gender, for a total of four subsamples: high school males (HSM), $N = 3,694$; high school females (HSF), $N = 3,657$; seventh-grade males (7M), $N = 4,341$; and seventh-grade females (7F), $N = 4,538$.

Instrument

The SAT-Mathematics test, form DSA016HM, was divided into two sections, each with a thirty-minute time limit. The entire test was composed of fifty-nine rather than sixty items because one item had been found to be defective. Among the fifty-nine, thirty-nine were standard multiple-choice items with five options each and twenty were quantitative comparison items in a multiple-choice format with four options each. As in all forms of the SAT-M, the questions were designed to measure developed mathematical reasoning ability in students who have had some algebra and geometry (Donlon, 1984).

Procedure

SAT-M item difficulties, computed separately for males and females and by grade, were transformed by Probit into normal deviates, Z (Snedecor & Cochran, 1980). The value of Z corresponding to any proportion p is such that the area of a standard normal curve to the left of Z is p. For example, $Z = 0$ for $p = .5$ (where 50 percent of the students got an item correct); $Z = 1.282$ for $p = .9$. Percent correct and percent omitted for each item were transformed separately; the resulting normal deviates for the four subgroups are reported in the appendix to this chapter, as are the differences in Z between any two groups in the study. The use of normal deviates ensured that differences in percent correct were kept nearly constant, irrespective of how difficult the item was for the students.

Because of the large sample sizes and because both sections of the test were highly speeded, significance testing was not meaningful. Therefore, to judge the relative magnitude of differences in normal deviates between males and females, gender differences in normal deviates were compared to age differences (i.e., between seventh and twelfth graders). Because items rather than individuals were the units of analysis, it was not reasonable to compute effect sizes (Cohen, 1988). The variance components for each effect in an analysis of variance, using SAT-M items as "subjects," were compared, as were correlation coefficients, in order to determine the relative magnitude of the effects.

Results

Gifted Seventh Graders

The correlations of SAT-M item difficulty (percent correct) and percent omitting the item between seventh-grade males and females were .98 and .99, respectively. This implies that about 98 percent of the variance in item difficulty for males and females was shared; item difficulty maintained the same rank order for males and females. The mean item difficulty was −.241 (standard deviation = .72; this means that about 40 percent obtained the correct answer for an item) for such males and −.432 (standard deviation = .71; 33 percent got the item correct) for such females. Males found the SAT-M problems to be easier than did the females. The difference in percent omitted, in normal deviate format, was much smaller: .097 (for males: −1.190 [standard deviation = .62]; on average, 12 percent omitted an item; for females: −1.093 [standard deviation = .65]; on average, 14 percent omitted an item).

The gender differences in item difficulty for the seventh graders are illustrated in figure 19.1. Three items were easier for females, but by a marginal amount (less than a −.07 difference in normal deviates, or less than 3 percentage points), with the remaining fifty-six all being easier for males. For those test items favoring males, all but four (7 percent) had a difference in normal deviates that was less than .36 (14 percentage points). This indicated a pattern of consistent small differences favoring males in SAT-M item difficulty.

As noted, however, there were four SAT-M items for which the performance advantage of males was rather substantial. Although this number is probably not higher than what would be expected if item difficulties were normally distributed (see figure 19.1), we inspected the content of those questions. The test item exhibiting the largest gender difference favoring males (with a normal deviate difference of .47; 18 percentage points) involved calculating a simple percentage. That item was a word problem, contained a female character, and was the second problem on the first math subtest. Among the remaining three, one (with a normal deviate difference of .39; 15 percentage points) was a word problem, involved a track meet, and was gender neutral. It

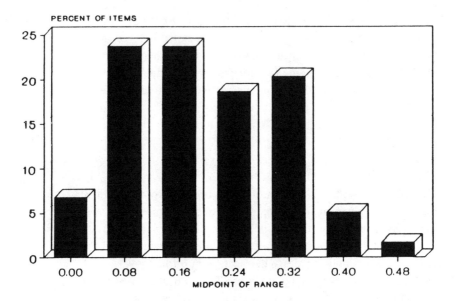

Figure 19.1. Distribution of differences in item difficulties on the SAT (percentage correct transformed into normal deviates) between junior high school males and females.

was the thirteenth item out of twenty-five on the first subtest. One was a quantitative comparison (with a normal deviate difference of .38; 15 percentage points), asking students to judge which simple fraction was larger. It was the eighteenth item out of thirty-five on the second subtest. The last item exhibiting a rather substantial male advantage (with a normal deviate difference of .37; 14 percentage points) was a geometry problem asking students to judge which angle in a figure was greater. Its placement was twenty-third out of thirty-five on the second subtest.

Two out of the three items that marginally favored females (with a normal deviate difference of less than −.07; 3 percentage points) were computation problems. All three contained no characters; they were placed fourth and twenty-third out of twenty-five on the first subtest and fourteenth out of thirty-five on the second subtest.

High School Students

The correlations of percent correct (item difficulty) and percent omitting the item between the high school males and females were both .99. Thus, at least 99 percent of the variance in item difficulty for high school males and females was shared; that is, the items maintained the same rank order of difficulty for both males and females. The mean item difficulty was .023 (on average, 51 percent got the item correct) for high school males and −.221 (on average, 42 percent got the item correct) for high school females, revealing that problems posed on the SAT-M were easier for males than females. The difference in percent omitted (for males: −1.530 [standard deviation = .64], or 6 percent; for females: −1.395 [standard deviation = .624], or 8 percent) was smaller: .14.

The gender differences in item performance for the high school students are illustrated in figure 19.2. One item favored females, but by a marginal amount (less than .05 difference in normal deviates, or 2 percentage points), with the remaining fifty-eight all favoring males. There were eight items (14 percent) for which the gender difference in item difficulty was greater than .36 (14 percentage points).

The eight SAT-M items that favored the high school males by the largest margin included three of the four test items that also favored the seventh grade males by the largest margin. The one exception (the nonoverlapping test item that only favored the seventh-grade males by a good margin) was the eighteenth item on the second subtest, which involved judging which simple fraction was larger. For the remaining five questions, on which only high school males

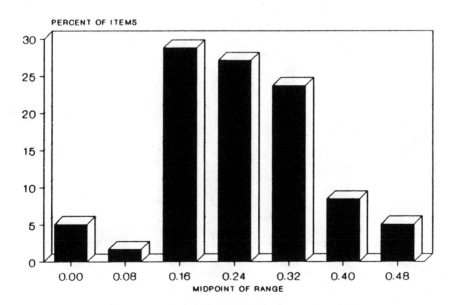

Figure 19.2. Distribution of differences in item difficulties on the SAT (percentage correct transformed into normal deviates) between high school males and females.

demonstrated a substantial performance advantage, one involved reasoning with mechanical objects (the ninth item out of twenty-five on the first subtest), one was an algebraic word problem about mixing punch (the fourteenth item out of twenty-five on the first subtest), one was a geometry problem (the twenty-fifth item out of twenty-five on the first subtest), one asked which decimal number was larger (the eighth item out of thirty-five on the second subtest), and the final one was a word problem involving algebra and the distance traveled by a car (the thirty-second item out of thirty-five on the second subtest).

Seventh-Grade Students versus High School Students

The correlations between the high school students and the seventh graders were .95 for both males and females for item difficulty and .91 and .92, respectively, for males and females for percent omitted. Thus, at least 91 percent of the variance in item difficulty was shared by high school students and seventh graders. The difference in mean item difficulty for the two groups of males (.023 versus −.241) was .26 (10 percentage points), while the difference between high school females and female seventh graders (−.221 versus −.432)

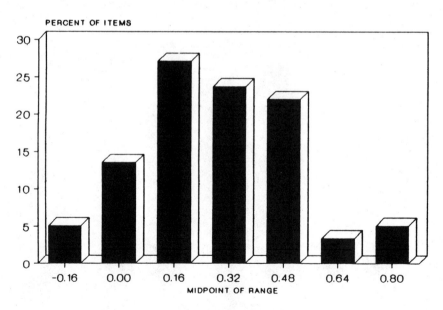

Figure 19.3. Distribution of differences in item difficulties on the SAT (percentage correct transformed into normal deviates) between high school males and junior high school males.

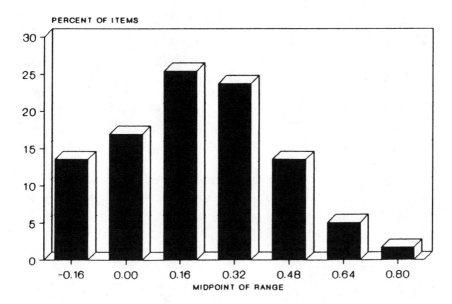

Figure 19.4. Distribution of differences in item difficulties on the SAT (percentage correct transformed into normal deviates) between high school females and junior high school females.

was .21 (8 percentage points). The respective differences in percent omitted were .34 and .30 (13 and 12 percentage points, respectively). Clearly, the high school students, both male and female, found the test items easier.

The differences in SAT item performance between the high school students and the gifted seventh graders are shown in figures 19.3 and 19.4. Almost all the items were easier for the high school students. Nine items (15 percent), however, favored the seventh graders. Significantly, about half of those items also exhibited some of the largest gender discrepancies in SAT-M item difficulty that favored males (see the appendix to this chapter).

Age and Gender

Finally, we assessed the relative contributions of the interactions of gender and item performance and age and item performance in explaining SAT-M scores. Through an analysis of variance, we determined the variance component of each effect. In this analysis it was not meaningful to deal with statistical significance because of the large sample size. First we looked at item difficulty; we compared the main effects of gender and age with their respective interaction terms (an indicator of item bias). The variance component for the gender-by-item interaction (.0044) was less than one-fifth the size of the variance component due to gender (.0235), while the age-by-item variance component (.0248) was about the same size as that for age (.0279). For the percent omitting an item, the gender-by-item variance component (.0022) was one-third the size of the variance component for gender (.0066). In contrast, the variance component for age-by-item interaction (.0304) was three-fifths the size of that for age (.0514). Thus, age related differentially to item difficulty to a much greater extent than did gender; the gender-by-item interaction in turn was much less than the main effect of gender.

Similar conclusions can be drawn from the correlations among the various groups, which correlations were presented earlier. The amount of shared variance in item difficulty was greater between males and females of the same approximate age (about 98 percent) than between the two age groups (about 92 percent). Yet the rank order of item difficulty was relatively constant across genders and age groups.

Discussion

The purpose of this investigation was (1) to determine the comparative precision with which the SAT-M measures meaningful individual differences, across both genders, in high school students and gifted seventh graders; and (2) to ascertain whether the gender differences consistently revealed by this instrument (Benbow, 1988; Benbow & Stanley, 1980, 1981, 1983; Lubinski & Benbow, 1992) might, in part, be a function of item bias. Our overall conclusion is that item bias does not appear to have contaminated this instrument; gender bias on the SAT-M was not demonstrated at the item level.

For the gifted seventh graders, 95 percent of the SAT-M items favored males, with only four items exhibiting moderately large differences. Thus, for this group of students, there was a consistent pattern of small differences in item performance that favored males. When the SAT-M item performance of high school students was studied, the advantage displayed by males was seen to be much larger. Nonetheless, the variance component for the gender-by-item interaction (an indicator of item bias) was less than one-fifth the size of the variance component due to gender. Moreover, at least 98 percent of the variance in item difficulty was shared by the males and the females; item difficulty maintained the same rank order for both genders at both age levels.

It should be noted that the item difficulty was similar for males and females within a grade, but was less similar between males and females across grades. The relationship between age and item performance was stronger than the one for gender, with the SAT-M being easier for high school students. Nonetheless, roughly the same rank order of item difficulty was found for high school students and gifted seventh graders. The SAT-M measured individual differences with comparable precision for seventh graders and high school students.

Those nine SAT-M items that favored the seventh graders rather than the twelfth graders were also the ones exhibiting some of the largest gender differences in item difficulty favoring males. Their common element appeared to be that they required abstract reasoning skills, rather than advanced mathematical knowledge, in order to be solved. It should be noted, however, that an exhaustive analysis of item content was not conducted. With so few test items being especially difficult for females compared to males, such an analysis seemed fruitless. Nonetheless, we could determine the item characteristics that were *not* found to be related to performance: (1) the gender of the characters in a problem, (2) the placement of an item in the test, (3) the geometric or spatial content of an item, and (4) the gender appropriateness of a problem topic.

We also explored the possibility that females may take fewer risks and, therefore, omit more of the test items than do males (see Kimball, 1989). The gender difference in items omitted was negligible, however, for both age groups. The seventh graders omitted more items than did the high school students.

Thus, in this study we identified no item characteristics or patterns of omission that served to bias ability assessment when the SAT-M was used with intellectually gifted students. Consequently, findings from recent cross-sectional and meta-analytic reviews (Feingold, 1988; Friedman, 1989; Hyde, Fennema, & Lamon, 1990), indicating that males and females are converging toward a common mean on a variety of intellectual parameters, might appear at odds with this observed gender difference favoring males on the SAT-M at extreme cutting scores. These results would be predictable, however, if the hypothesis of greater male variability were drawn upon. It is well known that on a variety of measures of intellectual functioning, even on measures for which females consistently display larger means, males tend to be more variable (Feingold, 1992; Lubinski & Humphreys, 1990b; Stanley, Benbow, Brody, Dauber, & Lupkowski, 1992). As a result, there tends to be a disproportionate number of males at both the upper and lower tails of score distributions on many measures of cognitive ability (cf. Becker & Hedges, 1988; Benbow, 1988; Feingold, 1992; Humphreys, 1988; Jensen, 1988; Lubinski & Benbow, 1992; Lubinski & Dawis, 1992).

It should be noted that item bias, as investigated in this study, is only one type of bias that can result when a psychological scale is used. Although the SAT-M does not appear to be contaminated by item bias, bias can occur in several ways. An example is the bias that involves the accuracy of inferences in relation to external criterion variables. These forms of bias involve intercept, slope, and standard-error differences as a function of group membership (e.g., gender or race; see Jensen, 1980). We did not address those issues.

In conclusion, then, item difficulty on the SAT-M maintained the same relative rank order for seventh graders and high school students and was not moderated by gender. Thus, gender bias at the item level does not seem to be a plausible explanation for the greater proportion of males compared to females at the upper tail of the SAT-M score distribution (Benbow, 1988).

Acknowledgments

This research was funded by grants MDR-8651737 and MDR-8855625 from the National Science Foundation and a grant from the College Board to Camilla Persson Benbow. We gratefully acknowledge their support.

References

Battista, M. T. (1990). Spatial visualization and gender differences in high school geometry. *Journal for Research in Mathematics Education* 21:47–60.

Becker, B. J. (1978). *The relationship of spatial ability to sex differences in the performance of mathematically precocious youths on the mathematical section of the Scholastic Aptitude Test.* Unpublished master's thesis. Johns Hopkins University, Baltimore.

Becker, B. J. (1990). Item characteristics and gender differences on the SAT-M for mathematically able youths. *American Educational Research Journal* 27:65–88.

Becker, B. J., & Hedges, L. (1988). The effects of selection and variability in studies of gender differences. *Behavioral and Brain Sciences* 11:183–184.

Benbow, C. P. (1988). Sex differences in mathematical reasoning ability in intellectually talented pre-adolescents: Their nature, effects, and possible causes. *Behavioral and Brain Sciences* 11:169–232.

Benbow, C. P. (1992). Academic achievement in mathematics and science of students between ages thirteen and twenty-three: Are there differences among students in the top one percent of mathematical ability? *Journal of Educational Psychology* 84:51–61.

Benbow, C. P., & Arjmand, O. (1990). Predictors of high academic achievement in mathematics and science by mathematically talented students: A longitudinal study. *Journal of Educational Psychology* 82:430–441.

Benbow, C. P., & Stanley, J. C. (1980). Sex differences in mathematical ability: Fact or artifact? *Science* 210:1262–1264.

Benbow, C. P., & Stanley, J. C. (1981). Mathematical ability: Is sex a factor? *Science* 212:114–121.

Benbow, C. P., & Stanley, J. C. (1983). Sex differences in mathematical reasoning ability: More facts. *Science* 222:1029–1031.

Boldt, R. F. (1983). *Status of research on item content and differential performance on tests used in higher education.* Princeton: Educational Testing Service.

Burnett, S. A., Lane, D. M., & Dratt, L. M. (1979). Spatial visualization and sex differences in quantitative ability. *Intelligence* 3:345–354.

Chipman, S. F., Marshall, S. P., & Scott, P. A. (1991). Content effects on word problem performance: A possible source of test bias? *American Educational Research Journal* 28:897–915.

Cohen, J. (1988). *Statistical power analysis for the behavioral sciences* (2nd ed.). Hillsdale, N.J.: Erlbaum.

Cohn, S. J. (1991). Talent searches. In N. Colangelo & G. A. Davis (Eds.), *Handbook of gifted education* (pp. 166–177). Needham Heights, Mass.: Allyn & Bacon.

Diamond, E. E., & Tittle, C. K. (1985). Sex equity in testing. In S. S. Klein (Ed.), *Handbook for achieving sex equity through education* (pp. 167–188). Baltimore: Johns Hopkins University Press.

Donlon, T. F. (1973). *Content factors in sex differences in test questions* (Research Memorandum No. 73–28). Princeton: Educational Testing Service.

Donlon, T. F. (Ed.). (1984). *The College Board technical handbook for the Scholastic Aptitude Test and Achievement Tests.* New York: College Entrance Examination Board.

Donlon, T. F., Ekstrom, R. B., Harris, A. M., & Lockheed, M. E. (1977). *Performance consequences of sex bias in the content of major achievement batteries* (Final Rep. No. PR 77–11). Princeton: Educational Testing Service.

Donlon, T. F., Ekstrom, R. B., & Lockheed, M. E. (1979). The consequences of sex bias in the content of major achievement test batteries. *Measurement, Evaluation, and Guidance* 11:202–216.

Feingold, A. (1988). Cognitive gender differences are disappearing. *American Psychologist* 43:95–103.

Feingold, A. (1992). Sex differences in variability in intellectual abilities: A new look at an old controversy. *Review of Educational Research* 62:61–84.

Friedman, L. (1989). Mathematics and the gender gap: A meta-analysis of recent studies on sex differences in mathematical tasks. *Review of Educational Research* 59:185–213.

Humphreys, L. G. (1988). Sex differences in variability may be more important than sex differences in means. *Behavioral and Brain Sciences* 11:195–196.

Hyde, J. S., Fennema, E., & Lamon, S. J. (1990). Gender differences in mathematics performance: A meta-analysis. *Psychological Bulletin* 107:139–155.

Jensen, A. R. (1980). *Bias in mental testing.* New York: Free Press.

Jensen, A. R. (1988). Sex differences in arithmetic computation and reasoning and prepubertal boys and girls. *Behavioral and Brain Sciences* 11:198–199.

Keating, D. P., & Stanley, J. C. (1972). Extreme measures for the exceptionally gifted in mathematics and science. *Educational Researcher* 1:3–7.

Kimball, M. M. (1989). A new perspective on women's math achievement. *Psychological Bulletin* 105:198–214.

Lubinski, D., & Benbow, C. P. (1992). Gender differences in abilities and preferences among the gifted: Implications for the math-science pipeline. *Current Directions in Psychological Science* 1:61–66.

Lubinski, D., & Dawis, R. V. (1992). Aptitudes, skills, and proficiencies. In M. D. Dunnette & L. M. Hough (Eds.), *The handbook of industrial/organizational psychology* (2nd ed., Vol. 3, pp. 1–59). Palo Alto: Consulting Psychologists Press.

Lubinski, D., & Humphreys, L. G. (1990a). Assessing spurious "moderator effects": Illustrated substantively with the hypothesized ("synergistic") relation between spatial and mathematical ability. *Psychological Bulletin* 107:385–393.

Lubinski, D., & Humphreys, L. G. (1990b). A broadly based analysis of mathematical giftedness. *Intelligence* 14:327–355.

McGee, M. G. (1979). Human spatial abilities: Psychometric studies and environmental, genetic, hormonal, and neurological influences. *Psychological Bulletin* 86:889–918.

McLarty, J. R., Noble, A. C., & Huntley, R. M. (1989). Effects of item wording on sex bias. *Journal of Educational Measurement* 26:285–293.

Mundy, J. F. (1982). *Spatial ability and calculus: The role of spatial training programs for males and females.* Paper presented at the annual meeting of the American Educational Research Association, New York.

Rowell, E. H., & Hennen, F. G. (1978). *The interaction between sex referents in test items and reading performance on individualized reading tests.* (ERIC Document Reproduction Service No. ED 191 009)

Sappington, J., Larsen, C., Martin, J., & Murphy, K. (1991). Sex differences in math problem solving as a function of gender specific item content. *Educational and Psychological Measurement* 51:1041–1048.

Snedecor, G. W., & Cochran, W. G. (1980). *Statistical methods* (7th ed.). Ames: Iowa State University Press.

Stanley, J. C., Benbow, C. P., Brody, L. E., Dauber, S., & Lupkowski, A. E. (1992). Gender differences on eighty-six nationally standardized aptitude and achievement tests. In N. Colangelo, S. G. Assouline, & D. L. Ambroson (Eds.), *Talent development: Proceedings from the 1991 Henry B. and Jocelyn Wallace National Research Symposium on Talent Development* (pp. 42–65). Unionville, N.Y.: Trillium Press.

Strassberg-Rosenberg, B., & Donlon, T. F. (1975). *Content influences on sex differences in performance on aptitude tests.* Paper presented at the annual meeting of the National Council of Measurement in Education, Washington, D.C.

Sweeney, E. J. (1953). *Sex differences in problem solving* (Tech. Rep.). Stanford: Stanford University, Department of Psychology.

20   Construct Validity of the SAT-M

A Comparative Study of High School Students and Gifted Seventh Graders

LOLA L. MINOR AND

CAMILLA PERSSON BENBOW

The Scholastic Aptitude Test (SAT) was designed to measure the reasoning ability of above-average high school juniors and seniors (Donlon & Angoff, 1971). It was assumed that this ability would grow "slowly over the years through interaction with the student's total environment" (p. 16). The mathematics section (SAT-M) was designed so that only the knowledge gained through grade nine would be required to answer the questions successfully.

In the past twenty-five years, however, the use of the SAT for the identification of gifted students aged thirteen and younger has increased dramatically. This enables the discrimination of the able from the very able, among young students already known to be in the top percentiles on national norms on standardized achievement tests. In 1972, Julian C. Stanley initiated this type of talent search by using the mathematics section of the SAT to select from a sample of 396 boys and girls those students who would receive the opportunity to attend special classes and become a part of his longitudinal research study (Stanley, 1977–1978; Lubinski & Benbow, 1994). During the January 1984 testing, more than 70,000 young students nationwide took the SAT-Verbal and Mathematics portions (Educational Testing Service, 1984), and by 1994 this number had risen to almost 150,000. Throughout the past two decades the validity of this use of the SAT has been documented and become accepted

(Benbow, 1992; Benbow & Stanley, 1983; Cohn, 1991; Stanley, 1977–1978; Stanley & Benbow, 1981–1982; see also chapter 15 above).

In reporting their findings, Benbow and Stanley hypothesized that the SAT-M functions more at the "analysis" level of Bloom's (1956) taxonomy for this age group, whereas it functions more at Bloom's next-lower level, "application," for the high school students (Benbow & Stanley, 1981, 1983; Lubinski & Benbow, 1994). They hypothesized that since few of the students have been exposed to much abstract mathematics and since most do not even know algebra, they have not developed the specialized reasoning skills used by the older students in solving problems in precalculus mathematics, but rather must depend on a more general mathematical reasoning ability. The purpose of the present study was to investigate the validity of this hypothesis by comparing the factor structures of high school students and gifted seventh-grade students for one testing of the SAT-M.

Developmental studies of the structure of intelligence have noted trends supporting age- and sex-differentiation hypotheses. Briefly, these studies have shown that the factor structure of intelligence becomes more differentiated with increasing age (Anastasi, 1970, 1983; Atkin et al., 1977; Dye & Very, 1968; Khan, 1970; Mukherjee, 1961; Reinert, 1970). Moreover, within an age group males are more differentiated than females (Atkin et al., 1977; Mukherjee, 1961; Very, 1967).

Since substantial sex differences on the SAT-M have been reported for gifted seventh graders (Benbow, 1988; Benbow & Stanley, 1980, 1981, 1983; Lubinski & Benbow, 1992, 1994) and developmental studies have indicated possible sex differences in factorial structure, a comparison of the factor structures of the males and the females within an age group also was performed.

These comparisons were conducted to investigate the construct validity of the SAT-M for different age groups and within an age group for males and females. Construct validity is the extent to which a test can be said to measure a theoretical trait. The existence of an a priori theory is implicit in this definition. For this study, the hypothesis was of developmental change involving mathematical reasoning processes related to the curricular areas being tested. Therefore, the procedure used was confirmatory, not exploratory, factor analysis.

Method

Subjects

Subject data for this study were provided by the Educational Testing Service from the January 1981 SAT testing. To be eligible to take the SAT in the seventh grade, most students had to score at least at the 97th percentile on a nationally normed achievement test, such as the Iowa Test of Basic Skills or the California Achievement Test, in mathematics, verbal areas, or overall ability. Most students of high school age who take the SAT are college bound, and thus represent academically able high school students. Due to the stricter requirements, however, the seventh-grade group should be more homogeneous in ability.

The sample was grouped into subsamples based on grade, and within grade by sex, for a total of six subsamples: the total high school group (HS),[1] $N = 7,357$; the total seventh-grade group (7), $N = 8,879$; high school males (HSM), $N = 3, 694$; high school females (HSF), $N = 3,657$; seventh-grade males (7M), $N = 4,341$; and seventh-grade females (7F), $N = 4,538$.

Instrument

The SAT-Mathematics test, form DSA016HM, was made up of two sections, each with a thirty-minute time limit. The entire test was made up of fifty-nine items (twenty-four and thirty-five items, respectively, for the two sections; one item was flawed and hence omitted), of which thirty-nine were standard multiple-choice questions with five options each and twenty were quantitative comparison items in a multiple-choice format with four options each. The questions were designed for students who had had one year of algebra and some geometry. Following Braswell (1978), the questions on this form were classified into four content areas: arithmetic (simple computation, percent, average, prime numbers, odd/even numbers), nineteen items; algebra (negative/positive numbers, factoring, inequalities, integer exponents, roots), seventeen items; geometry (area, perimeter, circumference, volume, triangles, angles, properties of parallel and perpendicular lines, coordinate grids), sixteen items; and miscellaneous, seven items.

Procedure

Factor analysis of item variables presents certain problems. The score range of dichotomous variables is so narrow that correlations computed may be seriously affected by changes in response pattern throughout the test (Barrett & Kline, 1981). The two correlations most often used in item-level analyses are the phi coefficient and the tetrachoric correlation. Unfortunately, both may lead to difficulties. The magnitude of the phi coefficient may be affected by the difficulty of the items; the tetrachoric does not produce a product-moment correlation matrix, and thus may not yield meaningful results (Reckase, 1981).

---

1. Six students did not specify their sex.

TABLE 20.1.   *Equated Delta Difficulty Indices by Content Area and within Area by Parcel*

Content Area	Index	Parcel	N Items per Parcel	Index
Miscellaneous	13.130	M1	4	13.075
		M2	3	13.200
Arithmetic	12.120	AR1	4	12.100
		AR2	4	12.125
		AR3	4	12.125
		AR4	4	12.100
		AR5	3	12.200
Algebra	13.765	AL1	4	13.800
		AL2	4	13.750
		AL3	5	13.760
		AL4	4	13.750
Geometry	14.700	G1	4	14.700
		G2	4	14.775
		G3	4	14.750
		G4	4	14.575
SAT	13.410			

The factor analysis of such items may lead to the appearance of spurious factors—artifactual factors—due to the nonlinearity of the response data to the underlying trait (McDonald, 1981; McDonald & Ahlawat, 1974).

An alternative to the factor analysis of item-level variables is the analysis of item parcels, or minitests, composed of several items of the same dimension. In this analysis, such item parcels were used. If parcels are to be used, the differing levels of difficulty of the items in each parcel must be considered; otherwise, artifactual difficulty factors may appear (Cook, Dorans, Eignor, & Petersen, 1983; Gorsuch, 1983).

Therefore, the items were divided according to the classification system described above into four content areas: arithmetic, algebra, geometry, and miscellaneous. Within each of the four subsets, items were placed into parcels of comparable difficulty based on their equated delta difficulty indices as established by the item analysis data provided by the Educational Testing Service (see table 20.1). (For a fuller explanation of equated delta difficulty indices, see Hecht & Swineford, 1981.)

Analysis

Scores for each subject on these item parcels were calculated based on the number correct, and then covariance matrices for the parcels were computed.

These covariance matrices were used as input data for the LISREL VI program (Jöreskog & Sörbom, 1984). Using the LISREL model, it is possible to postulate a priori structural relationships among observed and latent variables.

LISREL VI is a structural-equation model program, initially developed and introduced by Jöreskog (1971) and Jöreskog and Sörbom (1984). The program estimates the unknown coefficients in a set of linear structural equations for which the variables may be observed or latent. The model assumes a causal relationship between observed and latent variables. The latent variables may be treated as the cause of the observed variables, as caused by the observed variables, or as intervening variables (Jöreskog & Sörbom, 1984).

For this study, the factor-analysis model of the LISREL equations was used:

$$X = \Lambda_x \xi + \delta$$

where X is a (q X 1) vector of observed variables, Λ_x a (q X n) matrix of loadings of the Xs on the ξs, and δ a (q X 1) matrix of the errors of measurement in x. The errors of measurement are assumed to be uncorrelated with ξ. The population covariance matrix Σ is represented by

$$\Sigma^g = \Lambda^g \Phi^g \Lambda'^g + \Theta_\delta^g$$

where Φ is an (n X n) covariance matrix of the common factors, Θ_δ is a (q X q) covariance matrix of the residual factors, and the superscript (g) denotes the gth group. Of these, the elements in Λ_x, Φ, and Θ_δ may be of three kinds: fixed parameters that have been assigned values; constrained parameters for which the values are unknown, but equal to one or more other parameters; and free parameters for which the values are unknown and not constrained. The a priori designation of these parameters makes it possible to test hypothesized models, both within and across groups.

Assessment of Fit

LISREL supplies several ways of assessing the "goodness of fit" of the model to the data. One is the overall χ^2 measure, for which a nonsignificant χ^2 is indicative of a good fit. Since the sample size in this study is large, most models would be rejected. Therefore, the differences in χ^2 between models relative to changes in the degree of freedom were used as an important determiner of overall goodness of fit.

Two other measures of fit are the goodness-of-fit index (GFI) and the root mean square residual (RMS). Both of these measures should be between zero and one. The GFI is a measure of the amount of the variances and covariances jointly accounted for by the model. It is independent of sample size and relatively robust to departures from normality. The RMS is the square root of the average squared difference between elements in each group's observed covariance matrix and the covariance matrix reproduced from the model.

An additional statistic, described by Bentler and Bonett (1980), also was used in determining the goodness of fit. This statistic was defined as

$$\Delta_{kl} = (\chi_k^2 - \chi_l^2) \div \chi_0^2$$

where χ_k^2 is the overall χ^2 for the more constrained model, χ_l^2 is the χ^2 for the less constrained model, and χ_0^2 is the χ^2 for the null model. When $\chi_k^2 = \chi_0^2$, the statistic provides a normed-fit index (Δ), which makes a comparison between a given model and the null model (referred to as M0). The null model represents a severely restricted case in which all variables are assumed to be mutually independent. This statistic ranges in value from 0 to 1, with a value greater than or equal to 0.9 usually being indicative of a good fit.

When χ_k^2 is not equal to χ_0^2, but the χ^2 from another competing model, the statistic becomes a measure of the improvement in fit (Δ_I) and is used in comparing two hierarchical models relative to a common null model. This index will be larger when the less constrained model fits better than the more constrained model.

Determination of Invariance

Baltes and Nesselroade (1973) suggest two types of developmental change: *structural*, which refers to the number of factors, the pattern of factor loadings, and the factor intercorrelations; and *quantitative*, which refers to the differences in magnitude, such as the size of factor loadings and the standard errors of measurement. Thus, groups would be considered to be relatively invariant (the null hypothesis) if it could be shown that the parcels were measuring the same traits across groups, in the same units, and with the same accuracy. If differences were to be found, the type of developmental change would be determined by the point at which the variance is found.

To test for invariance, a series of three hierarchical models was tested in sequence for each of the comparisons using the LISREL procedure:

$H_n=3$:

X	X	X	M1
X	X	X	M2
X	0	0	AR1
X	0	0	AR2
X	0	0	AR3
X	0	0	AR4
X	0	0	AR5
0	X	0	AL1
0	X	0	AL2
0	X	0	AL3
0	X	0	AL4
0	0	X	G1
0	0	X	G2
0	0	X	G3
0	0	X	G4

X = factor defining parameter

0 = parameter fixed equal to zero

Figure 20.1. Hypothesized factor loading pattern matrix.

1. There are the same number of factors in each group with a factor pattern of similar form. The hypothesis for this analysis is of three factors, one for each of the main content areas with the miscellaneous item parcels loading on one or more of these, of the approximate form shown in figure 20.1.

To fix the scale, one element of the factor-defining parameters was set equal to one, while the other elements were free for all groups. Also, the Φ matrices were free, as were the diagonal elements of Θ_δ in the groups. No equality constraints were set on the parameters across groups, since this is a hypothesis of equal numbers of factors and similarity—not equality—of pattern. (This least constrained model is referred to as M3 in the tables in this chapter.)

In accordance with the Baltes and Nesselroade definitions, if this hypothesis were accepted, the groups would be considered structurally the same, but not necessarily quantitatively equal.

2. Assuming that the groups have the same factor model, the factor loadings are equal. The only additional constraint to the previous hypothesis is the declaration of the invariance of Λ_x. (This model is referred to as M2.)

$$H_\Lambda : \Lambda_x^1 = \Lambda_x^2 = \ldots \Lambda_x^g$$

This is a test of the equality of scale units. If these units are found to be different, the interpretation of the observed scores would not be equivalent across groups. Such a finding will be defined as structural, but not quantitative, invariance. If the units are found to be equal, the groups will be considered structurally equal and quantitatively similar.

3. Assuming similarity of factor pattern and equality of units of measurement, the standard errors of measurement are the same across groups. The construction of the invariance qd is added to test this hypothesis. (This model is referred to as M1.)

$$H_{\Lambda\Theta} : \Theta_\delta^1 = \Theta_\delta^2 = \ldots \Theta_\delta^g$$

If they were different, the parcels would not be measuring the latent variables with the same accuracy across groups. If equal, the groups will be considered both structurally and quantitatively invariant.

Results

The results of the five comparisons are shown in tables 20.2 through 20.4. These tables give the goodness-of-fit statistics for the null model and the three less constrained models. As noted above, primarily of interest are the goodness-of-fit index (GFI), the root mean square residual (RMS), the normed-fit index (Δ), and the improvement-of-fit index (Δ_1). Generally, the three-factor model hypothesized fits the data well.

The comparison of models across the two age groups (table 20.2) clearly shows that the model of similarity of factor loading (M3) fits very well, and is the best fitting of the three models. The GFI reaches 0.990 only for M3, and the RMS shows that the residuals are smallest for this model. There was very little

TABLE 20.2.   *Evaluation of Submodels across Age Groups, High School versus Seventh Grade*

	Model Test		GFI		RMS	
Model	C2	df	HS	7	HS	7
M0	67459.14	210	.293	.504	.437	.231
M1	1783.38	203	.984	.987	.096	.093
M2	1532.68	188	.986	.989	.095	.090
M3	572.68	172	.995	.996	.012	.012
	Model Comparison					
Comparison	C2	df	D	DI.		
M0–M1	65675.76	7	.974			
M0–M2	65926.46	22	.977			
M1–M2	250.82	15		.004		
M0–M3	66886.46	38	.992			
M2–M3	959.16	16		.014		

Note: $p < .001$ for all χ^2 statistics. GFI = Goodness-of-fit index. RMS = Root mean square residual.

TABLE 20.3.   *Evaluation of Submodels within Age Groups, High School Males versus High School Females*

| | | | Model Test | | | |
| | | | GFI | | RMS | |
Model	C2	df	HSM	HSF	HSM	HSF
M0	40375.00	210	.276	.339	.466	.370
M1	538.69	203	.990	.991	.044	.049
M2	471.65	188	.991	.992	.042	.048
M3	357.79	172	.993	.994	.014	.013

| | Model Comparison | | | |
Comparison	C2	df	D	DI
M0–M1	39836.31	7	.987	
M0–M2	39903.35	22	.988	
M1–M2	67.04	15		.002
M0–M3	40027.21	38	.991	
M2–M3	113.86	16		.003

Note: $p < .001$ for all χ^2. GFI = Goodness-of-fit index. RMS = Root mean square residual.

TABLE 20.4.   *Evaluation of Submodels within Age Groups, Seventh-Grade Males versus Seventh-Grade Females*

| | | | Model Test | | | |
| | | | GFI | | RMS | |
Model	C2	df	7M	7F	7M	7F
M0	24244.37	210	.460	.592	.261	.181
M1	653.99	203	.990	.991	.040	.041
M2	530.25	188	.991	.993	.036	.035
M3	376.74	172	.994	.995	.014	.010

| | Model Comparison | | | |
Comparison	C2	df	D	DI
M0–M1	23590.38	7	.973	
M0–M2	23714.12	22	.978	
M1–M2	123.74	15		.005
M0–M3	23867.63	38	.984	
M2–M3	153.51	16		.006

Note: $p < .001$ for all χ^2. GFI = Goodness-of-fit index. RMS = Root mean square residual.

change between the M1 and M2 models, but an approximate .08 improvement for the M3 model. The Δ indices also support this finding. The Δ for the M3 model is largest, and the Δ_I is a noticeably larger improvement than the Δ_I for the more constrained models. Therefore, only M3 is accepted.

In contrast, the comparisons of models within age groups (tables 20.3 and

20.4) demonstrate that all models can be accepted. Although the M3 model has the largest values for the GFI and the Δ, the improvement is not very great over the M2 and M1 models. The RMSs are small, and the largest change is .035 for the HSF group. The Δ_I is small, and essentially equal for the two comparisons, indicating that the least constrained model does not fit much better than the more restricted models.

A parcel-correlation matrix was computed and was submitted to the LISREL VI program for separate confirmatory analyses to be performed. By letting the Φ matrix remain free, an oblique solution with high factor intercorrelations was obtained. The factor-generated loadings of the parcels on the three hypothesized factors are shown for the total high school and gifted seventh-grade sample in table 20.5. Clearly, the patterns of loadings are similar for the two groups, although the loadings are consistently higher for the high school sample than for the gifted seventh graders. Factor loadings did not appear to differ for the three content areas for the high school students. The seventh graders, however, had the highest loadings on the arithmetic items. Thus, seventh graders showed a stronger reliance on arithmetic processes. The factors correlated very highly, especially for the high school group. For the high school group phi, the correlation between each set of factors ranged from .91 to .97, whereas for the seventh graders the range was from .84 to .92. These results indicate that performance on the SAT-M may be accounted for by one factor,

TABLE 20.5.   *Factor Loadings for the Total Sample of High School and Gifted Seventh-Grade Students*

	High School			Seventh Grade		
Parcel	Factor 1	Factor 2	Factor 3	Factor 1	Factor 2	Factor 3
M1	.70	−.33	.25	.61	−.38	.20
M2	1.30	−.89	.26	.86	−.54	.17
AR1	.64			.50		
AR2	.80			.74		
AR3	.70			.53		
AR4	.69			.48		
AR5	.67			.56		
AL1		.61			.44	
AL2		.61			.44	
AL3		.77			.55	
AL4		.78			.57	
G1			.71			.48
G2			.76			.54
G3			.55			.38
G4			.87			.57

TABLE 20.6.   *Factor Loadings for High School Males and Females*

	High School Males			High School Females		
Parcel	Factor 1	Factor 2	Factor 3	Factor 1	Factor 2	Factor 3
M1	.80	−0.35	.19	.62	−.27	.19
M2	1.71	−1.27	.27	1.02	−.63	.22
AR1	.66			.61		
AR2	.79			.76		
AR3	.68			.69		
AR4	.68			.67		
AR5	.66			.65		
AL1		.65			.56	
AL2		.64			.57	
AL3		.81			.69	
AL4		.79			.72	
G1			.79			.57
G2			.80			.67
G3			.57			.49
G4			.90			.81

presumably mathematical reasoning. Moreover, since the factor correlations were higher for the high school group than for the seventh graders, they revealed a developmental trend in SAT-M scores. It appears as if ability on the SAT-M becomes more integrated with age.

The above procedure was then repeated by sex but separately for the high school and seventh-grade students. The resulting factor loadings for the high school males and females are shown in table 20.6. The patterns are quite similar, although generally the loadings were slightly higher for males than females. The intercorrelations of the factors, however, were essentially of the same magnitude (from .91 to .98 for males and from .91 to .97 for females). The results for the seventh graders are shown in table 20.7. Quantitatively, the seventh-grade males appeared slightly more different from the seventh-grade females than was found for the comparison of high school students by sex. Moreover, there may be a sex difference in development of the ability measured by the SAT-M. The magnitude of the correlations among factors was slightly higher for the seventh-grade males (.88 to .95) than for the seventh-grade females (.79 to .88). It appeared as if the ability on SAT-M of males had become slightly more integrated and similar to the high school sample than that of seventh-grade females. These are, however, only trends in the data. The most restrictive model (i.e., that the SAT-M measures the same thing with equal scale units and with equal accuracy) accounting for sex did apply.

TABLE 20.7.　*Factor Loadings for Gifted Seventh-Grade Males and Females*

Parcel	Seventh-Grade Males			Seventh Grade Females		
	Factor 1	Factor 2	Factor 3	Factor 1	Factor 2	Factor 3
M1	.77	−.54	.22	.49	−.24	.11
M2	1.01	−.58	.08	.71	−.47	.21
AR1	.54			.46		
AR2	.74			.68		
AR3	.53			.51		
AR4	.53			.44		
AR5	.57			.54		
AL1		.47			.41	
AL2		.47			.41	
AL3		.58			.49	
AL4		.61			.49	
G1			.54			.40
G2			.61			.44
G3			.39			.33
G4			.62			.50

Discussion

The SAT was designed for above-average high school juniors and seniors to measure their mathematical and verbal reasoning abilities. Julian C. Stanley pioneered its use with intellectually talented seventh graders (Stanley, 1977–1978; see also chapter 14 above). Benbow and Stanley (1981, 1983) and Stanley and Benbow (1986) postulated that for talented seventh-grade students the SAT functions far more as a reasoning test than it does for high school students. Because these seventh-grade students have not been exposed to much abstract mathematics, and most do not even know first-year high school algebra (Benbow & Stanley, 1982a, 1982b, 1983), it was hypothesized that they would solve the problems on the SAT-M at the analysis level of Bloom's (1956) taxonomy rather than at the lower application level thought to be used by high school students, which leads to a hypothesis of developmental change across age groups. This is consistent with Donlon and Angoff (1971), who stated that the SAT-M measures mathematical reasoning ability that is developed through interaction with the total environment (as all abilities are).

A difference in the problem-solving approach of younger and older students as postulated by Benbow and Stanley (1981, 1983) and Stanley and Benbow (1986) was supported by the results of this study. Thus, the SAT-M scores of seventh-grade students should probably not be interpreted nor used as would the scores for high school students. Gifted seventh-grade students seem to display a stronger reliance on arithmetic processes. The high school students, in contrast, appear to have integrated more of the processes concerned with handling the various content-related tasks. Perhaps as learning (and overlearning, in the case of mathematics) occurs, the reliance on arithmetic reasoning is overcome in favor of particular knowledge gained (theorems, identities, etc.). An exploratory factor analysis of these data (not presented here) also supported this viewpoint. Moreover, using a different paradigm, Pollins (1984) also concluded that the SAT-M functions as a reasoning test for gifted seventh-grade students. This may imply that the SAT-M should be a better predictor of mathematics-learning ability for seventh graders than for high school students. Regardless of the exact nature of the differences between gifted seventh-grade students and high school students, it is clear that age is an important variable when interpreting the ability measured by the SAT-M. Our results indicated that the two age groups can be considered structurally, but not quantitatively, similar.

In contrast to the findings of age effects on the ability to solve problems on the SAT-M, there were no differences by sex. Within each age group the SAT-M appears to be measuring the same thing with equal scale units and accuracy for both sexes. Rock and Werts (1979) found a similar invariance of factor structure for ethnic groups within the high school population when the analysis was based on item types. It was expected that the males would be more differentiated than the females; that is, they would have more factors to explain their performance on the SAT-M. It should be noted, however, that previous works (Atkin et al., 1977; Mukherjee, 1961; Very, 1967) used variables designed to measure a greater range of abilities. It may be that the SAT-M measures an underlying trait that becomes more integrated with increasing age, with little variance due to sex beyond the possibility of differential rate of development.

Large sex differences on the SAT-M have been reported for the seventh-grade students (Benbow, 1988; Benbow & Stanley, 1980, 1983; Lubinski & Benbow, 1992, 1994). Similar results have also been found for the high school students by the Educational Testing Service (Admissions Testing Program, 1984). The reasons for these sex differences are by no means clear. The present results provide some evidence for some quantitative variance (differences in size of factor loadings, ordering of variables within a factor, etc.). The seventh-grade boys were more similar to the high school students than the seventh-grade girls were. Although few sex differences in mathematics training have been found among these gifted seventh graders (Benbow & Stanley, 1982a, 1982b), this may indicate that the mathematical reasoning ability of young, talented males is more fully developed than that of females at comparable ages.

This evidence, however, was not sufficient to reject the hypothesis of invariance between the boys and the girls. It may, however, offer a clue as to why males achieve higher scores on the SAT-M than females do.

In conclusion, the construct validity of the SAT-M for an age group appears to be supported. The construct, however, may be somewhat different for younger students than for older students and is in accord with developmental-change hypotheses (see, e.g., Benbow & Stanley, 1981, 1983). Structural differences between the sexes were not found, especially not among the high school students.

Acknowledgments

We thank Steven J. Breckler, Bert F. Green, and Julian C. Stanley for their comments and statistical aid in the preparation of this manuscript. We also thank Nancy Burton of the Educational Testing Service for her assistance in obtaining the data used in this study.

References

Admissions Testing Program. (1984). *College-bound seniors, 1983–1984*. Princeton: Educational Testing Service.

Anastasi, A. (1970). On the formation of psychological traits. *American Psychologist* 25:899–910.

Anastasi, A. (1983). Evolving trait concepts. *American Psychologist* 38:175–184.

Atkin, R., Bray, R., Davison, M., Herzberger, S., Humphreys, L., & Selzer, U. (1977). Ability factor differentiation, grades five through eleven. *Applied Psychological Measurement* 1:65–76.

Baltes, P. B., & Nesselroade, J. R. (1973). The developmental analysis of individual differences on multiple measures. In J. R. Nesselroade & H. W. Reese (Eds.), *Life-span developmental psychology: Methodological issues*. New York: Academic Press.

Barrett, P. T., & Kline, P. (1981). Radial parcel factor analysis. *Personality and Individual Differences* 2:311–318.

Benbow, C. P. (1988). Sex differences in mathematical reasoning ability in intellectually talented preadolescents: Their nature, effects, and possible causes. *Behavioral and Brain Sciences* 11:169–232.

Benbow, C. P. (1992). Academic achievement in mathematics and science of students between ages thirteen and twenty-three: Are there differences among students in the top one percent of mathematical ability? *Journal of Educational Psychology* 84:51–61.

Benbow, C. P., & Stanley, J. C. (1980). Sex differences in mathematical ability: Fact or artifact? *Science* 210:1262–1264.

Benbow, C. P., & Stanley, J. C. (1981). Mathematical ability: Is sex a factor? *Science* 212:114–121.

Benbow, C. P., & Stanley, J. C. (1982a). Consequences in high school and college of sex differences in mathematical reasoning ability: A longitudinal perspective. *American Educational Research Journal* 19:598–622.

Benbow, C. P., & Stanley, J. C. (1982b). Intellectually talented boys and girls: Educational profiles. *Gifted Child Quarterly* 26:82–88.

Benbow, C. P., & Stanley, J. C. (1983). Sex differences in mathematical reasoning ability: More facts. *Science* 222:1029–1031.

Bentler, P. M., & Bonett, D. G. (1980). Significance tests and goodness of fit in the analysis of covariance structures. *Psychological Bulletin* 88:588–606.

Bloom, B. S. (Ed.). (1956). *Taxonomy of educational objectives*. Handbook I: The cognitive domain. New York: David McKay.

Braswell, J. S. (1978). The College Board Scholastic Aptitude Test: An overview of the mathematical portion. *Mathematics Teacher* 71:168–180.

Cohn, S. J. (1991). Talent searches. In N. Colangelo & G. A. Davis (Eds.), *Handbook of gifted education* (pp. 166–177). Needham Heights, Mass.: Allyn & Bacon.

Cook, L. L., Dorans, N. J., Eignor, D. R., & Petersen, N. S. (1983). An assessment of the relationship between the assumption of unidimensionality and the quality of IRT true-score equating. Paper presented at the annual meeting of the American Educational Research Association, Montreal.

Donlon, T. F., & Angoff, W. H. (1971). The Scholastic Aptitude Test. In William H. Angoff (Ed.), *The College Board Admissions Testing Program: A technical report on research and development activities relating to the Scholastic Aptitude Test and Achievement Tests*. Princeton: College Entrance Examination Board.

Dye, N. W., & Very, P. S. (1968). Growth changes in factorial structure by age and sex. *Genetic Psychology Monographs* 78:55–88.

Educational Testing Service (1984). Talent search update. *Examiner* 14:5.

Gorsuch, R. L. (1983). *Factor analyses* (2nd ed.). Hillsdale, N.J.: Erlbaum.

Hecht, L., & Swineford, F. (1981). *Item analysis at the Educational Testing Service*. Princeton: Educational Testing Service.

Jöreskog, K. G. (1971). Simultaneous factor analysis in several populations. *Psychometrika* 36(4): 409–426.

Jöreskog, K. G., & Sörbom, D. (1984). *LISREL VI: Analysis of linear structural relationships by maximum likelihood, instrumental variables, and least squares methods* (3rd ed.) [Computer program]. Mooresville, Ind.: Scientific Software.

Khan, S. B. (1970). Development of mental abilities: An investigation of the "differentiation hypothesis." *Canadian Journal of Psychology* 24:199–205.

Lubinski, D., & Benbow, C. P. (1992). Gender differences in abilities and preferences among the gifted: Implications for the math-science pipeline. *Current Directions in Psychological Science* 1:61–66.

Lubinski, D., & Benbow, C. P. (1994). The Study of Mathematically Precocious Youth: The first three decades of a planned fifty-year study of intellectual talent. In R. F. Subotnik & K. D. Arnold (Eds.), *Beyond Terman: Contemporary longitudinal studies of giftedness and talent* (pp. 255–281). Norwood, N.J.: Ablex.

McDonald, R. P. (1981). The dimensionality of tests and items. *British Journal of Mathematical and Statistical Psychology* 34:100–117.

McDonald, R. P., & Ahlawat, K. S. (1974). Difficulty factors in binary data. *British Journal of Mathematical and Statistical Psychology* 27:82–99.

Mukherjee, B. N. (1961). The factorial structure of aptitude tests at successive grade levels. *British Journal of Mathematical and Statistical Psychology* 15:59–69.

Pollins, L. D. (1984). *The construct validity of the Scholastic Aptitude Test for young gifted students*. Unpublished doctoral dissertation, Duke University.

Reckase, M. D. (1981, April). *Guessing and dimensionality: The search for a unidimensional latent space*. Paper presented at the annual meeting of the American Educational Research Association, Los Angeles.

Reinert, G. (1970). Comparative factor analytic studies of intelligence throughout the human life-span. In L. R. Goulet & P. B. Baltes (Eds.), *Life-span development psychology: Research and theory*. New York: Academic Press.

Rock, D. A., & Werts, C. E. (1979). *Construct validity of the SAT across populations—an empirical confirmatory study* (Report No. CEEB RR-79–2). Princeton: Educational Testing Service.

Stanley, J. C. (1977–1978). The predictive value of the SAT. *College Board Review* 106:31–37.

Stanley, J. C., & Benbow, C. P. (1981–1982). Using the SAT to find intellectually talented seventh graders. *College Board Review* 122:3–27.

Stanley, J. C., & Benbow, C. P. (1986). Youths who reason exceptionally well mathematically. In R. J. Sternberg & J. E. Davidson (Eds.), *Conceptions of giftedness* (pp. 361–387). Cambridge: Cambridge University Press.

Very, P. E. (1967). Differential factor structures in mathematical ability. *Genetic Psychology Monographs* 75:169–207.

21

The Generalizability of Empirical Research Results

BETSY JANE BECKER

A primary goal of social science research is to provide information that will be interesting and useful beyond the specific context in which it was obtained. In short, we want to be able to generalize from our results. Campbell and Stanley's classic work on experimental and quasi-experimental research puts it simply: "Generalization always turns out to involve extrapolation into a realm not represented in one's sample" (1966, p. 17). The question that arises is, how can one assess the generalizability of empirical research results?

Generalizations are invoked in social science for two somewhat different purposes. The first case involves extensive generalizations about how relationships between variables that are found for one set of people in one context might apply to a different set of people in a different context. In either context, the meanings of the variables and of the relationships are well understood. The second use of generalizations is more intensive than extensive. It involves cases in which the variables of interest are not those that are explicitly measured, but those that are defined implicitly by generalization across indicators or operations of a relationship. For example, a variety of tests may measure mathematical ability, but no one test *defines* mathematical ability. Rather, the ability is defined by the construct that generalizes across the set of tests, each of which is an (imperfect) indicator of the ability. The context and persons involved may not vary at all, because the generalization of interest is made across multiple operationalizations of the construct.

In this chapter I propose a systematic theory of the generalizability of research results, drawing on formal quantitative methods for research synthesis and on the theory of generalizability of measurements. The proposed theory

362

provides a model for describing the characteristics or facets of studies that may have an impact on generalizability, and suggests a statistical method for evaluating the importance of those facets. Specifically, variation in the parameters of interest is estimated and partitioned into quantities that can be attributed to differences in operationalizations of the constructs or variables of interest. The information gained can be valuable in the interpretation of existing research and in planning future studies. I focus on the question of how to assess the generalizability of findings concerning relationships among variables (constructs) expressed as correlation coefficients. However, the analyses I propose also can be applied when other parameters (such as treatment effects) are of interest.

The concept of generalizability is introduced using Cronbach's (1982) model of inference and generalization in program evaluation. The role of multiple operationism in generalization is discussed, as is the connection between meta-analysis and multiple operationism. Cronbach's generalizability theory (Cronbach, Gleser, Nanda, & Rajaratnam, 1972) is then used to develop a parallel theory for the generalizability of study results. These ideas are illustrated using data from a meta-analysis by Friedman (1992), who examined interrelationships among mathematical, spatial, and verbal skills.

Assessing Study Generalizability

Generalizability concerns breadth of applicability. It asks, if a finding is based on a study that meets some mutually agreeable criteria for internal validity, how broadly can that finding be applied across different persons, treatment implementations, locations, and the like? This question is particularly important for evaluation studies, which examine potentially ameliorative treatments for social, educational, and medical problems. The knowledge that a treatment works well for many different people in a variety of locations or when implemented by diverse agents suggests that if the treatment is applied in a new context, it may continue to work well. But the researcher must ask: given existing evidence, how certain is it that the research result will hold in the new context?

Cronbach's Conception of Causal Generalizability

Cronbach (1982) described a framework for the generalizability of evaluation studies that is useful for conceptualizing a wide variety of research studies. The framework includes four elements, shown in table 21.1 as units (U), treatments (T), observing operations (O), and the setting or social context (S). This scheme is similar to Cook and Campbell's (1979) scheme, which considers persons, treatments, and settings.

TABLE 21.1.   *Cronbach's Framework for Generalization*

	Units	Treatments	Observing Operations	Setting/ Context
Domain of application	$^*U$	$^*T$	$^*O$	$^*S$
Target populations	U	T	O	S
Sampled instances of the populations	u	t	o	$-$

Source: Based on concepts described by Cronbach (1982).

Cronbach argued that making inferences about target populations of units, treatments, and observing operations (UTO) involves sampling specific instances from those populations (represented by lowercase u, t, and o) and (assuming the study is conducted without serious compromises) generalizing to the sampled domain $UTOS$. The setting S serves as a context for each study or set of studies; Cronbach treated S as fixed before sampling specific UTO combinations.

However, the more interesting and difficult question concerns how to assess the generalizability of results to $^*UTOS$. In this formulation, $^*UTOS$ represents situations not necessarily included in the set of units, treatments, and operations in the target population $UTOS$; in other words, a domain of interest beyond that explicitly sampled in the study or studies at hand.

Thus the question becomes one of assessing whether and how well research results can be extrapolated to the domain of application, $^*UTOS$. This question is complicated because $^*UTOS$ can be a broad domain that includes the situations studied, a narrow domain that is completely distinct from the situations studied, or a very narrow domain, such as a single school, community, or child.

Multiple Operationism

Cronbach's idea of sampling from populations of treatments and populations of observing operations makes explicit the idea of multiple operationism (Campbell, 1969), the process by which a theoretical construct, such as a treatment or outcome, is exemplified in multiple ways. Each realization of the theoretical entity should be different in terms of theoretically *irrelevant* characteristics. Multiple operationism works through the incorporation of "heterogeneous irrelevancies" (Cook, 1993, pp. 50–53) in the special procedures used to collect construct-relevant data.

The idea of multiple operationism has a long history in social science research methodology. Campbell and Fiske's argument that "any single operation, as representative of concepts, is equivocal" (1959, p. 101) has become a fundamental premise of research and evaluation practice. Because all treatments and measures are imperfect representations of the constructs they stand for, multiple instantiations of each construct are used to build a more complete understanding. Webb, Campbell, Schwartz, and Sechrest put it clearly in *Unobtrusive Measures*: "Once a proposition has been confirmed by two or more independent measurement processes, the uncertainty of its interpretation is greatly reduced. . . . If a proposition can survive the onslaught of a series of imperfect measures, with all their irrelevant error, confidence should be placed in it" (1966, p. 3).

By using a variety of different methods of measuring each construct, researchers hope to tap what is common and fundamental to the construct itself and to eliminate what is not. However, the use of different operationalizations also adds some variability or uncertainty to research results, because the irrelevant components of each operation tend to strengthen or weaken particular relationships based on that operation. In the context of questions about generalizability, one must ask whether and how much the use of different operationalizations of constructs contributes to the uncertainty of research findings.

Campbell and Fiske's (1959) convergent and discriminant validation techniques, based on the multitrait-multimethod matrix, provide a means of assessing similarities between different methods of measuring a single construct. Campbell and Fiske were not optimistic about the convergence of multiple methods, noting that "method or apparatus factors make very large contributions to psychological measurements" (p. 104).

Meta-analysis and Generalization

Many authors have noted the potential that the quantitative synthesis of research results, or meta-analysis (Glass, 1976), has for strengthening generalizations. Cook and Campbell foresaw the usefulness of multiple studies, stating that "a case can be made, therefore, that external validity is enhanced more by a number of smaller studies with haphazard samples than by a single study with initially representative samples if the latter could be implemented" (1979, p. 73). Cordray more recently noted: "While the statistical aggregation of results across studies does not circumvent the logical problems of induction, it does provide an empirical footing from which to judge the likely generalizability of findings" (1987, p. 6).

Part of the strength of meta-analysis for making generalizations comes from meta-analysis being an embodiment of multiple operationism. Cook notes that "meta-analysis has the potential to test propositions about highly general cause and effect constructs and to generate empirically grounded research questions about why some operational representations produce results different from others. No single study could match such richness" (1991, p. 257).

The Theory of Generalizability in Meta-analysis

Although these authors and other evaluation theorists and methodologists have argued that meta-analysis can strengthen or inform our generalizations, to date no one has proposed a specific theoretical framework and corresponding statistical model for understanding the process of generalization in meta-analysis. However, if we consider Cronbach's model of construct generalization and how meta-analyses have typically been conducted, a new statistical approach will become apparent.

A fundamental premise of meta-analysis is, to borrow a phrase from Light (1979), to capitalize on variation in study results. In meta-analysis we typically try to understand the sources of variation that lead to differences in study results and to attribute those differences to substantively important characteristics of subjects, treatments, or methods (i.e., the specific Us, Ts, and Os that have been studied). Meta-analysts often test hypotheses about the factors that explain variation in study outcomes (e.g., Hedges, 1982) or adjust for method-related artifacts such as unreliability or range restriction (e.g., Hunter & Schmidt, 1990). However, even in meta-analyses in which hypotheses are tested about method-related variation in effects, estimates of the amounts of parameter variation associated with specific method factors are rarely obtained.

By estimating the amount of variation in the effects of interest, we explicitly measure the uncertainty in our results. Minimal uncertainty in a set of findings, combined with information about the character of those findings, can suggest that a finding can be generalized broadly. Perhaps more important is the discovery of situations in which large amounts of parameter variation make research findings variable, or conditional, so that sharp conclusions are not highly generalizable.

Some uncertainty arises because researchers use different methods to study the same phenomena (in Cronbach's framework, different Os). By estimating those portions of variation that can be attributed to different measures of the constructs of interest, we can gauge the effects of using multiple operationalizations of the constructs. If research findings are to be practically useful, variation attributable to theoretically important characteristics of units, treatments, and operations should exceed variation due to theoretically irrelevant factors (such as the exact way in which a construct is measured).

An Analogue to Generalizability Theory

A useful framework for thinking about the generalizability of research results is provided by generalizability theory. Cronbach, Gleser, Nanda, and Rajaratnam (1972) proposed generalizability theory for use in the development of tests and measures, as well as for assessing their reliability. The aim of generalizability theory is to model explicitly and examine any sources of measurement error, such as observers, items, or occasions, which are called facets,[1] that contribute to variation in the estimation of persons' scores on a construct. Generalizability theory provides a systematic way to examine the impact of different observers, items, or occasions, and their interactions.

Loosely, if it is determined that a large amount of variation in students' scores is attributable to different observers rating students differently (that is, if the observer facet has a big variance component), then to get a reliable score we would need to have several, perhaps many, observers rate each student. The mean of several observers' ratings would be more stable than a single observer's rating.

Generalizability theory is used in measurement not just to describe the variability or reliability of measures, but also to plan and evaluate studies used for decision making. Its conceptual strength is that the methodological study (the G or generalizability study) is used to plan or evaluate substantive studies (the D or decision studies).

Figure 21.1 shows a parallel conceptualization of how accumulated evidence about *utoS* and *UTOS* can be used to generalize to **UTOS*. Analyses of the accumulated literature serve as a G study, in which sources of variation among the *U*s, *T*s, and *O*s are studied (via the *u*s, *t*s, and *o*s). This information can be used in a number of ways, in the analogue to the D or decision study. Information about **UTOS* becomes relevant in the D study. Information about **UTOS* suggests which components of variation are most relevant to the kinds of generalizations we wish to make. We may make generalizations directly on the basis of the D study itself. Alternatively, information from the G study might be used in the D study to interpret existing results or to plan further research. These ideas are illustrated below.

1. Note that the term *facet* is used by Cronbach, Gleser, Nanda, and Rajaratnam to refer to what might be called factors in a more traditional analysis-of-variance framework. The use of the term *facet* differs from that in Guttman's facet theory; Guttman refers to the combination or intersection of factor levels as a facet.

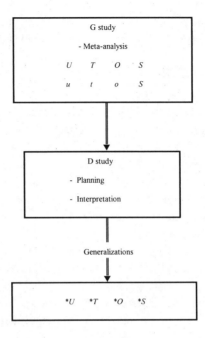

Figure 21.1. Empirical analysis of generalizability.

In the context of research generalizability, we are interested in the generalizability of certain theoretical parameters or effects such as relationships or treatment effects. Here we focus on the generalizability of results concerning relationships, represented as zero-order correlations in the primary studies. Thus we model the sources of variation in the correlations (rather than in student scores, as in generalizability theory), and then estimate the amounts of variation or uncertainty that could be attributed to those sources.

Imagine we have a series of k studies, each examining the relationship between two constructs, X and Y. We have gathered the studies, evaluated the measures used, and decided that all of the studies indeed appear to have used reasonable measures of those constructs. Therefore we need a model for variation in the population correlations that underlie the sample correlations we observe.

In the ith study the sample correlation r_{imn} is measured using measure m of construct X and measure n of construct Y, and estimates population correlation ρ_{imn}. That is,

$$r_{imn} = \rho_{imn} + e_{imn} \tag{1}$$

for $i = 1$ to k studies, $m = 1$ to M measures of construct X, and $n = 1$ to N measures of construct Y. Each sample correlation differs from its own population value only because of sampling error (e_{imn}). For simplicity, assume also that X and Y are free of measurement error and that no samples are subject to range restriction (i.e., that all samples are drawn from one population of subjects). The sample correlations are treated as asymptotically normally distributed variables with known variances and covariances, which have been given for instance by Olkin and Siotani (1976).

Next consider this simple model for the population correlations. Let

$$\rho_{imn} = \rho + \alpha_m + \beta_n + \gamma_{mn} + u_{imn} \tag{2}$$

for $i = 1$ to k, $m = 1$ to M, and $n = 1$ to N. The population correlation ρ_{imn} from study i, measured using measure m of construct X and measure n of construct Y, can be depicted as consisting of a fixed but unknown parameter ρ, which represents the true correlation between constructs X and Y (the construct correlation), a term α_m that indicates how much the correlations obtained using measure m of construct X deviate from the construct correlation value, an analogous term for the effect of the measure of Y, and a term for the interaction between the two measures.

Also, the model shows a residual term u_{imn}, which contains other deviations from ρ not attributable to measure effects. The residual term might contain differences due to theoretically important variables, such as features of the subjects studied or interventions that were administered. The effects included in the residuals in (2) are not unimportant or uninteresting, but they simply are not included in this model because it represents differences due only to measures. In an application of these methods that focused on factors other than measures, one would include other terms in the model.

First, however, consider an even simpler model, specifically

$$\rho_{im} = \rho + \alpha_m + u'_{im} \tag{3}$$

for $i = 1$ to k studies and $m = 1$ to M measures of X. This example shows the simplest possible case, where we are only considering the effects of measures of one construct (X). If the k studies had used a variety of tests of both X and Y, the effects β_n and the interaction would be subsumed in the residual. But in the example used below, this model applies because one construct is measured in the same way, in other words using the same test, in each study. We are holding constant the measure of construct Y by using only one test of Y. The sources of variation in this very simple model are given as

$$\text{Var}(\rho_{im}) = \text{Var}(\alpha_m) + \text{Var}(u'_{im}),$$

or

$$\sigma^2_\rho = \sigma^2_\alpha + \sigma^2_{w/\alpha}, \tag{4}$$

where σ^2_ρ is total parameter variation, σ^2_α represents between-measures variation and $\sigma^2_{w/\alpha}$ is an estimate of within-measure variation. The within-measure variation is here assumed to be equal in all measure groups, although this is not essential.

A Bivariate Example:
The Relationship between Mathematical and Spatial Tasks

To illustrate the application of these ideas, I use data drawn from Friedman (1992), who synthesized studies of correlations among mathematical, spatial, and verbal tasks. Researchers have studied the nature of mathematical abilities for quite some time (e.g., Smith, 1964). Mathematicians and others who have studied mathematical problem solving have noted that some people use visual

TABLE 21.2. *Correlations among Math, Verbal, and Spatial Performance Measures*

		Correlations		
Study	Sample Size	Math SR	Math Verbal	SR Verbal
1	688	.59	.51	.37
2	632	.51	.50	.29
3	90	.17	.05	−.07
4	300	.18	.18	.25
5	168	.52	.61	.45
6	114	.41	.38	.20
7	51	.42	.48	.23
8	18	.41	.74	.44
9	35	.50	.64	.33
10	34	.21	.28	−.07
11	74	.47	−.21	−.15
12	153	.28	.19	.18

Note: Data drawn from Friedman (1992). SR = Space relations.

TABLE 21.3. *Measures Used in Example Studies*

Study	Authors (Date)	Math	Verbal
		\multicolumn{2}{c}{Measure Used}	

Study	Authors (Date)	Math	Verbal
1	Fennema & Sherman (1978)	MCT	CAT
2	Fennema & Sherman (1978)	MCT	CAT
3	Filella (1960)	Math reasoning	Verbal reasoning
4	Filella (1960)	Math reasoning	Verbal reasoning
5	Pearson & Ferguson (1987)	ACT	ACT
6	Pearson & Ferguson (1987)	ACT	ACT
7	Rosenberg (1981)	SAT	SAT
8	Rosenberg (1981)	SAT	SAT
9	Weiner (1984)	SAT	SAT
10	Weiner (1984)	SAT	SAT
11	Becker (1978)	SAT	SAT
12	Becker (1978)	SAT	SAT

Note: ACT = American College Testing Program, CAT = Cognitive Abilities Test, MCT = Mathematics Concepts Test, SAT = Scholastic Aptitude Test.

(or geometric) approaches and strategies in solving math problems, whereas others use algebraic or analytic strategies (e.g., Krutetskii, 1976, p. 315). Because a fairly strong gender difference has been noted on measures of spatial ability, some researchers have proposed that spatial ability plays a role in the persistent finding of a gender difference in mathematical performance (Sherman, 1967). Others have argued that the relationship between spatial and mathematical skills is spurious (Lubinski & Humphreys, 1990). Yet others have wondered whether verbal skills also may play a role in mathematical performance, especially since findings of gender differences favoring females have been reported for some verbal skills.

Friedman collected more than a hundred studies of correlations among measures of performance on mathematical, spatial, and verbal tasks. I have used a small subset of her results to illustrate some analyses of generalizability; the data are shown in table 21.2. These studies all measured spatial ability via the Differential Aptitude Test of Space Relations (SR), while four different mathematical and verbal measures were used, as shown in table 21.3.

As above, the correlations are treated as though they are not subject to either measurement error or range restriction, to simplify the illustration. Score variances suggest that some of Friedman's studies may be subject to range restriction; however, this information was not available for all measures or all studies. Friedman collected no information about measure reliability.

Below I use these data to illustrate the computation of variance components, the meta-analytic analogue to a G study. I then use the computed values of these various components to estimate the generalizability of findings that could be obtained in research studies of the sort investigated here, if they used various research designs.

Estimation of Variance Components: The G Study

In generalizability theory the purpose of the G study is to assess the contribution of as many facets as possible to variation in student performance. In this example, the purpose is to assess the contribution of one study facet (the measurement of construct X) to variation in the parameters of interest—here, the population correlation coefficients.

We first estimate overall variation in the ρ_{im} parameters for the relationship of SR to mathematical performance. An unbiased, weighted method-of-moments estimator of the overall variance component is used. Details of the estimation method are described by Becker (1992). For Friedman's data, we obtain $\sigma = .0188$. This may seem small, but it may be more easily interpreted scaled as a standard deviation, which is .137. This result indicates, for instance, that if the true average mathematical-SR correlation were .49, which is the estimated weighted mean of the sample correlations, about 95 percent of the mathematical-SR *population* correlations would lie between .22 and .76, or within plus or minus 1.96 standard deviations of the true correlation. This range is rather broad; a correlation of .22 would have a considerably different substantive meaning about the space-math relationship than would a correlation of .76.

The overall parameter variance gives an initial assessment of the generalizability of the results. If the variance is very small in an absolute sense, then the result of interest would appear quite stable (i.e., generalizable) across all units, treatments, observing operations, and settings that have been studied. In the example of the correlations between mathematical and spatial ability, this does not appear to be the case.

Next we ask what part of the parameter variation can be attributed to differences in how the construct "mathematical performance" was operationalized. A standard meta-analysis homogeneity test (e.g., Hedges, 1982) would suggest whether the amount of variation between measures was significant, but would give no idea of how much variation exists. For these data the variation is greater than what would be expected due to sampling variation alone ($H = 70.42$, $df = 11$, $p < .001$).

Weighted method-of-moments estimators also are used here to obtain the between-measures and the pooled within-measure parameter variance estimates. For the correlations of spatial ability and mathematical performance the two estimates are $\hat{\sigma}^2_\alpha = .0176$ and $\hat{\sigma}^2_{w/\alpha} = .0012$. Expressed as standard deviations, those variances are more interpretable. The between-measures standard deviation is about .13, and the within-measure standard deviation is .03. Clearly a fair amount of variation can be attributed to the use of different measures (or to factors that, in this data set, happen to be confounded with the measure used). The proportion of parameter variance attributable to differences between measures can be estimated via the intraclass correlation coefficient, which is .936. Nearly all of the between-studies variation is related to differences in results based on different measures of mathematical performance.

When a finding shows low generalizability across operations (that is, a large between-measures variance), we must either narrow the construct and eliminate certain operationalizations as less relevant (e.g., we may select a particular instrument as our focus), or claim low generalizability for the result. If we do the latter, we should incorporate the uncertainty due to measures into our analyses. On the other hand, modifying the construct is consistent with Cook and Campbell's (1979) suggestion that one should "use the obtained pattern of data to edit one's thinking about both the cause and effect constructs" (p. 69). The most extreme version of "editing" one's construct is to reduce it to a single operation.

If a finding shows large within-measure variation, it suggests that other variables, such as characteristics of the units, treatments, or settings studied, may relate to differences in effects. The reviewer would certainly wish to examine the roles of substantively important study characteristics in explaining within-measure variation.

Using Variance Components to Estimate Uncertainty of Results: The D Study

The estimates of between- and within-measure variation can be used to assess the uncertainty of our results in a number of cases, or to a number of different *UTOSs. First consider the uncertainty in the results if we wished to generalize across all samples about the relationship between mathematical and spatial relations using any of the measures of mathematical performance. In other words, we wish to generalize to the broad construct represented by any of the mathematical measures, but any one study would have used only one measure of mathematical performance. In this case each study's population parameter deviates from the construct correlation because of both between-measures variation (since each study may use a different measure) and within-measure variation.

Consider an exemplary study that examined the relationship between mathematical and spatial tasks for one hundred students. Further imagine that a sample correlation of .50 has been obtained. Then, using the results of Olkin and Siotani (1976), the sampling variance of this correlation is estimated to be $\hat{\sigma}^2(\rho_{im}) = (1 - r^2_{im})^2/100 = .0056$, which gives a standard error of .075 based only on sampling variation. This variance is small relative to the parameter variance, and it considerably underestimates the uncertainty in the single study because it completely overlooks parameter variation.

We can assess the effect of this uncertainty on the precision of the correlation via an analysis of the data in which our estimate of σ^2_ρ is added to the sampling error variance for each correlation—that is, we use $\hat{\sigma}^2(\rho_{im}) + \hat{\sigma}^2_\rho$ as our variance estimate for r_{im}. For the exemplary study described just above, the new augmented variance would be $(.0056 + .0188) = .0244$, for a new standard error of .1562, double that computed when parameter variation is ignored. The proportion of variance in the exemplary study that is due to variation in operationalizations (and other parameter variation) can also be computed, as $.0188/(.0056 + .0188) = .7705$, or more than three-fourths of the study's uncertainty. The usual analysis vastly underestimates the uncertainty of the result *as a measure of the correlation between constructs.* This analysis also shows that not only can we can use the data from the G study (meta-analysis) as a D study per se, but also we can use the G-study analysis to understand a single study's uncertainty.

If we add the parameter variance to each of the studies in the example data set, we can incorporate parameter variation into the computation of the mean correlation and its variance. The revised mean correlation and its standard error would thus more accurately reflect the uncertainty about the mathematical-spatial relationship that arises because different measures of mathematical performance have been used. For Friedman's data the standard error of the mean *r* incorporating parameter variability is .047. The standard error estimate roughly triples when the total parameter variance is considered; that is, it is about three times .015, the standard error of the mean from a fixed-effects analysis. The estimate of the average strength of relationship between the SR and mathematical performance is less precise when parameter variation is included, primarily because different measures of the construct mathematical performance seem to give different results.

We might next ask how much uncertainty we should expect if we wished to generalize (across samples) to a narrower conception of mathematical performance, represented by only one measure of mathematical performance. We can gauge this by examining the standard error of the mathematical-SR correlation when the sampling error is augmented by adding only the within-measure component of variation (i.e., $\hat{\sigma}^2_{w/\alpha} = .0012$).

Again consider the exemplary study with one hundred subjects. In this case we would compute that study's error variance as $.0056 + .0012 = .0068$, giving a standard error of $.0825$, which is only ten percent larger than the original standard error incorporating only sampling variation. Thus focusing the definition of the mathematical construct by selecting a single measure of mathematical performance allows us to make more-precise statements about the relationship of mathematical performance to spatial ability.

If we reanalyze Friedman's data, adding $\hat{\sigma}^2_{w/\alpha} = .0012$ to each study's sampling variance, the standard error of the estimated (average) population correlation is $.022$. This is less than half of that computed based on total parameter variation, and is only slightly larger than the standard error from the fixed-effects analysis. By narrowing the construct definition through the choice of a single measure we gain precision, but in a narrower domain of "mathematical performance." To obtain a greater degree of generalizability of the relationship to a broader construct domain, we must accept a lower overall degree of precision.

There is a trade-off between breadth of domain and degree of generalizability. Thus in interpreting existing data we are faced with a choice. We can claim a low degree of generalizability (i.e., high uncertainty or variance in findings) over a broad domain or we can claim a high degree of generalizability (i.e., low uncertainty or variance of findings) over a narrower domain.

Finally, what might happen if we were to design a new study to allow us to generalize across all measures of the construct, but which used several measures of mathematical performance in order to get a more stable result within each study? In this case, if we designed a study using p measures, we would augment each study's sampling error with an estimate of $\sigma^2_{w/\alpha} + \sigma^2_\alpha/p$. The more measures that are used, the less uncertainty that arises from between-measures variation.

To continue with the example of the study with one hundred subjects, we ask what level of precision could be achieved if we conducted the study using p measures of mathematical performance. The variance[2] would be approximately $.0056 + .0012 + (.0176/p) = .0068 + .0176/p$. Table 21.4 shows values of the

---

2. The sampling error variance of the study would also change if multiple measures of math performance were used because the reported correlation value would be a mean of several values rather than a single value. The proper sampling variance would depend on the values of those sample correlations. However, the sampling variance based on a single correlation should be a conservative estimate of the proper variance value.

TABLE 21.4.   *Variance of Exemplary Study*
when Multiple Measures are Used

Number of Measures (p)	Study Variance
1	.0244
2	.0156
4	.0112
5	.0103
10	.0086
20	.0077

study's approximate variance, computed assuming different numbers of math measures used. Even the addition of a second measure decreases the study's variance by more than 30 percent. The variance is limited by the amount of variation that arises simply due to sampling, or equivalently, due to the size of the sample.

However, it is also apparent that the precision of any study cannot be increased solely by increasing the size of the sample. If the amount of parameter variation is estimated to be quite large, increasing the study sample size will diminish only the sampling-error component of the study's proper variance. The use of multiple measures to obtain a more precise result thus has limitations determined by the relative magnitudes of the three components of the variance (sampling error, within-measure variation, and between-measures variation).

The above example is very simple, but it illustrates some of the principles of this analysis. Although it could not be applied to this set of data, a different option in a real application would be to consider the slightly more complex two-factor model for the correlations between spatial ability and math presented in (2) above. If we were interested in the strength of the relationship of mathematical to spatial ability when spatial ability is represented by a variety of measures, not only the SR, we would also want to examine a component of variation attributable to differences in measures of spatial ability. Also, if the data permitted it, we could look for evidence of interactions between the mathematical and spatial measures used.

A Trivariate Example:
Mathematical, Spatial, and Verbal Performance

Consider next an example that is more realistic in a different way. In particular, consider the situation in which we are interested not only in the bivariate relationship between spatial ability and mathematical performance, but also in the prediction of mathematical performance from both spatial and verbal skills. That is, we are interested in a system of relationships. Again, the example data from Friedman (1992) include the correlations examined above plus the correlations between the SR and verbal outcomes and between mathematical and verbal outcomes. The additional correlations are displayed in the last two columns of table 21.2.

When relationships among several variables are involved, it is possible to partition both the variation and the covariation among the study parameters into between-measures and within-measure components. Therefore we can account for the influence of multiple operations on the uncertainty of more-complex interrelationships, such as the partial relationships of spatial and verbal skills together as predictors of mathematical performance.

G Study

As before, the initial step is to estimate the extent of parameter variation and covariation for each correlation or pair of correlations. For simplicity, denote the correlations from each study as a vector so that the elements in the correlation matrix are listed in lexicographic order

$$\mathbf{r} = (r_1, r_2, r_3)' = (r_{\text{Math-SR}}, r_{\text{Math-Verbal}}, r_{\text{SR-Verbal}})'.$$

Then introduce the subscript i to denote the study, so that the vector of correlations from study i is $\mathbf{r}_i = (r_{i1}, r_{i2}, r_{i3})'$. Corresponding to each vector $\mathbf{r}_i$ of sample correlations is a vector of correlation parameters $\rho_i = (\rho_{i1}, \rho_{i2}, \rho_{i3})$, and a vector of sampling errors $\mathbf{e}_i = \mathbf{r}_i - \rho_i$. The unconditional covariance matrix Σ_e can be can be computed from analytic results; the covariance matrix Σ_r depends on Σ_e and the covariance matrix Σ_ρ of ρ_i between studies.

Our goals in this context are to estimate the parameter covariance matrix Σ_ρ and to partition it into between- and within-measure components. That is, we wish to estimate $\Sigma_{w/\alpha}$, the covariance matrix of the ρ_i within measure categories, and Σ_α, the covariance matrix between measure categories, so that

$$\Sigma_\rho = \Sigma_\alpha + \Sigma_{w/\alpha}.$$

Methods for estimation of Σ_α and $\Sigma_{w/\alpha}$ are discussed, for example, by Dempster, Rubin, and Tsutakawa (1981) and Becker (1992). The estimate of the overall Σ_ρ matrix is

$$\hat{\Sigma}_\rho = \begin{bmatrix} .0188 & .0198 & .0118 \\ .0198 & .0338 & .0225 \\ .0118 & .0225 & .0161 \end{bmatrix}.$$

The matrix Σ_ρ informs us about the relative generalizability of the strength of association estimated for each relationship. The large parameter variances shown in the estimate of Σ_ρ imply that any accurate model must take the large variation in ρ_i values across studies into account. For instance, the parameter variation for the mathematical-verbal correlations (the second diagonal entry) is considerable, with a standard deviation of 0.184. Given an average correlation of .45 (the average computed assuming a fixed-effects model), 95 percent of the population correlations would be expected to lie between .09 and .81, a larger range than was estimated for the mathematical-spatial ability correlations.

The variance components are estimated next. The between- and within-measure variance-covariance matrices are

$$\hat{\Sigma}_\alpha = \begin{bmatrix} .0176 & .0176 & .0100 \\ .0176 & .0075 & .0054 \\ .0100 & .0054 & .0021 \end{bmatrix}, \text{ and } \hat{\Sigma}_{w/\alpha} = \begin{bmatrix} .0012 & .0022 & .0019 \\ .0022 & .0263 & .0171 \\ .0019 & .0171 & .0139 \end{bmatrix}.$$

The patterns of between- and within-measure variation differ for the three relationships. The between-measures variances for the mathematical-verbal and SR-verbal rs (.0075 and .0021, respectively) are much smaller than that for the mathematical-SR rs (.0176). In an absolute sense the mathematical-verbal and SR-verbal correlations have less measure-related variation. Thus, unlike what was found for the mathematical-SR correlations, the absolute amount of variation that can be attributed to the use of different measures is relatively small for these two relationships. This suggests that the use of multiple measures of the constructs of interest will not greatly improve the precision of the study results for those two relationships.[3]

The relative portions of variance and covariation that result from the use of different measures (i.e., variation between measures divided by total parameter variation) are shown in the matrix of intraclass correlations, for each relationship and each pair of correlations. That matrix is

3. In these studies, the measures of math performance are completely confounded with the measures of verbal performance used, since most often two subtests of the same test battery were used. In a larger data set, the data might not be constrained in this way.

$$\begin{array}{c} & \begin{array}{ccc} \text{M-S} & \text{M-V} & \text{S-V} \end{array} \\ \begin{array}{c} \text{M-S} \\ \text{M-V} \\ \text{S-V} \end{array} \left[\begin{array}{ccc} .934 & .888 & .842 \\ .888 & .221 & .241 \\ .842 & .241 & .133 \end{array} \right] \end{array}.$$

The smaller values of the second and third diagonal elements in the intra-class correlation matrix confirm that both the mathematical-verbal and SR-verbal relationships show relatively less measure-related variation than did the mathematical-SR correlations. Additionally, the variances in the estimated $\Sigma_{w/\alpha}$ matrix show that although the mathematical-verbal rs show *relatively* more between-measures variance than the SR-verbal correlations, they also show the greatest absolute amount of within-measure variation of the three relationships. This suggests that other variables may be needed to explain fully the patterns of relationships between mathematical and verbal performance seen in these data.

D Study

These matrices of estimates of uncertainty also can be incorporated into other analyses of multivariate relationships. In Becker (1992) I have developed esti-mates of a standardized regression model to predict one outcome variable based on the others in a system of related variables. In this example we may be interested in the relative importance of spatial and verbal skills in the predic-tion of mathematical performance. The model that I examined for Friedman's data is

$$z_{\text{Math}(i)} = b_s z_{\text{SR}(i)} + b_v z_{\text{Verbal}(i)} + e_{(i)},$$

for $i = 1$ to k studies, where the slope coefficients b_s and b_v indicate the relative importance of spatial ability (here the SR) and verbal ability in predicting mathematical performance, and $z_{\text{Math}(i)}$, $z_{\text{SR}(i)}$, and $z_{\text{Verbal}(i)}$ represent standard-ized scores on the respective measures in the ith study.

Before examining the standardized regression analysis, we consider the three average correlations based on a fixed-effects analysis, which are .48, .45, and .28, for the mathematical-SR, mathematical-verbal, and SR-verbal rela-tionships. The mathematical-SR and mathematical-verbal correlations are fairly similar, suggesting that the contributions of spatial and verbal skills to mathematical performance are roughly equivalent.

As a reference point, consider also the standardized regression slopes

TABLE 21.5. *Slopes and Standard Errors when Parameter Variation and Covariation Are Analyzed*

Predictor	Fixed-Effects Analysis	Random-Effects Analysis	Within-Measure Analysis
Spatial skill (SR)			
b_s	0.38	0.34	0.38
$SE(b_s)$	.016	.038	.026
Verbal skill			
b_v	0.34	0.28	0.28
$SE(b_v)$	.016	.044	.045

based on a model that assumes *no* parameter variation. These "fixed-effects" slopes are shown in the first column of table 21.5. The slopes b_s and b_v are fairly similar and both moderate in size. The standard errors are rather small, but a hypothesis test for the difference between the two slopes (under the fixed-effects model) was not significant.

The random-effects analysis incorporates the estimates of total parameter variation and covariation. This analysis represents one in which we use a single measure of each construct, but wish to generalize to the broader construct represented by the whole collection of measures. As was true for the analysis of the mathematical-SR correlations above, the standard errors in this analysis, shown in column two of table 21.5, are much larger than those for the fixed-effects analysis. Also, the standard error of the coefficient b_v for verbal performance increased more than that for SR. This is consistent with the mathematical-verbal correlations showing the largest parameter variance.

The final multivariate analysis, which incorporates only within-measure variation, portrays the level of uncertainty we would expect to find if we wished to generalize to very narrowly defined constructs. Here one could imagine selecting a single measure of each construct (i.e., of mathematical, spatial, and verbal performance). Again, both standard-error values are larger than those from the fixed-effects analysis, and the difference between the standard errors for b_s and b_v is greater than in the previous random-effects analysis.

The differences in the standard errors from the fixed versus the "within-measure" analyses arise because of the patterns of between- and within-measure variation shown above. Not only was the total parameter variation for the mathematical-SR correlations less than that for the mathematical-verbal *r*s, but most of the mathematical-SR variance was between-measures variation. So our inference can become more precise about the role of SR as a predictor of mathematical performance if we select a single measure or a narrow construct of mathematical performance. But the same is not true for our evaluation of the role of verbal ability in mathematical performance because the mathematical-verbal correlations showed a large amount of within-measure variation.

Conclusion

What is to be gained from the empirical analysis of generalizability? One benefit is the ability to quantify the uncertainty in collections of research results that arises from adhering to the principles of multiple operationism. Multiple operationism is a dominant epistemological principle in much of social science. It holds that constructs are multiply defined by the set of measures that are accepted as operations. The goal of multiple operationism is to get more-valid measures of constructs and therefore more-convincing results by using different ways of measuring or representing constructs. However, the use of different measures may introduce so much variation or uncertainty into the results that it is practically impossible to overcome it by simply adding more measures within a study.

Repeated application of the kinds of analyses I have described will contribute to a base of evidence about how much different ways of measuring important constructs contribute to uncertainty about relationships among them. Though the idea of multiple operationism is in theory quite reasonable, we may find that it introduces excessively large amounts of uncertainty into estimates of relationships between variables. If we repeatedly find that the amount of between-measures variation is large, we may have to narrow our constructs, and learn to live with generalizations that are more circumscribed in their domain of application than we would like, but which entail reasonably precise statements or conclusions within that domain.

The model I present here also provides information that can be used in developing research designs. Although many have argued that meta-analysis can be used for that purpose, these methods give one of the first concrete methods for doing so, by using the G study to determine the properties of various D studies that could be conducted. For example, the G study can provide data suggesting whether to use multiple measures of a given construct or constructs in a new study.

We often think of increasing the precision of studies by increasing the sample size. But when the between-studies parameter variation is great, decreasing the sampling error of any given study may do little to decrease the overall uncertainty. Hence, there may be a point of diminishing returns on increasing the sample size, limited by the extent of parameter variation. This was made clear in the illustrative exemplary study, and by Friedman's data, in which most studies were large enough so that the sampling variance was less, sometimes much less, than the total parameter variance.

Finally, the application of the kinds of analyses I have described can shed light on the results of existing research. Finding a great deal of between-measures variation for measures of a particular construct suggests that it may be a mistake to generalize too broadly the results of a single study involving a single measure of that construct. Because researchers naturally want to make sweeping statements in their conclusions and discussions, we as readers may have to learn to temper their generalizations in light of evidence that is gathered from studies like those demonstrated above.

References

Becker, B. J. (1978). *The relationship of spatial ability to sex differences in the performance of mathematically precocious youths on the mathematical sections of the Scholastic Aptitude Test.* Unpublished master's thesis, Johns Hopkins University, Baltimore.

Becker, B. J. (1992). Using the results of replicated studies to estimate linear models. *Journal of Educational Statistics* 17:341–362.

Campbell, D. T. (1969). Definitional versus multiple operationism. *et al.* 2:14–17.

Campbell, D. T., & Fiske, D. W. (1959). Convergent and discriminant validation by the multitrait-multimethod matrix. *Psychological Bulletin* 56:81–105.

Campbell, D. T., & Stanley, J. C. (1966). *Experimental and quasi-experimental designs for research.* Chicago: Rand McNally.

Cook, T. D. (1991). Meta-analysis: Its potential for causal description and causal explanation within program evaluation. In G. Albrecht & H. Otto (Eds.), *Social prevention and the social sciences: Theoretical controversies, research problems, and evaluation strategies* (pp. 245–285). Berlin: Walter de Gruyter.

Cook, T. D. (1993). A theory of the generalization of causal relationships. *New Directions for Program Evaluation* 57:39–82.

Cook, T. D., & Campbell, D. T. (1979). *Quasi-experimentation: Design and analysis for field settings.* Boston: Houghton Mifflin.

Cordray, D. S. (1987). *Strengthening causal interpretations of nonexperimental data: The role of meta-analysis.* Paper presented at the National Center for Health Services Research and Health Care Technology Assessment Conference, Tucson, Az.

Cronbach, L. J. (1982). *Designing evaluations of educational and social programs.* San Francisco: Jossey-Bass.

Cronbach, L. J., Gleser, G. C., Nanda, H., & Rajaratnam, N. (1972). *The dependability of behavioral measurements: Theory of generalizability for scores and profiles.* New York: Wiley.

Dempster, A. P., Rubin, D. B., & Tsutakawa, R. (1981). Estimation in covariance components models. *Journal of the American Statistical Association* 76:341–353.

Fennema, E., & Sherman, J. (1978). Sex-related differences in mathematics achievement, and related factors. *Journal for Research in Mathematics Education* 9:189–203.

Filella, J. F. (1960). Educational and sex differences in the organization of abilities in technical and academic students in Columbia, South America. *Genetic Psychology Monographs* 61:116–163.

Friedman, L. (1992). *A meta-analysis of spatial and mathematical tasks.* Unpublished doctoral dissertation, University of Chicago.

Glass, G. V. (1976). Primary, secondary, and meta-analysis of research. *Educational Researcher* 5:3–8.

Hedges, L. V. (1982). Fitting categorical models to effect sizes from a series of experiments. *Psychological Bulletin* 92:490–499.

Hunter, J. E., & Schmidt, F. L. (1990). *Methods of meta-analysis: Correcting error and bias in research findings*. Beverly Hills: Sage Publications.

Krutetskii, V. A. (1976). *The psychology of mathematical abilities in schoolchildren*. Chicago: University of Chicago Press.

Light, R. J. (1979). Capitalizing on variation: How conflicting research findings can be helpful for policy. *Educational Researcher* 8:3–8.

Lubinski, D., & Humphreys, L. G. (1990). Assessing spurious "moderator effects": Illustrated substantively with the hypothesized ("synergistic") relation between spatial and mathematical ability. *Psychological Bulletin* 107:385–393.

Olkin, I., & Siotani, M. (1976). Asymptotic distribution of functions of a correlation matrix. In S. Ideka (Ed.), *Essays in probability and statistics* (pp. 235–251). Tokyo: Sinko Tsusho.

Pearson, J. L., & Ferguson, L. R. (1987). Gender differences in patterns of spatial ability, environmental cognition, and math and English achievement in late adolescence. *Adolescence* 24:421–432.

Rosenberg, J. H. (1981). *The ability of selected cognitive, affective, and educational variables to predict the presence of anxiety related to mathematics*. Unpublished doctoral dissertation, University of Connecticut, Storrs.

Sherman, J. A. (1967). Problems of sex differences in space perception and aspects of intellectual functioning. *Psychological Review* 74:290–299.

Smith, I. (1964). *Spatial ability: Its educational and social significance*. San Diego: Robert R. Knapp.

Webb, E. J., Campbell, D. T., Schwartz, R. D., & Sechrest, L. B. (1966). *Unobtrusive measures: Nonrestrictive research in the social sciences*. Chicago: Rand McNally.

Weiner, N. C. (1984). *Cognitive aptitudes, personality variables, and gender difference effects on mathematical achievement for mathematically gifted students*. Unpublished doctoral dissertation, Arizona State University, Tempe.

22 Possible New Approaches to the Study of Mathematically Precocious Youth

N. L. GAGE

My impression, based on an examination of the major publications of the Study of Mathematically Precocious Youth (SMPY), is that the most frequently used, if not the only, approach of the study has been what is currently called "positivist," "postpositivist," "scientific"—and, often pejoratively, "mainstream," "establishmentarian," and "quantitative." To many, these adjectives, especially the adjective "scientific," have favorable connotations. This is particularly true for psychologists, including educational psychologists. It is not only that scientific knowledge is knowledge obtained empirically, objectively, communicably, reliably, replicably, cumulatively, and systematically; those criteria would also be met by the telephone book. Most important, such knowledge has value for the explanation, prediction, and control of phenomena. Most psychologists were raised to value and respect such knowledge and to try to meet its criteria. We grew up with such ideas, wanted to be scientists, and wanted to apply scientific method to the study of human nature, human behavior, the human mind, and human society.

Criticisms of Scientific Approaches

But recent years have seen much questioning and even outright rejection of the scientific method in the study of human affairs. The questioning and rejection have come, first, from certain philosophers of science; second, from those who call themselves phenomenological, interpretive, hermeneutic, naturalistic, or qualitative researchers; and third, from those who call themselves critical theorists.[1] In this chapter I will briefly detail the nature of this critique, applying it to the study of mathematically precocious youth whenever appropriate. This is followed by a response, or a counterargument, and a discussion of what we can learn from this new direction being taken in the social sciences.

Some Philosophers' Criticisms

Some philosophers have held that scientific, especially "social scientific," findings have no fixed and immutable character. The concepts and findings of science come and go, in this view, as science progresses, as paradigms change, as new research traditions emerge. These philosophers hold that scientific theories, rather than representing truth, are mere intellectual tools exploited for their temporary value in guiding research and revealing otherwise indeterminable relationships. Moreover, the theories produced by science are relative to, and dependent on, the scientists' conceptual framework. So it becomes erroneous to claim that any of these theories is true. What the scientist finds or believes depends on his or her point of view or perspective. There can be no objective observations that are neutral and true. Theories precede observations as well as follow upon them. So our ideas about reality are constructed by us rather than determined in any objective and veridical way by what is "out there."

Further, by an act of will or by the application of human knowledge of social science laws, those "laws" can be invalidated (Gewirth, 1954). For this reason, especially, social science cannot hope for immutable laws of the kind yielded by the natural sciences.

The Qualitativists' Critique

Consider next the qualitativists', interpretivists', or phenomenologists' critique. In their view also, the *social* sciences are not dealing with any objective reality—certainly nothing even approaching what, as I have just noted, is the questionably objective status of even what is studied by the natural sciences. Rather, the social sciences study matters that can be understood only through a kind of empathy, whereby the investigator enters into, or participates in, so to speak, the lives, feelings, actions, hopes, and fears of the persons or groups being

1. The interested reader can find a brief introduction to the literature on these issues in Soltis (1992).

studied. In this view, subjectivity is not only unavoidable but desirable. Herme-neutics, consisting of an endless alternation between understanding the whole in terms of its parts and understanding the parts in terms of the whole, is employed by interpretive investigators. What is studied and how it is studied are not independent of the values, interests, and purposes of investigators. Students of human action must rely on their own interests, values, and purposes in coming to understand those of other persons; that is, their own perspectives become indispensable tools for understanding those of other persons.

Thus, the interpretive researchers check and recheck their interpretations with their subjects. They build "thick descriptions" based on their immersion in the field. And these techniques are not mere alternatives to the positivists' use of standardized tests, estimates of reliability and validity, representative sam-ples, and so on. They are epistemologically different, based on different concep-tions of what is being studied, for what purpose, and under what conditions.

The Critical Theorists' Attack

I turn now to a third kind of criticism of postpositivism—the one that goes by the name of "critical theory." This orientation consists of examining and chal-lenging the whole framework of the society in which individual and social action goes on: its economic, political, and social structure. Economically, the framework may be capitalist or socialist. Politically, it may refer with greater or less validity to democracy or authoritarianism. Socially, it may constitute more or less sharply demarcated bourgeois and proletarian classes. How these di-mensions of society affect the social sciences, including educational psychology, is part of what concerns the critical theorists.

In their view, educational psychology focuses on merely "technical" issues rather than the fundamental concerns and goals of education. In doing so, the critical theorists say, educational psychology helps preserve rather than chal-lenge the status quo. And the status quo in the United States, they say, is one in which the dominant capitalist class exercises power over the whole educational enterprise, which it bends to its own purposes and needs. Educational psychol-ogy has neglected the critical examination of the resultant educational system and the society in which it is embedded. For example, it has neglected the causes and effects of the recent widespread unemployment among holders of the Ph.D. in physics. So, say the critical theorists, educational psychology has helped perpetuate the unjust social systems that now prevail in the United States, in other industrialized societies, and in many developing nations.

Thus, when critical theorists examine the curriculum, they see ways in which it serves to reproduce an inequitable social class structure. When they examine teaching materials, they see instructional packages depriving teachers of decision-making power and thus "deskilling," or proletarianizing, the teaching staff. The critical theorists concern themselves with how every aspect of capitalism influences not only the administration and financing of schools but also, subtly and pervasively, the largest and smallest features of what is taught and how it is taught to whom and for what purpose. Tinkering with technical details is what they see as the present function of educational psychology—a kind of fiddling while the people struggle with the basic questions of how a more just society and educational system can be achieved. They would say, I think, that aptitude testing, guidance, and acceleration in themselves will never rectify the severe social class, rural/urban, ethnic, and gender inequities now deeply embedded in American society.

Counterattacking the Critics

How can educational psychologists, who predominate among those studying mathematically precocious youth, respond to the criticisms of the antipostpositivist philosophers, the interpretivists, and the critical theorists? One alternative is to ignore the criticisms. But that response would leave the issues unmet and unresolved, would be tantamount to capitulation, and would miss an opportunity to benefit from criticism. My own response has two aspects: counterattack and accommodation.

Counterattacking the Philosophers

Our counterattack against the philosophers can point out that many of the issues they raise are centuries old, intractable until now, and never capable of halting scientific progress. We can point to the distinction between facts and interpretations and show that their arguments fail to diminish the force and strength of a myriad of facts, ranging from the reality of the Holocaust to the reality of the always-positive correlations between academic aptitude and academic achievement. Students of mathematically precocious youth can demand that qualitativists or interpretivists show the ways in which many facts about such youth depend completely for their veridicality on an arbitrary choice of theoretical and methodological procedures and how equally reasonable but different or contradictory facts can be generated by some alternative sets of such procedures. The critics of all three kinds could be asked to defend their low estimation of the yield of educational psychology in studying precocious youth against the evidence from bodies of replications that have yielded consistent and important results that compare favorably, as Hedges's findings (1987) suggest, with the consistency of results from replications of studies in the hard sciences. The whole attack on the fruitfulness of scientific work in social and educational research needs to be reexamined in the light of what we have learned in the years since Glass's meta-analysis (1976) invigorated the whole enterprise of accumulating evidence across roughly similar studies of relationships between variables.[2]

Counterattacking the Qualitativists

The attacks of the interpretivists need to be confronted with comparisons of the yield of their research orientations with the yield of positivistic educational psychology. Have their orientations and methods contributed as much to the understanding, identification, and beneficent treatment of any disadvantaged groups in our schools, including mathematically precocious youth? Of course, definitions of such outcomes of research may not be altogether comparable as between postpositivism and interpretivism, but surely a higher authority can be consulted to make such judgments of the contributions.

Counterattacking the Critical Theorists

By way of counterattacking the critical theorists, we could express skepticism about their claim that the failure, in every sense, of the Soviet Union provided no fair test of the validity of their Marxist conceptions of the nature of capitalism, the relationships between bourgeois and working classes, and the relationships between education and the capitalist state. They should be asked to spell out the ways in which education in a society that implemented their Marxist orientations would differ from education in capitalist societies. They should be asked to go beyond their criticism to concrete proposals for the reorganization of society and the schools, including the schools' treatment of mathematically precocious youth.

Accommodative Responses to the Criticisms

But beyond counterattacks, postpositivist educational psychologists can react accommodatively. Educational psychologists ought to look carefully at, and perhaps try out, the orientations and methods of the interpretivists, the eth-

2. For a defense of the possibility of long-lasting generalizations in the behavioral sciences, see Gage (1996).

nographers, the connoisseurs and critics on the qualitative side of methodology in social and educational research. Perhaps more in-depth studies of mathematically precocious youth, using methods similar to those of psychiatrists, clinical psychologists, assessment-of-personnel case-study researchers, and anthropologists, would yield better insights into the nature of such precocity.

Similarly, to accommodate to the critical theorists, studies of such youth might look at the ways in which the economic and political arrangements in our society have militated against the optimal achievement, and recognition of the full potential, of mathematically precocious youth. For example, evidence collected by SMPY has shown that such youth come disproportionately more often from educated parents providing middle-class homes in urban or suburban environments. We should not accept an unprovable hereditarian explanation of these findings—unprovable because the environmental and genetic variations producing *group* (as against *individual*) differences between culturally diverse groups are inextricably confounded. So the constructive action in the face of the group differences is to seek better ways of identifying the precocious youth who now languish neglected in our slums, rural areas, and ghettoes, just as in recent decades we have at last begun to redress the inequities in our identification and treatment of talent in the long-neglected female half of our population.

In short, criticisms of scientific approaches to human affairs have been made by philosophers, qualitativists, and critical theorists. Rather than ignoring, and beyond counterattacking, our critics among philosophers, interpretivists, and critical theorists, we should consider the possibility of learning from them.

References

Gage, N. L. (1996). Confronting counsels of despair for the behavioral sciences. *Educational Researcher* 25(3): 5–15, 22.

Gewirth, A. (1954). Can men change laws of social science? *Philosophy of Science* 21:229–241.

Glass, G. V. (1976). Primary, secondary, and meta-analysis of research. *Educational Researcher* 5:3–8.

Hedges, L. V. (1987). How hard is hard science, how soft is soft science? The empirical cumulativeness of research. *American Psychologist* 42:443–455.

Soltis, J. F. (1992). Inquiry paradigms. In M. Alkin (Ed.), *Encyclopedia of educational research* (6th ed., pp. 620–622). New York: Macmillan.

VI Giftedness ≠ Genius

I n this contribution, which brings the volume to a close, Arthur Jensen provides a thought-provoking piece on the nature of genius, with particular emphasis on the realm of nonintellectual personal attributes. We learn that in early treatments of genius (e.g., Galton, 1869), it was keenly appreciated, as it is today, that sheer intellectual power is insufficient for greatness. Large amounts of mental energy also are needed, and they are seen by many as second in importance, following ability. Some early writers actually formalized their thinking in this regard and provided labels for these constructs that involved some form of endurance or perseverance (what Spearman, and others, called "conative," as distinct from "cognitive"). Jensen synthesizes these concepts in an insightful manner to give us a new twist on genius. Many of Jensen's ideas mesh well with Paul E. Meehl characterization of first-rate intellects: "brains, facts, and passion" (see Sines, 1993). But Jensen adds more. His model of creativity is more multifaceted and explicitly multiplicative. Jensen adds to his critical makeup of genius a certain unconventional, abrasive self-centeredness (which many other observers have discussed in connection with genius), and he claims that these attributes are assessable via Eysenck's (1995) psychoticism scale. Perhaps Jensen's picture of genius is best construed as an emergenic phenomenon (see Lykken, McGue, Tellegen, & Bouchard, 1992), whereby the manifestation of certain (especially highly abstract) traits are dependent on the appropriate *configuration* of certain personal attributes in ideal amounts.

References

Eysenck, H. J. (1995). *Genius: The natural history of creativity*. Cambridge: Cambridge University Press.

Galton, F. (1869). *Hereditary genius: An inquiry into its laws and consequences*. London: Macmillan.

Lykken, D. T., McGue, M., Tellegen, A., & Bouchard, T. J. (1992). Emergenesis. *American Psychologist* 47:1565–1577.

Meehl, P. E. (1991). Preface. *Selected philosophical and methodological papers*. Minneapolis: University of Minnesota Press.

Sines, J. O. (1993). Paul E. Meehl: Brains, facts, and passion. *Contemporary Psychology* 38:691–692.

23   Giftedness and Genius

Crucial Differences

ARTHUR R. JENSEN

The main difference between genius and stupidity, I am told, is that genius has limits. A simple answer, and undoubtedly true. But my assignment here is to reflect on the much more complex difference between intellectual *giftedness* and *genius*, using the latter term in its original sense, as socially recognized, outstandingly creative achievement. In this think-piece (which is just that, rather than a comprehensive review of the literature), I will focus on factors, many intriguing in and of themselves, that are characteristic of genius. My primary thesis is that the emergence of genius is best described using a multiplicative model.

I will argue that exceptional achievement is a multiplicative function of a number of different traits, each of which is normally distributed, but which in combination are so synergistic as to skew the resulting distribution of achievement. An extremely extended upper tail is thus produced, and it is within this tail that genius can be found. An interesting two-part question then arises: how many different traits are involved in producing extraordinary achievement, and what are they? The musings that follow provide some conjectures that can be drawn on to answer this critical question.

As a subject for scientific study, the topic of genius, although immensely fascinating, is about as far from ideal as any phenomenon one can find. The literature on real genius can claim little besides biographical anecdotes and speculation, with this chapter contributing only more of the same. Whether the study of genius will ever evolve from a literary art form into a systematic science is itself highly speculative. The most promising efforts in this direction are those by Simonton (1988) and Eysenck (1995), with Eysenck's monograph leaving little of potential scientific value that can be added to the subject at present, pending new empirical evidence.

Intelligence

Earlier I stated that genius has limits. But its upper limit, at least in some fields, seems to be astronomically higher than its lower limit. Moreover, the upper limit of genius cannot be described as characterized by precocity, high intelligence, knowledge and problem-solving skills being learned with speed and ease, outstanding academic achievement, honors and awards, or even intellectual productivity. Although such attributes are commonly found at all levels of genius, they are not discriminating in the realm of genius.

My point is perhaps most clearly illustrated by the contrast between two famous mathematicians who became closely associated with one another as "teacher" and "student." The reason for the quotation marks here will soon be obvious, because the teacher later claimed that he learned more from the student than the student had learned from him. G. H. Hardy was England's leading mathematician, a professor at Cambridge University, a Fellow of the Royal Society, and the recipient of an honorary degree from Harvard. Remarkably precocious in early childhood, especially in mathematics, he became an exceptionally brilliant student, winning one scholarship after another. He was acknowledged the star graduate in mathematics at Cambridge, where he remained to become a professor of mathematics. He also became a world-class mathematician. His longtime friend C. P. Snow relates that Hardy, at the peak of his career, ranked himself fifth among the most important mathematicians of his day, and it should be pointed out that Hardy's colleagues regarded him as an overly modest man (Snow, 1967). If the Study of Mathematically Precocious Youth (SMPY) had been in existence when Hardy was a schoolboy, he would have been a most prized and promising student in the program.

One day Hardy received a strange-looking letter from Madras, India. It was full of mathematical formulations written in a quite unconventional—one might even say bizarre—form. The writer seemed almost mathematically illiterate by Cambridge standards. It was signed "Srinivasa Ramanujan." At first glance, Hardy thought it might even be some kind of fraud. Puzzling over this letter with its abstruse formulations, he surmised it was written either by some trickster or by someone sincere but poorly educated in mathematics. Hardy sought the opinion of his most highly esteemed colleague, J. E. Littlewood, the other famous mathematician at Cambridge. After the two of them had spent several hours studying the strange letter, they finally realized, with excitement and absolute certainty, that they had "discovered" a major mathematical genius. The weird-looking formulas, it turned out, revealed profound mathematical insights of a kind that are never created by ordinarily gifted mathematicians. Hardy regarded this "discovery" as the single most important event in his life. Here was the prospect of fulfilling what, until then, had been for him only an improbable dream: of ever knowing in person a mathematician possibly of Gauss's caliber.

A colleague in Hardy's department then traveled to India and persuaded Ramanujan to go to Cambridge, with all his expenses and a salary paid by the university. When the youth arrived from India, it was evident that, by ordinary standards, his educational background was meager and his almost entirely self-taught knowledge of math was full of gaps. He had not been at all successful in school, from which he had flunked out twice, and was never graduated. To say, however, that he was *obsessed* by mathematics is an understatement. As a boy in Madras, he was too poor to buy paper on which to work out his math problems. He did his prodigious mathematical work on a slate, copying his final results with red ink on old, discarded newspapers.

While in high school, he thought he had made a stunning mathematical discovery, but he later learned, to his great dismay, that his discovery had already been made 150 years earlier by the great mathematician Euler. Ramanujan felt extraordinary shame for having "discovered" something that was not original, never considering that only a real genius could have created or even re-created that discovery.

At Cambridge, Ramanujan was not required to take courses or exams. That would have been almost an insult and a sure waste of time. He learned some essential things from Hardy, but what excited Hardy the most had nothing to do with Ramanujan's great facility in learning the most advanced concepts and technical skills of mathematical analysis. Hardy himself had that kind of facility. What so impressed him was Ramanujan's uncanny mathematical intuition and capacity for inventing incredibly original and profound theorems. That, of course, is what real mathematical genius is all about. Facility in solving textbook problems and in passing difficult tests is utterly trivial when discussing genius. Although working out the proof of a theorem, unlike discovering a theorem, may take immense technical skill and assiduous effort, it is not itself a hallmark of genius. Indeed, Ramanujan seldom bothered to prove his own theorems; proof was a technical feat that could be left to lesser geniuses. Moreover, in some cases, because of his spotty mathematical education, he probably would have been unable to produce a formal proof even if he had wanted to. But a great many important theorems were generated in his obsessively active brain. Often he seemed to be in another world. One might say that the difference between Ramanujan creating a theorem and a professional mathematician solving a complex problem with standard techniques of analysis is like the difference between St. Francis in ecstasy and a sleepy vicar reciting the morning order of prayer.

After his experience with Ramanujan, Hardy told Snow that if the word *genius* meant anything, he (Hardy) was not really a genius at all (Snow, 1967, p. 27). Hardy had his own hundred-point rating scale of his estimates of the "natural ability" of eminent mathematicians. Though regarding himself at the time as one of the world's five best pure mathematicians, he gave himself a rating of only 25. The greatest mathematician of that period, David Hilbert, was rated 80. But Hardy rated Ramanujan 100, the same rating as he gave Carl Frederick Gauss, who is generally considered the greatest mathematical genius the world has known. On the importance of their total contributions to mathematics, however, Hardy rated himself 35, Ramanujan 85, and Gauss 100. By this reckoning Hardy was seemingly an overachiever and Ramanujan an underachiever. Yet one must keep in mind that Ramanujan died at age thirty, Hardy at seventy, and Gauss at seventy-eight.

Of course, all geniuses are by definition extreme overachievers, in the statistical sense. Nothing else that we could have known about them besides the monumental contributions we ascribe to their genius would have predicted such extraordinary achievement. In discussing Ramanujan's work, the Polish mathematician Mark Kac was forced to make a distinction between the "ordinary genius" and the "magician." He wrote:

> An ordinary genius is a fellow that you and I would be just as good as, if we were only many times better. There is no mystery as to how his mind works. Once we understand what he has done, we feel certain that we, too, could have done it. It is different with the magicians. They are, to use mathematical jargon, in the orthogonal complement of where we are and the working of their minds is for all intents and purposes incomprehensible. Even after we understand what they have done, the process by which they have done it is completely dark. (Quoted in Kanigel, 1991, p. 281; Kanigel's splendid biography of Ramanujan is highly recommended)

To come back to earth and the point of my meandering, genius requires giftedness (consisting essentially of *g*, often along with some special aptitude or talent, such as mathematical, spatial, musical, or artistic talent). But obviously there are other antecedents (to the magic of Ramanujan's "thinking processes") that are elusive to us. Nonetheless, we do know of at least two key attributes, beyond ability, that appear to function as catalysts for the creation of that special class of behavioral products specifically indicative of genius. They are productivity and creativity.

Creativity

Although we can recognize creative acts and even quantify them after a fashion (MacKinnon, 1962), our understanding of them in any explanatory sense is practically nil. Yet one prominent hypothesis concerning creativity (by which I mean the bringing into being of something that has not previously existed) seems to me not only unpromising, but extremely implausible and probably wrong. It is also inherently unfalsifiable and hence fails Popper's criterion for a useful scientific theory. I doubt that it will survive a truly critical examination. Because ruling out one explanation does further our understanding of creativity, I will focus on this theory.

I am referring here to what has been termed the *chance configuration theory* of creativity (well explicated by Simonton, 1988, ch. 1). Essentially, it amounts to expecting that a computer that perpetually generates strictly random sequences of all the letters of the alphabet, punctuation signs, and spaces will eventually produce *Hamlet* or some other work of creative genius. The theory insists that *blind chance* acting in the processes of memory searches for elements with which to form random combinations and permutations, from which finally there emerges some product or solution that the world considers original or creative. It is also essential that, although this generating process is operating entirely by blind chance, the random permutations produced thereby are subjected to a critical rejection/selection screening, with selective retention of the more promising products. This theory seems implausible, partly because of the sheer numerical explosion of the possible combinations and permutations when there are more than just a few elements. For example, the letters in the word *permutation* have 11! = 39,916,800 possible permutations. To discover the "right" one by randomly permuting the letters at a continuous rate of one permutation per second could take anywhere from one second (if one were extremely lucky) up to one year, three thirty-day months, and seven days (if one were equally unlucky). Even then, these calculations assume that the random generating mechanism never repeated a particular permutation; otherwise it would take much longer.

The combinatorial and permutational explosion resulting from an increase in the number of elements to be mentally manipulated and the exponentially increased processing time are not, however, the worst problems for this theory. The far greater problem is that, just as "nature abhors a vacuum," the human mind abhors randomness. I recall a lecture by the statistician Helen M. Walker in which she described a variety of experiments showing that intelligent people, no matter how sophisticated they are about statistics or how well they understand the meaning of randomness, and while putting forth their best conscious efforts, are simply *incapable* of selecting, combining, or permuting numbers, letters, words, or anything else in a truly random fashion. For example, when subjects are asked to generate a series of random numbers, or repeatedly to make a random selection of *N* items from among a much larger number of different objects spread out on a table, or take a random walk, it turns out no one can do it. This has been verified by statistical tests of randomness applied to their performance. People even have difficulty simply reading aloud from a table of random numbers without involuntarily and nonrandomly inserting other numbers. (Examples of this phenomenon are given in Kendall, 1948.)

Thus, randomness (or blind chance, to use the favored term in chance configuration theory) seems an unlikely explanation of creative thinking. This theory seems to have originated from what may be deemed an inappropriate analogy, namely the theory of biological evolution creating new living forms. According to the latter theory, a great variety of genetic effects is produced by *random* mutations and the screening out of all variations except those best adapted to the environment—that is, natural selection. But a genetic mutation, produced perhaps by a radioactive particle hitting a single molecule in the DNA at random and altering its genetic code, is an unfitting analogy for the necessarily integrated action of the myriad neurons involved in the mental manipulation of ideas.

The Creative Process

The implausibility of randomness, however, in no way implies that creative thinking does not involve a great deal of "trial-and-error" mental manipulation, though it is not at all random. The products that emerge are then critically sifted in light of the creator's aim. The individuals in whom this mental-manipulation process turns out to be truly creative most often are those who are relatively rich in each of three sources of variance in creativity: (1) *ideational fluency*, or the capacity to tap a flow of relevant ideas, themes, or images, and to play with them, also known as "brainstorming"; (2) what Eysenck (1995) has termed the individuals' *relevance horizon*; that is, the range or variety of elements, ideas, and associations that seem relevant to the problem (creativity involves a wide relevance horizon); and (3) *suspension of critical judgment*.

Creative persons are intellectually high risk takers. They are not afraid of zany ideas and can hold the inhibitions of self-criticism temporarily in abeyance. Both Darwin and Freud mentioned their gullibility and receptiveness to highly speculative ideas and believed that these traits were probably characteristic of creative thinkers in general. Darwin occasionally performed what he called "fool's experiments," trying out improbable ideas that most people would have instantly dismissed as foolish. Francis Crick once told me that Linus Pauling's scientific ideas turned out to be wrong about 80 percent of the time, but the other 20 percent finally proved to be so important that it would be a mistake to ignore any of his hunches.

I once asked another Nobel Prize winner, William Shockley, whose creativity resulted in about a hundred patented inventions in electronics, what he considered the main factors involved in his success. He said there were two: (1) he had an ability to generate, with respect to any given problem, a good many hypotheses, with little initial constraint by previous knowledge as to their plausibility or feasibility; and (2) he worked much harder than most people would at trying to figure out how a zany idea might be shaped into something technically feasible. Some of the ideas that eventually proved most fruitful, he said, were even a physical impossibility in their initial conception. For that very reason, most knowledgeable people would have dismissed such unrealistic ideas immediately, before searching their imaginations for transformations that might make them feasible.

Some creative geniuses, at least in the arts, seem to work in the opposite direction from that described by Shockley. That is, they begin by producing something fairly conventional, or even trite, and then set about to impose novel distortions, reshaping it in ways deemed creative. I recall a demonstration of this by Leonard Bernstein, in which he compared the early drafts of Beethoven's Fifth Symphony with the final version we know today. The first draft was a remarkably routine-sounding piece, scarcely suggesting the familiar qualities of Beethoven's genius. It was more on a par with the works composed by his mediocre contemporaries, now long forgotten. But then two processes took hold: (1) a lot of "doctoring," which introduced what for that time were surprising twists and turns in the harmonies and rhythms, along with an ascetic purification, and (2) a drastic pruning and simplification of the orchestral score to rid it completely of all the "unessential" notes in the harmonic texture, all the "elegant variations" of rhythm, and any suggestion of the kind of filigree ornamentation that was so common in the works of his contemporaries. This resulted in a starkly powerful, taut, and uniquely inevitable-sounding masterpiece, which, people now say, only Beethoven could have written. But when Beethoven's symphonies were first performed, they sounded so shockingly deviant from the prevailing aesthetic standards that leading critics declared him ripe for a madhouse.

One can see a similar process of artistic distortion in a fascinating motion picture using time-lapse photography of Picasso at work (*The Picasso Mystery*). He usually began by sketching something quite ordinary—for example, a completely realistic horse. Then he would begin distorting the figure this way and that, repeatedly painting over what he had just painted and imposing further, often fantastic, distortions. In one instance, this process resulted in such an utterly hopeless mess that Picasso finally tossed the canvas aside, with a remark to the effect of "Now I see how it should go." Then, taking a clean canvas, he worked quickly, with bold, deft strokes of his paintbrush, and there suddenly took shape the strangely distorted figure Picasso apparently had been striving for. Thus he achieved the startling aesthetic impact typical of Picasso's art.

It is exactly this kind of artistic distortion of perception that is never seen in the productions of the most extremely gifted idiot savants, whose drawings often are incredibly photographic, yet are never considered works of artistic genius. The greatest artists probably have a comparable gift for realistic drawing, but their genius leads them well beyond such photographic perception.

Other examples of distortion are found in the recorded performances of the greatest conductors and instrumentalists, the re-creative geniuses, such as Toscanini and Furtwängler, Paderewski and Kreisler. Such artists are not primarily distinguished from routine practitioners by their technical skill or virtuosity (though these are indeed impressive), but by the subtle distortions, within fairly narrow limits, of rhythm, pitch, phrasing, and the like, that they impose, consciously or unconsciously, on the works they perform. Differences between the greatest performers are easily recognizable by these "signatures." But others' attempts to imitate these idiosyncratic distortions are never subtle enough or consistent enough to escape detection as inauthentic; in fact, they usually amount to caricatures.

Psychosis

What is the wellspring of the basic elements of creativity listed above—ideational fluency, a wide relevance horizon, the suspension of inhibiting self-criticism, and the novel distortion of ordinary perception and thought? All of these features, when taken to an extreme degree, are characteristic of psychosis. The mental and emotional disorganization of clinical psychosis is, however, generally too disabling to permit genuinely creative or productive work, especially in the uncompensated individual. Eysenck, however, has identified a trait, or dimension of personality, termed *psychoticism*, which can be assessed by means of the Eysenck Personality Questionnaire (Eysenck & Eysenck, 1991). Trait psychoticism, it must be emphasized, does not imply the psychiatric diagnosis of psychosis, but only the predisposition or potential for the development of psychosis (Eysenck & Eysenck, 1976). In many creative geniuses, this potential for actual psychosis is usually buffered and held in check by certain other traits, such as a high degree of ego strength. Trait psychoticism is a constellation of characteristics that persons may show to varying degrees; such persons may be aggressive, cold, egocentric, impersonal, impulsive, antisocial, unempathic, tough-minded, and creative. This is not a charming picture of genius, perhaps, but a reading of the biographies of some of the world's most famous geniuses attests to its veracity.

By and large, geniuses are quite an odd lot by ordinary standards. Their spouses, children, and close friends are usually not generous in their personal recollections, aside from marveling at the accomplishments for which the person is acclaimed a genius. Often the personal eccentricities remain long hidden from the public. Beethoven's first biographer, for example, is known to have destroyed some of Beethoven's letters and conversation books, presumably because they revealed a pettiness and meanness of character that seemed utterly inconsistent with the sublime nobility of Beethoven's music. Richard Wagner's horrendous character is legendary. He displayed virtually all of the aforementioned features of trait psychoticism to a high degree and, to make matters worse, was also neurotic.

Trait psychoticism is hypothesized as a key condition in Eysenck's (1995) theory of creativity. Various theorists have also mentioned other characteristics, but some of these, such as self-confidence, independence, originality, and nonconformity, to name a few, might well stem from trait psychoticism. (See Jackson & Rushton, 1987, for reviews of the personality origins of productivity and creativity.)

Productivity

A startling corollary of the multiplicative model of exceptional achievement is best stated in the form of a general law. This is Price's Law, which says that if K persons have made a total of N countable contributions in a particular field, then $N/2$ of the contributions will be attributable to $\sqrt{K}$ (Price, 1963). Hence, as the total number of workers (K) in a discipline increases, the ratio $\sqrt{K}/K$ shrinks, increasing the elitism of the major contributors. This law, like any other, only holds true within certain limits. But within fairly homogeneous disciplines, Price's Law seems to hold up quite well for indices of productivity— for example, in math, the empirical sciences, musical composition, and the frequency of performance of musical works. Moreover, there is a high rank-order relationship between sheer productivity and various indices of the importance of a contributor's work, such as the frequency and half-life of scientific citations, and the frequency of performance and staying power of musical compositions in the concert repertoire. (Consider such contrasting famous contemporaries as Mozart and Salieri; Beethoven and Hummel; and Wagner and Meyerbeer.)

If productivity and importance could be suitably scaled, however, I would imagine that the correlation between them would show a scatter-diagram of the "twisted pear" variety (Fisher, 1959). That is, high productivity and triviality are more frequently associated than low productivity and high importance. As a rule, the greatest creative geniuses in every field are astoundingly prolific, although, without exception, they have also produced their share of trivia. (Consider Beethoven's *King Stephen* Overture and Wagner's "United States Centennial March," to say nothing of his ten published volumes of largely trivial prose writings—all incredible contrasts to these composers' greatest works.) But such seemingly unnecessary trivia from such geniuses is probably the inevitable effluvia of the mental energy without which their greatest works would not have come into being. On the other hand, high productivity is probably much more common than great importance, and high productivity per se is no guarantee of the importance of what is produced. The "twisted pear" relationship suggests that high productivity is a necessary but not sufficient condition for making contributions of importance in any field. The importance factor, however, depends on creativity—certainly an elusive attribute.

What might be the basis of individual differences in productivity? The word *motivation* immediately comes to mind, but it explains little and also seems too intentional and self-willed to fill the bill. When one reads about famous creative geniuses one finds that, although they may occasionally have to force themselves to work, they cannot *will* themselves to be *obsessed* by the subject of their work. Their obsessive-compulsive mental activity in a particular sphere is virtually beyond conscious control. I can recall three amusing examples of this, and they all involve dinner parties. Isaac Newton went down to the cellar to fetch some wine for his guests and, while filling a flagon, wrote a mathematical equation with his finger on the dust of the wine keg. After quite a long time had passed, his guests began to worry that he might have had an accident, and they went down to the cellar. There was Newton, engrossed in his mathematical formulas, having completely forgotten that he was hosting a dinner party.

My second example involves Richard Wagner. Wagner, while his guests assembled for dinner, suddenly took leave of them and dashed upstairs. Alarmed that something was wrong, his wife rushed to his room. Wagner exclaimed, "I'm doing it!"—their agreed signal that she was not to disturb him under any circumstances because some new musical idea was flooding his brain and would have to work itself out before he could be sociable again. He had a phenomenal memory for musical ideas that spontaneously surfaced, and could postpone writing them down until it was convenient, a tedious task he referred to not as composing but as merely "copying" the music in his mind's ear.

Then there is the story of Arturo Toscanini hosting a dinner party at which he was inexplicably morose and taciturn, just as he had been all that day and the day before. Suddenly he got up from the dinner table and hurried to his study; he returned after several minutes beaming joyfully and holding up the score of Brahms's First Symphony (which he was rehearsing that week for the NBC Symphony broadcast the following Sunday). Pointing to a passage in the first movement that had never pleased him in past performances, he exclaimed that it had suddenly dawned on him precisely what Brahms had intended at this troublesome point. In this passage, which never sounds "clean" when played exactly as written, Toscanini slightly altered the score to clarify the orchestral texture. He always insisted that his alterations were only the composer's true intention. But few would complain about his "delusions"; as Puccini once remarked, "Toscanini doesn't play my music as I wrote it, but as I dreamed it."

Mental Energy

Productivity implies actual production or objective achievement. For the psychological basis of intellectual productivity in the broadest sense, we need a construct that could be labeled *mental energy*. This term should not be confused with Spearman's *g* (for general intelligence). Spearman's theory of psychometric *g* as "mental energy" is a failed hypothesis and has been supplanted by better explanations of *g* based on the concept of neural efficiency (Jensen, 1993). The energy construct I have in mind refers to something quite different from cognitive ability. It is more akin to cortical arousal or activation, as if by a stimulant drug, but in this case an endogenous stimulant. Precisely what it consists of is unknown, but it might well involve brain and body chemistry.

One clue was suggested by Havelock Ellis (1904) in *A Study of British Genius*. Ellis noted a much higher than average rate of gout in the eminent subjects of his study; gout is associated with high levels of uric acid in the blood. So later investigators began looking for behavioral correlates of serum urate level (SUL), and there are now dozens of studies on this topic (reviewed in Jensen & Sinha, 1993). They show that SUL is only slightly correlated with IQ, but is more highly correlated with achievement and productivity. For instance, among high school students there is a relation between scholastic achievement and SUL, even controlling for IQ (Kasl, Brooks, & Rodgers, 1970). The "over-achievers" had higher SUL ratings, on average. Another study found a correlation of +.37 between SUL ratings and the publication rates of university professors (Mueller & French, 1974).

Why should there be such a relationship? The most plausible explanation seems to be that the molecular structure of uric acid is nearly the same as that of caffeine, and therefore it acts as a brain stimulant. Its more or less constant presence in the brain, although affecting measured ability only slightly, considerably heightens cortical arousal and increases mental activity. There are probably a number of other endogenous stimulants and reinforcers of productive behavior (such as the endorphins) whose synergistic effects are the basis of what is here called mental energy. I suggest that this energy, combined with very high g or an exceptional talent, results in high intellectual or artistic productivity. Include trait psychoticism with its creative component in this synergistic mixture and you have the essential makings of genius.

To summarize:

Genius = High Ability × High Productivity × High Creativity.

The theoretical underpinnings of these three ingredients are:

—Ability = g = efficiency of information processing

—Productivity = endogenous cortical stimulation

—Creativity = trait psychoticism

Other Personality Correlates

There are undoubtedly other personality correlates of genius, although some of them may only reflect the more fundamental variables in the formula given above. The biographies of many geniuses indicate that, from an early age, they are characterized by great sensitivity to their experiences (especially those of a cognitive nature), the development of unusually strong and long-term interests (often manifested as unusual or idiosyncratic hobbies or projects), curiosity and exploratory behavior, a strong desire to excel in their own pursuits, theoretical and aesthetic values, and a high degree of self-discipline in acquiring necessary skills (MacKinnon, 1962).

The development of expert-level knowledge and skill is essential for any important achievement (Rabinowitz & Glaser, 1985). A high level of expertise involves the automatization of a host of special skills and cognitive routines. Automatization comes about only as a result of an immense amount of practice (Jensen, 1990; Walberg, 1988). Most people can scarcely imagine (and are probably incapable of) the extraordinary amount of practice that is required for genius-quality performance, even for such a prodigious genius as Mozart.

In their *self*-assigned tasks, geniuses are not only persistent but also remarkably able learners. Ramanujan, for example, disliked school and played truant to work on math problems beyond the level of anything he was offered at school. Wagner frequently played truant so he could devote his whole day to studying the orchestral scores of Beethoven. Francis Galton, with an estimated childhood IQ of around 200 and an acknowledged genius in adulthood, absolutely hated the frustrations of school and pleaded with his parents to let him quit. Similar examples are legion in the accounts of geniuses.

In reading about geniuses, I consistently find one other important factor that must be added to the composite I have described so far. It is a factor related to the direction of personal ambition and the persistence of effort. This factor channels and focuses the individual's mental energy; it might be described best as personal ideals or values. These may be artistic, aesthetic, scientific, theoretical, philosophical, religious, political, social, economic, or moral values, or something idiosyncratic. In persons of genius, especially, this "value factor" seems absolutely to dominate their self-concept, and it is not mundane. People are often puzzled by what they perceive as the genius's self-sacrifice and often egocentric indifference to the needs of others. But the genius's value system, at the core of his or her self-concept, is hardly ever sacrificed for the kind of mundane pleasures and unimaginative goals commonly valued by ordinary persons. Acting on their own values—perhaps one should say *acting out* their self-images—is a notable feature of famous geniuses.

Characteristics of Genius: Some Conclusions

Although this chapter is not meant to provide an exhaustive review of the literature on geniuses and highly creative individuals, it has raised some consistent themes that might be worthy of scientific study. I propose that genius is a multiplicative effect of high ability, productivity, and creativity. Moreover, many of the personality traits associated with genius can be captured by the label "psychoticism." Although geniuses may have a predisposition toward such a disorder, they are buffered by a high degree of ego strength and intelligence. A number of the remaining personality correlates of genius may best be captured by the idea that genius represents an acting-out of its very essence.

Giftedness and Genius: Important Differences

Although giftedness (exceptional mental ability or outstanding talent) is a *threshold* trait for the emergence of genius, giftedness and genius do seem to be crucially different phenomena, not simply different points on a continuum. It has even been suggested that giftedness is in the orthogonal plane to genius. Thomas Mann (1947), in his penetrating and insightful study of Richard Wagner's genius, for instance, makes the startling point that Wagner was not a musical prodigy and did not even seem particularly *talented*, in music or in anything else for that matter, compared to many lesser composers and poets. He was never skilled at playing any musical instrument, and his seriously focused interest in music began much later than it does for most musicians. Yet Mann is awed by Wagner's achievements as one of the world's stupendous creative geniuses, whose extraordinarily innovative masterpieces and their inescapable influence on later composers place him among the surpassing elite in the history of music, in the class with Bach, Mozart, and Beethoven.

It is interesting to note the words used by Mann in explaining what he calls Wagner's "vast genius"; they are not "giftedness" or "talent," but "intelligence" and "will." It is the second word here that strikes me as most telling. After all, a high level of intelligence is what we mean by "gifted," and Wagner was indeed most probably gifted in that sense. His childhood IQ was around 140, as estimated by Catherine Cox (1926) in her classic, although somewhat flawed, study of three hundred historic geniuses. Yet that level of IQ is fairly commonplace on university campuses.

We do not have to discuss such an awesome level of genius as Wagner's, however, to recognize that garden-variety outstanding achievement, to which giftedness is generally an accompaniment, is not so highly correlated with the psychometric and scholastic indices of giftedness as many people, even psychologists, might expect. At another symposium related to this topic, conducted more than twenty years ago, one of the speakers, who apparently had never heard of statistical regression, expressed dire alarm at the observation that far too many students who scored above the 99th percentile on IQ tests did not turn out, as adults, among those at the top of the distribution of recognized intellectual achievements. He was dismayed at many of the rather ordinary occupations and respectable but hardly impressive accomplishments displayed in midlife by the majority of the highly gifted students in his survey. A significant number of students who had tested considerably lower, only in the top quartile, did about as well in life as many of the gifted. The speaker said the educational system was to blame for not properly cultivating gifted students. If they were so bright, should they not have been high achievers? After all, their IQs were well within the range of the estimated childhood IQs of the three hundred historically eminent geniuses in Cox's (1926) study. Although education is discussed in more detail below, the point here is that giftedness does not assure exceptional achievement; it is only a necessary condition.

To reinforce this point, I offer an additional example that occurred on the very day I sat down to write this chapter. On that day I received a letter from someone I had never met, though I knew he was an eminent professor of biophysics. He had read something I wrote concerning IQ as a predictor of achievement, but he was totally unaware of the present work. The coincidence is that my correspondent posed the very question that is central to my theme. He wrote:

> I have felt for a long time that IQ, however defined, is only loosely related to mental achievement. Over the years I have bumped into a fair number of MENSA people. As a group, they seem to be dilettantes seeking titillation but seem unable to think critically or deeply. They have a lot of motivation for intellectual play but little for doing anything worthwhile. One gets the feeling that brains were wasted on them. So, what is it that makes an intelligently productive person?

This is not an uncommon observation, and I have even heard it expressed by members of MENSA. It is one of their self-perceived problems, one for which some have offered theories or rationalizations. The most typical is that they are so gifted that too many subjects attract their intellectual interest and they can never commit themselves to any particular interest. It could also be that individuals drawn toward membership in MENSA are a selective subset of the gifted population, individuals lacking in focus. After all, most highly gifted individuals do not join MENSA.

We must, then, consider some of the ways in which *achievement* contrasts with *ability* if we are to make any headway in understanding the distinction between giftedness (i.e., mainly high *g* or special abilities) and genius. Genius involves actual achievement and creativity. Each of these characteristics is a quantitative variable. The concept of genius generally applies only when both of these variables characterize accomplishments at some extraordinary socially recognized level. Individual differences in countable units of achievement, unlike measures of ability, are not normally distributed, but have a very positively skewed distribution, resembling the so-called J-curve. For example, the number of publications of members of the American Psychological Association, of research scientists, and of academicians in general, the number of patents of inventors, the number of compositions of composers, or the frequency of composers' works in the concert repertoire all show the same J-curve. More-over, in every case, the J-curve can be normalized by a logarithmic transforma-tion. This striking phenomenon is consistent with a multiplicative model of achievement, as developed and discussed above. That is, exceptional achieve-ment is a multiplicative function of a number of different traits, each of which may be normally distributed, but which in combination are so synergistic as to skew the resulting distribution of achievement. Thereby, an extremely extended upper tail of exceptional achievement is produced. Most geniuses are found far out in this tail.

The multiplication of several normally distributed variables yields, there-fore, a highly skewed distribution. In such a distribution, the mean is close to the bottom and the mode generally *is* the bottom. For any variable measured on a ratio scale, therefore, the distance between the median and the 99th percentile is much smaller for a normally distributed variable, such as ability, than for a markedly skewed variable, such as productivity. Indeed, this accords well with subjective impressions: the range of individual differences in ability (g or fluid intelligence) above the median level does not seem nearly so astounding as the above-median range of productivity or achievement.

In conclusion, giftedness, a normally distributed variable, is a prerequisite for the development of genius. When it interacts with a number of other critical characteristics, which also are normally distributed, exceptional achievement is produced. Exceptional achievement, however, is a variable that is no longer normal; it is highly skewed, with genius found at the tip of the tail.

Educational Implications

At this point in my highly speculative groping to understand the nature of genius as differentiated from giftedness, I should like to make some practical recommendations. First, I would not consider trying to select gifted youngsters explicitly with the aim of discovering and cultivating future geniuses. Julian Stanley's decision (Stanley, 1977) to select explicitly for mathematical gifted-ness—to choose youths who, in Stanley's words, "reason exceptionally well mathematically"—was an admirably sound and wise decision from a practical and socially productive standpoint. The latent traits involved in exceptional mathematical reasoning ability are mainly high g plus high math talent (inde-pendent of g). These traits are no guarantee of high productivity, much less of genius. But the threshold nature of g and math talent is so crucial to excelling in math and the quantitative sciences that we can be fairly certain that most of the *productive* mathematicians and scientists, as well as the inevitably few geniuses, will come from that segment of the population of which the SMPY students are a sample. Indeed, in Donald MacKinnon's (1962) well-known study of large numbers of creative writers, mathematicians, and architects (certainly none of them a Shakespeare, Gauss, or Michelangelo), the very bottom of the range of intelligence-test scores in the whole sample was at about the 75th percentile of the general population, and the mean was at the 98th percentile (MacKinnon & Hall, 1972).

However, it might eventually be profitable for researchers to consider searching beyond high ability per se and identify personality indices that also will aid in the prediction of exceptional achievement. The proportion of those gifted youths selected for special opportunities who are most apt to be productive professionals in their later careers would thereby be increased. Assuming that high achievement and productivity can be predicted at all, over and above what our usual tests of ability can predict, it would take extensive research indeed to discover sufficiently valid predictors to justify their use in this way. Lubinski and Benbow (1992) have presented evidence that a "theoretical orientation," as measured by the Allport, Vernon, and Lindzey Study of Values, might be just such a variable for scientific disciplines.

Conclusion

Certainly, the education and cultivation of intellectually gifted youths has never been more important than it is today, and its importance will continue to grow as we move into the next century. The preservation and advancement of civilized society will require that an increasing proportion of the population have a high level of educated intelligence in science, engineering, and technology. Superior intellectual talent will be at a premium. Probably there will always be only relatively few geniuses, even among all persons identified as gifted. Yet this is not cause for concern. For any society to benefit from the fruits of genius requires the efforts of a great many gifted persons who have acquired high levels of knowledge and skill. For example, it takes about three hundred exceptionally talented and highly accomplished musicians, singers, set designers, artists, lighting directors, and stage directors, besides many stagehands, to put on a production of The Ring of the Nibelung, an artistic creation of surpassing genius. Were it not for the concerted efforts of these performers, the score of Wagner's colossal work would lie idle. The same is true, but on an much larger scale, in modern science and technology. The instigating creative ideas are seldom actualized for the benefit of society without the backup and follow-through endeavors of a great many gifted and accomplished persons. Thus, a nation's most important resource is the level öf educated intelligence in its population; it determines the quality of life. It is imperative for society to cultivate all the high ability that can possibly be found, wherever it can be found.

References

Cohn, S. J., Carlson, J. S., & Jensen, A. R. (1985). Speed of information processing in academically gifted youths. *Personality and Individual Differences* 6:621–629.

Cox, C. M. (1926). *The early mental traits of three hundred geniuses*. Stanford: Stanford University Press.

Ellis, H. (1904). *A study of British genius*. London: Hurst & Blackett.

Eysenck, H. J. (1995). *Genius: The natural history of creativity*. Cambridge: Cambridge University Press.

Eysenck, H. J., & Eysenck, S. B. G. (1976). *Psychoticism as a dimension of personality*. London: Hodder & Stoughton.

Eysenck, H. J., & Eysenck, S. B. G. (1991). *Manual of the Eysenck Personality Scales (EPS Adult)*. London: Hodder & Stoughton.

Fisher, J. (1959). The twisted pear and the prediction of behavior. *Journal of Consulting Psychology* 23:400–405.

Jackson, D. N., & Rushton, J. P. (Eds.). (1987). *Scientific excellence: Origins and assessment*. Beverly Hills: Sage Publications.

Jensen, A. R. (1990). Speed of information processing in a calculating prodigy. *Intelligence* 14:259–274.

Jensen, A. R. (1992a). The importance of intraindividual variability in reaction time. *Personality and Individual Differences* 13:869–882.

Jensen, A. R. (1992b). Understanding *g* in terms of information processing. *Educational Psychology Review* 4:271–308.

Jensen, A. R. (1993). Spearman's *g*: From psychometrics to biology. In F. M. Crinella & J. Yu (Eds.), *Brain mechanisms and behavior*. New York: New York Academy of Sciences.

Jensen, A. R., Cohn, S. J., & Cohn, C. M. G. (1989). Speed of information processing in academically gifted youths and their siblings. *Personality and Individual Differences* 10:29–34.

Jensen, A. R., & Sinha, S. N. (1993). Physical correlates of human intelligence. In P. A. Vernon (Ed.), *Biological approaches to the study of human intelligence*. Norwood, N.J.: Ablex.

Kanigel, R. (1991). *The man who knew infinity: A life of the genius Ramanujan*. New York: Scribners.

Kasl, S. V., Brooks, G. W., & Rodgers, W. L. (1970). Serum uric acid and cholesterol in achievement behaviour and motivation: 1. The relationship to ability, grades, test performance, and motivation. *Journal of the American Medical Association* 213:1158–1164.

Kendall, M. G. (1948). *The advanced theory of statistics* (Vol. 1). London: Charles Griffin.

Lubinski, D., & Benbow, C. P. (1992). Gender differences in abilities and preferences among the gifted: Implications for the math-science pipeline. *Current Directions in Psychological Science* 1:61–66.

MacKinnon, D. W. (1962). The nature and nurture of creative talent. *American Psychologist* 17:484–495.

MacKinnon, D. W., & Hall, W. B. (1972). Intelligence and creativity. In H. W. Peter, *Colloquium 17: The measurement of creativity. Proceedings, Seventeenth International Congress of Applied Psychology, Liege, Belgium, 25–30 July, 1971* (Vol. 2, pp. 1883–1888). Brussels: Editest.

Mann, T. (1947). Sufferings and greatness of Richard Wagner. In T. Mann, *Essays of three decades* (H. T. Low-Porter, Trans., pp. 307–352). New York: Knopf.

Mueller, E. F., & French, J. R., Jr. (1974). Uric acid and achievement. *Journal of Personality and Social Psychology* 30:336–340.

Price, D. J. (1963). *Little science, big science*. New York: Columbia University Press.

Rabinowitz, M., & Glaser, R. (1985). Cognitive structure and process in highly competent performance. In F. D. Horowitz & M. O'Brien (Eds.), *The gifted and talented: Developmental perspectives* (pp. 75–98). Washington, D.C.: American Psychological Association.

Simonton, D. K. (1988). *Scientific genius: A psychology of science*. New York: Cambridge University Press.

Snow, C. P. (1967). *Variety of men*. London: Macmillan.

Stanley, J. C. (1977). Rationale of the Study of Mathematically Precocious Youth (SMPY) during its first five years of promoting educational acceleration. In J. C. Stanley, W. C. George, & C. H. Solano (Eds.), *The gifted and the creative: A fifty-year perspective* (pp. 75–112). Baltimore: Johns Hopkins University Press.

Walberg, H. J. (1988). Creativity and talent as learning. In R. J. Sternberg (Ed.), *The nature of creativity: Contemporary psychological perspectives* (pp. 340–361). Cambridge: Cambridge University Press.

Appendix

TABLE A.1. *Item Difficulties and Percent Omitted, Transformed into Normal Deviates, for Seventh Graders and High School Students, by Gender*

Item No.	Group							
	7MR	7MO	7FR	7FO	HMR	HMO	HFR	HFO
1	0.958	−1.977	0.852	−1.995	1.243	−2.878	0.982	−2.457
2	0.662	−1.977	0.192	−1.960	0.659	−2.326	0.256	−2.144
3	0.105	−2.366	−0.148	−2.197	0.527	−2.652	0.345	−2.457
4	0.842	−1.522	0.908	−1.580	0.904	−1.655	0.772	−1.589
5	0.476	−1.812	0.220	−1.751	0.634	−1.825	0.350	−1.706
6	−0.053	−1.645	−0.300	−1.419	0.562	−2.144	0.253	−1.896
7	0.451	−1.774	0.118	−1.825	0.568	−2.034	0.225	−1.852
8	−0.277	−0.697	−0.375	−0.583	0.391	−1.270	0.256	−1.175
9	0.502	−1.572	0.184	−1.522	0.499	−1.626	0.126	−1.454
10	0.018	−1.522	−0.053	−1.468	0.179	−1.598	0.146	−1.514
11	0.116	−1.555	−0.131	−1.366	0.287	−1.717	0.058	−1.589
12	−0.287	−1.385	−0.580	−1.160	0.136	−1.995	−0.204	−1.665
13	0.189	−1.866	−0.204	−1.799	0.123	−1.751	−0.410	−1.685
14	0.176	−1.685	−0.088	−1.598	0.233	−1.825	−0.174	−1.706
15	−0.690	−0.393	−0.999	−0.256	0.030	−1.067	−0.287	−1.003
16	−0.313	−1.896	−0.493	−1.774	−0.068	−1.799	−0.282	−1.881
17	−0.499	−1.270	−0.616	−1.136	−0.350	−1.774	−0.542	−1.506
18	−0.580	−0.681	−0.769	−0.595	−0.277	−1.032	−0.502	−0.867
19	−0.908	−0.287	−1.032	−0.189	−0.539	−0.665	−0.716	−0.539
20	—	−0.548	—	−0.418	—	−0.942	—	−0.842
21	−0.813	−1.675	−1.103	−1.514	−0.653	−1.685	−0.874	−1.607
22	−1.276	−0.313	−1.405	−0.238	−0.810	−0.742	−1.063	−0.571
23	−1.341	0.025	−1.299	0.098	−1.019	−0.166	−1.282	−0.035
24	−1.626	−0.225	−1.655	−0.240	−1.282	−0.631	−1.232	−0.637
25	−1.392	−0.285	−1.572	−0.251	−0.950	−0.356	−1.311	−0.295
26	0.510	−1.461	0.340	−1.440	0.931	−1.960	0.779	−1.852
27	0.468	−1.717	0.412	−1.866	0.716	−1.960	0.586	−2.197
28	−0.220	−1.146	−0.335	−1.094	0.233	−1.762	0.005	−1.635
29	0.184	−0.900	0.060	−0.779	0.637	−1.379	0.321	−1.094
30	0.215	−1.049	−0.083	−0.806	0.372	−1.329	0.073	−1.028
31	−0.716	−0.476	−0.863	−0.429	0.133	−1.270	−0.098	−1.200
32	−0.665	−0.927	−0.935	−0.732	−0.176	−1.572	−0.396	−1.461
33	1.405	−2.197	1.117	−2.226	1.506	−2.457	1.028	−2.409
34	1.175	−2.512	0.915	−2.652	1.155	−2.748	0.817	−2.652
35	0.634	−1.190	0.332	−0.896	0.931	−1.995	0.759	−1.762
36	−0.212	−1.751	−0.279	−1.695	0.548	−2.144	0.364	−2.014
37	0.732	−1.762	0.646	−1.675	0.550	−2.290	0.473	−2.014
38	0.215	−1.287	−0.053	−1.067	0.202	−1.751	−0.033	−1.572
39	0.305	−1.598	0.329	−1.655	0.684	−2.366	0.562	−2.366
40	0.050	−1.353	−0.085	−1.175	0.194	−1.896	0.005	−1.706
41	0.136	−1.751	−0.123	−1.799	0.332	−2.226	0.008	−2.075
42	0.090	−1.131	−0.060	−1.076	0.313	−1.626	0.111	−1.514
43	0.118	−1.762	−0.259	−1.706	−0.063	−2.197	−0.277	−1.896
44	−0.473	−1.461	−0.726	−1.276	0.053	−1.825	−0.261	−1.514

TABLE A.1. *Continued*

Item No.	Group							
	7MR	7MO	7FR	7FO	HMR	HMO	HFR	HFO
45	−0.065	−1.108	−0.253	−0.974	0.396	−1.728	0.116	−1.499
46	−0.574	−1.058	−0.628	−0.912	−0.222	−1.359	−0.383	−1.175
47	−0.908	−0.765	−0.999	−0.589	−0.393	−1.293	−0.568	−1.112
48	−1.024	−1.067	−1.392	−0.954	−0.565	−1.372	−1.024	−1.329
49	−0.852	−0.970	−0.986	−0.806	−0.719	−1.293	−0.970	−1.098
50	−1.032	−1.317	−1.254	−1.175	−0.772	−1.329	−1.067	−1.131
51	−1.098	−0.459	−1.190	−0.259	−1.175	−1.379	−1.347	−1.287
52	−1.514	−0.539	1.616	−0.356	−1.165	−0.999	−1.317	−0.776
53	−0.070	−0.739	−0.228	−0.589	0.040	−0.927	0.233	−0.776
54	0.259	−1.287	0.199	−1.366	0.013	−1.131	0.010	−1.216
55	−0.610	−0.550	−0.893	−0.335	−0.372	−0.867	−0.568	−0.803
56	−0.631	−1.126	−0.693	−0.970	−0.530	−0.962	−0.662	−0.954
57	−0.631	−0.690	−0.958	−0.385	−0.516	−0.550	−0.915	−0.418
58	−1.195	−0.111	−1.491	0.065	−0.927	−0.311	−1.165	−0.266
59	−1.335	−0.653	−1.616	−0.583	−1.045	−0.637	−1.359	−0.574
60	−1.372	−0.040	−1.499	0.028	−0.946	−0.169	−1.305	−0.156

Note: 7 = Seventh grade
H = High school
M = Males
F = Females
O = Percent omitted in normal deviates
R = Percent correct in normal deviates
Example: 7MR = percent of seventh-grade males getting item correct (in normal deviates).

TABLE A.2. *Differences in Item Difficulties (Percent Correct and Percent Omitted, Transformed into Normal Deviates)*

Item No.	MF7R	MFHR	H7MR	H7FR	MF7O	MFHO	H7MO	H7FO
1	0.106	0.261	0.285	0.130	0.018	−0.421	−0.901	−0.462
2	0.470	0.403	−0.003	0.064	−0.017	−0.182	−0.349	−0.184
3	0.253	0.182	0.422	0.493	−0.169	−0.195	−0.286	−0.260
4	−0.066	0.132	0.062	−0.136	0.058	−0.066	−0.133	−0.009
5	0.256	0.284	0.158	0.130	−0.061	−0.119	−0.013	0.045
6	0.247	0.309	0.615	0.553	−0.226	−0.248	−0.499	−0.477
7	0.333	0.343	0.117	0.107	0.051	−0.182	−0.260	−0.027
8	0.098	0.135	0.668	0.631	−0.114	−0.095	−0.573	−0.592
9	0.318	0.373	−0.003	−0.058	−0.050	−0.172	−0.054	0.068
10	0.071	0.033	0.161	0.199	−0.054	−0.084	−0.076	−0.048
11	0.247	0.229	0.171	0.189	−0.189	−0.128	−0.162	−0.223
12	0.293	0.340	0.423	0.376	−0.225	−0.330	−0.610	−0.505
13	0.393	0.533	−0.066	−0.206	−0.067	−0.066	0.115	0.114
14	0.264	0.407	0.057	−0.086	−0.087	−0.119	−0.140	−0.108
15	0.309	0.317	0.720	0.712	−0.137	−0.064	−0.674	−0.747
16	0.180	0.214	0.245	0.211	−0.122	0.082	0.097	−0.107
17	0.117	0.192	0.149	0.074	−0.134	−0.268	−0.504	−0.370
18	0.189	0.225	0.303	0.267	−0.086	−0.165	−0.351	−0.272
19	0.124	0.177	0.369	0.316	−0.098	−0.126	−0.378	−0.350
20	—	—	—	—	−0.130	−0.100	−0.394	−0.424
21	0.290	0.221	0.160	0.229	−0.161	−0.078	−0.010	−0.093
22	0.129	0.253	0.466	0.342	−0.075	−0.171	−0.429	−0.333
23	−0.042	0.263	0.322	0.017	−0.073	−0.131	−0.191	−0.133
24	0.029	−0.050	0.344	0.423	0.015	0.006	−0.406	−0.397
25	0.180	0.361	0.442	0.261	−0.034	−0.061	−0.071	−0.044
26	0.170	0.152	0.421	0.439	−0.021	−0.108	−0.499	−0.412
27	0.056	0.130	0.248	0.174	0.149	0.237	−0.243	−0.331
28	0.115	0.228	0.453	0.340	−0.052	−0.127	−0.616	−0.541
29	0.124	0.316	0.453	0.261	−0.121	−0.285	−0.479	−0.315
30	0.298	0.299	0.157	0.156	−0.243	−0.301	−0.280	−0.222
31	0.147	0.231	0.849	0.765	−0.047	−0.070	−0.794	−0.771
32	0.270	0.220	0.489	0.539	−0.195	−0.111	−0.645	−0.729
33	0.288	0.478	0.101	−0.089	0.029	−0.048	−0.260	−0.183
34	0.260	0.338	−0.020	−0.098	0.140	−0.096	−0.236	0.000
35	0.302	0.172	0.297	0.427	−0.294	−0.233	−0.805	−0.866
36	0.067	0.184	0.760	0.643	−0.056	−0.130	−0.393	−0.319
37	0.086	0.077	−0.182	−0.173	−0.087	−0.276	−0.528	−0.339
38	0.268	0.235	−0.013	0.020	−0.220	−0.179	−0.464	−0.505
39	−0.024	0.122	0.379	0.233	0.057	0.000	−0.768	−0.711
40	0.135	0.189	0.144	0.909	−0.178	−0.190	−0.543	−0.531
41	0.259	0.324	0.196	0.131	0.048	−0.151	−0.475	−0.276
42	0.150	0.202	0.223	0.171	−0.055	−0.112	−0.495	−0.438
43	0.377	0.214	−0.181	−0.018	−0.056	−0.301	−0.435	−0.190
44	0.253	0.314	0.526	0.465	−0.185	−0.311	−0.364	−0.238
45	0.188	0.280	0.461	0.369	−0.134	−0.229	−0.620	−0.525

TABLE A.2. *Continued*

Item No.	MF7R	MFHR	H7MR	H7FR	MF7O	MFHO	H7MO	H7FO
46	0.054	0.161	0.352	0.245	−0.146	−0.184	−0.301	−0.263
47	0.091	0.175	0.515	0.431	−0.176	−0.181	−0.528	−0.523
48	0.368	0.459	0.459	0.368	−0.113	−0.043	−0.305	−0.375
49	0.134	0.251	0.133	0.016	−0.164	−0.195	−0.323	−0.292
50	0.222	0.295	0.260	0.187	−0.142	−0.198	−0.012	0.044
51	0.092	0.172	−0.077	−0.157	−0.200	−0.092	−0.920	−1.028
52	0.102	0.152	0.349	0.299	−0.183	−0.223	−0.460	−0.420
53	0.158	0.273	0.110	−0.005	−0.150	−0.151	−0.188	−0.187
54	0.060	0.003	−0.246	−0.189	0.079	0.085	0.156	0.150
55	0.283	0.196	0.238	0.325	−0.215	0.064	−0.317	−0.468
56	0.062	0.132	0.101	0.031	−0.156	−0.008	0.164	0.016
57	0.327	0.399	0.115	0.043	−0.305	−0.132	0.140	−0.033
58	0.296	0.238	0.268	0.326	−0.176	−0.045	−0.200	−0.331
59	0.281	0.314	0.290	0.257	−0.070	−0.063	0.016	0.009
60	0.127	0.359	0.426	0.194	−0.068	−0.013	−0.129	−0.184

Note: 7 = Seventh grade
    H = High school
    M = Males
    F = Females
    O = Percent omitted in normal deviates
    R = Percent correct in normal deviates
Example: MF7R = difference between seventh-grade males and females on percent correct.

Index

Library of Congress Cataloging-in-Publication Data

Intellectual talent : psychometric and social issues / edited by
    Camilla Persson Benbow and David Lubinski.
        p.   cm.
    Includes index.
    Chiefly papers originally presented at a symposium titled From
Psychometrics to Giftedness conducted in honor of Julian C. Stanley
in San Francisco on April 19, 1992.
    ISBN 0-8018-5301-X (cloth : alk. paper). — ISBN 0-8018-5302-8
(pbk. : alk. paper)
    1. Intellect—Congresses.   2. Nature and nuture—Congresses.
3. Genius—Congresses.   4. Psychometrics—Congresses.   5. Gifted
children—Education—Congresses.   6. Educational psychology—
Congresses.   I. Benbow, Camilla Parsson.   II. Lubinski, David
John.   III. Stanley, Julian C.
BF432.C48I58   1996
153.9—dc20   96-8377